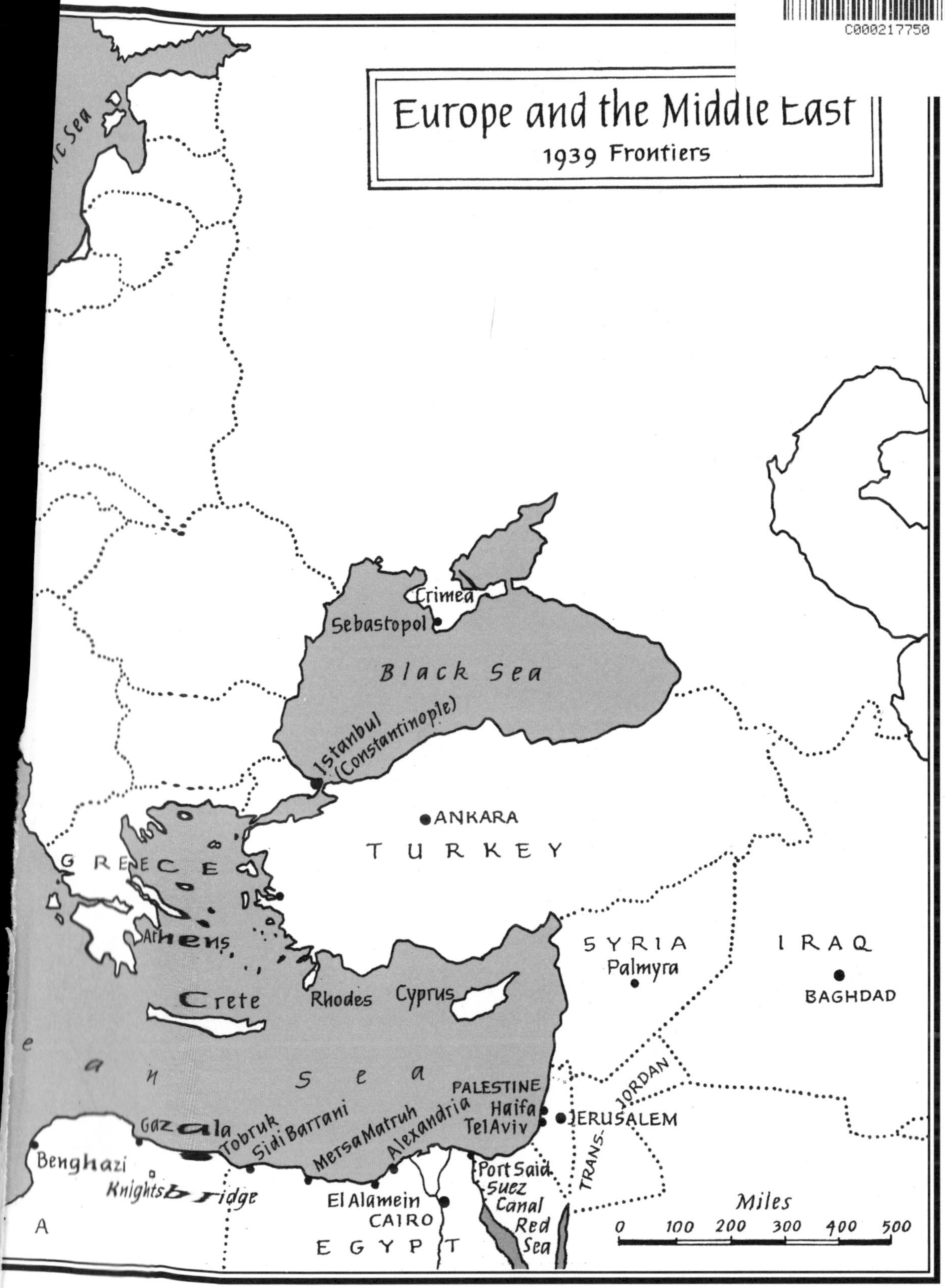
Europe and the Middle East
1939 Frontiers
Crimea
Sebastopol
Black Sea
Istanbul
(Constantinople)
ANKARA
TURKEY
GREECE
Athens
Crete
Rhodes
Cyprus
SYRIA
Palmyra
IRAQ
BAGHDAD
PALESTINE
Haifa
Tel Aviv
JERUSALEM
TRANS-JORDAN
Gazala
Tobruk
Sidi Barrani
Mersa Matruh
Alexandria
Benghazi
Knightsbridge
El Alamein
CAIRO
EGYPT
Port Said
Suez Canal
Red Sea
Miles
0 100 200 300 400 500

SECOND TO NONE

The Colonel-in-Chief at the Presentation of Colours to the Regiment at Windsor Castle on 22 May 1999.

SECOND TO NONE

THE COLDSTREAM GUARDS 1650–2000

Edited by
JULIAN PAGET

LEO COOPER

First published in Great Britain in 2000 by
LEO COOPER
an imprint of
Pen & Sword Books
47 Church Street
Barnsley, South Yorkshire. S70 2AS

A CIP record for this book is available from the British Library

ISBN 085052 769 4

Typeset in Sabon by
Phoenix Typesetting, Ilkley, West Yorkshire.

Printed by
Redwood Books Ltd, Trowbridge, Wilts.

Dedicated
by Gracious Permission
to
HER MAJESTY THE QUEEN
Colonel-in-Chief
of the
Coldstream Guards

CONTENTS

MAPS

The 28th Colonel of the Regiment, General Sir Michael Rose, KCB, CBE, DSO, QGM, standing in front of the portrait of the 1st Colonel, General George Monck, Duke of Albemarle.

FOREWORD

by
General Sir Michael Rose
KCB, CBE, DSO, QGM

Colonel of the Regiment

It has been said that history is but the biography of great men. However this most recent history of the Regiment which has been written to mark the 350th Anniversary of the founding of the Regiment is the story of all men, – both great and small, who have served in the Coldstream Guards. It is a story of fortitude, courage and the indomitable will to succeed both in times of war and peace. Since 1650 when the Coldstream Guards was formed by General Monck, this 'small Company of Men whom God made the instrument of Great Things' has on more than one occasion literally held the fate of the nation and the monarchy in its hands. Success or failure in these instances did not depend on the superiority of weapons or technology but on the fighting spirit and character of those men serving in the Regiment at the time, – men who were formidable in battle but compassionate in victory. They were men who, over the centuries, have always been proud to call themselves Coldstreamers.

As a result of political, social and technological change many of the requirements of modern soldiering are today different from those of the seventeenth century. Yet, because the fundamental demands of the battlefield have not changed, much can be gained by today's soldiers and officers from reading about the past. The need for good leadership, discipline, duty and service to others are all made evident in this latest history of the Coldstream Guards.

The Regiment owes an immense debt of gratitude to the many authors who, in writing this history, have ensured that future generations of Coldstreamers will be inspired to achieve the same high ideals as their forebears. A special word of thanks, however, must go to Lieutenant Colonel Sir Julian Paget and Major Edward Crofton who between them so encouraged others to put pen to paper, and who with such skill were then able to transform the many different contributions into a thoroughly fascinating and readable book.

I commend this history to all those who aspire to be true Coldstreamers.

PREFACE

by
Professor Sir Michael Howard,
CBE, MC, D. Litt, FBA

Every regiment in the British Army can claim to be unique, but the claim of the Coldstream is better than most.

In the first place, it is the only infantry regiment to have survived from Oliver Cromwell's New Model Army, which was itself the first entirely professional force ever to be raised in Britain; a stark contrast to the quasi-feudal levies and casual mercenaries with which England and Scotland had previously fought their wars and civil wars. In the second, it was raised and commanded not, as was usual at that time, by a 'gentleman of quality', but by a professional soldier who knew his trade inside out, and one who commanded the total loyalty of his men – George Monck, later first Duke of Albemarle. Monck was a figure who would have been as much at home in the world of the twentieth century as in the seventeenth. An honourable man whose trade was war and who wanted only to be left to practise it, he found the structure of society disintegrating around him and took the immensely courageous decision to use the force at his disposal to restore and maintain order. Such men in their time have either founded their own dynasties, as Cromwell attempted, or instituted more or less benevolent dictatorships that seldom outlived them. Monck, on the contrary, used his power quite selflessly to restore and sustain the only form of government that was acceptable to the peoples of England and Scotland after twenty years of civil war: a hereditary monarchy whose legitimacy was incontestable, but which was placed under constitutional constraints that made it politically acceptable. That monarchy Monck served loyally to the end of his days and his Regiment has served it ever since. The Coldstream retain some historic quirks. Unlike other Regiments in the Household Division it has rarely had a member of the Royal Family as its Regimental Colonel, that honour usually going to a senior officer in the Regiment. The loyal toast is not drunk in the Mess unless the Monarch is present. No seniority is yielded to the regiment formed from the King's personal followers in exile which became the First Foot Guards, later the Grenadiers: *Nulli Secundus*, the Coldstream say, and mean it. The Coldstream Guards has played a quite distinctive role in our island history and nobody should be allowed to forget it.

Probably few people join the Coldstream for ideological reasons or ever have, though research might show a slight bias towards Whig rather than Tory during its first century of recruitment. Regulars, both officers and men, normally join from family or local loyalties and the same names recur through centuries of the regimental history. During the vast and sudden expansions occasioned by the two World Wars recruitment was more random and opportunistic. Motives for joining may sometimes have been highly discreditable – the frank confession by Evelyn Waugh's anti-hero Basil Seal that he was attracted to a regiment that was not so stuffy as the Grenadiers and had none of the bogus original connections of the other three may have struck home with some – and sometimes frankly bizarre. The present writer, for one, felt that a regiment that had selected Figaro's aria *Non piu andrai* as its slow march must be civilized above the ordinary and found that he was perfectly right. But whatever their reasons for joining, they all found themselves in company that combined efficiency and panache with totally unassuming friendliness, and look back on their years with the Regiment as among the most rewarding in their lives.

The Coldstream's initial task was one very familiar to our own times. It was 'peacekeeping', or rather 'peace-making'. Monck's regiment was the only force preserving order in the chaotic interregnum that preceded Charles II's return to power. Today it has found itself doing much the same throughout the world, not least in Northern Ireland; not fighting, but preventing other people from fighting each other. Since then the history of the Regiment has been that of land warfare as a whole. It partook in the formal yet murderous battles of eighteenth-century Europe. It distinguished itself in the rough-houses of the Napoleonic Wars, notably the skirmish at Hougoumont, and the 'soldiers' battles' of the Crimea when no senior commander had the faintest idea what was going on. It adjusted itself to modern war the hard way on the Modder River. It endured the ordeal of the First World War with the stalwart courage commemorated so impressively in the Guards Memorial on Horse Guards Parade. In the Second World War its battalions served in the deserts of North Africa, the mountains of Italy, the *bocage* of Normandy and the muddy forests of the Rhine in conditions that, though often harsh, gave all ranks opportunities to show independent initiative such as their predecessors had rarely enjoyed. And after that . . .

After that there is practically nothing that Coldstreamers have not been required to do and few corners of the world where they were not required to do it. Hunting terrorists in the jungles of Malaya; peace-keeping in Palestine and Cyprus with, alas, little success in the former; preserving order in Kenya and Guyana and, repeatedly, Northern Ireland; garrison duties in Hong Kong and Belize; preparing to fight an inconceivable war on the plains of North Germany; fighting an actual war in the deserts of Iraq, and finally attempting to restore peace to the shattered communities of Bosnia: nothing has been too difficult or outlandish for the Regiment to undertake. Monck might have understood much of it, but few of his successors as Colonel of the Regiment would have recognized it as soldiering as they knew it. But by the end of the second millennium keeping the peace is more important than fighting wars, and first-rate soldiers are no less necessary to do it.

Meanwhile the Regiment regularly returns to the function for which the Household Division is best known throughout the world: 'public duties' in London and Windsor, and above all performing the annual ceremony watched with fascinated admiration from all over the world; Trooping the Colour. Anyone who believes that this immaculate performance has nothing to do with real soldiering has never seen a battalion stumble back to its billets, muddy, exhausted and thoroughly bloody-minded after enduring ten days of rain and shell-fire in slit trenches on a freezing mountain; only to be summoned by the drill-sergeants early next morning on to an improvised barrack-square and finding themselves within a few hours capable of mounting a parade that would do them credit at Wellington Barracks. It is perhaps only then that one can experience the full pride of being a Guardsman. It is a pride that sustains those lucky enough to have known it throughout their lives, in peace as well as in war.

ACKNOWLEDGEMENTS

Many individuals have contributed to this history in various ways, and it is very much a consolidated Coldstream effort. First of all, there are the authors (some of them first-timers) who have taken tremendous trouble and care over their research and their contribution. There are also many members of the Regiment, who have provided invaluable first-hand information, diaries, photographs and illustrations, and they are listed later on.

Our grateful thanks go to many others who have helped in different ways: Brigadier Myles Frisby for his help in finding contributors; Lieutenant Colonel Bill Corbould for obtaining and organizing all the illustrations; John Mollo and Stuart Rutherford for their original illustrations, drawn specially for this History; Captain David Horn, Curator of the Guards Museum, who has not only provided much information and help, but has also organized the Coldstream exhibition in the Museum; *The Guards Magazine* for several quotations and illustrations; Andy Cockrill who has photographed many items as illustrations for the book; Major General Colin Wallis-King for invaluable comments; Brigadier Henry Wilson, Publishing Manager of Pen and Sword Books for giving guidance and support on many matters; Tom Hartman of Pen and Sword who has most thoroughly and skilfully edited everything with great patience.

The book could not have been completed without the tremendous work done by the Regimental Adjutant, Major Edward Crofton, who, on top of being responsible for organizing much of our 350th Anniversary programme, has still managed to put in many hours of overtime as Assistant Editor, author and adviser. Also at Regimental Headquarters, Matilda White has typed and re-typed with both skill and patience.

The Editors also wish to acknowledge the invaluable contributions of the following Coldstreamers:

Lieutenant Colonel J.N. Agnew, D. Ainslow, Captain M. Bendix OBE JP DL, Major W. Birkbeck DL, the Rt Hon R.T. Boscawen MC, Lieutenant Colonel J.J.S. Bourne-May, Wing Commander G.H. Briggs DFC, Captain S. Brooksbank, Major General R.J.D.E. Buckland CB MBE DL, Major M.M. Bull MBE, I.G. Butler CBE, Captain M. Buxton, Major R.C. Carr-Gomm OBE, Major R. de L. Cazenove, Major J.G.B. Chester MC, C. Chew, Captain A.S. Clowes DL, Major the Lord Coleridge, Major N.S.C. Collin, Captain L.H.T. Court, Major J.C. Cowley OBE DCM, C.E. Crace, C.H. d'Ambrumenil, Brigadier Sir Jeffrey Darell Bt MC, Major the Duke of Devonshire KG MC PC, Captain the Lord Digby KCVO JP DL, Major N. Duckworth MBE MM, J. Elliott, J.B. Faller, Captain the Viscount Falmouth, F. Farnhill DCM, Captain E.W. Faure-Walker DL, Captain R.E. Faure-Walker, W. Fitness, Major D. Fletcher, L.A. Fortune, Captain A.G. Foucard MC, Captain C.F. Fuglesang, Major D.H.J. Glisson MBE,

P. Gourd, Major M. Hall, Captain Sir Michael Hamilton, the late Major W.B. Harris QC, Major D.C.E. Helme, the late Colonel E.R. Hill DSO, Professor Sir Michael Howard CBE MC, the Earl Jellicoe KBE DSO MC PC, Major C.W. Lambton, C.J.M. Langley, Captain R.P. Laurie OBE JP DL, J. Lawton, Major Sir Victor Le Fanu KCVO, Lieutenant Colonel J.R. Macfarlane, Major P.J.D. Macfarlane ERD JP, Major General A.P.W. MacLellan CB CVO MBE, Colonel M.W.F. Maxse LVO DL, Captain R.J.R. McDougall ERD, Brigadier I.H. McNeil OBE, Major the Lord Middleton MC, K. Millman, General Sir John Mogg GCB CBE DSO DL, A Napier OBE, Captain M.H.J. Nicholas, J. Nixon, Captain Sir Michael Palliser GCMG, Colonel A.B. Pemberton CVO MBE, The Rt Rev S.W. Phipps MC, J. Pipkin BEM, Major J.B. Priestley MC, Colonel the Viscount Ridley KG GCVO TD JP, Captain A.C. Sainthill, Major J.G. Savelle MBE, Captain C.C.I. Schofield MBE, Major Sir Reginald Secondé KCMG CVO, Captain D.L. Sheldon, D.W. Shenton, Captain B.H.G. Sparrow MC, Captain the Lord Stanley of Alderley DL, Major M.W. Stilwell CBE MC, Captain the Hon P.A. Strutt MC, Colonel R.G. Style, Major the Lord Suffield MC, Sir Adrian Swire DL, D. Thompson, Major General D.A.H. Toler OBE MC DL, Captain D.C. Tudway-Quilter DL, the late S. Webb, Major J.I. Whitaker, Brigadier the Hon H.E.C. Willoughby, the late Colonel E.I. Windsor Clive, Brigadier R.C. Windsor Clive and Major General Sir John Younger Bt CBE.

We are also most grateful to: I. Carter (Imperial War Museum), Major General Sir Robert Corbett KCVO CB, Brigadier F.H. Coutts CBE (late KOSB), N. Crichton-Stuart, V. Croft MM, C. Dodkin MBE, Mrs A. Dunlop, Lieutenant Colonel K. Edlin, Major D. Fletcher, Sir Alexander Glen KBE DSC, J. Harding MBE (Historical Branch (Army) MOD), Brigadier F.R. Henn CBE (late 11th Hussars), Dr J.B. Ingram (late RAMC), Miss A. Kelsall, Major General D. Lloyd-Owen CB DSO OBE MC, Mrs L. Llewellyn, I.G. MacPherson, Spike Milligan CBE (late RA), J. Montgomerie (RUSI Library), Ms J. Mullin (Imperial War Museum), Mrs A. O'Neill, Major R. Powell, Major R. Rylance (RAPC Museum), A.M. Roding (Archivist of Enschede), Captain P.H. Starling (Army Medical Services Museum), D. Sarkar (Author *Guards VC*), H.E. Schulman MBE, Miss M. Simpson (MOD Library), Lieutenant Colonel D. Sutherland MC, Lieutenant Colonel M. Tomkin MC, Dr I. Toptani, the Marquess Townshend DL, Major J.N.P. Watson, Miss A. Ward OBE (Historical Branch (Army) MOD), Ms L. Windmill, S. Wood (Scottish United Services Museum).

ILLUSTRATIONS

We would like to express our humble thanks to Her Majesty The Queen for her gracious permission to allow us to reproduce pictures from the Royal Collection.

We would also like to express our very sincere thanks to all those who have allowed us to reproduce photographs, and who are listed below:

G. Allcock, Colonel Sir Brian Barttelot Bt OBE DL, Wing Commander G.H. Briggs DFC, Major M.C.A. Codrington, Captain L.H.T. Court, H.G. Currie, A.N.G. Duckworth-Chad, J. Farrar, Brigadier R.J. Heywood OBE, Major S.D. Holborow, P. Humber, Imperial War Museum, London, the Earl Jellicoe, KBE, DSO, MC, PC, Mrs M. Jordan, Captain J.A. Kerr, Major C.K. Macfarlane, Major Sir Fergus Matheson of Matheson Bt, Major G.A. Philippi, N. Potts, The Trustees of the National Museums of Scotland, A. Radcliffe, H. Szymanski, Ms L. Windmill, Major J.M. Vernon, Brigadier R.J.S. Wardle OBE, Major J.I. Whitaker.

CHAPTER ONE

FORMATION, 1650–1661

by Julian Paget

Origins

The great military historian Sir John Fortescue, referring to the origins of the Coldstream Guards in 1650 as part of Oliver Cromwell's New Model Army, described them as "the oldest of our existing national regiments".[1]

The year 1650 was a troubled and turbulent moment in the history of Britain, for the country had just ended seven years of bitter civil war, lasting from 1642 to 1649, and arousing fiercely conflicting convictions throughout the land. On the Royalist side were those who believed devoutly in the King as the supreme, autocratic ruler in the country, while the Roundheads believed equally strongly that the nation should be democratically governed through an elected Parliament. So wide was the gap between them that there were even occasions when fathers and sons fought on opposite sides.

In 1649 the struggle ended with victory for the more highly organized and professional Roundhead forces of Oliver Cromwell, known as the New Model Army. On 1 January 1649 England witnessed the terrible sight of King Charles I being publicly beheaded outside Whitehall Palace. From that moment Oliver Cromwell and the Roundheads dominated the country.

But it did not lead to peace. The Royalists had been crushed, but their cause lived on and they had not lost heart. The future King Charles II had fled with a following of loyal supporters to Holland, which was at war with England, as was France. Scotland naturally still strongly supported the Stuart cause, and so the Roundhead Government faced opposition from many directions.

Cromwell depended for his power on his New Model Army, the first whole-time, professional army that the country had ever known. One of the most promising officers in it was one Colonel George Monck, known to Cromwell as an experienced commander and one of the leading military theorists of the day.

He had been born in 1609 at Torrington in Devon, the second son of Sir Thomas Monck, a respected local figure and a staunch Royalist. Soldiering was in young George's blood and at the age of sixteen he began his military career by serving with the Spanish and then the Dutch armies overseas. In 1640 he came home and joined the Royalist forces, whereupon he was sent to Ireland to fight the Roundheads there. He did well, but in 1644 was captured at the Battle of Nantwich and was imprisoned in the Tower. While there he used his enforced idleness to write a treatise entitled

[1] *History of the British Army*, Vol I, page 240.

"Observations upon Military and Political Matters",[2] a knowledgeable and authoritative manual which attracted the attention of Oliver Cromwell.

In 1646 Monck was offered his freedom on condition that he would join the New Model Army and serve with it in Ireland. He agreed to do so and soon showed his military worth commanding Parliamentary forces in Ulster. Cromwell was so impressed by his qualities that he decided to give him command of a regiment of his own. He chose a Yorkshire regiment of foot already in existence and belonging to a Colonel John Bright[3], who was resigning. But it transpired that, by a remarkable coincidence, this was the very regiment that had captured Monck in 1644 when he was a Royalist and they understandably refused to accept him now as their Commanding Officer. "We'll have none of him," they declared, and Cromwell had to think again.

The Dunbar Medal. It bears the head of Oliver Cromwell on one side and a sitting of the House of Commons on the other.

He solved the problem by forming a new regiment specially for Monck, taking five companies from Sir Arthur Hazelrigg's Regiment[4] and five companies from Colonel Fenwick's Regiment.[5] The amalgamation took place in late July and early August 1650 near Morpeth in Northumberland and was officially approved by Parliament on 13 August 1650. The new regiment was given the title Monck's Regiment of Foot, later to become the Coldstream Guards.

Service in Scotland

At this time Scotland remained strongly loyal to the Royalist cause and when Charles Stuart, the exiled son of King Charles I, landed at Speymouth in June 1650 to reclaim the throne of England, he was warmly welcomed by the Scots, who raised an army to support him. As soon as Cromwell heard the news, he marched north with an army of 16,000, including Monck's Regiment, and the Scots were decisively defeated at Dunbar on 3 September 1650.

He then had a special medal struck and awarded to all officers and men who had taken part in the great victory. It was the first campaign medal ever awarded in the British Army and the Coldstream Guards is the only surviving regiment to have been awarded it. A specimen of the Dunbar Medal belonging to the Regiment is today in the Guards Museum in Wellington Barracks.

[2] Published posthumously in 1671.

[3] In those days regiments not only bore the name of their Commanding Officer, but literally belonged to him, and he had to recruit, organize, feed, clothe and pay them.

[4] Originally raised in 1645 as Weldon's Regiment of Foot, it became Lilburne's and after that Hazelrigg's.

[5] Originally formed in 1645 as Lloyd's 7th Regiment of Foot, it became Herbert's, Overton's, and finally Fenwick's. Colonel Fenwick was the son of Sir George Fenwick of Brinkburn, Co Northumberland.

Despite their setback at Dunbar, the Scots continued to support the Royalist cause and were a considerable problem to Cromwell. In August 1651 he appointed Colonel Monck to command the 6000 Parliamentary troops that were still in Scotland and gave him orders that he was to bring the country firmly under control. This he did very effectively, subduing all but the far north.

In March 1652 Monck had to leave Scotland due to ill health, but he recovered and was then appointed as one of Cromwell's generals at sea[6] during the war of 1652–1654 against the Dutch. He seems to have proved successful in his new role, even though he issued an order to the fleet during one battle to "Wheel to the Right. Charge!"

In 1654 he was sent back to Scotland to suppress risings in the Highlands, which he did within a year. Meanwhile, much was happening back in England. Oliver Cromwell died in 1658 and was succeeded by his son Richard; but he had none of his father's convictions nor his strength of character, with the result that the country slid steadily into more internal conflict.

Loyalties were becoming divided again and officers in the Army found themselves faced with three possible options. First, there was the existing regime of the Commonwealth under Richard Cromwell, which in effect meant rule by the military commanders known as the 'Major Generals'. Second, there could be a proper democratic Parliament in the shape of the ineffectual Rump of the Long Parliament. Finally, there was the possibility of the restoration of the Monarchy with a new Constitution.

Monck firmly refused to commit himself at this stage, except to declare that, as a matter of principle, he supported the Government of the day, but he nevertheless kept a weather eye on possible developments. He was in a strong position, being away from the capital, with a powerful army under his command and a corps of officers who were, as far as he could determine, loyal to him and would follow whatever line he took. He was careful to keep politics out of his army as far as he could and he made it clear to all his officers that he expected them to obey the civil power from which they had received their commission.

In view of his actions during the Restoration, it is perhaps of interest to try to assess Monck's motives in these troubled times. He might appear to be something of an opportunist who trimmed his sails to every changing wind for his personal advantage, but this does not do him justice, for his motives went deeper than that. He was a sincere man and is probably better termed a realist and a pragmatist who held firm views as to the duties and loyalties required of him both as a soldier and as a citizen[7]. He believed strongly in the rule of a freely elected Parliament and in a civil power free of military pressure; he did *not* believe in military rule nor in military men seeking power for their own advantage.

He set out his views in a letter to Parliament in 1659, in which he declared:

> "Obedience is my great principle and I have always and ever shall reverence the Parliament's resolution in civil things as infallible and sacred."[8]

In that year events began to move rapidly towards a crisis, as Richard Cromwell lost control of his Major Generals. In October two of them, Charles Fleetwood and John Lambert, took matters into

[6] It was common practice in those times for generals to be sent to sea to command a fleet.

[7] He himself wrote. "The profession of a soldier is so famous and honourable amongst men, that Emperors and Kings do account it a great honour to be of the profession and to have experience in it."

[8] Clarke Papers IV.22–23.

their own hands and ejected the Long Parliament, once more imposing military rule on the country Monck was strongly opposed to such a development and declared his support for Parliament. On 12 November he wrote to the Lord Mayor of London:

> "I take God to witness that I have no other end than to restore the Parliament to its former freedom and authority, and the people to their just rights and liberties."[9]

Then in December 1659 came two significant developments. First, an order was issued by the military authorities in London requiring Monck and all his officers to sign a 'treaty' testifying to their loyalty to the Commonwealth. Monck resented this as an unwarranted imposition and responded by summoning a Grand Council of Officers in his army in Scotland to obtain their views for himself. The outcome was that he was able to report that "all present concurred in rejecting the treaty and swore to live and die with their general".

The second event was that on 8 December 1659 Monck moved his headquarters from Berwick-upon-Tweed to the small town of Coldstream on the Scottish bank of the River Tweed, where he was well placed to take action in Scotland or England as the need arose. The concentration of his army of some 7000 men in the area caused severe administrative problems, however, for the local inhabitants. There was only just enough food or accommodation for everyone and the troops suffered considerable hardships during the winter, not only from short rations but also from the limited quarters available.

Monck himself suffered from the general discomfort, and his loyal chaplain, Thomas Gumble, wrote of life in Coldstream at the time:

> "The general's palace was a little smoaky cottage that had two great dunghills at the door, a hall or entry so dark and narrow as a man could not turn in it; the rooms were worse than I can describe."[10]

Monck remained there, however, throughout December, watching developments and receiving many visitors of widely differing views. But he refused to disclose his own intentions, if indeed he had any, other than to wait and see what happened next.

He did not have to wait long. London and other cities were soon demanding the return of the Long Parliament. The loyalty of the army was under severe strain, with officers and men alike either publicly declaring their neutrality or else expressing their support for the ever-growing calls for the return of a proper Parliament.

Finally, on 26 December Richard Cromwell and his generals bowed to public opinion and Parliament was recalled. This was what Monck had been waiting for and as soon as the news reached Coldstream he gave orders for his famous march south. It was a historic moment for the country and also for the Coldstream Guards, and, to quote Thomas Gumble once more:

> "The town of Coldstream, because the general did it the honour to make it the place of his residence for some time, hath given title to a small company of men whom God made

[9] Old Parliamentary History xxii page 47

[10] *The Life of General Monck, Duke of Albemarle*, Thomas Gumble, pp.177–179

the instruments of great things; and though poor, yet honest as ever corrupt nature produced into the world, by the no dishonourable name of Coldstreamers."[11]

The March to London, 1660

On 2 January 1660 General Monck and an army of some 6000 crossed the Tweed and set out on their 350-mile march to London. On the 4th they reached Morpeth, where Monck's Regiment had been formed almost ten years before, and the next day they entered Newcastle. Then it was on to Durham (6th) and on the 11th they arrived in York, where they rested for five days; Nottingham was reached on the 19th, Leicester on the 23rd, Northampton on the 25th and St Albans on the 28th.

It was a triumphant progress all the way, for in every town the troops were met with the ringing of bells and congratulatory addresses welcoming them as liberators. It was clear that they had strong public support, but Monck "kept his counsel and none knew his intentions".[12]

On 3 February 1660 Monck and his Regiment entered London; the General took up his quarters in Whitehall, while his troops were billeted for the first (but far from the last) time around St James's Palace.

The primary challenge was to solve the problem of the government of the country. The Rump Parliament was still in power, but had become thoroughly unpopular and unrepresentative. In a speech to Parliament on 6 February Monck told them bluntly that his evidence was that the country wanted them dissolved and a new start made; but this was not accepted. He was supported, however, by the Common Council of London, who declared that they would refuse to pay any taxes until Monck's demands were met.

Parliament retaliated by ordering Monck, as their military commander, to march against the City, to destroy the City gates and to arrest ten leading figures on the Council. This put Monck in a difficult position and he decided that, much as he resented such an order, he had no option at this stage but to obey it. His troops therefore began to carry out the demolition work, but they felt much the same as Monck did, and it was reported that "never did soldiers with so much regret obey their general".[13]

When they were about half-way through their unwelcome task Monck proposed to Parliament that they should come to terms with the City, but they firmly refused, even though this brought them increased unpopularity. That night some of Monck's senior officers came to him to declare that they had not marched from Scotland to make themselves "odious to the whole nation" and that they would resign rather than continue to support a thoroughly unrepresentative Parliament.

This was just the expression of support that Monck wanted and he immediately wrote a formal letter to Parliament demanding their dissolution, followed by free elections. He then finally confirmed where his sympathies lay by declaring his backing for the City's defiance and reinforcing it by marching his troops into the City again, but this time to offer his protection to the City Council.

The reaction was described by Samuel Pepys in his Diaries:[14]

[11] Gumble, p 105

[12] *Early History of the Coldstream Guards*, G. Davies, 1923, p.102

[13] Price. pp 762–763.

[14] Diary, 11 February 1660, Gumble, p 250.

"It was very strange how the countenance of men in the hall was all changed with joy in half an hour's time . . . Monck came out after telling the Mayor and Aldermen he would stand by his men . . . Such a shout I never heard in all my life, crying out 'God bless your excellence'. I saw many people give the soldiers drink and money, and all along the streets cried 'God bless them' and extraordinary good words . . . the common joy was everywhere to be seen . . . It was past imagination, both the greatness and the suddenness of it. From being cursed as tyrants, the redcoats were now hailed as deliverers."[15]

A first step had been taken to restore civil liberties, but it was not the end of the story. There was now a growing, though not universal, clamour for the restoration of the Monarchy, but Monck did not himself promote it publicly, maintaining that it was for Parliament and the people to decide.

The new freely elected Parliament that he had demanded duly met on 25 April and Monck took his seat as the member for his native county of Devon. One of the first acts of the new House of Commons was to vote for the return of the Monarchy and Monck was among those who voted in favour.

The Restoration, 1660

So it was that on 25 May 1660 King Charles II landed at Dover, where he was welcomed, among many others, by General Monck, and they exchanged warm greetings. The Royal party set off immediately for London, but they stopped on the 27th at Canterbury.

There the King showed his gratitude to Monck by bestowing on him the Order of the Garter, the highest honour in the country and only rarely granted to a commoner. As a further sign of Royal favour, the King personally placed the ribbon on Monck, rather than leaving it to the Garter King of Arms.

Further honours followed on 7 July when Monck was created Duke of Albemarle and also appointed Lord General of the Land Forces. His regiment of foot now became 'The Duke of Albemarle's Regiment' or 'The Lord General's Regiment', and so it continued to be until Monck's death in 1670. It took as its badge the Star of the Order of the Garter, which has remained the badge of the Regiment ever since.[16]

So the King was back on the throne, but the situation was far from secure. A substantial part of the New Model Army was still under arms and their loyalty to Charles was, to put it mildly, highly questionable. His only personal troops at the moment were his one Troop of Life Guards, some eighty strong, together with the Duke of Albemarle's Regiment of Foot and also his Regiment of Horse;[17] the King needed them all, for the country was still in a state of turmoil and he was highly vulnerable to attacks on his life.

Not surprisingly, the King decided that the whole army must be rapidly and thoroughly purged of all doubtful elements and then be reorganized. As a first move, he dismissed all officers whose

[15] The Skinners Company generously invite senior officers of the Regiment to lunch with them to commemorate the occasion when Monck lunched with them in April 1660. In 1952 the Regiment was granted the Freedom of the City of London and in 2000 exercised the rights and privileges involved by marching through the City with drums beating, Colours flying and bayonets fixed.

[16] It was officially granted to the Regiment as their badge by King William III in 1695.

[17] His Royal Regiment of Guards under Colonel Wentworth, who would become the First Guards, were at this stage still in Bruges where the King had been in exile.

General George Monck, Duke of Albemarle KG (1608–1669), 1st Colonel of the Regiment.

loyalty was in question and replaced them by loyal Royalists.

Charles would have liked to retain a small standing army, but Parliament, with memories of the Civil War still very much in their minds, opposed any form of permanent military power in the hands of the Monarch. They therefore passed an Act on 26 August 1660 ordering the disbandment of the entire New Model Army. No exceptions whatsoever were to be permitted and every single unit in England, including Monck's two regiments, was listed for disbandment.

One concession only was made and that was that Monck's Regiments of Horse and Foot should, in recognition of their services to the King, be the last to disappear. This must have seemed at the time to be a somewhat dubious honour, but, as events turned out, it was to have far-reaching results, for it would mean that both these regiments not only survived, but also became part of the Household Division.

On Sunday, 6 January 1661, two days before Monck's two regiments were due to be disbanded, came a minor event that was to have major repercussions for both the Household Division and the British Army in the future. On that day a London wine cooper called Thomas Venner led some sixty fanatical armed supporters in a revolt against both the King and Parliament. His followers called themselves the 'Fifth Monarchy Men' or the 'Millenarians', and they managed to cause so much trouble that neither the City Trained Bands nor the few troops available could cope with them.

Parliament was forced very reluctantly to call on Monck's Regiment of Foot for help, whereupon these veterans, supported by some of the King's Life Guards, soon rounded up the rebels and the Venner Riots were quelled. The incident served, however, to make two points clear to both Parliament and the King. The first was that there was definitely a need to maintain a larger, professional standing army in the country, both to protect the Sovereign and to maintain law and order. The second was that Monck's two regiments were too valuable to lose and they should be retained as part of any such permanent force.

The Creation of the Standing Army, 1661

So the disbandment of these two regiments was averted and on 26 January 1661 King Charles II signed what has been called 'the birth certificate of the British Army'. It was a Royal Warrant authorizing the establishment of the first Standing Army in the country, as opposed to the temporary armies that had till then been raised only as and when required.

The Act of Parliament disbanding the New Model Army was, however, still on the Statute Book and had to be formally complied with. So it came about that at 10 o'clock on the morning of St Valentine's Day, 14 February 1661, Monck's Regiment of Horse and his Regiment of Foot both paraded at Tower Hill. There they symbolically laid down their arms as units of the New Model Army and were immediately ordered to take them up again as Royal troops in the new Standing Army, and also as 'an extra-ordinary guard to his Royal person'.

Monck's Regiment of Horse was at once re-named 'Lord Albemarle's Troop of His Majesty's Life Guards' and became the Third Troop, after 'The King's' and the 'Duke of York's'. As such, it became Household Cavalry from that moment.

Monck's Regiment of Foot received the title of 'The Lord General's Regiment of Foot Guards' and is considered to have become Household Troops from that moment, with seniority immediately after Lord Wentworth's and Colonel John Russell's Regiments (now the First or Grenadier Guards).

'The Lord General's Regiment of Foot Guards' of course accepted the Royal Command as to seniority, but at the same time did not want it to be forgotten that it was the oldest English regiment still in existence. To avoid any doubt on this point it took as its Regimental motto 'Nulli Secundus' or 'Second to None',[18] and to this day the Regiment does not accept that it should ever be referred to as 'Second Guards', a point that was confirmed by the Secretary of War in January 1830.

Death of General Monck, 1670

On 3 January 1670 General Monck, Duke of Albemarle, died, aged 62, and was buried in Westminster Abbey.[19] His son duly handed back his father's insignia of the Order of the Garter, but, to quote the *London Gazette* of 6 January 1670: "His Majesty, to express the great value he had for the incomparable merits of that great and glorious person towards His Majesty and his people, immediately ordered the Garter to be carried back to his sons". It was an unprecedented honour.

Monck's Regiment was now officially given the title of 'His Majesty's Coldstream Regiment of Foot Guards' and this continues today.

Note on Author

Lieutenant Colonel Sir Julian Paget Bt, CVO, MA, served in the Regiment 1940–1968 and commanded the 2nd Battalion 1960–1962. He served in the Guards Armoured Division 1941–45 and also in Palestine, Kenya and Aden. He was Editor of *The Guards Magazine* 1976–1993.

[18] It is the only Regiment in the British Army officially to have a Regimental motto.

[19] A suit of his funeral armour still exists in the Museum at Westminster Abbey.

CHAPTER TWO

WAR AFTER WAR, 1660–1815

by Julian Paget

During the 155 years from 1660 to 1815 one war followed another with grim regularity, as England, France, Spain and the Netherlands fought for supremacy in Europe and overseas. As a result, the Regiment was on active service with one or other of its battalions for around sixty of the 155 years, taking part in fifteen campaigns and earning fourteen Battle Honours. But we shall in this chapter not recount every battle in detail and will instead pick out the highlights. A table on page 22 summarizes the lengthy list of conflicts.

War Against the Dutch, 1662–1667

Strangely, the Regiment's first active service after 1660 was on the high seas. This was not as surprising as it may sound, for it was normal practice in the seventeenth century for soldiers to fight on board naval ships. So it was that in 1662 500 men from the Duke of Albemarle's Regiment were detailed by Royal Warrant for service at sea during the continuing war against the Dutch. The Coldstream can therefore claim to be the parent of that distinguished Corps, the Royal Marines, created in 1664.

In the same year came an intriguing incident when some fifty Coldstreamers took part in an expedition that was sent to fight the Dutch in North America. It was commanded by Captain Robert Holmes of the Royal Navy[1] and succeeded in capturing the capital of the Dutch Settlement in North America, which was called New Amsterdam. Captain Holmes promptly re-named it New York in honour of the King's brother, The Duke of York, and so it has remained ever since.[2]

Tangier, 1680

In 1680 the Regiment acquired its first Battle Honour of **Tangier 1680**. This chief city of Morocco had been presented to King Charles II as part of the dowry of Catherine of Braganza whom he married in 1662. The Moors not unnaturally strongly resented seeing their capital in infidel hands and they raided it persistently.

In 1680 the Governor called for reinforcements to the regular garrison in order to be able to deal with the Moors once and for all. A Composite Battalion composed of First and Coldstream

[1] He later became Admiral Sir Robert Holmes. He is also shown in the Regimental Roll of Officers as a Captain in the Regiment as at April 1667 to 1669. (MacKinnon. Vol 2. p 460/1)

[2] A Coldstream badge was recently discovered in the foundations of a skyscraper in New York.

Guards[3] was formed and called 'The King's Battalion'; it was sent out to Tangier the same year, whereupon the Moors were decisively defeated and peace was established. The garrison then remained there for four years, after which the King decided that this outpost was too costly to maintain (an early Defence Review!) and handed it back to the Moors.

Organization

Until now regiments had been known by the name of their commander (e.g. 'Monck's Regiment') but towards the end of the seventeenth century they began to be formed into 'battalions' and referred to by numbers. Thus, in 1684, the Regiment formed a 1st Battalion.

The battalions at this time consisted of a varying number of companies, each around 100 strong, and each named after the officer who commanded it. This custom continues today, with men being members, for example, of 'Number 2 or Major Willoughby's Company'. Each company also had its own Colour with its own distinctive badge, similar in style to those of the Colonel, Lieutenant Colonel and Major of the Regiment, but smaller in size. (See *Appendix D*)

Around 1680 there were three significant changes to the organization of the Regiment. First, in 1678 a 'grenadier company' was formed in each battalion. These men were armed with grenades and hatchets, and they wore mitre caps instead of broad-brimmed hats, so that they could more easily sling their firelocks over either shoulder and then hurl their grenades. Evelyn described them in his diaries as wearing "furred hats with coped crowns, which gave them a fierce expression . . . their clothing was piebald yellow and red." Their special role was to lead the assault on fortifications, which was a demanding task, and they were therefore normally men of above average height and physique. The Foot Guards were pioneers of this innovation and it was not until the reign of James II that all infantry regiments were similarly organized.

Second, it was about this time that 'double rank' became more general. This privilege had already been granted to The Life Guards, because many of their officers had held senior ranks in the Royalist Army during the Civil War of 1642–49. When they went into exile with the King in 1650 they loyally agreed to serve in a lower rank and, to compensate them, Charles II ordered in 1661 that they should be allowed to hold a rank one above that of their actual appointment in the Army.

The same privilege was extended to the Foot Guards in 1687, when Captains were granted the 'double rank' of Lieutenant Colonel[4]; four years later Lieutenants also received 'double rank', but it was not extended to the junior rank of Ensign until 1815. The system continued for almost two centuries until it was abolished as part of the Cardwell reforms in 1871.

The third and perhaps most important event came in 1684 when the Regiment formed a 2nd Battalion,[5] that would continue to exist for over 300 years until reduced to a company in 1994.

Divided Loyalties Once Again

The dramatic year 1688 saw the loyalties of the country, and particularly of the Household Troops, sorely tested once again. The determination of King James II, who had come to the throne in 1685, to convert England back to Catholicism had already alienated many of his subjects, among them

[3] The Regiment provided two officers and 130 men.

[4] The rank of Major did not exist at this time, being introduced at the end of the century.

[5] They are mentioned as taking part in a review on Putney Heath in front of King Charles II on 1 October 1684.

some Army officers who had been dismissed on religious grounds, together with others who had resigned on grounds of conscience.

The climax came when the Protestant Prince of Orange landed in Devon on 5 November 1688 with the aim of driving James II from the throne and restoring Protestantism in England. This situation forced all ranks of the Household Troops to make the hard choice between loyalty to their unpopular, Catholic-minded Sovereign and loyalty to a foreign Protestant invader.

In the event most of the Guards Regiments stood by their King, though some of the Third Guards were so strongly opposed to Catholicism that they declared for Prince William. The Colonel of the Coldstream at the time was the 82-year-old Earl of Craven and he loyally asked leave to send his Regiment to confront the Dutch forces, which were advancing on London, but the King personally forbade him to do so.

Finally, on 18 December 1688 James II fled and the Prince of Orange entered London to be crowned as King William III. A difficult time inevitably followed for the Household Troops whose loyalties were highly suspect in the eyes of the new Sovereign and the Royal Guards' duties were taken over by his Blue Dutch Guards. The Coldstream were particularly unpopular, following their known support of King James II, and within a year both battalions were sent overseas. In addition, the Earl of Craven was dismissed as Colonel and replaced by Colonel Thomas Tolemache.[6]

The Regiment was not alone in being sent out of the country to fight in Flanders. Indeed, all five regiments of Household Cavalry and Foot Guards ended up there, the first time they had ever all been together on active service.[7] It was not a successful campaign and the army was twice defeated (Landen, 29 July 1692 and Steenkirk, 3 August 1692), neither of which became Battle Honours. Landen is, however, noteworthy as the first occasion on which the Foot Guards fought in Guards Brigades under their own officers, a system that has been successfully followed ever since.

In June 1694 Thomas Tolemache (now a Lieutenant General) died of wounds received during a raid on the French coast in which a detachment of the Regiment took part. His place as Colonel of the Regiment was taken by Lieutenant General Lord Cutts, an officer renowned for such exceptional coolness and bravery under fire that he was given the nickname throughout the Army of 'Salamander Cutts'. He commanded two Guards Brigades at the capture of **Namur**[8] on 16 August 1695 and after the action was appointed a 'Brigadier of the Guards', an honour never previously granted to any officer.

The war finally ended with the Peace of Ryswick on 11 September 1697, and both battalions of the Regiment returned home.

The War of the Spanish Succession, 1702–13

The War of the Spanish Succession began in 1702 and saw the British Army under John Churchill, the future Duke of Marlborough, win a series of brilliant successes. The Regiment was not involved

[6] There have been several variations of spelling and it is now 'Tollemache'. At least eight generations of the family have served in the Coldstream and they must surely be the longest-serving family in the Regiment.

[7]

1st Guards Brigade	*2nd Guards Brigade*
1st Battalion First Guards	2nd Battalion First Guards
2nd Battalion Third Guards	1st Battalion Coldstream Guards
2nd Battalion Dutch Guards	1st Battalion Third Guards

[8] The Regiment's second Battle Honour, although it was not awarded until 1910.

for the first six years of the main campaign in Europe, but nevertheless won a third Battle Honour – at **Gibraltar**.

In September 1704 a Composite Battalion, composed of 200 First Guards and 600 Coldstreamers, was sent first to Lisbon and then to Gibraltar. The Rock had been captured from the Spanish in July by a detachment of Marines[9] under Admiral Sir George Rooke, but it was then closely besieged and reinforcements were called for. The Composite Battalion landed on 20 January 1705 and was involved in repelling several attacks; it then remained as part of the garrison until the siege was lifted in April 1705.

Meanwhile, on the mainland Marlborough won his 'famous victory' at Blenheim on 13 August 1704; the Regiment did not take part, but was well represented by its Colonel, General 'Salamander' Cutts, who led the crucial attack with his usual bravery.[10]

The Regiment only became involved in 1708 when six companies were sent to Flanders as part of a Composite Battalion with the First Guards and took part in the Battle of **Oudenarde** on 11 July 1708, which became the fourth Battle Honour.

In April 1709 a further Coldstream detachment was sent to join the war, whereupon a Guards Brigade was formed, consisting of a First Guards battalion and a Coldstream battalion. On 11 September 1709 both these battalions took part in the Battle of **Malplaquet**; it was an exceptionally bloody contest and the Regiment's losses were among the heaviest of the twenty battalions involved. They undoubtedly distinguished themselves and it became a well-deserved Battle Honour.

Thereafter the war petered out and when the Treaty of Utrecht was signed in 1713 the Regiment returned home in March for a welcome period of twenty-seven years of peace and home service.

The War of the Austrian Succession, 1740–1748

The peace was broken by the outbreak in 1740 of the War of the Austrian Succession. The origins are complex and the campaign only concerns us because the expeditionary force sent to the Continent in 1742 included a Guards Brigade consisting of the 1st Battalions of all three regiments of Foot Guards.

In 1743 King George II not only joined the army in Flanders but also assumed command. On 27 June 1743 he fought the Battle of **Dettingen**, well known as the last occasion on which a King of England personally led his troops into action. He led them, in fact, into a dangerous trap, carefully prepared by the French, and the situation was only saved by several gallant charges made by the cavalry, including, for the first time, a Household Cavalry Brigade.

The Guards Brigade formed the rearguard and so was not involved in the battle until the later stages. The French finally suffered a severe defeat, losing 5,000 men, and **Dettingen** became the Regiment's sixth Battle Honour.

In 1745 the King handed over command to his 25-year-old son, The Duke of Cumberland, whose first action as a commander was the Battle of Fontenoy on 11 May 1745. Things did not go well and the Allied army was forced to make a frontal assault against the enemy centre, which involved

[9] Although the Royal Marines have fought worldwide for over 300 years, they carry only one Battle Honour on their Colour, which is 'Gibraltar'.

[10] When he died in 1707 he was succeeded as Colonel of the Regiment by General Charles Churchill (brother of the Duke of Marlborough) who had served in the Regiment in Flanders and in Gibraltar.

an advance of half a mile across flat, open country under intense fire from their front and also from French strongpoints on both flanks.

The Guards Brigade was on the right of the leading line, with the regiments in their customary positions, that is the First Guards on the right, the Coldstream on the left and the Third Guards in the centre. The brigade was commanded by Colonel George Churchill, Coldstream Guards. With shouldered arms the three battalions marched steadily forward, despite the fierce fire from three sides. Finally, as they topped a slight ridge, now seriously reduced in numbers, they found, thirty yards in front of them, four complete battalions of French Guards, as yet unscathed.

It was the first time that the British and French Guards had met in battle and it was a dramatic confrontation. The French fired first, but to little effect. Then the Guards replied and their first volley laid low nineteen French officers and 600 men. Steadily they reloaded, firing in disciplined sequence six platoons at a time, so that the volleys never ceased. Finally the French gave way and the Guards advanced. But they did not receive any support and found themselves isolated; for three hours they had to hold their positions against both infantry and cavalry attacks, but finally were forced to withdraw, having lost around half their strength. It had been a bloody and bitter defeat, and was not allowed to count as a Battle Honour, though it was perhaps deserved.

The 'Forty-Five', 1745

July 1745 saw a new threat, this time at home, as the Scots rebelled in support of Charles Stuart, grandson of King James II, who was claiming the English Crown. The Guards Brigade in Flanders was hurriedly recalled, while in London the grenadier companies of the Guards battalions stationed there were formed into a scratch force for the defence of the capital.

The threat faded, however, and The Duke of Cumberland pursued the Jacobite Army back into Scotland, where they were crushed at the Battle of Culloden on 16 April 1746. With Scotland subdued, he then returned in 1747 to the campaign in Flanders, taking with him a new Guards Brigade, composed this time of the 2nd Battalions of each Regiment. They did not, however, see any major action and returned home in 1748 when the war was ended by the Treaty of Aix-la-Chapelle.

The Seven Years War, 1756–1763

The peace that followed lasted only eight years and in 1756 another campaign began, again against the French. The Foot Guards were not involved initially, but in 1758 the 1st Battalions of each Regiment were formed into a Guards Brigade and took part in several rather abortive raids on the French coast.

In 1760 another Guards Brigade, composed of the 2nd Battalion of each Regiment, was sent to Germany under the command of a Coldstreamer with the unusual name of Major General Julius Caesar. A year later the grenadier companies of each Regiment were formed into a composite Grenadier Battalion, which became the fourth battalion of the brigade, a practice that would continue over the next fifty years.

In 1763 the 2nd Battalion returned home, landing at Yarmouth, which meant that the Regiment had spent twenty-four out of the last sixty years fighting somewhere on the Continent. Its next campaign would be on the other side of the Atlantic.

The American War of Independence, 1775–1783

In 1775 the British settlers in the colonies of North America became highly dissatisfied with their treatment by the Government at home and began to demand their independence. The Whitehall response was to send a military force across the Atlantic "to teach the rebels a lesson". The expedition included a Composite Guards Battalion from all three Regiments, commanded by a Coldstreamer, Colonel Edward Mathew. The Coldstream contingent, consisting of nine officers and 298 other ranks, was reviewed on Wimbledon Common by King George III before it set sail in March 1776. The voyage lasted no less than five months and it was August before the troops thankfully set foot on dry land.

Almost immediately they were involved in the seizure of New York, and no doubt the Coldstreamers present enjoyed reminding the First and Third Guards that the Coldstream had already carried out this operation once before, just 111 years earlier. (see page 9)

Early in 1777 the Composite Battalion was reorganized into a brigade of two battalions with Colonel Mathew as the Brigade Commander. The brigade fought throughout the campaign and was involved in most of the engagements of 1776–77. This was followed by two years of garrison duty in New York, before they were sent south to join General Cornwallis in Carolina.

Throughout the war the British troops in their distinctive uniforms found themselves at a distinct disadvantage against the unorthodox mobile tactics of the American settlers whose camouflaged sharpshooters caused undue casualties to the 'redcoats'. In an attempt to counter this, the Guards formed a 'light company', consisting of men specially trained and equipped to act as skirmishers and so protect the vulnerable, immobile ranks of infantry. This was the first time that the rigid parade-ground manoeuvring of the last 100 years was modified and it led to the acceptance of 'light companies' as a normal part of regular infantry battalions.[11]

In February 1781 the Guards Brigade distinguished itself when the troops waded waist-high for 500 yards across the flooded Catawba River in North Carolina under heavy fire from the opposite bank and then drove back the American defenders.

Six weeks later, on 15 March, both battalions took part in the Battle of Guildford Court House where they helped to defeat a numerically superior American force. It was an expensive victory, however, and they lost almost half their strength, a setback that their general, Lord Cornwallis, could ill afford.

It was in fact the beginning of the end for the British forces in the south. Soon afterwards Cornwallis found himself trapped in Yorktown and, after a brief defence, he surrendered on 19 October 1781 with his entire force of 6,000 men, including 500 men of the Guards Brigade.

The American Colonies were granted their independence in November 1782 and the next year England also came to terms with France, Spain and Holland. A peace of general exhaustion ensued, but within a decade Europe would be plunged into war once again, this time against Napoleon Bonaparte.

Formation of the Nulli Secundus Club, 1783

On 4 May 1783 five officers of the Regiment decided to form a Dining Club, appropriately named the Nulli Secundus Club. There were originally fourteen members and they dined once a month for

[11] The 'grenadier company' formed the right flank of the battalion when in line; the light company was on the left.

five shillings a head. One of the rules was that "Any member of this Club entering into the Holy State of Matrimony shall give the members of the Club a Dinner".

In June 1807 a uniform was agreed which was basically the dark blue Nulli Coat still worn today.

From 1830 until the end of his reign King William IV invited the members (now numbering twenty-three) to hold their Dinners at St James's Palace, and he himself attended.

Today there are around 750 members and a Dinner is held annually in June before the Sovereign's Birthday Parade.

The Struggle against Napoleon, 1793–1815

The French Revolution of 1789 led to over twenty years of conflict between England and Napoleonic France that would only end at Waterloo in 1815. It is a war that is of particular historical interest because of the series of remarkable parallels between the struggle against Napoleon and that against Adolf Hitler and Nazi Germany 146 years later.

In both cases a ruthless, ambitious dictator conquered and dominated all Europe, and Britain stood alone against him for several long years. The British Army was driven from the Continent at Corunna in 1809 as it was at Dunkirk in 1940. There was a recurring threat of invasion that was only thwarted by our sea power and in both struggles the nation was inspired by the oratory of a great leader, be it William Pitt or Winston Churchill. Both dictators tried and failed to defeat Russia. Above all, our supremacy at sea enabled us not only to thwart invasion threats and blockades, but in due course to take the offensive by attacking the enemy's possessions overseas and finally launching our own invasion of Occupied Europe.

The actual campaigning against Napoleon began in 1793 when the French Government sent an expeditionary force against Holland who was an ally of England at that time. The British Army had as usual been reduced to a dangerously low level as soon as there was a moment of peace and it was only with the greatest difficulty that an effective force could be raised at all. The troops most ready for action were the Foot Guards and they were hurriedly formed into a Guards Brigade consisting of the 1st Battalion of each Regiment, together with a fourth or Flank Battalion formed from the grenadier and light companies.

They sailed for Holland in February 1793 and the Regiment thus had the dubious honour of being among the first troops to engage those of Revolutionary France on the Continent. They were extremely ill-equipped, with no transport, no reserve ammunition and few stores; shipping was so short that they had to be transported across the Channel in Thames coal barges.

It was not a particularly successful campaign, but there was one moment of glory when the Guards Brigade was sent to support the Prince of Orange, whose troops had been driven out of the village of **Lincelles**. On arrival there was no sign of the Dutch force that was supposed to reinforce them and they found themselves expected to attack 5,000 strongly entrenched enemy even though they had only 1,100 men. Despite heavy artillery and musket fire, the three Guards battalions stormed the defences and cleared the village, thereby earning one more Battle Honour. It was the Regiment's seventh and was the first to be awarded at the time, rather than much later.

The campaign dragged on, but little was achieved and no one was sorry when the force was withdrawn in April 1795. During the next three years Napoleon established his dominating position in Europe, just as Hitler did between 1939 and 1941, and by 1797 Britain stood alone, facing an apparently invincible dictatorship.

Determined to defeat this impudent island, Napoleon planned invasion. But although he assembled a large invasion fleet off Dunkirk, he was prevented by the Royal Navy from using it. Then in February 1797 the fleet of his ally, Spain, was destroyed off Cape St Vincent and in October his Dutch fleet was defeated at Camperdown. So, as in 1940, the invasion barges never left France and England breathed again.

Just as Hitler attacked Egypt in 1940 when his invasion plans failed, so Napoleon in 1798 struck in the Middle East and occupied Egypt. Even though his fleet was destroyed by Nelson in Aboukir Bay on 11 August 1798, he pushed on into Palestine, only to be halted in 1799 by the defiant garrison of Acre under Sidney Smith. He thereupon decided to cut his losses, abandoned his army in Egypt and returned to Europe to continue his conquests there.

So by 1801 Britain stood alone yet again and the daunting prospect was made worse by the imposition of a monstrous new 'income tax' at the exorbitant rate of two and a half per cent. But by skilful use of her sea power, she started operations at opposite ends of Europe that would within the next twelve months dramatically change the situation.

In January 1801 Nelson destroyed the Danish fleet in Copenhagen, while General Sir Ralph Abercrombie set sail from Minorca on an expedition that was intended to drive the French out of Egypt. He had with him a Guards Brigade consisting of 1st Battalion Coldstream Guards and 1st Battalion Third Guards. They sailed with him to the Bay of Marmorice on the coast of Turkey where they were relentlessly trained with the Royal Navy in carrying out an opposed landing until everything ran like clockwork. It was an early instance of thorough combined operations planning and training and it would pay good dividends.

On 8 March 1801 the assault force landed at Aboukir Bay, a beach some ten miles east of Alexandria. It was covered by the guns of Aboukir Fort and was such a strong position that the French commander had allotted only 2,000 men to its defence.

As dawn broke three lines of assault boats, each containing fifty men, moved slowly inshore towards the two-mile-long beach, in perfect formation, as if on parade. There was no firing and no cheering, only the rattle of the rowlocks. Then with a roar the guns in Aboukir Fort opened up with a storm of grapeshot, round and chain shot. A direct hit sank a boat of fifty Coldstreamers, then a Third Guards boat was hit and it looked as if the landing might fail.

But without reply the flotilla pushed steadily on and at last they reached the shore. Despite heavy enemy fire the men formed up in line and prepared to advance inland. But the battle was not yet won. There was some confusion, due to the heavy casualties, and a French cavalry charge almost drove them back into the sea. But it was repulsed and the three brigades advanced. The French withdrew and a bridgehead was safely established. It had been a highly hazardous operation, but, thanks to the fine discipline, leadership and training, it was an impressive victory.

Cairo was captured on 27 June and on 28 September a force that included the Guards Brigade seized Alexandria. This marked the end of a highly successful campaign that left Egypt in our hands and ended French expansion in North Africa. In December 1801 the 1st Battalion sailed home with the brigade, stopping briefly en route in Malta.

For their 'conspicuous service' in this campaign both the Coldstream and Third Guards were awarded the distinction of carrying on their Colours a badge of a Sphinx, superscribed with the word **'Egypt.'**

Threat of Invasion

Despite his setback in Egypt Napoleon still dominated Europe and in 1802 England signed the Treaty of Amiens, which it was hoped would lead to peace. But within a year it became clear that Napoleon remained set on world domination and by May 1803 Britain and France were again at war.

Britain stood alone in defying the Emperor and, as in 1798, there was a very real threat of invasion. But as in 1940 Britannia ruled the waves and, although Napoleon assembled a Grand Army of 160,000 and a fleet of 2,100 barges, he was still thwarted by the Royal Navy.

"Let us be masters of the Channel for six hours," he demanded angrily of his admirals, "and we shall be masters of the world." But Admiral Villeneuve could no more grant him that than could Admiral Raeder and Field Marshal Goering grant it to Hitler 137 years later.

In England almost a tenth of the population joined the Volunteers, the equivalent of the Home Guard of 1940, only to find to their indignation that, as in 1940, there were not enough muskets to go round and many were issued with pikes! Martello Towers were built to defend the coast, while among the forces defending the capital were three Guards Brigades, the 1st and 2nd formed from the Regular battalions while the 3rd contained the depot battalion of each Regiment.

The threat reached its peak in the first days of 1804. All Press mention of troop movements was forbidden and any editor who disobeyed was liable to arrest. Plans were made for the gold in the Bank of England to be moved to Worcester Cathedral and the Volunteers hurried to their posts. Invasion seemed inevitable, but the Royal Navy was not dismayed.

"I do not say the French cannot come," growled Lord St Vincent, the First Sea Lord. "I only say they cannot come by water."

He was right. As 1804 passed, Napoleon's fleets dared not put to sea and his hopes of a successful conquest of England steadily dwindled. Then, when a combined French and Spanish fleet finally ventured out of Cadiz on 21 October 1805, it was promptly destroyed by Nelson off Cape Trafalgar and the threat of invasion was ended.

Britain immediately began to think once more of using her sea power for offensive operations and in October 1805 2nd Guards Brigade, which included the 1st Battalion, was sent to Hanover to join an Allied force there, but the campaign petered out and the troops returned home in February 1806.

Undaunted, the same brigade was sent in August 1807 on a daring but this time successful expedition to Denmark. Copenhagen was captured and the entire Danish fleet was removed, just ahead of Napoleon, who had also planned to seize it.

The Peninsular War, 1808–1814

Having failed to crush England by invasion, Napoleon now tried to starve her into submission (as did Hitler with his U-Boats from 1940). He issued the Berlin Decrees, which forbade any European country to trade with us, and he enforced it ruthlessly. But there was one defiant exception, Portugal, who was not only England's oldest ally,[12] but also did most of her trade with us.

When Portugal defied Napoleon he promptly sent an army to invade the country in November 1807. The following spring he also invaded Spain, whereupon both countries appealed to England

[12] The Treaty of Windsor 1386.

for help. Eager to support any nation that was prepared to stand up against the French, the British Government boldly agreed to send troops to Portugal. So, on 1 August 1808 14,500 men under the command of a promising young general called Sir Arthur Wellesley landed at Figueiro and the Peninsular War had begun.

There were no Coldstreamers involved at this stage, but the force included 1st Guards Brigade composed of the 1st and 2nd Battalions of the First Guards. Wellesley successfully drove the French out of Portugal, but was then ordered home, and handed over to Major General Sir John Moore. He was ordered to advance into Spain to support the Spanish army there, but this provoked Napoleon to intervene himself at the head of an army of 200,000. His 'blizkrieg' forced Moore to retreat in haste in January 1809 to the port of Corunna in order to save his army (the only one that England possessed).

The retreat over mountains in midwinter involved extreme hardships and, as the demoralized 15,000 survivors straggled into Corunna on 11 January 1809, there occurred a famous incident, much valued by Guardsmen of all Regiments. It cannot be better described than in the words of the military historian, Sir John Fortescue:

> "A brigade caught the General's eye at a distance, for they were marching like soldiers. 'Those must be the Guards,' he said, and presently the two battalions of the First Guards, each of them still 800 strong, strode by in column of sections, with drums beating, the drum major twirling his staff at their head and the men keeping step as if in their own barrack yard. The senior regiment of the British infantry had set an example to the whole army."[13]

They also established a tradition that day that would inspire future generations of Guardsmen of all Regiments in years to come. The 1st, 2nd and 3rd Battalions of the Coldstream set the same standards of discipline on the Retreat from Mons in 1914 (see page 46) and so did the 1st and 2nd Battalions on the beaches of Dunkirk in 1940. (see page 90).

Undaunted by the disaster of Corunna, the British Government resolved, as in 1940, that they would fight on regardless, and within a mere three months a second expeditionary force was on its way to Portugal, again commanded by Sir Arthur Wellesley. This time it included 2nd Guards Brigade, composed of the 1st Battalions of the Coldstream and Third Guards, who would together fight on for the rest of the Peninsular War.

The Crossing of the Douro, 12 May 1809

The Guards Brigade was part of Sherbrooke's 1st Division, and on 12 May it took part in Wellesley's remarkably bold Crossing of the Douro and the capture of the Portuguese city of Oporto. The Guardsmen were due to be among the first troops to cross in the main assault, but the 29th Foot (Worcester Regiment) were in front of them in the assembly area and sent back word that the streets were so narrow that such big men as the Guardsmen would never get through. It was not true, but it gave the 29th the satisfaction of beating the Guards to it!

[13] *History of the British Army*, Vol iv, p 375.

Talavera, 28 July 1809

Having driven the French out of Portugal for the second time by his capture of Oporto, Wellesley turned south and boldly advanced towards Madrid. But he had now to cooperate with the Spanish Army, which proved far from easy, and as a result of their incompetence he found himself having to fight the Battle of **Talavera** on 28 July 1809, although outnumbered two to one.

"Never was there such a murderous battle," he himself declared, but at the end of the day it was the French who withdrew, despite their superiority in numbers. The Guards Brigade was again in the 1st Division and at one moment the battalions advanced too far and found themselves cut off and under fire from both flanks. They were rescued by a timely charge by the 48th Foot (Northamptonshire Regiment) and rallied in time to join in the final victory. Talavera was awarded as a Battle Honour and a special medal was struck for issue to 'meritorious officers'.

Wellesley withdrew after the battle back into Portugal, where he remained on the defensive until he felt strong enough to take the initiative again.

Battle of Barrosa, 5 March 1811[14]

In March 1810 three companies of the 2nd Battalion of the Regiment joined the Peninsular Army as part of a Composite Guards Brigade of all three Regiments.[15] It was, however, used to reinforce the garrison of Cadiz and so found itself besieged there for the next two and a half years.

But they did have one moment of glory, which was the Battle of **Barrosa**, one of the finest actions against overwhelming odds in the history of the Regiment. In 1811 part of the garrison, including the Composite Guards Brigade, was withdrawn from Cadiz and sent by sea to Tarifa, west of Gibraltar, with the aim of then marching back towards Cadiz and attacking the besieging French force from the rear.

But, again due to Spanish incompetence, the rearguard of the force was ambushed by some 9,000 French near the village of Barrosa and was cut off from the main body. The British were only 5,000 strong, but they were commanded by a fine, fighting soldier, Lieutenant General Thomas Graham,[16] who decided that the only hope lay in a bold counter-attack. The 2nd Battalion of the Regiment and the 2nd Battalion First Guards were involved in desperate close-quarter fighting, led by General Graham himself. They were outnumbered almost two to one, but finally it was the French who withdrew, and the enemy commander spoke afterwards of "the incredibility of so rash an attack".[17]

It was not a major battle, but it was a great victory and a fine feat of arms, which became a very well-earned Battle Honour for the Regiment.

[14] There are various spellings.

[15] It was commanded by Major General W.T.Dilkes, Third Guards, and consisted of:
Six companies, 2nd Bn First Guards.
Three companies, 2nd Bn Coldstream Guards.
Three companies, 2nd Bn Third Guards.

[16] Later Lord Lynedoch.

[17] The Coldstream lost about a third of its strength.

Battle of Fuentes d'Onor, 3–5 May 1811

The 1st Battalion meanwhile, as part of 1st Guards Brigade, took part in the Battle of **Fuentes d'Onor** (3–5 May 1811), a hard-fought two-day contest on the Portuguese border, which Wellington[18] described as "a near-run thing". The Regiment was not too heavily involved, but it was awarded another Battle Honour.

On to the Offensive, 1812

By the beginning of 1812 Napoleon had withdrawn troops from Spain to build up his army for the invasion of Russia in June and, as a result, Wellington was at last in a position to go on to the offensive in the Peninsula. In January 1812 he captured the key fortress of Ciudad Rodrigo and the 1st Battalion took part. This was followed by his dramatic victory of **Salamanca** on 22 July 1812 when "40,000 Frenchmen were defeated in 40 minutes". Again, the 1st Battalion was involved and the light companies of the Guards Brigade received a special mention in Wellington's Despatches for seizing the key village of Los Arapiles and holding it against constant counter-attacks. Salamanca became the Regiment's eleventh Battle Honour.

From there Wellington went on to liberate Madrid on 12 August, which forced the French to lift their two-and-a-half-year siege of Cadiz. The liberated garrison, including the Coldstream Detachment, promptly marched north, determined not to miss any more fighting. They covered 400 miles in nineteen days but only reached the main army on 18 October, in time to return with it to winter quarters in Portugal.

In October 1812 1st Battalion First Guards arrived in the Peninsula from England and thus made a total of five Guards battalions in the Peninsular Army. Wellington therefore formed two Guards Brigades[19] both of which were placed in 1st Division, now commanded by General Graham of Barrosa fame.

The Great Advance, 1813–14

So we come to 1813 when Wellington decided that, following Napoleon's disastrous losses in Russia,[20] there was now a chance of the Peninsular Army finally driving the French out of Spain altogether. The parallels with 1944 are striking at this point, for Napoleon, like Hitler, was now committed to a war on two fronts against confident, well-trained Allied armies that were steadily liberating the occupied countries of Europe and advancing towards the enemy's homeland.

Wellington set off from Portugal on 22 May 1813 and by the end of the year had advanced 500 miles, crossed the Pyrenees and established his army deep in French territory. The last eighteen

[18] He had been created Baron Douro of Wellesley and Viscount Wellington soon after his victory at Talavera.

[19] *1st Guards Brigade.* (Major General K.A.Howard, Coldstream Guards)
- 2nd Bn First Guards.
- 3rd Bn First Guards.
- Composite Bn, Coldstream and Third Guards.

2nd Guards Brigade. (Major General the Hon. E. Stopford, Third Guards)
- 1st Bn Coldstream Guards.
- 1st Bn Third Guards.

[20] It is intriguing that Napoleon set off for Moscow on 22 June 1812 and Hitler in 1941 started on 24 June.

months of the war brought both triumphs and disasters for the Regiment, who were represented by the 1st Battalion and also their detachment in the Composite Battalion. Both fought in the overwhelming victory of Vitoria on 21 June 1813, but then suffered severe losses in the costly siege of San Sebastian, where a detachment of one officer and fifty-three men volunteered for the storming party on 21 August and suffered over fifty per cent casualties.

Both Guards Brigades took part in the series of operations in the Pyrenees, including three bold river crossings over the Bidassoa (7 October 1813), the Nivelle (10 November) and the **Nive** (9 December;) the last encounter becoming the Regiment's twelfth Battle Honour.

The advance continued in 1814 and 2nd Guards Brigade distinguished itself at the Crossing of the Adour on 23 February 1814, when two Coldstream companies and six from the Third Guards held a precarious bridgehead across the river through the night against constant attacks.

On 5 April 1814 Napoleon abdicated and on the 12th an armistice was signed between Wellington and the French commander, Marshal Soult, at Toulouse. But the war ended on a tragic note, particularly for the Regiment, because of the Sortie from Bayonne. The bulk of the Allied Army began enjoying the end of hostilities, but the 1st and 5th Divisions were still besieging Bayonne, 140 miles to the west, where the French garrison of 14,000 was still holding out under its fanatical commander, General Thouvenot. He had been told of Napoleon's abdication and the armistice, but refused to believe it and vowed to fight on.

1st and 2nd Guards Brigades both formed part of the besieging force and were positioned to the north of Bayonne. Having been told of the armistice, security seem to have been relaxed. Unfortunately, the French had other ideas and at 0300 on 14 April they launched a powerful sortie northwards from the citadel with 6,000 men.

The attack achieved complete surprise and the brunt of it fell on the two Guards Brigades. There was fierce, confused fighting throughout the night and, although by dawn the sortie had been repulsed, this was not achieved without heavy casualties. The Allies lost 826 men with 231 taken prisoner. Out of this total the Coldstream lost two officers and thirty-two men killed and five officers and 122 men wounded – a tragic end to a highly successful campaign.

The dead from the Guards Brigades were buried by their regiments in military cemeteries on the outskirts of Bayonne, one for the Coldstream and one for the Third Guards, on the sites of their battalion camps in 1814. They still exist today and are thought to be the oldest British Army cemeteries.[21]

So the Peninsular War was over at last and in July 1814 the Coldstreamers in the two Guards Brigades returned home after five years of active service overseas. They had certainly played their part in the final victory, earning six Battle Honours.[22]

But there was one final round yet to be fought against Napoleon at Waterloo on 18 June 1815.

[21] The Coldstream Guards cemetery is located in the Rue de Laharie, just east of the village of St Bernard, and is marked on maps as 'Cimetière des Anglais'.

[22] **Talavera. Barrosa. Fuentes d'Onor. Salamanca. Nive. Peninsula.**

COLDSTREAM CAMPAIGNING. 1664–1815

Serial	Dates	Campaign	Battles	Date	Bn
1	1664–67	Second Dutch War	Naval Actions.	1662	1st
			Capture of New Amsterdam	1664	1st
2	1680–84	Tangier	**Tangier**	1680	1st
			Walcourt	1689	1st
3	1689–97	War of the League of Augsburg	Steenkirk	1692	1st & 2nd
			Landen	1693	1st
			Namur	1695	Composite
4	1702–13	War of the Spanish Succession	**Gibraltar**	1704-5	Composite
			Oudenarde	1708	1st
			Malplaquet	1709	1st
5	1740–48	War of the Austrian Succession	**Dettingen**	1743	1st
			Fontenoy	1745	1st
6	1745	The '45		1745	1st
7	1756–63	Seven Years War	St Malo	1758	1st
			Wilhelmstal	1762	2nd
			Omöneberg	1762	2nd
8	1775–83	American War of Independence	New York	1776	Composite
			Catawba River	1781	Composite
			Guildford Court House	1781	Composite
			Yorktown	1781	Composite
9	1793–1807	Napoleonic Wars	**Lincelles**	1793	1st
10			**Egypt**	1801	1st
11			Hanover	1805	1st
12			Copenhagen	1807	1st
13	1808–14	**Peninsular War**	Crossing of the Douro	1809	1st
			Talavera	1809	1st
			Barrosa	1811	2nd
			Fuentes D'Onor	1811	1st
			Salamanca	1812	1st
			Vitoria	1813	1st & 2nd
			San Sebastian	1813	1st & 2nd
			Bidassoa	1813	1st & 2nd
			Nivelle	1813	1st & 2nd
			Nive	1813	1st & 2nd
			Adour	1814	1st & 2nd
			Bayonne	1814	1st & 2nd
14	1815	Waterloo	Quatre Bras	1815	2nd
			Waterloo	1815	2nd

CHAPTER THREE

WATERLOO

by Julian Paget

At the beginning of 1815 life in England was just beginning to return to normal after nearly 28 years of unrelenting war against Napoleon Bonaparte and everyone was looking forward to a period of peace. Then on 26 February 1815 Napoleon escaped from Elba, landed in the South of France and was soon back in Paris as Emperor once more, with most of the country supporting him.

The Allies (Britain, Prussia, Russia and Austria) began assembling an Allied Army under the supreme command of the Duke of Wellington to deal with Boney once and for all, but it was a slow process, for the troops had, as usual, been disbanded as soon as possible after the end of hostilities. The 1st Battalion of the Regiment was in London, but the 2nd Battalion was sent in May to join Wellington's army in Belgium as part of 2nd Guards Brigade, commanded by Major General Sir John Byng of the Third Guards. The brigade was in 1st Division, commanded by Major General Sir George Cooke of the First Guards, together with 1st Guards Brigade.[1]

On 15 June 1815 Napoleon suddenly launched a 'blitzkrieg' across the frontier at Charleroi and advanced rapidly in a two-pronged attack towards Brussels, where Wellington had his head-quarters. The Duke was taken completely by surprise and exclaimed "Napoleon has humbugged me, by God. He has stolen 36 hours march on me." He was at that stage uncertain as to where Napoleon's main blow would fall, but he deployed his troops during the night of the 15th and awaited developments.

16 June 1815

The next day, the 16th, Napoleon attacked and defeated the Prussian army at Ligny. The Prussian commander, Marshal Blücher, retreated to Wavre in order to be able to support Wellington, as he had promised to do. Napoleon at the same time ordered Marshal Ney to capture the important crossroads at Quatre Bras on the main route to Brussels. Quatre Bras was defended by only 8,000 Dutch and Belgian troops, and they were attacked on the morning of the 16th by some 20,000 French. Somehow they managed to hold their ground until the afternoon when the British

[1] *1st Division.* (Major General Sir George Cooke. First Guards.)
1st Guards Brigade. (Major General Sir Peregrine Maitland. First Guards.)
2nd Battalion First Guards.
3rd Battalion First Guards.
2nd Guards Brigade. (Major General Sir John Byng. Third Guards.)
2nd Battalion Coldstream Guards.
2nd Battalion Third Guards.

reinforcements sent by Wellington began to arrive. By the evening the Allies outnumbered the French and Quatre Bras was secure.

Among the British troops sent to Quatre Bras were the two Guards Brigades. 2nd Battalion Coldstream Guards had been encamped at Enghien and orders were received at 0130 on the 16th to move immediately with all speed to Braine le Comte. The Battalion set off at 0430 and when it arrived was promptly told to hurry on to Quatre Bras.

It was a flaming hot June day, but by marching non-stop for thirteen hours, the men covered twenty-six miles and finally reached Quatre Bras at about 1700. The battle was still on and they were thrown straight into the fray. The brunt of the fighting fell on 1st Guards Brigade, who were in the lead; the 2nd Battalion was not heavily engaged. By nightfall the French withdrew and the crisis was over, leaving the exhausted troops to snatch some welcome rest.

17 June

The next day Wellington ordered all the troops at Quatre Bras to withdraw to his previously selected defensive position along the ridge at Mont St Jean, some three miles south of the village of Waterloo, where he now had his headquarters. The move was carried out successfully, though there was a sharp rearguard action on the way at Genappe, in which the battalion's light company was engaged.

Just as the army reached its positions there was a tremendous thunderstorm with torrential rain, so that within minutes everyone was soaked to the skin. There was no shelter, they had received no rations that day and they were exhausted, having marched almost non-stop for the last two days. But thankfully they threw off their packs and tried to get some rest in the waterlogged fields.

2nd Guards Brigade was positioned on the west end of the ridge of Mont St Jean, with 1st Guards Brigade on its left. It formed the right of the Allied line and some 500 yards to its front lay the château and farm of Hougoumont, a key outpost halfway between the British and French lines.

Just as the men were settling down, despite the steady rain, the unwelcome order came at about 1900 that the four light companies of the two Guards Brigades[2] were to move forward immediately and occupy the farm and orchard of Hougoumont.

The light companies had been the last to arrive at Mont St Jean, having been with the rearguard, and they were more exhausted than most. But they now set off into the driving rain with the prospect of a sleepless night ahead.

The 2nd Battalion light company was commanded by Lieutenant Colonel Henry Wyndham, and it was given the task of occupying the actual château and farm buildings of Hougoumont. The Third Guards light company occupied the large garden and the area round the farm, while the two light companies of the First Guards held the orchard some 500 yards to the east.

They were only just in time, for soon after they moved into the farm some French cavalry appeared, hoping to seize the position, but they were driven off with a few volleys. The men in the farm buildings may well have thought that they would enjoy a comfortable night under cover, but they were soon disillusioned, for they were put to work fortifying the buildings in every way possible. Loopholes were made in the walls and firesteps constructed; all the entrances were closed, and where

[2] Each infantry battalion consisted at full strength of six to ten companies, each up to 100 strong. One of them was a 'light company' which consisted of picked men trained as mobile troops and skirmishers. They operated either as a company within their own battalion or were amalgamated to form a 'light battalion'.

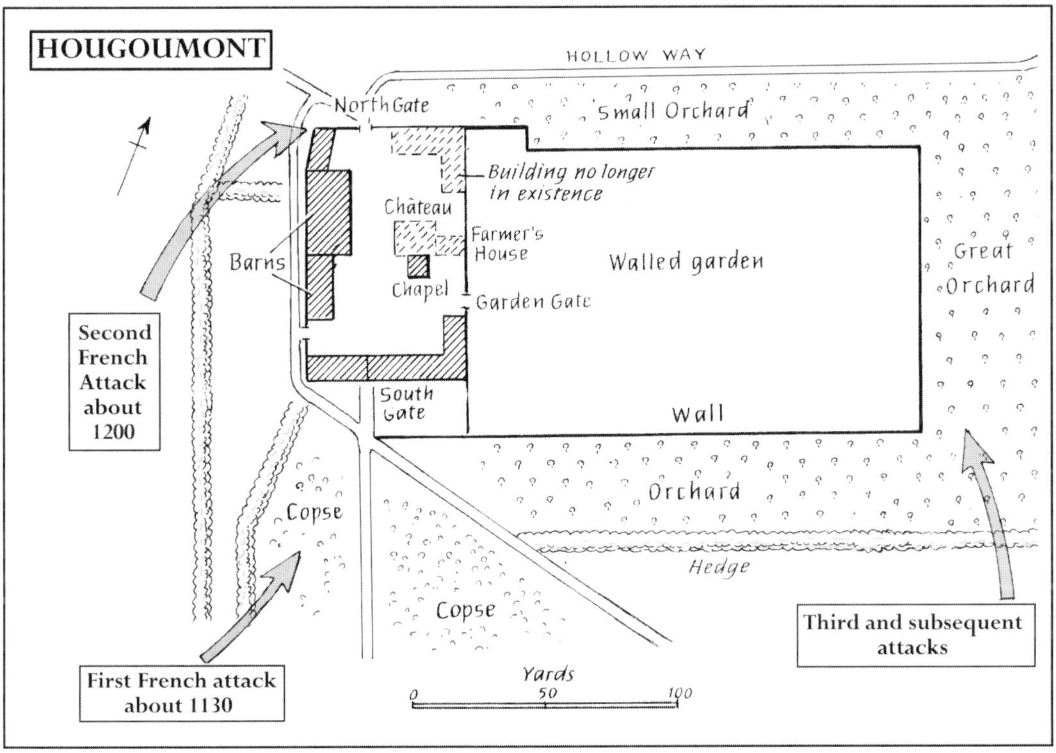

possible barricaded. Only the North or Great Gate was deliberately left open, so that reinforcements, supplies and ammunition could reach the farm from the main position behind.

Those in Hougoumont were certainly better off than their comrades on the ridge. Ensign Charles Short, aged only sixteen and a half, described his uncomfortable night:

> "We were under arms the whole night expecting the attack and it rained to that degree that the field where we were was halfway up our legs in mud; nobody, of course, could lie down. The ague got hold of some of the men. I with another officer had a blanket and with a little more gin we kept up very well. We had only one fire and you cannot conceive the state we were in. We formed a hollow square and prepared to receive Cavalry twice, but found it was a false alarm both times. Soon after daylight the Commissary sent up with the greatest difficulty some gin, and we found an old cask full of wet rye leaves which we breakfasted upon. Everyone was in high spirits."

18 June

The torrential rain finally eased off as dawn broke on Sunday, 18 June 1815 and everyone 'stood to' ready for the expected French attack. It was a miserable, muddy morning, and 72,000 sodden Allied troops faced an equally sodden 68,000 French veterans a mere 1,000 yards away across the valley.

Ten miles to the east, unknown to Napoleon, 60,000 Prussians under the indomitable 73-year-old warrior Marshal Blücher set out at dawn from Wavre to march to support Wellington, as Blücher had promised they would. The crucial question was whether they could arrive in time.

All was set for the Battle of Waterloo.

All the troops in and around Hougoumont, both Coldstream and Third Guards, were under the overall command of Lieutenant Colonel James Macdonell, (pronounced Macdonell) of the 2nd Battalion. He was a large, powerful officer, renowned for his bravery, having been awarded a gold medal (the equivalent of a Victoria Cross) for his distinguished conduct at the Battle of Maida in 1806. He would certainly distinguish himself again at Waterloo.

Lieutenant Colonel James Macdonell.

Soon after dawn Wellington rode down to Hougoumont to make sure that all was well and he ordered up a force of around 1,000 Nassau and Hanoverian troops, whom he sent to occupy the copse just south of Hougoumont – a reinforcement that was very welcome.

Just before 1100 he came down again to see that his orders had been carried out. He was accompanied this time by his Prussian Liaison Officer, General Müffling, and together they had a word with Colonel Macdonell. The Duke stressed the vital importance of holding Hougoumont and told Macdonell that his troops must "defend the post to the last extremity".

Müffling, who rather fancied himself as a tactician and liked to discuss military matters with the Duke, questioned whether the farm really could be held, seeing how exposed it was and how few men, a mere 1,500 or so, had been allocated to its defence.

"Ah," replied the Duke. "But you do not know Macdonell."

Half an hour later, at about 1130, the first shot of the Battle of Waterloo was fired. It was directed against Hougoumont, and from then on until the end of the day a total of seven enemy attacks would be launched against this key position – but it held out.

Napoleon had intended that the assault on Hougoumont should only be a diversion, designed to make Wellington weaken his centre by sending reinforcement to the farm. But the ploy did not work, because the Duke declined to change his plans. Moreover the French commander concerned, Napoleon's brother Jerome, was determined to show his worth, and so, contrary to orders, went on attacking in the vain hope of capturing it.

The first attack against Hougoumont was made at 1130 by Bauduin's Brigade and it drove back the Nassauers and Hanoverians holding the copse. But as the French troops emerged from the wood, confident that Hougoumont was now within their grasp, they were stopped in their tracks. Between them and the farm was a thirty-yard strip of open ground, a veritable 'killing ground', swept by accurate musket fire from the windows and loopholed walls manned by the Coldstream.

Desperately, the French launched one attack after another against the South Gate, but in vain, and throughout the day the gate was never forced.

The Closing of the Gate

The French lost some 1,500 men in this first assault, but they soon attacked again with a second brigade. This time they swept round to the west of the farm, supported by cavalry, and came very close to success, being thwarted only by the famous Closing of the Gate.

The open ground to the west of the farm was held by the light company of the Third Guards who were heavily outnumbered and were forced back to the North Gate, through which they withdrew into the courtyard of the farm. They then attempted to shut the gate behind them against the pursuing French, who were close on their heels. The attackers were led by a giant of a man called Lieutenant Legros, known appropriately as *'L'Enfonceur'* or 'The Smasher'. Seizing an axe from one of the pioneers, he swung it against the panels of the gate and forced his way through, followed by between 50 and 100 men.

For a moment it seemed to them that the capture of Hougoumont was in sight. Desperate close-quarter fighting developed on all sides. Some French soldiers reached as far as the château, but they were heavily outnumbered and eventually every single one of them was killed, except for one unarmed drummer boy, who was spared.

But even as this bitter fighting was taking place inside Hougoumont, more of the enemy were trying to force their way in through the gate. Lieutenant Colonel Macdonell was by the Garden Gate and when he became aware of the danger he at once realized that it was vital that the great North Gate be closed.

Shouting to three other Coldstream officers[3] nearby to join him, he rushed towards the gate. As the four of them reached the area of the Draw Well they were joined by two more Coldstreamers[4] and four men from the Third Guards.[5] Shoulder to shoulder the group drove back any enemy in their way and fought their way through to the North Gate.

Colonel Macdonell put his shoulder to it, together with Corporal James Graham, who was also of sturdy build. Others joined in, either adding their weight to those at the gate or else hacking and firing at the Frenchmen who were still trying to force their way in.

Very slowly the two heavy panels were pushed together and then held in position until the massive crossbar could be dropped into place. Finally the entrance was barricaded and reinforced with any pieces of timber that could be found.

But the struggle was not yet over. Even while the gate was being secured, some of the enemy tried to scale the walls, and one French Grenadier, standing on the shoulders of a comrade, leaned over the top and took aim at Colonel Wyndham. Fortunately Wyndham[6] saw him out of the corner of

[3] Lieutenant Colonel Henry Wyndham.
Ensign James Hervey.
Ensign Henry Gooch.

[4] Corporal James Graham (promoted to Sergeant after the battle).
Corporal Joseph Graham (his brother).

[5] Sergeant Ralph Fraser.
Sergeant Bruce McGregor.
Sergeant Joseph Aston.
Private Joseph Lester.

his eye; he had no musket himself, but, picking one up, he handed it to Corporal Graham, who managed, just in time, to shoot the Frenchman.

So the Great Gate was closed and was never again forced, but it had been "a near run thing". The enemy never managed to penetrate into Hougoumont again during the rest of the day and it is not hard to appreciate why Wellington declared later that "The success of the Battle of Waterloo turned on the closing of the gates [at Hougoumont]."

Major General Byng, commanding 2nd Guards Brigade, had been keeping a close watch on the fighting round Hougoumont, and when he saw the mêlée at the North Gate he ordered the remainder of the 2nd Bn Coldstream Guards to move forward and counter-attack the French who had penetrated to the north side of the farm.

The Commanding Officer, Lieutenant Colonel Alexander Woodford, (a Peninsular War veteran, who would later become a Field Marshal) led three companies[7] down to the North Gate soon after it had been finally closed and, after some stiff fighting, they drove the French back down the lane and then into the wood.

"We found the enemy very near the wall," he recorded later, "and charged them, upon which they went off, and I took the opportunity of entering the farm by a side door in the lane" (the West Door).

The rest of the battalion (less two companies left on the ridge with the Colours[8]) then moved into the farm. Colonel Woodford was in fact now the senior officer in Hougoumont, but he generously declined to take over command from Colonel Macdonell, who was doing so well, and they fought the battle together for the rest of the day.

The 600 or so additional Coldstreamers were a welcome reinforcement for the hard-pressed light companies inside Hougoumont, and in particular their arrival made it possible for Colonel Macdonell to strengthen the defences along the east wall of the garden and so offer better support to the troops defending the orchard.

So far the fighting had all been around Hougoumont, but at 1300 Napoleon at last launched his main attack, advancing with 18,000 men against Wellington's centre after a murderous 30-minute bombardment by 80 guns. It was repulsed, largely thanks to the charge by two brigades of British Heavy Cavalry, and Napoleon had to think again, for his whole plan had been frustrated.

There was now a brief lull for the defenders of Hougoumont, but at 1445 a new threat developed when the French brought up a battery of howitzers and began to shell the buildings. They fired 'carcass projectiles' (incendiary devices), which soon set fire to many of the roofs of the farm. By 1500 the château, the chapel and the Great Barn were all ablaze. Napoleon no doubt hoped that the fire would drive out the defenders, where his troops had failed, but he would be thwarted yet again.

"The heat and smoke of the conflagration were very difficult to bear," wrote Colonel Woodford. "Several men were burnt as neither Colonel Macdonell or myself could penetrate to the stables where the wounded had been carried."

[6] His niece said of him that, because of his experience at Hougoumont, he would never thereafter for the rest of his life close any door and would, as a result, often sit in a howling draught for hours on end!

[7] Grenadier Company. Lieutenant Colonel D. MacKinnon.
No 1 Company. Lieutenant Colonel T. Sowerby.
No 4 Company. Lieutenant Colonel the Hon E. Acheson.

[8] Nos 7 and 8 Companies. The officers of these companies, however, left the Colours in the care of the Non-Commissioned Officers and themselves joined in the fighting at Hougoumont.

At this moment Corporal James Graham, who had helped to close the gate, approached Colonel Macdonell and asked permission to leave his post in the firing line in the garden. Well aware of Graham's bravery, the Colonel queried why he wanted to retire at such a critical moment.

"I would not," replied the Corporal. "Only my brother lies wounded in that building which has just caught fire."

Permission was promptly given, and his brother, Joseph (who had also been involved in the Closing of the Gate) was removed to safety, whereupon Corporal Graham immediately returned to his post.

There were wounded men from both sides in the burning buildings and many were burnt alive. Most of Hougoumont was now blazing fiercely and there was little that could be done about it. The chapel was ablaze and there are eye-witness accounts of how the flames licked through the wooden door and set fire to the feet of the life-size, wooden statue of Christ on the Cross that hung just above the door. But then they stopped, miraculously it seemed to some, leaving the feet charred and blackened, but the remainder of the body untouched.

The fire had meanwhile been noticed by Wellington, who immediately wrote a message repeating his original orders that Hougoumont must be held at all costs. It was written, as was his custom, in his own hand on a slip of ass's skin which provided a smooth surface that was largely waterproof and could be wiped clean (an early version of talc!).

"I see that the fire has communicated from the Hay Stack to the Roof of the château. You must however still keep your men in those parts to which the fire does not reach. Take care that no men are lost by the falling-in of the Roof or Floors. After they have both fallen in, occupy the ruined walls inside the Garden; particularly if it should be possible for the enemy to pass through the Embers in the inside of the House."

What a remarkable example of the Duke's personal attention to detail!

It was a grim scene indeed inside Hougoumont at this moment. Burning timbers crashed down on the men in their positions and thick, choking smoke billowed everywhere, making their eyes stream as they strained to watch for the next enemy move. Red-hot flying sparks burned their uniforms and started new fires. Through the roar of the flames came cries for help from the wounded and the wild neighing of panic-stricken horses. Enemy shells still crashed into the buildings and the musket fire was incessant. Yet the defenders stayed at their posts and fought on.

Private Matthew Clay of the Third Guards was among them, positioned in the château, and he described the scene:

> "I was told off with others under Lieutenant Gough (*sic.* probably Ensign Gooch) of the Coldstream Guards, and was posted in an upper room. This room was situated higher than the surrounding buildings and we annoyed the enemy's skirmishers from the window. The enemy noticed this and threw their shells among us and set the building which we were defending on fire. Our officer placed himself at the entrance of the room and would not allow anyone to leave his post until our position became hopeless and too perilous to remain. We fully expected the floor to sink with us every moment, and in our escape several of us were more or less injured."

So, while Hougoumont blazed and disintegrated round them, the defenders remained at their posts, and not a single Frenchman managed to penetrate into either the buildings or the garden.

But enemy pressure on the approaches to Hougoumont from the north was steadily increasing and it was only with the greatest difficulty that the vital line of communication to the North Gate was kept open by the 2nd Battalion, whose responsibility it was. It was just as well that they were successful in this task, for a new crisis now arose as supplies of ammunition began to run low.

The situation was saved by the heroic action of a Private of the Waggon Train, who was in charge of a tumbril of ammunition on the ridge. An officer on the staff recorded the incident:

> "I merely pointed out to him where he was wanted, when he gallantly started his horses and drove straight down to the farm, to the gate of which I saw him arrive. He must have lost his horses as there was severe fire kept on him. I feel convinced that to that man's service the Guards owe their ammunition."[9]

The Regimental History states that the tumbril arrived "about one o'clock" and "proved most seasonable".

Elsewhere the battle was steadily building up to a crisis. At 1600 Ney launched the first of the two great cavalry charges that the French would make that day. Over 4,500 horsemen pounded across the muddy valley and on up the slope where the Allied squares awaited them. Five times they attacked, but they could not break the squares, and five times they were beaten off.

For over an hour the attacks went on with the utmost gallantry and determination; but even when Napoleon threw in a further 5,000 horsemen the ever-dwindling squares stood firm. Finally it was the French who withdrew, with the vital breakthrough still not achieved.

The defence of Hougoumont can be said to have contributed to the defeat of these cavalry attacks. The fact that both Hougoumont and La Haye Sainte were still in Allied hands meant that as the French cavalry advanced they were under fire from both flanks. They were therefore forced to charge on a very restricted front of only 800 yards, thus losing some impetus as well as providing a better target for the Allied artillery. Hougoumont has been described as "a thorn in the side of all the French attacks" and this was certainly true of the two cavalry charges.

But the defenders were not allowed to remain mere spectators for long. Just about the same time as the two cavalry charges, a powerful attack by some three infantry regiments was made against the south-east corner of the orchard. The sector was held by the Third Guards, supported by two battalions of the King's German Legion (KGL), but they were forced back as far as the Hollow Way, where they rallied. The Commanding Officer of the Third Guards reported:

> "But when the attacking troops attempted to pass through the orchard they received so destructive a fire from the Coldstream Guards posted inside the Garden Wall that they were completely staggered, and we meanwhile advanced and regained our post."

The seventh and final attack on Hougoumont came at about 1830. The gallant KGL had been finally driven out of La Haye Sainte, when their ammunition ran out, and the French now had troops to spare for a final assault on Hougoumont. It again came in against the Third Guards in the orchard, and once more Colonel Hepburn, commanding the Third Guards, declared:

[9] A plaque by the North Gate commemorates the incident.

> "Again the fire of the Coldstream did us good service. In fact it was this fire that constituted the strength of the post. We once more advanced and resumed our station along the front edge, from whence there was no further effort to dislodge us."

At 1930 came the climax of the battle. The Prussians were now closing in in growing numbers against Napoleon's right flank and he had to take one final gamble, whether to withdraw while he could or to make one last desperate bid for victory. He decided to risk all and launched his invincible Imperial Guard against the centre of the Allied line. But it was too late. They were repulsed and withdrew back to the French lines.

"La Garde Recule"

These three words spelt in effect the defeat of France and the Grande Armée was soon in full retreat. But round Hougoumont the bitter fighting continued unabated, with neither side being aware of the fate of the Imperial Guard.

As the Allied line moved forward the weary troops in Hougoumont remained at their posts. Exhausted, they watched in the gathering gloom as the enemy, who for the last nine hours had done their best to kill them, now disappeared into the wood where at dawn that same day it had all started.

After a while the Coldstreamers in Hougoumont were ordered to move back and bivouack for the night in a field just behind the farm, where they joined Nos 7 and 8 Companies. The Third Guards too bivouacked nearby, joining up with their light company who had been with the Coldstream in Hougoumont all day.

At the Roll Call that evening there were many names that went unanswered in both battalions. The losses were not as grim as in some of the regiments on the main position, but they were heavy enough. The 2nd Battalion lost 348 all ranks, while the Third Guards' casualties were 236. Altogether the 6,000 or so Allied troops who were eventually involved in the defence of Hougoumont suffered around 1,500 casualties against French losses estimated at more than 5,000.

There are varying accounts of the numbers involved on each side in the struggle for Hougoumont. There is little doubt that the French committed 13–15,000 troops to their continuous attacks on the farm and orchard. This represented the major part of three divisions (Jerome, Foy and Bachelu) which might otherwise have been available elsewhere on the battlefield and might well have made a difference to the outcome.

Wellington committed altogether a maximum of 3,500 troops to the actual defence of Hougoumont itself, with perhaps a further 2,500 in support behind the farm. But even on the basis of around 6,000 Allied troops defending Hougoumont against 14,000 French, this was a most satisfactory and economical ratio from Wellington's point of view. He fed in reinforcements only as essential and yet tied down most of a French corps for the whole day. Nor did he weaken his centre as Napoleon had hoped he would.

That night Wellington wrote in his Despatch:

> "It gives me the greatest satisfaction to assure your Lordship that the army has never on any occasion conducted itself better. The Division of Guards . . . set an example which was followed by all."

Wellington's confidante, Thomas Creevy, related later that as the Duke was at work on his Despatch he "praised greatly those Guards who kept the farm against the repeated attacks of the French." He also commented:

> "You may depend upon it that no troops but the British could have held Hougoumont and only the best of them at that."

Nor had the Duke forgotten that General Müffling had, on the eve of the battle, ventured to question whether Hougoumont was defensible at all. He now could not resist making the brief comment when he next saw him: "You see, the Guards held Hougoumont."

"The Bravest Man in England"

All ranks who took part in the Battle of Waterloo received in 1816 a silver Waterloo Medal, the first general issue made to the British Army. In addition, they had the letters 'W.M.' (Waterloo Man) put after their name in the records; this was perhaps of even greater importance to them since it counted as two years' extra service.

Officers in the Household Cavalry and the Foot Guards benefited also in that the privilege of 'double rank' was extended to include Ensigns, who were now given the rank of Lieutenant.

Corporal James Graham (now a Sergeant) and Sergeant Fraser of the Third Guards were both awarded a special medal for their gallantry at Hougoumont. Sergeant Graham was also nominated by Wellington for an annuity of £10 a year which had been offered by a patriotic citizen, the Reverend John Norcross, Rector of Framlingham in Suffolk, to be given to "one of his brave countrymen who fought in the late tremendous but glorious conflict."

Unfortunately, after only two years, the Rector went bankrupt and the annuity ceased. But when he died some time later he left £500 to be given to "the bravest man in England". Wellington was invited to nominate this individual, and he wrote:

> "The success of the Battle of Waterloo turned on the closing of the gates at Hougoumont. The gates were closed in the most courageous manner at (sic) the very nick of time by the efforts of Sir J. Macdonell.[10] I cannot help thinking Sir James is the man to whom you should give the £500."

So it was settled, but the gallant Colonel immediately shared his award with Sergeant Graham, declaring:

> "I cannot claim all the merit due to the closing of the gates of Hougoumont, for Sergeant John[11] Graham, who saw the importance of the step, rushed forward and together we shut the gates."

[10] He had been knighted after Waterloo.

[11] This must be an error by the Colonel. It should be James.

Hougoumont Today

Hougoumont today is remarkably unchanged from what it was in 1815 and it is a most moving place to visit. Most of the buildings still stand and the Great Gate is still in position, though it is now of metal rather than wood; the outbuildings on either side are gone, but it is not difficult to envisage the dramatic Closing of the Gate.

The South Gate is much as it was (less the bullet holes!) and on the wall alongside it are two plaques to commemorate the 2nd Battalion's defence of it.[12] The upper one is simply a Coldstream star with the words 'Coldstream Guards' and was put up in 1965. Below it is an inscribed plaque that was erected in 1993 at the instigation of Lieutenant Colonel Sir Julian Paget, a former Commanding Officer of the 2nd Battalion (1960–1962).

The château was burnt down in 1815, but the tiny, simple chapel next to it survives virtually untouched, with the charred figure of Christ still hanging there, and it is a moving memorial to the men who fought and died in Hougoumont that day. The interior of the chapel was redecorated and restored in 1965 by the Pioneers of the 2nd Battalion as part of the celebrations of the 150th anniversary of the battle, and the Third Guards made a wooden cross for the altar.

Hougoumont rightly holds a very special place in the annals of the Regiment, and it is also remembered every year through the traditional ceremony of 'Hanging the Brick' in the Sergeants' Mess at Christmas.

[12] Two large locks taken from Hougoumont are held by the Regiment and have been loaned to the Wellington Museum at Waterloo.

CHAPTER FOUR

AN AGE OF EMPIRE, 1815–1914

by Julian Paget

The Long Peace, 1815–1853

Victory at Waterloo and the final overthrow of Napoleon brought England thirty-eight years of peace, the longest period without a war since the Regiment was formed. Campaigning gave way to an era of relaxation and social extravagance that became known as 'the Age of Elegance'. The pace was set by the Monarch, King George IV, who presided over a whirl of ceremonial and social activity centred not only on London but also on Windsor and Brighton, and the Household Troops were inevitably involved.

Home Service

The 2nd Battalion returned from France in 1818 and both battalions were then kept fully occupied on Royal duties. This consisted of guarding the Sovereign and his palaces, with Guard Mounting taking place daily on Horse Guards. From there the troops marched off to the Guard Room at St James's Palace (where it still is today). The King lived mainly at Kensington Palace and the Guard at Buckingham House was only a Sergeant's command until 1837 when Queen Victoria made it her 'main residence' and called it Buckingham Palace.[1] The Guard was then increased to one officer and forty-four men and the Changing of the Guard began to take place in the forecourt as today.

Until 1829 when Sir Robert Peel created the Metropolitan Police, the Army was responsible for the maintenance of law and order in the capital and it was quite a heavy commitment. The Foot Guards had to protect over thirty buildings including the Royal Mint, the Bank of England, the British Museum, the Savoy Prison and the Royal Academy. They not only had to provide picquets regularly at Covent Garden and Drury Lane theatres to prevent rowdyism at performances, but Guardsmen were also used as 'extras' for operas – especially productions of *Aida*[2]. Another duty was that troops were frequently called out on fire-fighting duties.[3]

A more serious task came in 1820 when the 2nd Battalion was called on to deal with a plot called the Cato Street Conspiracy, in which a group of ten dissidents were planning to assassinate several Cabinet Ministers when they were dining with Lord Harrowby at his house in Belgrave Square.

[1] Built in 1704 as the London home of the Duke of Buckingham, it was bought by King George III in 1762 as a Dower House for Queen Charlotte.

[2] There is still a small room at Drury Lane Theatre known as 'the Barracks'.

[3] A duty that has also occurred in the last fifty years during Fire Brigade strikes.

Their plan was fortunately discovered just in time and on 19 March 1820 the conspirators were surrounded in their hide-out at a house in Cato Street just off the Edgware Road.

A detachment from the 2nd Battalion, with two peace officers, closed in and captured nine of the ten men.[4] The tenth member of the gang, who was in fact the ringleader, escaped, but was caught soon afterwards, and they were all either hanged or transported.

Training

Training for war was minimal and was usually carried out in Hyde Park. It was still based on the tactics of the Peninsular War and concentrated on musketry and the ability to carry out the basic battlefield drills such as advancing in line and forming square. It was carried out in what we would call Home Service Order, i.e. a scarlet tunic, grey trousers and a shako, except for the grenadier companies who wore bearskins.

Living Conditions

Living conditions in the Army were not good early in the nineteenth century, but they improved steadily as the standard of living rose throughout the country. The Guards took a particular interest in the welfare of their men and indeed took the lead in instituting several new amenities in their regiments, for which the officers paid out of their own pockets.

Regimental schools were instituted in 1811, a Sergeant schoolmaster being appointed with a special allowance of £10 a year. In 1814 the Coldstream set up their own hospital, several years before the first Army hospitals were opened.

A particularly significant improvement was the provision of married quarters for the men. The wives and children of soldiers had till then lived in the barrack rooms, as was the custom throughout the Army, and the only possible privacy was a blanket or curtain stretched across the room. This unsatisfactory situation changed only because of an outbreak of cholera in 1832. The overcrowded barrack rooms were obviously a health threat and so some families were billetted out in cholera-free areas, while separate family quarters were arranged in barracks as an emergency measure.

In 1852 the Household Division led the way in setting up more permanent accommodation for families when a group of officers raised £9,000 privately to build a hostel for fifty-six families in Francis Street, just off the Vauxhall Bridge Road. They were bought out a few years later by the War Department, who pointed out that it was illegal for soldiers to pay rent to their officers for their accommodation, even though it was only the equivalent of twelve new pence a week.

Only three infantry barracks were available in London in 1821 and none of them could house a complete battalion. Most men and their families were therefore still billetted out in inns and on private citizens, and it was not until 1834, when Wellington Barracks was completed, that there was enough barrack accommodation for the five battalions stationed in the capital.[5]

[4] The detachment was commanded by Captain FitzClarence and included Sergeant Graham of Hougoumont fame, who again distinguished himself, this time by saving the life of his officer.

[5] Tower of London. Wellington Barracks. King's New Barracks (near the National Gallery). Portman Street. (in Granville Place, Portman Square). Knightsbridge Barracks (near St George's Place, Hyde Park Corner). Infantry Barracks, Windsor, now Victoria Barracks.

Jacob the Goose

No serious campaign disturbed the Long Peace, but in 1839 a Guards Brigade, consisting of the 2nd Battalions of the Grenadier and Coldstream Guards, was sent to Canada to deal with a revolt by the French element of the population there. They were not involved in any fighting, but were kept there on garrison duties until 1842.

The campaign is well known within the Coldstream Guards because it led to the acquisition of 'Jacob', a large, white goose who attached himself to the battalion and became a Regimental pet. Then one snowy night he saved many lives by giving the alarm when the rebels were just about to launch a surprise attack.

Thereafter he was taken on strength as an honoured Regimental mascot and was brought back to London, where he used to parade up and down alongside the sentry outside the barrack gate. He was eventually run over by a van in the Portman Square Barracks, but is still remembered. His head and neck were preserved and are on display in the Guards Museum, hung with an officer's gorget inscribed 'Jacob. 2nd Bn Coldstream Guards. Died on Duty'.[6]

Jacob the Goose.

The Crimean War, 1854–56

In March 1854 the Long Peace ended with the outbreak of the Crimean War, caused by Russian aggression against Turkey. Russia had always wanted a warm-water port, and so in 1853 the Tsar picked a quarrel with Turkey, with a view to gaining control of the Dardanelles and so acquiring access to the Mediterranean. On 30 November Russia destroyed the Turkish fleet in the Black Sea by attacking it while in harbour at Sinop (shades of Pearl Harbor in 1941!).

Britain and France (now allies, though on somewhat uneasy terms) declared war on Russia and agreed to send a joint naval and military force to the Crimea with the aim of destroying the Russian fleet based there. It was thought that this would teach the Tsar the 'short, sharp lesson' he needed and that the war would be over by Christmas.

A Guards Brigade was sent out, with 1st Bn Coldstream Guards alongside 3rd Bn Grenadier Guards and 1st Bn Scots Guards. They were a fine body of men, mostly Regulars, with 7 to 18 years'

[6] In 1995 Number 7 Company of the Regiment, the descendants of the 2nd Battalion, went on a training visit to Hungary and was presented by the Hungarian 62nd Mechanical Infantry Brigade with "Jacob Mk II", who duly returned to England, but unfortunately turned out to be a gander! (*Guards Magazine* 1996).

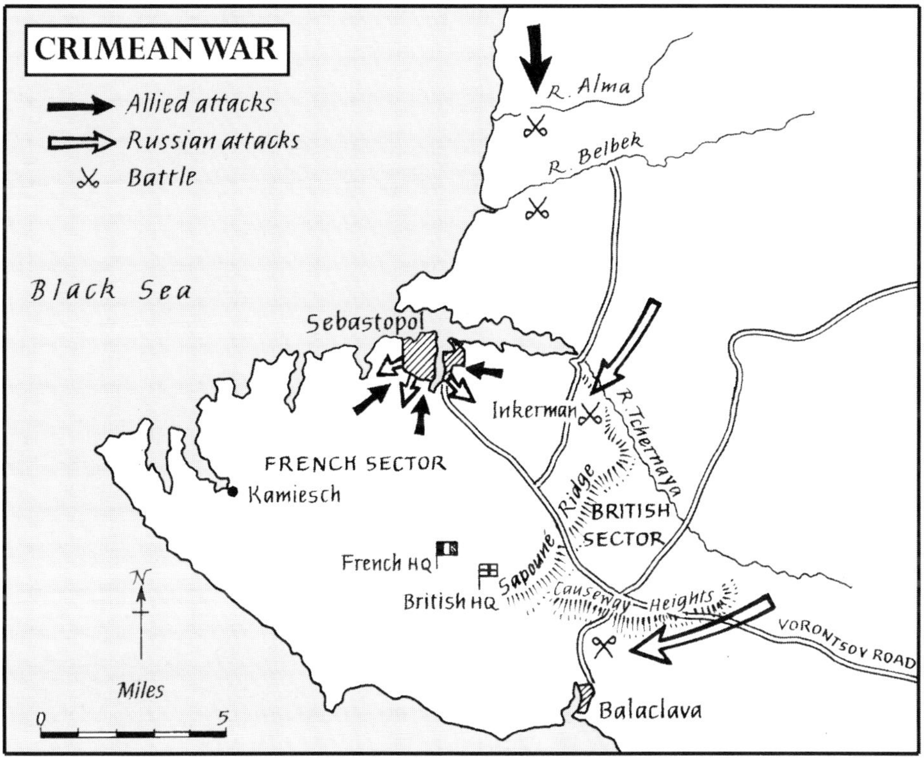

service, whose efficiency had been improved by training at the new camp set up the previous year at Chobham.

But the Army as a whole was disgracefully rusty and mismanaged after forty years of peace; organization and equipment were hopelessly inadequate, as would soon become painfully clear, at the expense, as always, of the troops. The commanders were old and out-of-date, and collaboration with the French, after some 700 years of fighting against them, proved decidedly difficult.[7]

The Allied armies landed at Calamita Bay, some 30 miles north of Sevastopol, and the first encounter was at the Battle of the **Alma** on 20 September 1854, when the Guards Brigade was in the thick of the fighting to capture the formidable strongpoint, the Great Redoubt. Although outnumbered, it forced the Russians to withdraw and became the Regiment's fifteenth Battle Honour.

The Allies then advanced on Sevastopol and the fatal decision was made not to attack it immediately but to invest it in preparation for a siege. The British base was at Balaclava, with the French on their left, and on 25 October the Russians launched a strong attack from the east against the British sector. They were stopped by the famous stand by the 93rd Foot, which became known as 'the Thin Red Line', and by the successful Charge of the Heavy Brigade of Cavalry. This was followed by the famous, but disastrous, Charge of the Light Brigade, and in the end the battle was a stalemate.

The Regiment was not involved at Balaclava, but certainly was in the Battle of **Inkerman** two

[7] Lord Raglan kept referring to 'the enemy' as 'the French'.

Private George Strong winning the Victoria Cross by throwing an unexploded shell out of the forward trenches at Sevastopol, September 1855.

weeks later. As dawn broke on 5 November a thick fog shrouded the battlefield and enabled 30,000 Russians to close in unseen on the 6,000 or so British troops holding the approaches to Balaclava. It was an area of very broken ground, covered in thick scrub and the fighting soon developed into a confused mêlée over which commanders had little control. It has fairly been called 'a soldiers' battle', for success depended on the determination and initiative of scattered bodies of troops all fighting on their own.

Lord Wantage VC, of the Scots Fusilier Guards (as they were then called), wrote:

> "Few battles have been fought in which the personal influence of the company officers had so much to do . . . no divisional, brigade or even regimental order was given. The men, headed by their officers, fought in companies or half-companies."

An example of the type of fighting was the Regiment's first Victoria Cross, won by Captain Goodlake of the 1st Battalion.[8] He was in command of the skirmishers out in front of the main Allied line and distinguished himself by holding off vastly superior numbers long enough for the other troops to get into position.[9]

[8] A party visiting the battlefield of Inkerman in 1998 found his name scratched on the wall of a cave in which he and his skirmishers must have hidden while out on operations.

[9] The Victoria Cross was instituted by Queen Victoria in 1856 for valour in action, and the first distribution was made by The Queen in Hyde Park on 26 June 1857. The medals were cast from the metal of captured Russian guns.

Another Victoria Cross was won by Private William Stanlake, who was a sharpshooter. On one occasion he crawled to within six yards of a Russian sentry, as a result of which a successful attack was launched on the enemy position. A third Victoria Cross went to Private George Strong, who picked up a live shell and threw it out of the trench. The fourth award was won by Lieutenant John Conolly, who displayed great gallantry while in the 49th Foot, and was promoted into the Coldstream Guards in addition to winning a Victoria Cross.

It was grim fighting, particularly round the Sandbag Battery, where the Guards Brigade was heavily involved, and the Regiment lost thirteen out of seventeen officers, eight of them being killed. Finally, it was the Russians who withdrew, but the Regiment had suffered 208 casualties.

Drummers in the Crimea 1855 (from a colour lithograph by Price-Watkins).

The campaign then stagnated into a prolonged and unsuccessful siege of **Sevastopol**[10] which dragged on until September 1855. The winter of 1854–55 was exceptionally severe and the troops suffered terrible hardships. On the night of 14 November 1854 an appalling storm sank twenty-one ships containing much of the Army's food, clothing, equipment, medical supplies and comforts. Tents were destroyed, frostbite was commonplace and many died of cholera and scurvy.[11]

Peace came at last in March 1856 and the 1st Battalion returned home in June. On 8 July it paraded at Aldershot and was inspected by Queen Victoria, who, it is recorded, "quite broke down and burst into tears". The next day it marched through London to loud cheers.

It had been a grim and also ill-managed war, due to the shameful incompetence of the authorities, both civil and military, in looking after their troops. But good did come out of evil. The first-ever war correspondent, William Russell of *The Times*, sent back a series of highly critical, first-hand despatches exposing the unacceptable suffering imposed on the troops, and these aroused public opinion. At the same time Florence Nightingale revolutionized the medical services and began a life-long campaign to provide more care and more respect for the British soldier both in war and in peace.

The result was a series of drastic and long overdue reforms to the whole Army, implemented largely due to the drive and imagination of Sidney Herbert, who was three times Secretary of State at War between 1846 and 1863, and Edward Cardwell, who held the post from 1868–74. Chelsea Barracks was built 1865–70 and those at Windsor were refurbished; the out-of-date accommodation at St John's Wood and Portman Square was given up and the first married quarters were built. Education was introduced for the troops, sixty per cent of whom were illiterate, while officers were

10 A Battle Honour, together with Alma and Inkerman.

11 There were around four deaths from sickness to every one due to enemy action.

sent as reluctant students to the new Military University at Camberley[12] to learn more about their profession.

Training was made more realistic, though it was still carried out in tunic and bearskin. But it was no longer limited to drills in Hyde Park. Manoeuvres up to divisional level were organized at Aldershot in 1871–73, while the Foot Guards set up their own training area at Pirbright. Signalling (with flags) was introduced and horse-drawn transport was provided at battalion level. In 1890 the Lee Enfield rifle was issued to replace the Brown Bess musket that had been the soldier's weapon for over 150 years.

Imperial Warfare

From 1856 to 1882 the Regiment saw no active service, but during the Zulu War of 1879 Captain the Hon Ronald Campbell of the Regiment distinguished himself by leading a suicidal attack on a Zulu position in a cave wide enough for only one person to enter. He was killed in what the C-in-C, Sir Evelyn Wood, described as "one of the bravest deeds I ever saw". Posthumous VCs were not awarded at that time, or he would certainly have won one, and so made two VCs in the family in two generations, for his son would win a Victoria Cross in the Great War. (See page 59.)

Egypt, 1882

In 1882 a Guards Brigade composed of 2nd Bn Grenadier Guards, 2nd Bn Coldstream Guards and 1st Bn Scots Guards was sent to **Egypt** as part of a force under Sir Garnet Wolseley to deal with a Colonel Arabi who had massacred 150 Europeans and actually dared to demand "Egypt for the Egyptians". The first and only action for the Regiment was the Battle of **Tel-el-Kebir** on 13 September, where the Eqyptian army was routed and Cairo occupied.[13]

Sudan, 1884

Peace in the Middle East was short-lived, however, and only two years later Sir Garnet Wolseley was called upon again to go to the rescue of General Gordon who was besieged in Khartoum in the Sudan by Mahomet Ahmed, better known as the Mahdi, the self-declared leader of the Moslem world.

The plan was for a two-pronged advance on Khartoum from the north. One force moved up the Nile in some of the tourist steamers belonging to an enterprising travel agent called Mr Thomas Cook. The other prong was a mobile force mounted mainly on camels, which was to move 150 miles across the desert to attack Khartoum from the west.

The Household Cavalry formed a Heavy Camel Regiment and the Foot Guards, not to be outdone, formed a rival Guards Camel Regiment (otherwise known as 'The Camelry Corps'!). It was commanded by Lt Col the Hon E.T.H. Boscawen of the Regiment[14] and consisted of detachments of two officers and forty men from each regiment.

Despite the disapproval of the C-in-C in Horse Guards, The Duke of Cambridge, (who declared

[12] Later to become the Staff College.

[13] Both 'Tel-el-Kebir' and 'Egypt 1882' became Battle Honours.

[14] His son, the Rt Hon Robert Boscawen MC, and his grandson, Lt Col Hugh Boscawen, both followed him into the Regiment.

that the idea of Guardsmen on camels was "unsound and distasteful to Regiments, officers and men") the force was formed and arrived in Cairo in December 1884. It then set off somewhat unsteadily and uncomfortably into the desert, wearing the new 'khaki' uniform for the first time (described unenthusiastically by The Queen as "a sort of café-au-lait shade"). It reached Khartoum on 28 January 1885, only to discover that it had been captured by the Mahdi two days before and General Gordon was dead.[15]

So ended what was expected to be the first and last official appearance of the Coldstream Guards on camels, but in fact the 3rd Battalion, when stationed in Egypt in the 1930s, mounted its Intelligence Section on the beasts.

Suakin, 1885

The Sudan campaign was not a Battle Honour, but the Regiment acquired one more when the 1st Battalion[16] was sent in March 1885 to **Suakin** in the Sudan to round up the remnants of the Mahdi's army. It was a comparatively minor operation, but noteworthy because a New South Wales battalion was attached to the Guards Brigade, the first time that Australian troops had fought as part of the British Army and outside their own country.

Ashanti, 1895

A similar imperial campaign occurred in 1895 when an expeditionary force was sent to Ashanti in West Africa; it included a Guards Composite Company, which had a Coldstream detachment, and successfully completed its mission of deposing the local ruler, King Prempeh, who had offended Victorian principles by running a flourishing slave trade.

Formation of 3rd Battalion

In 1897 the strength of the whole Army was increased and, as a result, the Coldstream and Scots Guards both received the welcome news that they could raise a third battalion. So the 3rd Battalion Coldstream Guards was formed at Woolwich on 1 December 1897 and received its Colours from Queen Victoria in Aldershot on 6 July 1898. By April 1899 the Battalion had an establishment of six companies and this was raised to eight in July 1900.

South African War, 1899–1902

On 10 March 1899 the 1st Battalion was sent to Gibraltar and when the South African War broke out on 12 October in the same year the 1st and 2nd Battalions were both shipped to Cape Town, together with 3rd Bn Grenadier Guards and 1st Bn Scots Guards. They there joined 1st Guards Brigade[17] which was part of 1st Division, commanded by Major General Lord Methuen, Scots Guards.

[15] A Coldstream Cup for polo dates back to this posting.
[16] It was part of a Guards Brigade consisting of 3rd Bn Grenadier Guards, 1st Bn Coldstream Guards and 2nd Bn Scots Guards, and was commanded by Major General A. Lyon Fremantle.
[17] Commanded by Major General Sir H.E. Colvile, Grenadier Guards.

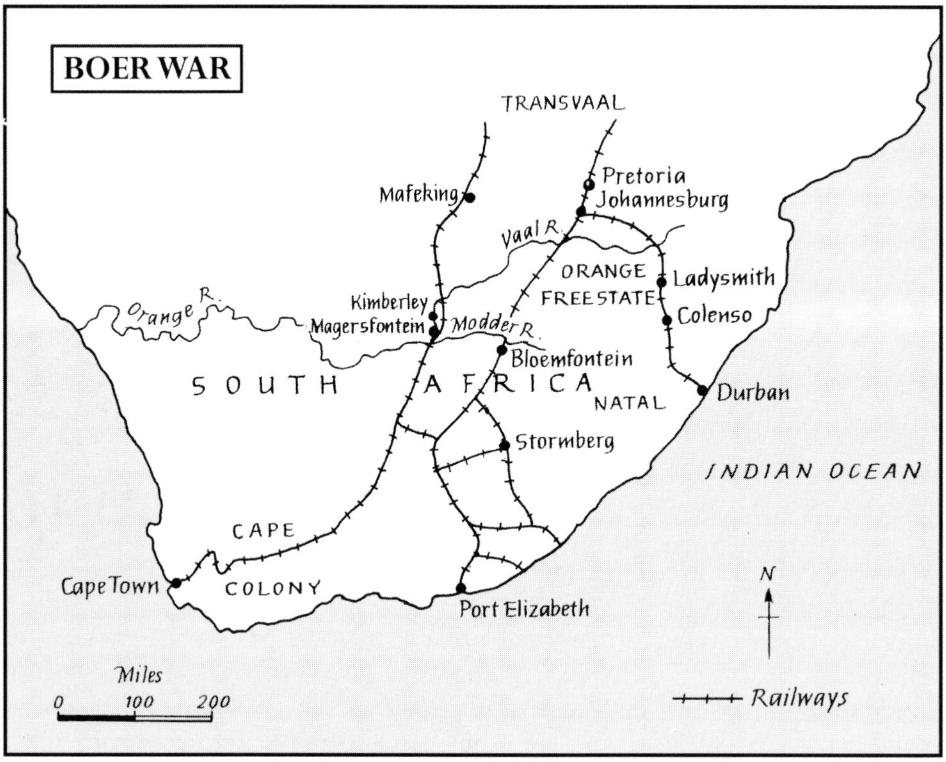

The war started disastrously with the Boers successfully besieging the British garrisons in Kimberley, Mafeking and Ladysmith.

The army began its advance northwards to relieve Kimberley on 21 November, and on the 23rd both Coldstream battalions were involved in the fighting at Belmont, followed by the Battle of **Modder River**[18], where they were under fire for twelve hours and suffered ninety-two casualties, including the Commanding Officer of the 2nd Battalion, Lt Col H.R. Stopford, who was killed. The advance continued and on 11 December they were involved in the costly battle at Magersfontein, where the Commanding Officer of the 1st Battalion, Lt Col A.E. Codrington, was wounded.

Things were not going well and this period became known as 'Black Week', when the British forces suffered three serious setbacks: Stormberg (10 December), Magersfontein (11th) and Colenso (15th). After this the advance was halted and the Guards Brigade returned to the Modder River area.

In the New Year the situation improved markedly when Lord Roberts took over as C-in-C. He relieved Kimberley on 15 February and forced the Boer commander, Cronje, to surrender shortly afterwards at Paardeberg. Ladysmith was relieved on 28 February and the Boer capital of Pretoria was captured on 5 June, with the 2nd Battalion leading the advance.[19]

The situation had swung dramatically against the Boers, but they were far from defeated and the

[18] A Battle Honour.

[19] Major General Pole-Carew of the Regiment took over command of 1st Guards Brigade on 12 February 1900 and of 11th Division on 13 April 1900.

Members of the 3rd Battalion Camel Company at Khartoum 1908, where the Battalion spent a year.

war now entered its second phase – mobile guerrilla operations. The problem was to get to grips with the elusive Boer 'commandos', who were extremely skilled and elusive, with no set positions or bases, and they proved remarkably difficult to defeat.

New mobile units were needed and, as the Household Cavalry had returned home in November 1900, the Foot Guards stepped rather smugly into the breach by forming two Guards Mounted Infantry Companies. All Regiments contributed, and the Coldstream found their share; after six weeks training at Aldershot they set sail for South Africa in November 1901.

But it proved a lengthy and frustrating task to round up the 'commandos' and it was 31 May 1902 when the Boers finally capitulated.

Both battalions spent the last period of the war operating in Cape Colony[20] and returned home in October 1902, having earned two Battle Honours, **Modder River** and **South Africa 1899–1902.**

Reforms

Although the campaign had ended in success, there was general disquiet over the serious weaknesses that it had exposed in the Army, despite the reforms initiated after the Crimean War of 1854–56. A further set of improvements were therefore set in hand, which led to the creation of the magnificent, professional army that would defy the Kaiser in 1914.

The driving force behind the reforms was Lord Haldane, who was Secretary of State for War from 1905 to 1913; he revitalized the Army at every level. He created the Army Council and a staff to serve it. He also organized an Expeditionary Force of one cavalry and six infantry divisions to be always ready for active service. The Brigade of Guards' contribution to it was 1st Guards Brigade at Aldershot and 4th Guards Brigade composed of battalions in London and Windsor.

[20] There is a village in Cape Colony which is called 'Coldstream', traditionally so named because two (unidentified) Coldstream officers spent a leave there during the war and the local inhabitants so enjoyed their company that they named the place 'Coldstream'. So it has remained ever since, and any visiting Coldstreamers will be made very welcome.

But, as always in times of peace, the Treasury axe fell on the Armed Forces and when a new Liberal Government came to power in 1905 they demanded the disbandment of two Guards battalions as part of extensive defence cuts. 3rd Bn Scots Guards was particularly vulnerable and was disbanded the next year.

3rd Bn Coldstream Guards was due to meet the same fate, but was saved at the last moment by a call for reinforcements for the garrison in Egypt. Coldstream recruiting was strong and so the battalion was sent off to Cairo, where it remained for the next five years. It was a case of 'out of sight, out of mind' and it would survive for almost half a century more.

The Colonel of the Regiment and three Coldstream officers visit Coldstream, South Africa, during a Battlefield Tour in 1992. *Left to right:* Lt Colonel Sir Julian Paget, Major General Sir George Burns, Captain R. Lucas, Major F. Matheson.

As well as reorganizing the structure of the Army Haldane infused it with a new spirit that affected and influenced all ranks. For the first time for centuries the soldier began to be treated far more as an individual, as someone who could be trusted to think and act for himself; education was encouraged and living conditions were improved. As a result, better men enlisted and the Regular soldier began to have greater pride in his skills and responsibilities.

Training followed a set pattern throughout the year, working up from individual skills to six weeks of large-scale manoeuvres in the autumn. 'Tactical Exercises Without Troops' (TEWTs) were introduced and promotion examinations became matters to be treated with new respect. The skills required of a soldier in those days were few compared to today. The only weapons in a battalion were rifles, pistols and perhaps a machine gun. What little transport existed was still horse-drawn, wirelesses were unknown and communications were by field telephones.

Fighting efficiency in the case of the infantry depended primarily on skill at arms and on marching ability, and very high standards were attained in both. Above all, the small professional Army consisted of men who were individuals, each ready to play his own part and to think for himself as never before. The motivation was patriotism and a strong sense of duty and Regimental pride.

Those who spoke of "an Army unequalled since the time of Cromwell" were not exaggerating. The dedication and spirit of the 'Contemptible Little Army' of 1914 had much in common with that of the New Model Army, and it would soon be put to the test.

CHAPTER FIVE

THE FIRST WORLD WAR

by Tony Maxse

A comprehensive history of the Regiment in the First World War entitled *The Coldstream Guards 1914–1918* was published in 1926 by Lieutenant Colonel Sir John Ross of Bladensburg in two volumes, each of 500 pages. From this we learn that some 20,000 Coldstreamers served with the four battalions on the Western Front, including 650 officers, and that the Regiment lost 3,860 killed and 10,277 wounded or taken prisoner, a total of 14,137, which compares with total casualties of under 5,000 in the Second World War. The scale of the tragedy of the First World War still haunts the country today, although it should not be forgotten that the spirit and bravery of the soldiers who lived and fought in appalling conditions eventually carried them through to final victory.

August 1914

All European countries had schemes to mobilize their armies at the start of war and these swung into action on 1 August 1914. By the 7th the three active Coldstream battalions, then in London, Windsor and Aldershot, could each muster over 1000 men, including their Reservists who had arrived by train from all parts of the country. For example, Private Wyatt, who had served four years from 1904 to 1908 in England and Egypt and had since then been an officer in the Barnsley Borough Police, rejoined the 3rd Battalion at Chelsea Barracks and was soon to make his name.

The three Commanding Officers, Lieutenant Colonels Ponsonby, Pereira and Feilding, were in their mid-forties and all had campaigning experience in the Boer War, from which they had learned valuable lessons. This was put to good use and all three would have distinguished careers.

The 1st Battalion was in 1st Guards Brigade under Brigadier General Maxse, a Coldstreamer, in the 1st Division, and the other two battalions were in 4th Guards Brigade in the 2nd Division under Brigadier General Scott-Kerr, Grenadier Guards.

Efficient plans had been laid in advance to ship an expeditionary force to France, and by 14 August all three battalions had landed at Le Havre. The French railways struggled valiantly to move large bodies of men and horses, and by the 20th the British Expeditionary Force (BEF) under General Sir John French had some 70,000 men in four divisions in position just over the Belgian frontier.

Lieutenant H.C.Loyd had been commissioned in 1910 and many years later, when Colonel of the Regiment, he published his experiences as a platoon commander in the 2nd Battalion for the first two months in France. On arrival at their billets in Belgium he reported that:

> "We do route marches each morning in order to get everyone's feet hardened. It is fortunate we do, particularly as the reservists are far from fit. On the 20th we move

towards Mons where we arrive after several long marches on the evening of 23rd August. That morning we first hear the sound of guns."

The Kaiser had just issued the order from his HQ at Aachen commanding his army to:

> "exterminate first the treacherous English and walk over General French's contemptible little army."

The arrogance of this remark demonstrates the advantage that a determined military nation has over a peaceable democracy such as Britain. A Coldstream officer visiting Hanover in 1886 was struck by the large number of soldiers in the street in uniform, the officers all carrying swords; he was amused by the frequent saluting and clicking of heels. Units were kept at full strength, always well equipped, and training could be carried out with little consideration for the civilian population.

Retreat from Mons

In early August the Kaiser had invaded Belgium with 750,000 men against 250,000 Belgian and French troops, and in under three weeks they had fought their way to Mons, near the French border. The guns that Lieutenant Loyd heard heralded the first attack on the British Army, but the troops were ready and their steady fire and determined defence held the line. Sadly this was temporary as the French had withdrawn on our right and on the 24th the Allies were forced to retreat. Over thirteen days the withdrawal covered some 200 miles, but training and discipline saw the British Army through, as demonstrated by numerous small exciting actions, including those involving 4th Guards Brigade on 25 August and on 1 September.

Landrecies, 25 August 1914

The brigade reached Landrecies in the afternoon of the 25th after a hurried and painful march and set about defending the town with its crossing of the River Sambre. Half the 3rd Coldstream, under the Second-in-Command, Major T.G. Matheson, was defending the road from the north, where it was repeatedly attacked for most of the night, but repulsed the enemy with well-aimed fire.

Unluckily a strawstack caught fire which lit up the position and a German field gun started shelling at short range. Private Wyatt bravely dashed out twice under heavy fire to extinguish the fire. A week later, as Lance Corporal Wyatt, he behaved again with great gallantry at the action at Villers Cotterets and was awarded the Victoria Cross for both incidents. After the war he was interviewed by his local newspaper about these actions and he was asked why he went to extinguish the fire. "Because Major Matheson told me to," he replied.

The 2nd Battalion was in the same brigade and 'Budget'[1] Loyd related:

> "Late in the afternoon of 25 August we enter Landrecies, hot and exhausted. . . . I get my men into quite a good place, arrange for their food and go off to find that I have been allotted a nice room with a good bed, at the top of a woman's clothes shop. It is full of

[1] So called because he joined the Regiment in 1910, the year of Lloyd George's Budget.

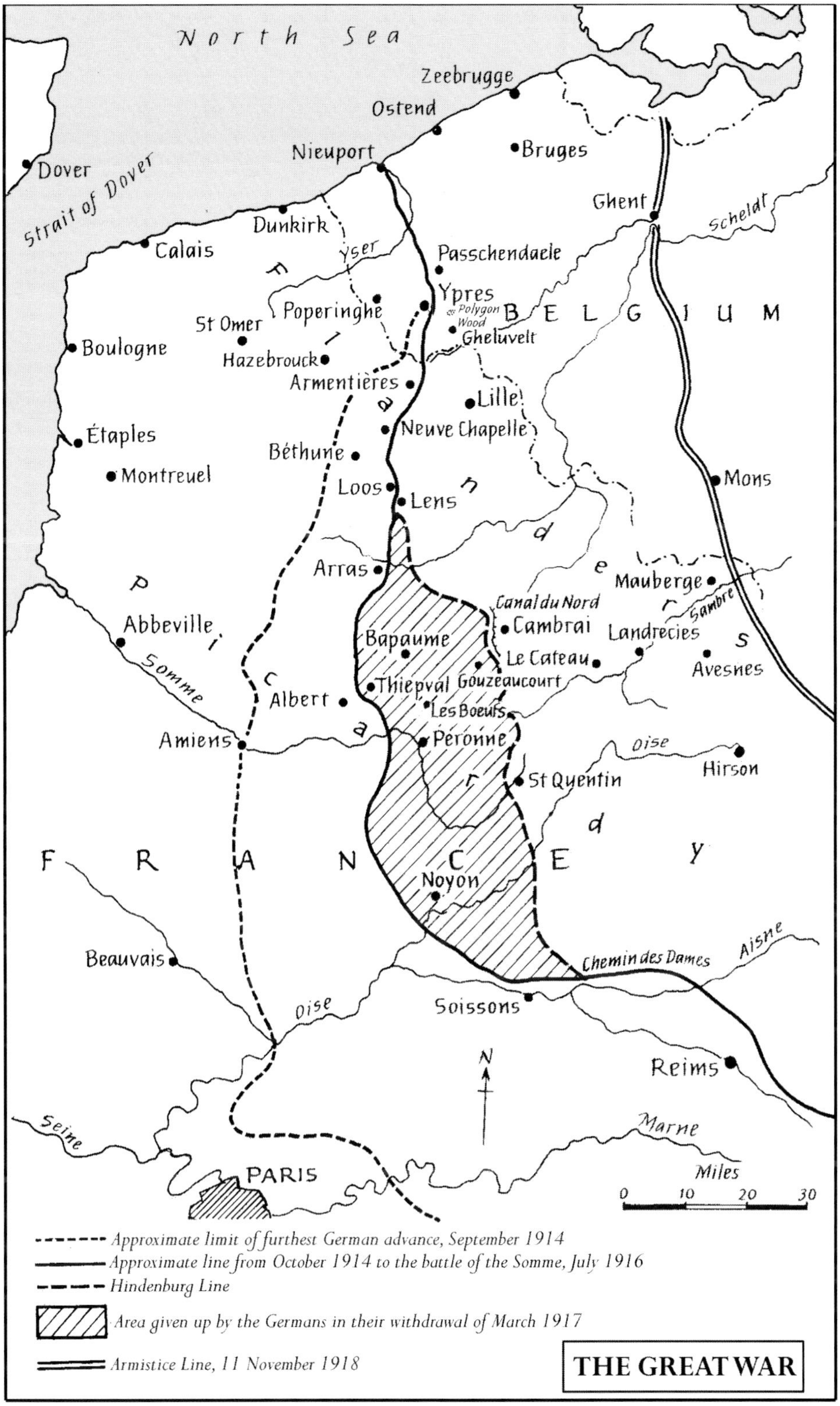
North Sea
Zeebrugge
Ostend
Nieuport
Bruges
Dover
Strait of Dover
Ghent
Scheldt
Dunkirk
Calais
Yser
Passchendaele
Ypres
Polygon Wood
Poperinghe
St Omer
BELGIUM
Gheluvelt
Boulogne
Hazebrouck
Armentières
Lille
Neuve Chapelle
Étaples
Béthune
Montreuel
Loos
Lens
Mons
Flanders
Arras
Picardy
Mauberge
Canal du Nord
Cambrai
Landrecies
Sambre
Abbeville
Bapaume
Le Cateau
Avesnes
Somme
Thiepval
Gouzeaucourt
Albert
Les Boeufs
Amiens
Péronne
Oise
Hirson
St Quentin
FRANCE
Noyon
Beauvais
Chemin des Dames
Aisne
Soissons
Oise
N
Reims
Seine
Marne
PARIS
Miles
0 10 20 30
Approximate limit of furthest German advance, September 1914
Approximate line from October 1914 to the battle of the Somme, July 1916
Hindenburg Line
Area given up by the Germans in their withdrawal of March 1917
Armistice Line, 11 November 1918
THE GREAT WAR

3rd Battalion Coldstream Guards at Landrecies August 1914 (from a painting by W.B. Woollen R.I).

girls who are clearly frightened and apprehensive. I manage to persuade one to produce a hip-bath with some hot water, into which I get with relief but with smarting blisters and I start to wash myself properly.

"Suddenly shots ring down the street and I hear the whizz of bullets outside. The girls rush into my room in a panic and the sight of me in my bath does nothing to calm them. I leap out, dress more quickly than I have ever dressed before and, expecting orders, rejoin my platoon, but it is a false alarm."

The retreat continued, as Loyd describes:

"We tramp on day after day, mile after mile. Nothing but minor skirmishes take place on our front, but on the morning of 1 September we are told that the enemy who are close on our heels are to be held on a certain line until 11.30 a.m.

"The company commander's plan is gradually to withdraw and he tells me that my platoon is to remain as rear party. The hour 11.25 arrives and I am alone with my platoon. I see heads lining up in considerable numbers on the ridge just outside the village. This is ominous. I tell my snipers to give them a few shots.

"It is 11.27. I order two sections under the platoon sergeant to crawl back for ten yards and then to collect 100 yards back and wait for me. More and more heads appear in front. My eye is on my watch. It is 11.29. Just before 11.30 I order a burst of aimed fire to keep the heads down. It is 11.30 exactly and with relief which it is impossible to describe I order the last section to crawl back.

"I assemble the whole of my platoon and hastily move off in the direction given me by the company commander. I have gone only a short distance when bursts of rifle fire open up in rear; the enemy must have attacked right on our heels.

"I push on, and eventually after a mile or two succeed in rejoining the battalion. We have been singularly lucky to emerge without losing a man from a very awkward and dangerous situation. We march on and after something like 35 miles we are halted at 3 a.m. on the side of the road. . . . At no time does it occur to us that the army is in any real danger. In spite of our acute fatigue our morale is good.

"We trek on day after day. On 5th September when in bivouac we are told we are to march back the way we have come. It is literally a case of 'About turn, Quick march'. Knowing nothing of the general situation, we are completely mystified as to what is happening. Later we learn that the great retreat is over, and that we are now pushing the enemy back."

A week earlier the French Government had abandoned Paris for Bordeaux and the general Allied position seemed critical. However, the Germans had suffered numerous casualties and were having problems supplying their forces over great distances on roads that were hopelessly congested. On 4 September their Commander in Chief, Von Moltke, observed that they had captured very few French guns which indicated that "they have withdrawn in good order and according to plan".

The Marne and Aisne, September 1914

Indeed General Joffre, the French commander, had planned the later stages of the withdrawal in order to fight on the Marne and this battle has justly been called one of the most significant of the twentieth century. If the Germans had won they would have taken Paris and the war might well have been lost.

The River Marne is a serious obstacle and runs from the champagne country round Epernay due west to join the Seine in Paris and the Germans were 20 miles south of the river in many places. On 6 September (a date celebrated in France until the occupation in 1940) the Allies advanced and the 1st Battalion led 1st Guards Brigade. All three Coldstream battalions were involved in the advance up to the Marne over the next two days. On the way the whole of 4th Guards Brigade fought a spirited action crossing a tributary, the Petit Morin, which resulted in the 2nd Coldstream capturing 100 prisoners with seven machine guns.

The Marne was crossed on 9 September and in the next three days our troops advanced thirty miles further to the River Aisne. The 2nd Battalion came under heavy fire as it approached a blown bridge at Chavonne, but after a while our artillery caused the enemy to retire, and Lance Corporal Milward ferried No 3 Company across in a very leaky boat. Soon afterwards the remains of the bridge were repaired enough for the rest of the battalion to cross man by man.

On the 14th the 1st Battalion saw its first major action when 1st Guards Brigade attacked up the steep wooded north bank of the Aisne and across the plateau to the Chemin des Dames, a road running along the top of a prominent ridge. The Brigadier described it as "a ding-dong battle under

Lance Corporal F.W. Dobson returning home to North Shields. He was awarded the Victoria Cross for conspicuous gallantry with the 2nd Battalion at Chavonne on the Aisne in September 1914.

heavy German artillery fire to which our gunners could not then reply. The result was that we lost about one third of my brigade in killed, wounded and missing in about a couple of hours or so. With the remainder we stuck to the ground we had gained" and this was "an indispensible bridgehead over the river". In the confusion Lieutenant Colonel Ponsonby gathered a party of 100 men, including some Black Watch, and pushed on over the Chemin des Dames before midday. Later they found themselves surrounded and had to make their way back at night, carrying their Commanding Officer who had been wounded in the foot. The battalion losses amounted to 388 that day.

Meanwhile the 2nd and 3rd Battalions crossed the Aisne further west and joined the 2nd Grenadiers who had taken La Cour de Soupir, a farmstead on high ground a mile north of the river. This prominent position was vital as our forces further west were unable to make any progress. In spite of continuous shelling and some of the buildings catching fire, the farm was tenaciously defended for nearly three weeks. This marked the start of static warfare in this area and, with continuous work, the defences were steadily improved, with deeper trenches providing vital protection.

During this time the 3rd Battalion sent out a patrol of three men on the 28th to check on German activity behind a wood. Early in the day they were fired on and two fell, but rather than leave them out until dark Private Dobson volunteered to cross a considerable piece of ground in view of the enemy. He found one man dead and the second badly wounded, so he dressed his wounds and crawled back. Fog now came down to provide some cover and, assisted by Corporal Brown, he took out a stretcher and retrieved the wounded man. He was awarded the Victoria Cross and Brown received the Distinguished Conduct Medal.

First Battle of Ypres, October–November 1914

At the beginning of October the front north of the Aisne was still fluid and attempts were made by each side to turn the flank of the other. This became the 'Race to the Sea' and each day the Germans seemed to be just ahead and often managed to occupy the most favourable ground. The opportunity was taken to rearrange the Allied armies and the French took over the Aisne, while the British Army moved north to Flanders to be accessible for supplies arriving through Calais and Boulogne. The battalions spent some twenty-eight hours on the train in closed cattle trucks loaded with forty men each.

For the rest of the war the British front spread across three areas, Flanders, Artois and Picardy. Nearest the coast, Flanders spans the French–Belgian border and includes Ypres. Arras, Cambrai and Loos are in Artois, while the Somme and Amiens are in Picardy to the south.

The Coldstream battalions arrived in Flanders to find a fluid front protecting Ypres, the only important Belgian town in our hands. The front (not yet a rigid trench line) formed a rough semi-circle facing east, and this became the notorious Ypres Salient, the scene of bitter fighting for over three years as the Germans attempted to capture the town and the British fought to improve its protection. On 20 October the 2nd and 3rd Battalions dug new positions in the northern part of the Salient, although much hindered by crowds of refugees who had been burnt out of their homes by the Germans.

The 1st Battle of Ypres lasted four weeks and was made up of a series of desperate struggles against heavy odds. On 23 October the Germans launched massive attacks on a wide front which involved all three battalions. Over four days the 1st Battalion lost 197 all ranks, and the wounded included Lieutenant Colonel Feilding, (commanding the 3rd Battalion) and Budget Loyd, who relates:

> "I am in process of getting one section into some sort of fire position when 'crack' I am hit in the head. Blood pours down my face and clothes. I take off my cap and find a large hole in the top. However, I do not feel any great pain and I continue disposing the platoon. Just as I have got things into some sort of shape, I suddenly feel a stunning blow over the heart, and looking down I see there is a hole in my mackintosh. I feel a good deal of pain, but the bullet – probably a ricochet – has evidently only glanced across my chest.
>
> "We are in a cauldron where we are, two or three men killed or wounded, and I am still bleeding profusely. I realize I must somehow try and stop the rest of the company from coming so far forward.
>
> "I run back into the wood and fortunately I run into the company commander. He looks at me horrified. I suppose I look far worse than I feel. I explain the position in front in detail. . . . He then orders me back to the Battalion First Aid Post where my wounds are attended to, but I still do not feel too bad, although I have a six-inch cut along the left side of my head, and a gash in the chest. . . . In a few days I am sent home.
>
> "In less than two months I rejoin my battalion in trenches with mud and water up to the knees."

Loyd had a wonderful war record, winning the MC and the DSO as well as three Mentions in Despatches. He demonstrated fine leadership commanding a company and from February 1917 was a valued Brigade Major to Brigadier General Ponsonby in 2nd Guards Brigade Headquarters.

Gheluvelt, October 1914

In spite of their losses, the 1st Battalion joined 1st Bn Scots Guards on 26 October in an attack on German positions in Poezelhoek, about 1,200 yards NE of Gheluvelt village. By the evening of the 28th the Battalions were dug in along the small road that ran north from the Gheluvelt crossroads on the Menin Road, a mile forward of the village. The 1st Coldstream, only 350 strong, was assigned a frontage of 800 yards, which meant that the positions were effectively a line of outposts; it did have some support from the Battalion Headquarters trench about 400 yards behind the right-hand companies and from machine gun sections in three other battalions. The artillery were very short of ammunition and were rationed to just nine rounds per gun per day.

The GHQ orders for 29 October were to "continue the offensive", but this proved optimistic for at 0530 hours six battalions from the *54th Reserve Division* appeared out of the mist in the Coldstream sector, while *16 Bavarian Division* attacked the Grenadiers south of the Menin Road. No 1 Company of the Coldstream, north of the crossroads, was almost destroyed; No 2 Company gave way only after all its officers were killed. The remaining companies formed a flank with the Scots Guards, enfilading the German attack, and beating off the *II/16 Bavarian Reserve Infantry Regiment*; 500 yards further south the Coldstream Headquarters position was overrun by 0900 hours. Survivors joined the Scots Guards and Cameron Highlander companies in Poezelhoek Wood, only to be driven out by further strong attacks.

Three hours later the 3rd Infantry Brigade drove the now depleted *54th Reserve Division* out of Gheluvelt. But 1st Guards Brigade suffered 1,100 casualties that day and was reduced to 275 all ranks. The 1st Coldstream lost every single one of its officers, and the Quartermaster, Lieutenant Jock Boyd, collected just sixty men that evening.

A further sixty men, who had escaped from Poezelhoek Wood rejoined the 1st Battalion the next day, and a draft of two officers and 100 men arrived on 1 November. But there was to be no respite, and on that same day the 200 or so men moved into trenches near Gheluvelt. The next day the Germans attacked again and took them in the rear; they lost both officers and 100 men and were overwhelmed.

Captain and Quartermaster J. Boyd after the First World War.

During the desperate battles of 29 October 4th Guards Brigade was brought up in support, and the 2nd and 3rd Battalions were grouped together under Lieutenant Colonel Pereira to defend the eastern edge of Polygon Wood. Little did they know that they would still be there twenty days later. The German attacks continued day after day and on 11 November they launched four divisions against just 10,000 weary British defenders. Despite two hours of heavy shelling, the Coldstream repulsed the assault on their front, and six days later they were finally relieved.

To say that life in Polygon Wood was difficult would be an under-statement. At that stage of the war there was no established defence system with dug-outs for protection and communication trenches for bringing up rations and supplies, so the food never arrived hot. A further unpleasantness was the presence of masses of German corpses, and in one clearing the men buried 800. Some gruesome examples of Prussian punishment were also revealed with the discovery of German soldiers who had been hanged or tied to a tree and shot.

News of the terrible losses to 1st Guards Brigade at Gheluvelt came as one of the first significant wartime shocks in England and gave an ominous foretaste of what was to come. On the German side too there would be an intriguing consequence. One of the company runners in *II/16 Bavarian Reserve Infantry Regiment* (which attacked Poezelhoek Wood) was called Adolf Hitler, and he was decorated for his bravery at Gheluvelt with the Iron Cross, Second Class. His wartime front-line experiences and a near-obsession with the battle were described in *Mein Kampf* and were to influence him throughout his life.[2]

From 17 November 4th Guards Brigade was commanded by a future CIGS and Field Marshal, Brigadier General Lord Cavan (Scott-Kerr having been wounded some weeks before).

The First Battle of Ypres ended in stalemate and proved to be the final spasm of mobile warfare. The line of trenches from the Swiss border to the Channel was being daily strengthened and fortified by both sides; firepower was going to be decisive from now on, especially artillery. The enemy was stronger in heavy guns and howitzers, but our 18-pounder field guns matched the German 77mms; our main problem was supply. The production of guns and ammunition by the factories at home became crucial, and shortages throughout 1915 would cause extreme frustration.

The Regiment was now having to think of another kind of supply, that of men to maintain its very existence. Over 3,000 men had originally landed in France and reinforcements of nearly 2,000 had been added since; but after just four months of fighting, losses totalled 2,418, as follows:

Battalion.	Killed.	Wounded.	Prisoner.	Total.
1st	322	678	188	1,188
2nd	116	313	15	444
3rd	193	581	12	786

Those killed represented about one quarter of the total casualties and this proportion was typical of operations throughout the war. Most of our infantry suffered similar losses, and as the Official History stated:

> "The old British Regular Army was gone past recall, leaving but a remnant to carry on the training of the New Armies."

Reinforcements

At the very start of the war Lord Kitchener had launched his famous appeal for volunteers to join the 'New Armies' and its success was due to the extraordinary enthusiasm for the war, demonstrated today in old films of men marching merrily off to join their trains for the port. A few years later

[2] Captain Thorne, Grenadier Guards (later General Sir Andrew), was Staff Captain in 1st Guards Brigade at the time and, having studied German sources, wrote an account of the battle in the Summer 1932 number of the Household Brigade Magazine. In 1934–35 he was Military Attaché in Berlin and Hitler discussed Gheluvelt with him on several occasions. A translation of the Household Brigade Magazine article was found in Hitler's bunker after his death.

Captain Cyril Falls wrote: "The modern intellectual is inclined to look with impatience upon the ardour with which they went to war. Looking back, the intensity – and I dare say the purity – of that spirit still moves me deeply."

In August 1914 a Coldstream Reserve Battalion was formed at Victoria Barracks, Windsor, to train and equip drafts of officers and other ranks for battalions in the field. Reservists or recruits (who had already done their initial twelve weeks' basic drill at the Guards Depot at Caterham) arrived at Windsor for thorough training in musketry, the Lewis gun, trench warfare and bombing. From 1915 an extra four companies were formed to receive the wounded and sick after discharge from hospital. The Barracks was built for 800 all ranks, but on occasions accommodation had to be found for many times this number.

Generally the system worked well and it was made easier by a conscious decision by all Foot Guards regiments that in order to maintain standards they would not expand on the scale of Line regiments. For example the Royal Fusiliers at one time had over seventy battalions.

Trench Warfare, 1915

In early 1915 all three battalions were in the industrial area between Lens and Béthune and reinforcements were soon to be needed again. On 25 January the 1st Battalion suffered 200 casualties from a German attack which opened with the explosion of four large mines. The following week the 2nd and 3rd Battalions were involved in successful attacks on high railway embankments and brickworks, and the line gained was held until our advance in 1918. These attacks out of the trench line started with the men rising simultaneously and advancing in line, in the formation that has now become familiar from films of the time. The authorities considered that traditional fire and movement was not suitable with two opposing parallel trench lines and also that the new civilian recruits were not trained to act in sections and platoons. Many commentators have since pointed out that there had been plenty of time for field training before drafts were sent to the front.

Two officers who were to become well-known now rejoined after recovering from wounds. Lieutenant A.F.Smith resumed as Adjutant of the 3rd Battalion and 2nd Lieutenant O.W.H.Leese returned to the front. Arthur Smith went as GS03 to the Guards Division in December, and became a Lieutenant Colonel on the staff in 1918.[3]

By early May both Pereira and Feilding had been promoted to command infantry brigades, and the 2nd and 3rd Battalions were commanded by Julian Steele and Torquhil Matheson, the latter being promoted to command a brigade just two months later, when John Campbell took over the 3rd Battalion.

Formation of the Guards Division

In August Lord Kitchener ordered the formation of a Guards Division under the command of the Earl of Cavan, and it included all Guards battalions in France. The sign of the 'Ever Open Eye' (originally called the 'Eye') was soon chosen and was to become famous through two world wars. A 4th Coldstream Battalion was formed to provide the Divisional Pioneers under Lieutenant Colonel R.C.E. Skeffington-Smyth, and the Reserve Battalion at Windsor, now 3780 strong, became the 5th

[3] Arthur Smith ended up as a Lieutenant General in the Second World War and Oliver Leese commanded 8th Army in Italy in 1944 and was Deputy Supreme Commander in the Far East, 1945.

Coldstream. Two of the three brigades in the new division were commanded by Coldstreamers, Feilding and Ponsonby.

Another important development was the formation of the Guards Machine Gun Company. At last this weapon's importance was recognized and these companies became standard throughout the BEF. They were armed with the water-cooled Vickers Gun which was capable of sustained rapid fire with ordinary .303 bullets and its great advantage over a platoon of riflemen was the ability to control its fire in the confusion and noise of battle. By the end of the war over 71,000 Vickers Guns were supplied, plus 133,000 Lewis Guns, a lighter air-cooled machine gun used within rifle companies.

Loos, September 1915

Meanwhile our allies, the French and the Russians, were being hard-pressed and it became important for us to attack to relieve the pressure and to keep up morale. Loos is in the coal-mining area near Lens, where the enemy defences were well established, using concrete and wire plus several trench systems in depth with well-sited machine guns. Britain now had thirty-five divisions in France and preparations for the attack were thorough, as this was to be our major contribution to the war in 1915. The aim was to capture Lens and its important railway junction.

On 25 September the Guards Division was in reserve for the initial attack, but this soon faltered and the Division moved forward, although frustrated by severe road congestion with thousands of wounded being carried back. The 1st Battalion was then involved in an attack on a point called Hill 70, which started well when a big chalk pit was rushed and held. Two days later the battalion was still in position when a heavy enemy bombardment caused 270 casualties including Lieutenant Colonel A.G.E.Egerton, the Commanding Officer, and Lieutenant the Hon M.H.D.Browne, the Adjutant, who were both killed, plus Captain Tommy Agar-Robartes MP who died of his wounds soon after.[4]

Lance Sergeant O. Brooks, VC

After a brief respite the Guards Division was back in the line and facing determined counter-attacks. The Germans gained a footing in some trenches of the 3rd Battalion, and Lance Sergeant Brooks, followed by six bombers, started bombing down the captured trench. After forty-five minutes of fierce fighting the intruders were driven out and it is estimated that the battalion used 5,000 bombs that afternoon. Brooks was awarded the Victoria Cross and the bombers with him each won the Distinguished Conduct Medal.

In spite of some isolated minor successes, Loos is generally considered a disaster due to the huge losses suffered in our attacks. Conditions at the end of the battle were horrific, with arms, heads and legs heaped in ghastly piles and many dead of both sides blocking the communication trenches, with active enemy sniping making it difficult to move.

[4] Agar-Robartes' belongings were returned to his mother at the family home, Lanhydrock in Cornwall, and she put his fine alligator skin case in the attic. The family died out, the house passed to the National Trust, and in 1999 the case was opened for the first time to reveal what an officer took with him to the war. The case with over twenty items is on exhibition there and includes a field periscope, a signalling lamp, wire cutters, a spirit stove with walnut case and a leather writing set.

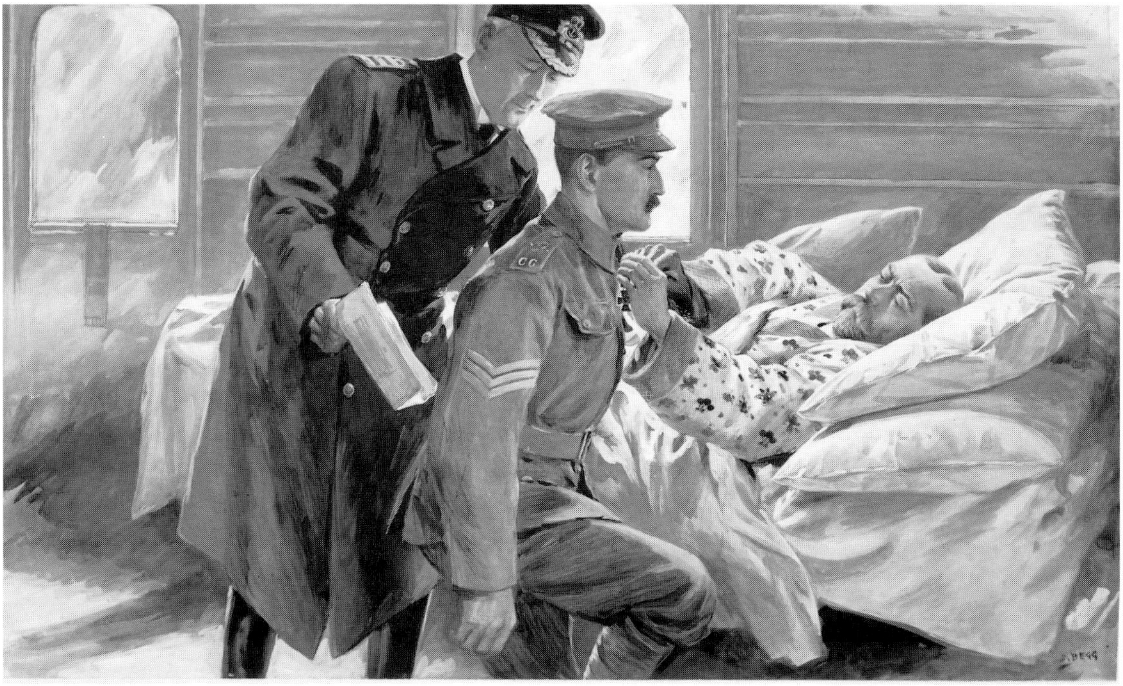

Lance Sergeant O. Brooks receiving his Victoria Cross from His Majesty King George V at Aire station on 1 November 1915. The King was recovering from a riding accident while in Flanders.

The trenches were apt to flood in the winter in this low-lying country and waders were issued in some areas. Both sides were active in tunnelling and mining and the 4th (Pioneer) Battalion lost two men who were drowned in a listening tunnel. Willie Baynes led a patrol into no-man's-land and wrote: "I went up to my waist in water in one place, and foolishly wet my revolver; special arrangements have now luckily been made so that all patrollers can get back to a safe place to get dry and a change of clothes."

In December Sir Douglas Haig took over as Commander-in-Chief of the BEF from Sir John French and a Fourth Army was formed under Lieutenant General Sir Henry Rawlinson, a distinguished Coldstreamer.[5]

Ponsonby's diary records that "Fatty Cavan has got command of the XIVth Corps. This is a great blow as it means he will leave us and we all swear by him." General Geoffrey Feilding took over the Guards Division, "a most popular appointment with everyone". 'Pinto' Pereira returned to succeed him at 1st Guards Brigade and on 1 January conscription came in, as the supply of volunteers for the Army was drying up.

The Division was out of the line for much of February and March 1916, but the men were kept busy with maintenance and training. Bombing drill was well practised, as grenades were proving more effective in the trenches than rifles. There was time for sport too, and there were football matches, boxing and even race meetings.

[5] Rawlinson's regimental service was, however, limited to a period in 1892 in between his exchange from the 60th Rifles and attending the Staff College.

Haig now commanded one and a half million men in four armies and a massive infrastructure had built up over two years to feed and supply them through the ports from Le Havre to Calais, and on by rail and lorry transport. Much road-building and repair was needed behind the front line and the material required often came from England, sometimes 3,000 tons a week. Light railways were built and many miles of waterpipes were laid. The postal service was remarkably reliable and letters from England would arrive in two or three days, although the post for home was deliberately slower as it had to be censored and the delay rendered any information on troop movements less valuable should it reach the enemy.

War has been described as ninety per cent boredom and ten per cent absolute hell, and 1914–18 was no exception. John Terraine[6] quotes a Captain Sidney Rogerson: "Life in the trenches was not all ghastliness. It was a compound of many things; fright and boredom, humour, comradeship, tragedy, weariness, courage and despair." Lieutenant Willie Baynes wrote home to say that "We have spent quite a lot of time ratting in the trenches as Ferguson brought back a ferret from home with him and we adopted someone's terrier that was wandering about on its own, and killed about forty rats in the two days; at night the great moment is to shoot them by the light of an electric torch with a revolver, but the results are not quite so good."[7]

Relief in the Line

In March 1916 the battalions returned to the line with a system of relieving each other on a regular pattern. Ian Hay was a popular author at the time because his books conveyed much of the spirit and humour of the trenches. His *Carrying On after the First Hundred Thousand*[8] was written in 1917 and gives a light-hearted but valuable insight into some of the problems of a battalion relief:

> "Under cover of night the [relieving] battalion sets out, forming a strange procession. By day the road is a wilderness, but after nightfall it is packed with troops and transport, and not a light is shown. If you can imagine what the Mansion House crossing would be like with its midday traffic at midnight, entirely unilluminated, paved with twelve inches of liquid mud, liberally pitted with 'crump holes' you may derive some faint idea of things at a busy road junction lying behind the trenches.
>
> "Until reaching what is facetiously termed 'the shell area', the troops plod along in fours at the right of the road. At any moment they may be called upon to halt and crowd into the roadside, while a transport train passes, carrying rations and coke up to the firing line. When this procession, consisting of a dozen limbered waggons, drawn by four mules and headed by a profane person on horseback (the Transport Officer) has rumbled past, the company, which has been standing respectfully in the ditch enjoying a refreshing shower bath of mud, sets out once more, only to take hasty cover as sounds of fresh and more animated traffic are heard approaching from the opposite direction. These are artillery waggons, returning empty from replenishing the batteries; scattering homely jests like hail, and proceeding wherever possible at a hand gallop.
>
> "Sometimes an axle breaks, or a waggon side-slips into the morass reserved for

[6] *The Western Front*
[7] Lieutenant Baynes letter, 8.12.16.
[8] Published by Blackwood, 1917.

infantry. The result is a block, which promptly extends forward and back for a couple of miles. A chorus of biting sarcasm and blasphemous humour surges up and down the line until plunging mules are unyoked and the offending vehicle man-handled out of sight. Everything has to make way for a ration train. To crown it all it is more than likely that the calmness and smooth working of the proceedings will be assisted by a burst of shrapnel overhead. It is a most amazing scrimmage altogether.

"And yet, though the scene is enacted night after night without a break, there is hardly a case on record of the transport being surprised upon these roads by the coming of daylight, and none whatever of the rations and ammunition failing to get through."

Somehow the system of supply did work, remarkable as it may now seem.

The Somme, July–November 1916

In February 1916 Germany launched massive and determined attacks on the French fortresses around Verdun which were defended at enormous cost. It became vital for the enlarged BEF to play a significant role in support, and so plans were laid for the Battle of the Somme.

The Guards Division was still in Flanders in July and so avoided the horrors of the first day when 57,000 men fell. Even on this day two divisions reached their objectives. One of them, the 18th, was trained and commanded by a Coldstreamer, Ivor Maxse, whose Brigade Major for Artillery was a Major Alan Brooke (later the Field Marshal). The thorough training of the infantry contributed to this success, and a significant factor was Brooke's advanced artillery programme with seventeen 'lifts' onto various targets, while many other divisional programmes that day had only two or three 'lifts'.

The rest of the Army was not slow to copy a good thing, as shells were now plentiful (1.7 million had been fired in the preliminary bombardment). The guns, well behind the front line, would usually fire at ranges from 3000 to 6000 yards. The term 'creeping barrage' came into use for an artillery programme that enabled the infantry to follow very closely behind the landing area of our shells, which kept the enemy down in their trenches until the last possible moment.

Haig and Rawlinson persisted with the attacks and gradually some significant advances were made. The Guards Division was transferred to the Somme and a major operation was planned for 15 September, known as Flers-Courcelette, carried out by the Fourth and Fifth Armies together with the French on the right. The division was to be launched from the area of Ginchy with the final objective being the village of Les Boeufs, by now just a heap of rubble after three months of intensive shelling. The obliteration of the countryside made for difficulties in keeping to the line of advance, especially as the start line was an irregular semi-circle and some troops had to change direction half-way through the attack.

Many lessons had been learnt since 1 July and the preliminary bombardment was fairly effective, while the formation developed for attacks was described as 'waves'. Two platoons formed a line and each company had two lines, with fifty yards between each. A battalion would have two companies in rear to make a total of four lines, and a brigade would have two battalions up and two in reserve to make four more waves. The 2nd and 3rd Battalions were the front line for 1st Guards Brigade, while the 1st Battalion led on the left of 2nd Guards Brigade. This battle entered the history books because it marked the first appearance of tanks. They were used on the flanks of the division and the initial reaction was that they showed promise, although on this occasion their achievements were limited to isolated incidents. Many broke down or ditched, but the few that reached the German trenches caused considerable alarm.

Zero hour was at 6.20 a.m. and the first waves of the 2nd and 3rd Battalions had a bad start with fire from enfilade machine guns hidden in a sunken lane on the left. This lane was close to a tank corridor which was left unshelled in order to avoid churning the ground, but the two tanks broke down and the enemy machine guns were unmolested. The 3rd Battalion's Second in Command and the Adjutants of both battalions were among those killed within 100 yards of the start.

Soon many units had direction problems and they found unexpected German trenches which had to be cleared. In the confusion the Division became two groups, the left being the larger part of all three Coldstream battalions, plus some Irish Guardsmen. Colonel Campbell, commanding the 3rd Battalion, realized the need to deal with the sunken lane machine guns and he rallied the survivors of the leading waves with his hunting horn. This carried the whole line forward in one headlong and irresistible rush onto the guns. Many Germans were bayonetted or taken prisoner and in one dug-out four machine guns were captured, plus several trench mortars.

The attack swept on over the road, over another unexpected trench and on to a third line, which dominated the area of advance and offered good protection. The three Commanding Officers decided to hold this line and Brigade Headquarters was informed by pigeon.

The troops were all mixed up in the German trenches, and the division on the right was held up. Colonel Baring, commanding the 1st Battalion, was trying to sort out his men when he was killed climbing over a trench barricade. Colonel Campbell then led the 2nd and 3rd Battalions on towards Les Boeufs, but they soon came under heavy artillery and machine-gun fire. A second call on his hunting horn rallied the whole line again to capture the next trenches, where they consolidated, as they were well in advance of the units on either flank.

Campbell was awarded the Victoria Cross for his gallantry and initiative at a very critical moment which turned the fortunes of the day.

Coldstream losses totalled 1219, including Captain Oliver Leese who was wounded again, and the 2nd Battalion was left with just three officers. Six weeks later Willie Baynes returned to the 2nd Battalion, having been wounded in the Ypres Salient on 22 July, and commented "that there is hardly an officer I know".

Pereira, the Brigade Commander, issued a special order, saying: "As Coldstreamers you have just taken part in what is certainly the biggest event in the military history of the Regiment. The 1st, 2nd and 3rd Battalions of the Regiment attacked in line; . . . you have left a mark on the German that he will never forget."

J.V.Campbell and his hunting horn captured the public imagination, so inevitably some wag wrote new words to the song "John Peel":

"D'ye ken J.V. in his coat khaki,
D'ye ken J.V. when he's out for a spree,
D'ye ken J.V. who makes Boches flee
With horn in his hand in the morning.

Chorus:
T'is the sound of his horn brought the Boche from
his trench,
Same as it does with his hounds from the bench,
For J.V.'s View Hulloa creates a wrench
In the heart of the Boche in the morning."

It has been said that the chief penalty of doing one job of work well is that you are promptly put on another. This is supposed to be a compliment, so the Regiment had just a few days out of the line to take in fresh drafts before the next attack by Fourth Army on 25 September, which again included Les Boeufs in its objectives. This time the Guards Division was only responsible for the northern section of the village. The Grenadier and Irish Guards took the first objectives and then our 2nd and 3rd Battalions followed through, bombing their way into the village and seeking out the enemy in dug-outs. The operation was described as "a thoroughly well-planned and admirably conducted feat of arms which reflected the greatest credit upon every unit in the Division".

Rawlinson, the Army Commander, reported to Lord Derby, the Minister of War: "The battles of the 15th and the 25th were certainly very successful, more so than I had dared to hope. . . . The result has been that not only have we gained the whole of the high ground which commands the plain right up to Bapaume, but have also secured an area of between 3,000 and 4,000 yards deep on the other side of the ridge."

The battalions returned to a section of the line north of Les Boeufs in November, to find gruesome debris of many more weeks of fighting, with all-pervasive mud and unburied bodies, together with the litter of smashed weapons and stores. Willie Baynes wrote that "It is quite astonishing that war can be carried on at all under present conditions and I wonder the men can survive it".[9] Trench fighting caused the loss of eighty men in eleven days, including the wounding of Follett, commanding the 2nd Battalion.

This officer had been wounded as an Ensign in the Boer War and had a remarkable record in 1914–18. He sailed in August 1914 in charge of a company and took command of the 2nd Battalion in March 1916, being wounded four months later in Flanders. He returned in September to take over the 1st Battalion, following the loss of Baring, for two months, before being transferred to the 2nd Battalion shortly before the incident just described. He returned to the 2nd Battalion in March 1917 and a year later was promoted to command a Guards Brigade, but was tragically killed in action in this post just six weeks before the Armistice. He won the DSO and was Mentioned in Despatches four times.

The British Army fought for four and a half months on the Somme and advanced about six miles at an appalling cost in men. But the Germans suffered too and Ludendorff commented at the end of 1916:

> "The strain during this year had proved too great. The endurance of the troops had been weakened by long spells of defence under the powerful enemy artillery fire. . . . We were completely exhausted on the Western Front. . . . We now urgently needed a rest. The army had been fought to a standstill and was utterly worn out."

Three months earlier Hindenburg and Ludendorff had visited the Somme and decided to withdraw to a fortified line to cut off a salient which had its south-west corner at Noyon. Construction took place over the winter and on 16 March 1917 the German Army quietly retreated to these well-prepared positions. The new line was ten miles back in places, with everything before it laid waste with Teutonic thoroughness. Our troops, wondering what had happened, found desolation, booby-trapped trenches and buildings, and the only inhabitants were the old and sick, who had little to eat. John Terraine in *The White Heat* called "the existence of the Hindenburg Line a measure of the

[9] Letter 16.12.16.

German defeat on the Somme". However, as we shall see, although the Germans had lost a battle, the war was far from over and they demonstrated impressive powers of recovery.

In the meantime the Allies' propaganda machine made the best of the German move, but Willie Baynes was not fooled: "I see our official communiqués are taking advantage of the Hun's withdrawal to make everyone think that we are doing an enormous push, but I don't suppose any intelligent person pays much attention to them nowadays. There are some cavalry dancing about again, which is always a source of much amusement here."[10]

The World War involved Germany's ally Turkey, whose Ottoman Empire extended into present-day Iraq where we sent forces to defend our oil supplies around the Persian Gulf. In August 1916 a Coldstreamer, Lieutenant General Sir Stanley Maude, was appointed Commander-in-Chief of this force, after it had suffered some serious setbacks. Reinforcements arrived from India and Sir Stanley planned and executed a major expedition up the length of the River Tigris to capture Baghdad in March 1917. Conditions were extremely difficult and this victory was a remarkable achievement that helped raise morale at home at a difficult stage of the war.

Passchendaele, The Opening, July 1917

In April and May 1917 the Coldstream battalions were busily engaged on the repair of roads and railways wrecked by the Germans in their withdrawal. Rawlinson congratulated them, saying "it was largely due to their labours that transportation services in this area are now in a satisfactory condition".

The French Army had suffered enormous losses over three years of war, but their new commander, General Nivelle, promised a revolutionary attack that would sweep through the German lines in a few days and set the Allies on the path to victory. It failed miserably and the loss of morale in the French Armies set off widespread mutinies, although the authorities managed to suppress any publicity. General Pétain was able to restore morale eventually, but it was clearly up to the British Army to take the strain.

Accordingly plans were made for a major attack which became known as the Third Battle of Ypres, or Passchendaele, the name of the village that was the final objective. The shape of the salient had changed little since the Germans had improved their positions in the Second Battle of Ypres in 1915 and the town was within range of their guns, so it was important to push them back and gain the high ground. The Guards Division moved north and the brigades took turns in the line during June and July to become familiar with the front, which included a stretch of the Yser Canal. Patrols went out to obtain information about the enemy and one in the 2nd Battalion was led by Lieutenant W.B.St Leger with 2nd Lieutenant Porritt, Sergeant Graham and forty men. They crossed the canal by mats[11] and, entering German trenches to right and left, they caused havoc by spirited bombing, and identified the German units. The raid lasted just fifteen minutes with an officer and two NCOs earning decorations.

Fortunately an opportunity arose to gain ground on the far side before the major assault due on 31 July. The 3rd Battalion was in the line on 27 July when two wounded British soldiers were seen

[10] Letter, 18.3.17.

[11] These 'mats' were a Belgian invention, consisting of a canvas strip the full width of the canal and one yard wide, backed with wire netting and wooden battens. They could be carried rolled up and were invaluable in getting troops across the muddy bottom of a canal.

across the canal and Lieutenant C.J.Hambro with Private Smith went across to bring them in. Hambro reported that the area seemed clear of enemy and this was confirmed by air reconnaissance.

That evening strong patrols with artillery support crossed over and established a line 500 to 600 yards beyond the canal. The engineers with the 4th Battalion Pioneers quickly built seventeen bridges of floating petrol tins and mats so that the brigade could form up on the new line for zero hour at 3.50 a.m. on the 31st. All this time our seven-day preliminary bombardment continued.

The Royal Flying Corps had provided full details of the German defences and each unit was thoroughly briefed for its task which was to capture a series of objectives, keeping close to their creeping barrage. The assault was successful and the 1st Battalion reached its second objective.

Private Whitham, VC

On the final advance an enemy machine gun was found to be enfilading the battalion from the right. Private Whitham, on his own initiative, immediately worked his way from shell hole to shell hole through our own barrage and rushed the machine gun. He captured the post, plus an officer and two soldiers, and was awarded the VC, the citation commenting that the action undoubtedly saved many lives and enabled the line to advance to the final objective 2000 yards from the start line.

The 2nd Battalion also achieved its objective near Steenbeck at about 9.30, but No 2 Company lost all its Sergeants, whereupon Corporal Kent took over as Company Sergeant Major "most efficiently".

This promising start was ruined that night by the weather and rain fell in torrents for four days. The whole of this part of Flanders is low-lying and criss-crossed by streams and irrigation ditches. Continuous shelling had wrecked the land drainage system and this, combined with heavy rain, produced conditions that even veterans of the Somme found atrocious. Parts of the country became a vast quagmire several feet deep and could only be crossed by duckboards. In the dark a man carrying a heavy load could miss his footing and very likely drown in the stinking mud to join numerous corpses of men and horses.

Passchendaele, October 1917

In spite of the conditions the battle continued with modest victories, step by step, including the recapture of Polygon Wood on 26 September.

The Regiment's second battle honour for the Third Battle of Ypres (**Passchendaele**) was awarded for the action on 9 October. The Guards Division made careful preparations for an attack to keep the pressure up and advance 2500 yards to the ridge to the left of Passchendaele. In spite of more rain the attack was successful, being conducted with the resolution and precision needed to follow an elaborate artillery plan. For example the barrage for the 2nd Battalion was static on the Broenbeck stream for four minutes, lifted 100 yards for six minutes and then moved forward at 100 yards each six minutes. It rested on the first objective for forty-five minutes, then advanced 100 yards each eight minutes and rested on the second objective for forty-five minutes. This must have given company officers and NCOs enough to think about in addition to controlling the advance of their platoons under enemy fire.

The 2nd Battalion set off by wading the Broenbeck up to the waist and No 2 Company lost all its officers early in the day due to heavy fire from pillboxes. However, some pillboxes lacked a good field of view and the Company NCOs led parties by a flank and captured thirty-five prisoners, plus three machine guns. At 9 a.m. the 3rd Battalion passed through and fought its way to the final objective. Similarly in 2nd Guards Brigade, the 1st Battalion passed through the Irish Guards to gain its objective.

The 4th Battalion was commended for sterling work providing hutting and tramlines, plus road repairs, but casualties in all four battalions for early October totalled 426. The village of Passchendaele was finally captured by the Canadians on 6 November.

Haig has been fiercely criticized for prolonging the battle for over three months with enormous losses in appalling conditions and the debate still continues eighty years later. The observation of a senior enemy commander, Lieutenant General Otto von Moser, is of interest:

> "Field Marshal Haig threw into this stupendous struggle everything . . . in the shape of weapons of war, especially shells, aircraft and tanks. The consequence was that these battles in Flanders constituted a veritable purgatory for the German troops, and they and their leaders suffered the most frightful martyrdom of the entire war."

The final tally of casualties is estimated at 250,000 British and 300,000 Germans.

Cambrai, November 1917

In fact Passchendaele was to be the last great battle of attrition. Numerous books over the past sixty years, including *The Donkeys* by Alan Clark, have told us that the appalling casualties of this period could easily have been avoided if the British Army had found itself a decent set of generals. Undoubtedly some were obstinate or stupid, but competent historians have made it clear that many were extremely able and imaginative officers. No commanders of the other nations involved in the war came up with that elusive battle-winning formula. Every attack made was thoroughly reviewed and the lessons were debated and learnt and put into practice.

One of these generals was John Ponsonby, now in command of the 40th Division, known as 'The Bantams' as it had been formed when the height requirement for recruits was reduced to 5ft 3ins. His diary for 19 November records:

> "Everything has now been arranged for the great battle tomorrow. It has been kept a profound secret. . . . The plot was I believe hatched three months ago."

This plot comprised a completely new sort of attack towards the important town of Cambrai, north of the Somme. It had become clear that a preliminary bombardment over several days gave the enemy ample warning and so, to achieve surprise, our guns opened up with a terrific barrage at zero hour. The disadvantage was that the enemy wire remained intact, but tanks were now available for the first time on a large scale and 400 joined the attack to flatten the wire.

The opening day of the battle on 20 November was a huge success and entered history as the first big tank victory. With infantry support they blasted through the Hindenburg Line and captured forty square miles of ground, 100 guns and 10,000 prisoners. The church bells were rung all over England in great rejoicing.

Unfortunately surprise had not been complete and fresh enemy divisions were already moving towards Cambrai when the battle opened and they continued to arrive in large numbers. Meanwhile, our initial attack had failed to capture Bourlon Wood, a prominent feature on our north flank.

The battle was to last ten days and involve three Coldstreamers commanding divisions. First into action was General Pereira of the 2nd Division which held the left flank, west of Bourlon Wood, and successfully repulsed a number of counter-attacks. Next came Ponsonby's 40th Division which on the fourth day of the battle captured much of Bourlon Wood with the support of thirty-two tanks. Enemy counter-attacks and shelling left them seriously weakened and the situation in the wood was so confused that our artillery could give little support; two days later the remnants had to withdraw.

General Feilding, commanding the Guards Division, was the third involved. He had been warned before a Corps Commander's conference[12] that he was to make a joint attack with the 62nd Division on Bourlon Wood and the village of Fontaine, and so he came armed with a written appreciation of the situation. He pointed out that the attack involved an advance across open country to capture an undemolished village which would be stoutly defended. Shelling and machine-gun fire could be expected from three sides from the well-organized German reinforcements that had now arrived.

The Corps Commander had not prepared any detailed plan for this attack and would not make a decision. He then announced that they were expecting General Byng, the Army Commander, who arrived in due course and ordered the attack to go ahead. Following these delays, the Company Commanders of the 1st Coldstream did not receive their orders until midnight to take over the line and prepare for an attack to start at 6.20 a.m. over ground they had not seen. The 2nd Battalion Irish Guards was on their left, commanded by Lieutenant Colonel Harold Alexander (later Field Marshal).

In spite of these difficulties 2nd Guards Brigade advanced close behind a creeping barrage with the support of twelve tanks and reached its first objective, the 1st Battalion capturing over 500 prisoners. However, as Feilding had foreseen, enemy fire caused heavy casualties and, with too few guards, half the prisoners escaped. Determined German counter-attacks threatened to surround the battalion, together with the 4th Grenadiers, so they were all ordered to withdraw, the losses in the 1st Battalion amounting to 220. The divisional history comments that "It is highly questionable whether a local attack, arranged in such a haphazard and casual manner, against a position of such strength as the Bourlon Ridge could have been successful."[13]

Meanwhile the enemy were gathering more divisions and ground attack aircraft for an assault on both sides of the British salient at dawn on 30 November. They achieved a quick success, recapturing all the land they had lost ten days before and in the south they swept on two miles beyond the old line.

Gouzeaucourt, November 1917

Luckily, 1st Guards Brigade was in billets nearby and was ordered to head for the village of Gouzeaucourt. On the way the Brigadier, riding ahead, met British soldiers fleeing, who reported that the enemy were in the village, looting our supply train there. An attack was launched at 12.30 p.m. and within an hour the 2nd and 3rd Coldstream swept through the village and towards the ridge beyond, but they were then held up by very heavy fire and so they consolidated.

They recaptured some British 60-pounder guns and a 12-inch howitzer and the unlooted rations on the supply train proved most welcome. The following day the same battalions advanced a further

[12] Quoted in *A Wood Called Bourlon*, William Moore, Leo Cooper, 1988, page 129.

[13] *The Guards Division in the Great War*, Headlam, Vol I, pages 319–320.

1500 yards. A dangerous situation had been saved, but the cost of the two days had been heavy – 470 all ranks.

The German advance on 30 November was a major setback, particularly so soon after the celebrations for the success ten days before, and a fierce outcry was voiced by the Prime Minister and the Press in London. General Sir Julian Byng, the Army Commander, stated in his account of the disaster:

> "I attribute the reason of the local success on the part of the enemy to one cause and one alone, namely – lack of training on the part of junior officers and NCOs and men."[14]

He concluded that:

> "The remedy seems to be a longer period of training and in this connection it is to be noted that in the Guards, where the course is longer, there is no likelihood of any lack of staunch behaviour."

The German Onslaught, 1918

The fearful casualties of the battles of 1917 caused concern in the Government at home which had to juggle with manpower for the Army, for the factories that made the tanks, guns and shells, and for the production of vital coal and steel. In addition Lloyd George now distrusted his generals and he restricted the numbers in the drafts for France, while agreeing with the French that Haig's army would take over more of the front. Meanwhile the Russian Revolution enabled Germany to start transferring troops from the east and by mid-March 1918 forty-six extra divisions faced the Allies on the Western Front.

In February many infantry battalions were disbanded in order to make others up to strength, and brigades were reduced from four to three battalions. The surplus battalions in the Guards Division formed a 4th Guards Brigade which included the 3rd Coldstream and this new brigade was posted to the 31st Division. Once again the Guards Brigades took turns to man the front line, but they were thinly stretched; our commanders were well aware that the Germans would launch a major assault, so the emphasis was on constructing a new system of defence in depth. This comprised a line of outposts each of four to six men with a Lewis Gun, all mutually supporting and with the main line behind.

On 20 March the Guards Division was relieved by the 4th Division, now commanded by Major General Torquhil Matheson, and the very next day the German offensive started with a devastating five-hour bombardment from 6,500 guns, 120 for each mile of front. Then sixty-four divisions attacked a British front of nineteen divisions, (plus thirteen in reserve). A thick mist helped the enemy as their storm troops infiltrated between our outposts.

Over the next ten days the Fifth Army opposite St Quentin was pushed back forty miles, but, in spite of heavy losses in men and materials, the front was not broken. Before the battle was over its commander, General Gough, was sacked, although it was hardly his fault that he had been denied sufficient troops to hold his line.

[14] Third Army Papers, quoted by Moore, p.170–1.

The fifty-mile-wide breakthrough had its north point near Arras and it was in this area that the Guards Division moved into the line on 23 March. The 3rd Battalion (in another division, but close by) was the first to face the onslaught and it was forced back on the 25th. Over the next three days all battalions faced renewed attacks and withdrew some 2–3000 yards, mainly due to much greater setbacks further south.

On the 28th the Germans launched their final big attack in this area, but with good visibility they were held and suffered substantial casualties from our machine guns. Coldstream casualties for these March battles amounted to 279 all ranks, and the Guards Division played a useful role at the left hinge of the retreat in maintaining the link with our static line further north.

Hazebrouck, April 1918

During this great battle Haig had moved divisions south from the Ypres area to hold the crumbling line and so when the Germans launched a fresh attack in the north on 9 April the weakened British line was quickly driven back. 4th Guards Brigade with the 3rd Battalion hurried to the area and took up a position twelve miles behind our original front line.

The brigade had not had a chance to recover from the previous battle, but a strong Australian division was due to arrive by train and take over the line late the next day to defend Hazebrouck, a crucial rail and road junction only twenty-two miles from the coast at Dunkirk. 4th Guards Brigade's task was simple – hold on until the Australians arrive – but not easy to execute in the general confusion of the retreat where it even had difficulty in locating the units on either flank.

The overall situation was extremely serious and Haig issued his famous Order of the Day, saying, "With our backs to the wall and believing in the justice of our cause, each one of us must fight on to the end". Each company had some 400 yards of front and at dawn on 12 April the Germans launched a big attack aimed at Hazebrouck which the 3rd Battalion halted with machine-gun and rifle fire. The battalion then tried to advance to a better position, but No 1 Company on the right could see no sign of any British on its flank, so its situation was critical after severe losses. Sergeant Vickers, DCM, now in charge, handled the forty survivors with considerable tactical skill and, in spite of violent attacks all day, 4th Guards Brigade prevented the enemy advance towards Hazebrouck.

At dawn on the 13th the brigade found itself holding a front of nearly two miles, with a fresh division now on the right.

The German attacks continued, including an armoured car with a mounted machine gun, and fog enabled them to infiltrate our positions. Our companies found enemy on three sides and all the men in the left outpost of No 3 Company became casualties, except Private Jacotine who continued single-handed to defend the position, holding the enemy back for twenty minutes before he was killed.

The struggle continued with fury throughout the day with many acts of splendid valour; finally the brigade was reduced to a series of isolated groups, unsupported and hemmed in by an overwhelming mass of Germans. However, the line held while the Australians were able to de-train and organize their defence in the rear. Congratulations were showered on 4th Guards Brigade by the Duke of Connaught and Generals Haig and Plumer, and, although the brigade was replenished with drafts, this was its last significant action for some months. For a period it provided an officers' training school in a pleasant seaside resort.

The Final Phase

German attacks continued through May and June but no further ground was given up; the enemy losses were estimated at well over 300,000, while Lloyd George consented to reinforcements being sent to France. The United States had declared war in 1917, and after a slow start their troops were now arriving in force.

The British prepared for open campaigning and it became important to change the attitudes of officers whose only experience was trench warfare. Ivor Maxse was now Inspector General of Training, preaching new tactics as well as the importance of training, with a team of twenty like-minded officers, one of whom summed up the new doctrine:

> "The Colonel Commanding the Bollockyboos
> Has strictly revised all his previous views . . .
> He keeps his battalion, untiring, approving,
> All moving and firing, and firing and moving;
> They know about guns, they know about tanks,
> They'll take any risk that you like with their flanks.
> They're perfectly sound on the use of the ground,
> They all are at one that training is fun
> And there's nought they don't know about killing the Hun."

As in 1914 the River Marne proved to be a turning point when the French and Americans scored a success in July which greatly helped Allied morale. Next came the British victory of Amiens on 8 August which Ludendorff called "the black day for the German Army". With the support of 400 of the latest Mark V tanks and 800 aircraft the Germans were driven back over six miles in a single day. At this stage the Kaiser asked to open negotiations for peace, but his expectations that he could retain Alsace-Lorraine and a full-strength German Army and Navy were soon rebuffed by the Allies.

Everything was shaping up towards victory. Production in the factories in Britain was now in full swing and in one day the British guns fired some 940,000 shells. The formidable new Mark V tank, although rather slow, was at its best on the first day of a battle. The fumes, noise and heat would totally exhaust a crew and after a day's action there was usually much repair and maintenance needed.

The Victory Campaign

The second major battle of this campaign started north of the River Somme on 21 August with the 5th and the 2nd Divisions alongside the Guards Division, and the three commanders, Major Generals Ponsonby, Pereira and Feilding, lined up in order of their commands back in August 1914, i.e. the 1st, 2nd and 3rd Battalions. At 4.55 a.m. the 1st Battalion led the advance with ten tanks in support and achieved surprise, so reaching the first objective by 6.30 a.m. This was followed by another large-scale attack two days later, when the battalion captured Moyenneville in spite of thick fog making direction-finding difficult. In three days the brigade advanced 5000 yards and captured 1260 prisoners.

The enemy had therefore in a few weeks been thrust back across the whole of the old Somme battlefields and on 27 August the attack was resumed. The 2nd Battalion was involved in the capture of St Leger (Battle Honour **Arras, 1918**). The right flank was held up by heavy fire, while the left company reached the objective, but finding itself on its own decided to withdraw. It was a confusing struggle and the Battalion was at one time down to 140 men, with the final tally of casualties at 308. However, the next day patrols found that the Germans had departed.

The Hindenburg Line

After over two and a half years at the head of the Guards Division, Geoffrey Feilding was now posted to command London District and Torquhil Matheson took over when the Division was facing the Hindenburg Line at a point where it made use of the Canal du Nord in a deep cutting with wire defences and the inevitable machine guns sited to cover its length.

The attack was fixed for 27 September and the 1st Battalion was given scaling ladders to climb down the steep walls of the canal. No 2 Company was held up by a machine-gun post hidden in the remains of a ruined iron bridge, so Captain Frisby, the Company Commander, sent 2nd Lieutenant Mallam with a party to outflank the post while he planned to rush it. Lance Corporal Jackson immediately volunteered to join him with two others. The flanking party were soon held up by wire, so Frisby's little group dashed forward and climbed down into the canal under point-blank fire. They scrambled through the wire and rushed the post to capture it with two machine guns and twelve men, Frisby receiving a bayonet wound in the leg.

Two more companies of the battalion were then able to cross, but, due to the delay, their artillery barrage had got too far ahead, allowing other enemy machine guns to open up. Many of the officers were now casualties and Frisby organized the battalion defence across the canal and continued to press the enemy support line, with the result that at 5 p.m. 300 Germans surrendered with thirty machine guns, compared with battalion losses of 151.

This brilliant action produced two Coldstream Victoria Crosses in one day, Frisby and Jackson. The latter, after the capture of the machine-gun post, continued to set an inspiring example and was the first to jump into a German trench which his platoon had been ordered to clear. He was killed later that day and so became the Regiment's only posthumous Victoria Cross of the war.

Another part of the Hindenburg Line made use of the St Quentin Canal, where there was a tunnel, so over the top seemed the best place to attack; but the Germans had thought of this too, so an

Major General G.P.T. Feilding CB CMG DSO, General Officer Commanding Guards Division 1916–1918.

alternative had to be found. John Campbell, VC, now commanding 137 Brigade, led a most original type of attack across the canal by the mouth of the tunnel with the help of ladders and makeshift bridges with many of the men wearing lifebelts.

General Sir Torquhil Matheson KCB CMG, General Officer Commanding Guards Division 1918–1919.

Cambrai, 1918

The Battle of **Cambrai** had not ended in success in 1917, but it was now to be the Regiment's final major battle honour of the war, following the capture of the town by the Canadians on 9 October. The 2nd Battalion led an advance of 4000 yards until held up by machine guns, sited in houses and clumps of trees in undamaged countryside. The 1st and 3rd Battalions also moved forward and within a few days the gain was seven miles up to the banks of the River Selle. A popular novelty for the troops was the availability of undestroyed houses for billeting overnight.

The River Selle was a real obstacle, some fourteen feet wide with banks over seven feet high. No 4 Company of the 1st Battalion was sent across in order to close a gap with the units on the left. Enemy counter-attacks met fierce Lewis and Vickers fire, but still threatened to surround the company, which lost all its officers. The NCOs displayed coolness and initiative and executed a skilful withdrawal back across the river.

The main attack over the Selle was planned for 20 October and during the previous night patrols went out to protect the Engineers and 4th Battalion Pioneers who brought forward eight infantry bridges which they managed to carry down a muddy slope and erect in silence by 2 a.m. Tapes were laid for two battalions to find the bridges, enabling the attack to go in at dawn. The Grenadier battalion later complained that the bridges were "very indifferent". No doubt a suitable riposte was made to this comment.

The attack succeeded and our line was now twenty miles east of Cambrai, but, as we have seen, some enemy troops continued to fight obstinately, retiring methodically, while our battalion officers and NCOs were unaware of the state of demoralization and confusion behind the lines. Ludendorff summed it up: "The number of shirkers behind the front increased alarmingly. . . . The men who fought at the front were heroes, but there were not enough of them."

Final Victory, November 1918

The final battle opened on 4 November on the River Sambre with twenty-two divisions and a full programme of artillery support. The distances were longer and cavalry patrols had to be sent out at one stage to locate the enemy. On the second day the 1st Battalion captured eight field guns, but, even so close to the end, the grief for families was not over and the Regiment's losses over three days included forty-five killed and 130 wounded.

Final success was achieved on the night of the 7th when the Grenadiers liberated Maubeuge, an important fortified city on the Belgian border which had held out for two weeks in 1914. The 2nd Battalion received a great welcome when it passed through the city next day to take up positions beyond.

At 11 a.m. on 11 November Commanding Officers announced to the men that hostilities had ended. The news was received with dignity, the men scarcely realizing that the end had really come and that an outstanding victory had crowned their efforts. The Guards Division had advanced fifty miles over three months, while the British Army had captured 187,000 prisoners, 2,850 guns and 29,000 machine guns, nearly half of the total haul of all the Allies put together.

The series of well-planned victories since the Battle of Amiens was described by John Terraine as "unparalleled in the history of the British Army". Learning from experience, the Army had become masters of the battlefield, employing a range of weaponry that would have amazed the professional army of 1914. Over fifty British divisions played their part, so is it possible to judge the contribution of just one? The troops from the Empire, including the Australians, won high acclaim and, in commenting on their success, John Terraine wrote: "The Guards Division . . . set standards of performance which were admired even by the Australians." On 22 November the great contribution that the Division had made to victory was recognized by King George V who ordered that the rank "Private" be replaced by "Guardsman".

COLDSTREAM COMMANDERS IN THE FIRST WORLD WAR

	The Guards Division	
Aug 1915–Jan 1916	Major-General	The Earl of Cavan, KP, CB, MVO, Grenadier Guards
Jan 1916–Sep 1918	" "	G.P.T.Feilding, CB, CMG, DSO
Sept 1918	" "	T.G.Matheson, CB, CMG
	Coldstreamers Commanding Guards Brigades	
1st Guards Brigade		
Aug–Sept 1914	Brigadier General	F.I.Maxse, CB, DSO
(4th Guards Brigade)	(Became 1st Guards Brigade in August 1915)	
June 1915–Jan 1916	Brigadier General	G.P.T.Feilding, CB, DSO
Jan–Dec 1916	" "	C.E.Pereira, CMG
2nd Guards Brigade		
July 1915–Nov 1916 and Mar–Aug 1917	Brigadier General	J. Ponsonby, CMG, DSO
Mar–Apr 1918	" "	G.B.S.Follett, DSO, MVO
3rd Guards Brigade		
Apr–Sept 1918	Brigadier General	G.B.S.Follett, DSO, MVO (Killed in Action)
Sept–Nov 1918	" "	C.P.Heywood, CMG, DSO (wounded)
Dec 1918	" "	J.V.Campbell, VC, CMG, DSO

Battalion Commanders

1st Battalion

August 1914	Lieutenant Colonel	J.Ponsonby, CMG
August 1915	" "	A.G.E.Egerton (Killed in Action)
October 1915	" "	Hon G.V.Baring, MP (Killed in Action)
September 1916	" "	G.B.S.Follett, DSO, MVO
November 1916	" "	E.B.G.Gregge-Hopwood, DSO (Killed in action)
July 1917	" "	J.C.Brand, MC

2nd Battalion

August 1914	Lieutenant Colonel	C.E.Pereira
May 1915	" "	J.McC.Steele
August 1915	" "	P.A.MacGregor, DSO
March 1916	" "	G.B.S.Follett, DSO, MVO (wounded)
July 1916	" "	R.B.J.Crawfurd, DSO
November 1916	" "	G.B.S.Follett, DSO, MVO (wounded)
November 1916	" "	L.M.Gibbs, MC
March 1917	" "	G.B.S.Follett, DSO, MVO
March 1918	" "	E.P.Brassey, MC

3rd Battalion

August 1914	Lieutenant Colonel	G.P.T.Feilding, DSO
April 1915	" "	T.G.Matheson
July 1915	" "	J.V.Campbell, VC, DSO
November 1916	" "	R.B.J.Crawfurd, DSO
October 1917	" "	F.Longueville, DSO, MC
April 1918	" "	R.B.J.Crawfurd, DSO

4th Battalion

August 1915	Lieutenant Colonel	R.C.E.Skeffington-Smyth, DSO
October 1917	" "	G.J.Edwards, MC

Note on Author

Captain Anthony Maxse was commissioned in 1952, following his father and grandfather in the Regiment. He saw service with the 1st Battalion. He retired from the Army in 1962.

CHAPTER SIX

BETWEEN THE WARS, 1919–1939

by Robin Alderson

It is tempting to regard the twenty years from 1919 to 1939 as a peaceful, uneventful and uninteresting interlude between the two fiercest and most destructive wars that the world has ever known. This would be wrong, for, although the service of the Coldstream Guards during these years may seem insignificant when compared with the war years, the changes that followed the First World War and the events which led up to the Second World War were as challenging for the Regiment as for the nation that it served.

The experience of war for those returning from France, and the sense of personal loss for families throughout Britain who had lost a son, a father or a brother during those four years, profoundly affected attitudes and social relationships. Women had proved themselves capable of fulfilling roles that would never have been contemplated in peace. The class attitudes and social barriers of earlier years were, if not swept away, at any rate irrevocably weakened by people's awareness of the human cost of war and by a renewed perception of common interests and shared aspirations.

Every fibre of the nation's effort had been involved in the struggle. Wartime demands on Britain's industrial output had altered employment patterns, products and productive capacity. The economy had been sustained by massive public borrowing. Britain's Dominions and Colonies were wholly committed to the war effort and extensive loans had been secured in the US. The aim of the post-war government was to establish a lasting international peace following the 'war to end all wars' and, at home, to create a country 'fit for heroes'. But the policies which they enacted were constrained by practical considerations: the need to rebuild the country's manufacturing and industrial base without weakening Britain's credit overseas and to secure the colonies and the sea routes upon which imperial commerce depended without detriment to the all-too-fragile economy. Successive governments struggled to balance such conflicting demands. The result was a period of complex and far-reaching change for the whole nation.

For the Army, too, these were years of change. Its organization, tactical doctrine and equipment as well as the less esoteric imperatives of recruiting and deployment were all shaped not only by the experience of four years of trench warfare but also by the Government's more immediate priorities and preoccupations. Following the Armistice and the Paris Peace Conference of 1919, the size and shape of the Armed Forces were reduced to peacetime establishments. Conscription ceased and those organizations created to meet the special needs of war soon disappeared from the order of battle. For the Brigade of Guards this meant an end to the Machine Gun Guards, while for the Coldstream the 4th (Pioneer) Battalion ceased to exist. By 1920 the peacetime organization of battalions was established at a strength of thirty-three officers and 1,000 rank and file, formed in four Companies each with four platoons of four sections, armed with the Lewis Gun and rifle with the long bayonet.

The rifle companies were supported by a Headquarters Wing, which incorporated machine-gun, signals and transport platoons, musketry instructors, the Quartermaster's Department and the Corps of Drums trained as stretcher bearers.

Home Service, 1919–1929

The pattern of peacetime soldiering quickly established itself. In England the ten Foot Guards battalions were stationed either in London District as part of 7th Guards Brigade or in 1st Guards Brigade, which was established in Aldershot by the mid-1920s. As a rule one or two battalions were stationed overseas, with one usually forming part of the strategically important Suez Brigade in Egypt. At home Wellington and Chelsea Barracks were two battalion stations, while single battalions occupied Waterloo Barracks in the Tower of London and Victoria Barracks, Windsor.

Home Service Clothing, with rolled greatcoats and capes, was reintroduced for Public Duties in 1921. Duties were mounted on a daily basis, the King's Guard being found in turn by battalions in Chelsea and Wellington Barracks with the Tower of London and Windsor Castle guards being found by the battalions in Victoria and Waterloo Barracks. Duties also involved guarding the Magazine in Hyde Park and the Bank of England Picquet.

Barrack rooms were crowded and spartan; food was plain though filling and discipline was rigid. Battalions undertook an annual training cycle. This started with a musketry camp, which usually took place on the ranges in the Pirbright area. Battalions were either billetted in the hutted training lines or camped under canvas. Great emphasis was placed on individual weapon-handling skills and on accurate shooting at ranges of more than 300 yards. Battalions would then move on to tactical training further afield, often on Salisbury Plain. This invariably involved prolonged route marching. Battalion- and brigade-level schemes took place all over the country, units and formations often exercising against each other, much to the entertainment of the local population. Equipment and supplies were carried on horse-drawn limbers until the introduction of mechanical transport for battalions in 1934. Changes of station usually took place at the conclusion of formation training, battalions moving directly to their new station, often by train.

3rd Battalion Guard Mounting, Wellington Barracks 1920. The Adjutant is Captain O.W.H. Leese.

1st Battalion Guard Mounting, Chelsea Barracks 1920. The Ensign is Second Lieutenant G.N. Scott-Chad.

In barracks sport offered a welcome relief from drill. A continuous round of battalion and brigade competitions for milling, tug of war, football, rugby, swimming, cricket and cross-country running took place. Evening smoking concerts provided entertainment on a regular basis. Officers took every opportunity for sport in the hunting and shooting seasons. In London District Drum Majors were particularly adept at finding commercial opportunities for their Corps of Drums in variety shows and theatre concerts. Battalions in Aldershot invariably participated in the Aldershot Tattoo which took place every year in Rushmoor Arena.

The General Election of 1924 brought a Conservative government to power whose economic policies included returning Sterling to the gold standard. This was intended to control inflation but its effects proved particularly damaging to British exports. During 1925 unemployment rose sharply as industry, starved of capital for investment, was forced to retrench. The manifest weakness of the British economy damaged public confidence and badly affected industrial relations. During the early months of 1926 economic and industrial conditions deteriorated further and the Trades Union Congress called a General Strike. This started on 4 May and the Government had little option but to call upon the Army to maintain public services.

The 1st Battalion Coldstream Guards, serving as the Headquarters Battalion in Wellington Barracks, was host to a variety of military technicians who had been ordered to the capital to maintain essential services. Life was considerably disrupted and troops not on duty were confined to barracks, although sport was allowed to continue in Green Park. Various well-known artistes visited the Battalion to take part in evening concerts.

The 3rd Battalion was confined to its barracks in the Tower of London. Here the men occupied themselves and passing members of the public by staging football matches and boxing competitions in the moat. On 8 May the Battalion was ordered to march to the Royal Victoria Docks, which it occupied until 17 May. Guards were mounted to secure the entrances and exits of the Docks whenever convoys of lorries came or went. A number of submarines provided power for the London electricity grid and their crews provided enthusiastic opposition for Coldstream teams at scratch cricket matches between the warehouses and cranes of London docks. Concert parties provided evening entertainment, one proving particularly popular in which Miss Maisie Grey brought the house down with her song "What love means to girls like me". Although the Strike was over by

12 May the disruption, which continued for some months, caused the cancellation of the King's Birthday Parade in June 1926. Following the General Strike, governments were more circumspect in the pursuit of their economic objectives.

By the mid 1920s the organization of the infantry battalion had been modified to include a Support Company, consisting of a medium mortar platoon, an anti-tank platoon and a medium machine-gun platoon. Unemployment had made military service popular for young men, but recruits for the Regiment had to meet a height standard of 5 foot 11 inches.

Overseas Service

Although inadequately resourced for the task, the Army faced the demanding role of garrisoning a widely dispersed Empire, securing British interests in a variety of situations and responding to events many of which seemed of little direct relevance to Britain. Battalions often served overseas under the most trying conditions. Conveyed aboard troopships which were often old, slow and cramped, battalions travelled as formed units, often complete with their own mules or horses. A voyage to the Far East could take more than six weeks, with little opportunity for exercise for man or animal alike. During the 2nd Battalion's journey to Shanghai in 1929 a violent storm in the Bay of Biscay confined almost every man to his bunk. On a similar voyage one of the mules reacted violently to the prospect of overseas service, necessitating unprecedented steps on the part of the ship's carpenter to secure the animal in close arrest. In contrast to troopships, some moves were made aboard chartered passenger liners; all enjoyed the services of the ships' stewards, the better cooking and the greater luxury which these afforded. The comparative leisure of these voyages was interrupted by coaling stops, usually at Suez and Colombo or Singapore. For 24 hours the ventilation of the entire ship would be sealed to prevent coal dust penetrating the living spaces while the ships bunkers were refilled. While the ship was alongside, battalions would take the opportunity to disembark for a route march or other physical exercise, which all would enjoy despite the unaccustomed climatic conditions.

Turkey, 1922, 3rd Battalion

Peace-keeping became a military task for the first time in 1921 when 1st Guards Brigade was despatched to Turkey to enforce the settlement achieved at the Paris Peace Conference in 1919. The politicians of the victorious nations had extensively recast both the political geography and economy of Central and Eastern Europe and the Near East by means of a number of linked international treaties and the imposition of reparations on the defeated nations. These arrangements were to be underpinned by a 'League of Nations' which would resolve international disputes without recourse to war.

In dismantling the Ottoman Empire, the Peace Conference had placed parts of Asian Turkey under Greek control, an outcome which proved completely unacceptable to the Turkish population. The resulting insurgency, in which Mustapha Kemal's Turkish Nationalist Party raised an army to drive the Greeks out of Asia, endangered the post-war settlement of the Balkans as well as the demilitarized status of the Bosphorus as an international waterway. In the face of this threat the British, French and Italian governments agreed to form an allied force to prevent the peace settlement unravelling completely. However, they were only able to reach agreement on the limited aim of safeguarding the status of the Bosphorus. It was as part of this force that the 3rd Battalion, commanded by Lieutenant Colonel W.St A. Warde-Aldam DSO, embarked on 10 September 1922 for Constantinople as part of 1st Guards Brigade.

The SS *Huntsgreen*, which carried the Coldstream Battalion and the 2nd Battalion Royal Fusiliers, was small and slow. The accommodation was cramped and uncomfortable. However, the sea was calm and the month-long voyage was uneventful. The Battalion arrived off Chanak, on the eastern shore of the entrance to the Dardanelles, where the Fusiliers disembarked, on 9 October. Here a number of Coldstream officers went ashore to visit the 1st Battalion Irish Guards, the first British battalion to arrive in Turkey, which had been holding a bridgehead on the Asian side. The French and Italian elements of the allied force had been ordered by their governments not to deploy on the eastern shore and British troops had therefore been alone in confronting the Turkish Nationalist army. Though the aggression of the Turkish soldiers was now somewhat mitigated by their early success against the Greeks, circumstances were still far from stable.

SS *Huntsgreen* reached Constantinople the following morning. Political negotiations were well in hand, but rumours of possible concessions were causing unrest among the local Christian population, particularly in the Pera district of the city. To reassure them, the 3rd Battalion was ordered to disembark that morning and undertake a route march through the hot and very uneven streets of the city with bayonets fixed and Colours flying. This impressive demonstration of British military effectiveness reached its climax with a march past their Commander-in-Chief. The Battalion then re-embarked on SS *Huntsgreen* and crossed to the Asiatic shore where they took up their allotted positions in the allied line. Two companies occupied defensive positions across the Ismid Peninsula whilst the remainder of the Battalion was quartered in an abandoned orphanage. The companies in the line lived in marginally greater comfort until it started to rain.

By November the Battalion had moved out of these positions and re-crossed the Bosphorus to undertake internal security duties in Pera and Galata, providing guards for GHQ and other key points. In early December the Battalion moved to Mashlak, about six miles north of Constantinople, where more salubrious quarters were available, whilst they continued to undertake security duties within the city. Incidents were rare and duties became increasingly routine, leaving time for training and sport. Local sporting diversions included welcome flights of duck and woodcock and outings with the Mashlak Hunt; clearly the operational emergency had now entirely receded.

On 3 June 1923 1st Guards Brigade honoured the King's birthday by Trooping the Colour at the Taxim Stadium; the 3rd Battalion provided Numbers 5 and 6 Guards. By early autumn negotiations to reach a permanent settlement to the dispute reached their conclusion with the signing of the Treaty of Lausanne on 2 October 1923. On the same day the Battalion boarded SS *Arabia* bound for England.

Shanghai, 1927, 2nd Battalion

In January 1927 the 2nd Battalion, commanded by Lieutenant Colonel P.R.B.Lawrence MC, embarked for service in China, thereby becoming the first Foot Guards battalion to serve 'East of Suez'. Although the causes of the Chinese Civil War had no direct bearing on Britain, the hostility of the Chinese towards foreigners threatened the prosperity of the European expatriate communities in Hankow and Shanghai. Following fighting in the Yangtse valley, the Cantonese rebel army occupied Hankow. As a result the British government felt obliged to protect British commercial interests in Shanghai and hastily dispatched a division to reinforce the Shanghai Defence Force.

As part of this force, the 2nd Battalion embarked on SS *Kinfauns Castle* on 22 January 1927 for the long voyage to China and arrived in Shanghai on 10 March 1927. 20th Indian Brigade, which had arrived some weeks earlier, had secured the perimeter of the International Concession. Its boundary followed the shore of Soochow Creek and the River Whangpoo to the north and east. The western boundary followed the line of the Hangchow–Shanghai Railway, while to the south the British bordered French and American settlements. Each settlement had its own national garrison. The perimeter was secured by barbed-wire entanglements with sandbag emplacements at crossroads and defensive positions at the entry points.

The Battalion was responsible for the foreshore of Soochow Creek, between Markham Road Bridge and Price's Candle Factory, and was quartered in a hutted cantonment in nearby Jessfield Park. It was the responsibility of the Shanghai City police to deal with subversive activities among the local population, but not even their methods were sufficient to calm public disquiet at the news on 22 March that Cantonese troops were advancing on Shanghai. Hundreds of refugees flooded into the city from the surrounding region and for three days the situation was extremely tense, with intermittent shooting occurring at various points around the perimeter. Although the Cantonese came within contact of the British positions, there were only minor skirmishes and the Coldstream were not involved.

However, No 1 Company did undertake an operation, supported by the police, to recover two police stations which were thought to have been overrun by rebel gunmen. This rather haphazard operation was launched along the narrow streets of the city following minimal consultation by the police and resulted in the capture of three rifles, a quantity of ammunition and some seditious literature. Four sorry-looking individuals were arrested and taken away by the police. It was not long before the situation became calmer and life settled down to regular company reliefs every six days. By May the atmosphere was sufficiently relaxed for the Battalion to begin preparations for the King's Birthday Parade. This took place on 3 June on the Kiang-Wan Race Course, which was on international territory; the salute was taken by Sir Miles Lampson KCMG, the British Minister for the Settlement.

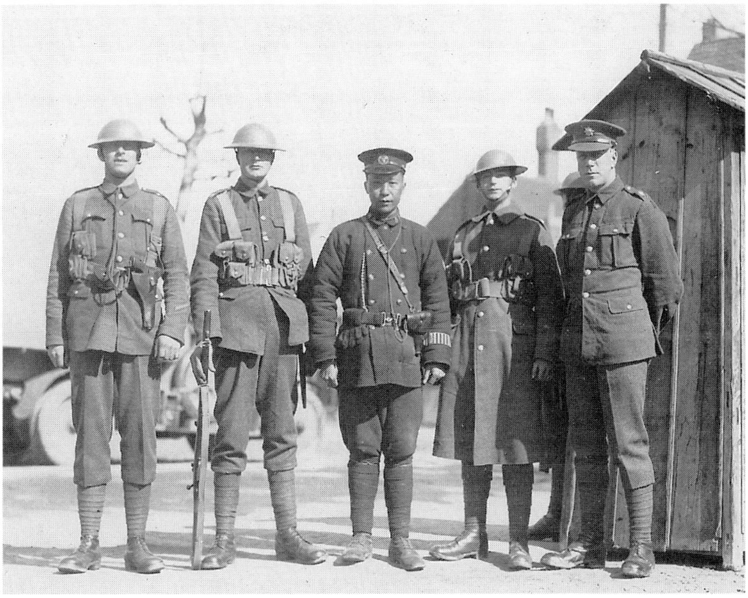

Number 1 Company 2nd Battalion; Guardsmen with Chinese Police, Shanghai, 1927.

2nd Battalion; King's Birthday Parade, Shanghai, 3 June 1927.

Drummer Fortune who was on the parade, aged twenty-two, wrote:

> "At the final dress rehearsal the Commanding Officer addressed the Battalion back in camp saying that on the following day he expected them to demonstrate to the American Marines, who had recently arrived, just how Ceremonial drill should be carried out. Little did we realize what lay ahead.
>
> "When we marched on to the racecourse the following morning, we were greeted by over 2000 people of all nationalities packed into the racecourse grandstand, and many thousands of Chinese lined the sides of the racecourse. When the first arms movement took place there was spontaneous applause from the grandstand – but it wasn't Horse Guards Parade – and spectators were showing real appreciation for what they were witnessing. This constant applause seemed to inspire the Battalion, so much so that despite the heat – something over 100° – this was arms skill to perfection such as I had not seen before on Horse Guards Parade, nor in the many years since. As the Battalion marched off the racecourse at the end of the Ceremony it was not only to applause, but to loud and prolonged cheering! The Commanding Officer certainly had his 'instructions' of the previous day carried out to the full!"[1]

By this time the Battalion had moved to a tented camp at Hungjao, seven miles from Shanghai, which enjoyed temperatures marginally below those in the city but was extensively infested with

[1] Letter from 2648527 Drummer L.A.Fortune February, 2000.

malarial mosquitoes. By July the Battalion was in more comfortable accommodation in huts in Kiachow Road, opposite the waterworks. Some excitement was caused during the summer when an RAF aeroplane crashed on Cantonese territory within sight of the British perimeter. Prompt action by British troops enabled the wrecked fuselage to be removed before the Cantonese authorities realized what had occurred. However, the wings were not to be secured so easily. Eventually a British 18-pounder emplacement was constructed astride the Shanghai–Nankin railway line; this resolute action achieved the desired purpose, enabling the RAF to recover their missing wings.

The summer climate in China proved both uncomfortable and unhealthy and sentries had to be posted wearing mosquito nets on their helmets. Throughout the remainder of the tour sports and physical training became a major preoccupation in order to counter the debilitating effects of an outbreak of enteric; nevertheless there were ten deaths from various causes during the tour. Less than a year after its arrival in China the Battalion embarked on TS *Assaye*, a small but relatively comfortable troopship, reaching Southampton after an uneventful voyage on 28 March 1928.

Sudan, 1932–1933, 1st Battalion

In 1932 the 1st Battalion had been due to undertake a two-year tour as part of the Suez Brigade. However, maintenance of a garrison in China had left the Army with shortages eleswhere and the Battalion was ordered to the Sudan garrison for six months prior to joining the brigade in the Canal Zone. Commanded by Lieutenant Colonel L.M.Gibbs DSO MC, it embarked on SS *Tuscania* at Liverpool on 22 March for an enjoyable voyage via Marseilles and Port Said, arriving in Port Sudan on 4 April. Battalion Headquarters with Numbers 1 and 2 Companies was based in barracks in Khartoum, on the northern bank of the River Nile. No 3 Company was located at Atbara, a railway junction on the Nile some 170 miles north of Khartoum. No 4 Company occupied an isolated camp at Gebeit, in the Red Sea hills eighty miles from Port Sudan.

Conditions in the Sudan were primitive, the climate was trying and it was recognized as a problem posting. However, the 2nd Battalion's experience in Shanghai had demonstrated the benefits of physical training in preventing illness and maintaining the operational capability of the Battalion. Throughout the six months of the 1st Battalion's tour in the Sudan, in addition to musketry and military training, the Battalion undertook a rigorous and varied programme of games and sport, with the result that not a single man's health suffered as a consequence of the climatic conditions. Light relief was provided for some of the officers by the Khartoum Foxhounds. It was as a conces-

1st Battalion; King's Birthday Parade, Cairo, 1933.

sion to the summer temperatures that the Battalion Trooped its Colour for the King's Birthday Parade at 0630 hours on 3 June, the Commanding Officer being mounted on a fine Arab pony.

Relieved in Sudan in October 1932, the Battalion arrived in Suez in early November to undertake the strategically important role of protecting this vulnerable link in the shipping route between Europe and India. After an uneventful year in Egypt, it finally returned to England two weeks before Christmas 1933.

Home Service, 1930–1936

The three Battalions of the Regiment had received new Colours from His Majesty King George V on Horse Guards in 1921. In 1926 the Guards Memorial had been unveiled by The Duke of Connaught. On a parade which was both impressive and moving, detachments from every Foot Guards battalion were joined by war veterans, detachments of Yeomen of the Guard and Chelsea Pensioners. The parade had ended with a march past in which scarlet, khaki and civilian dress mingled in a seemingly endless flow of Guardsmen.

Throughout the inter-war years the Regiment in England took part in a number of notable State and Ceremonial occasions; the years 1935–6, with the three Coldstream Battalions all serving together in London District, were particularly busy. On St George's Day 1935 the Colonel of the Regiment, Lieutenant General Sir Alfred Codrington, addressed all three Battalions of the Regiment at Pirbright. During the following twelve months Coldstream Guards of Honour, marching detachments or Street Liners participated in the celebrations for the wedding of The Duke of Kent, King George V's Silver Jubilee Parade and the State Funeral of The King in January 1936, as well as the Proclamation of King Edward VIII. Shortly after his accession The King reviewed all the Foot Guards Battalions in England and presented new Colours to all three Battalions of the Regiment in Hyde Park on 16 July. On 13 July 1936 the Colonel of the Regiment reviewed the Regiment on parade at Chelsea Barracks – the last time in the history of the Regiment that three Coldstream Battalions paraded together on their own.

This period saw other changes. The short bayonet was introduced for Public Duties and the rolled greatcoat ceased to be carried. Duties were formed in threes rather than in fours. Within battalions, horse transport had been replaced by motor transport during the winter of 1934, but it was not until 1936 that mechanical transport replaced the horses and limbers to deliver kits and rations to

2nd Battalion marching from Bustard Camp, Salisbury Plain, to Aldershot, September 1933.

2nd Battalion; Intelligence Section, 1934.

the Palace guards. It was some months before 15 cwt trucks proved as reliable as the horses they replaced.

During the 1930s international events were increasingly overshadowed by the rising military power of Germany. Hitler introduced conscription in March 1935 with the aim of raising an army of 500,000 men, in defiance of international arms agreements. The Italians flouted the League of Nations by invading and annexing Abyssinia. While Britain and France engaged in intense diplomatic and political efforts to stabilize the deteriorating international situation, the British government introduced a four-year rearmament plan. This was condemned by some as being an unnecessarily belligerent and expensive response to events and by others as being too little too late. Under this programme steps were taken to recruit additional officers and to prepare the Regiment for mobilization should the worst occur.

The Colonel of the Regiment, Lieutenant General Sir Alfred Codrington, inspecting Coldstreamers at Wellington Barracks, circa 1930.

2nd Battalion marching past His Majesty King Edward VIII, Wellington Barracks 1936. The Commanding Officer is Lieutenant Colonel the Earl of Romney (right of photograph). In attendance (centre of photograph), Major General Sir Bertram Sergison-Brooke and Colonel A.F. Smith, Regimental Lieutenant Colonel.

Inspection of the Regiment by the Colonel of the Regiment, Chelsea Barracks, 13 July 1936.

Palestine, 1936–39, 3rd Battalion

But these preparations had scarcely started when the 3rd Battalion received warning in September 1936 to embark for a short notice tour in Palestine. Britain had been involved in the region as a result of the Balfour Declaration in 1917 which was intended to attract Jewish support for the raising of war loans in the US; to achieve this the British Foreign Secretary had committed Britain to supporting "the establishment in Palestine of a national home for the Jewish People". Following the removal of Turkish suzerainty over Lebanon, Syria and Trans-Jordan in 1919, the administration of these countries was mandated to Britain and France by the League of Nations. A hostage to fortune, Balfour's declaration soon served to encourage Jewish immigration to Palestine from post-war Germany and Bolshevik Russia, where anti-Semitic pogroms provided a more immediate motive than Zionism itself. The fear that large numbers of Jews from Europe would undermine the interests of the Arab population of Palestine weakened British control of Trans-Jordan. Rioting broke out among the Arab populations in 1929 to protest against the influx of European Jews, and the British administration sought to defuse the situation by imposing controls on Jewish immigration. This caused a strong reaction in both Britain and America.

The 3rd Battalion, commanded by Lieutenant Colonel J.A.C.Whitaker, sailed for Haifa on board the SS *Laurentic*, landing on 1 October 1936. The situation was somewhat calmed, however, by news of the imminent arrival of a Commission to study the question of Jewish immigration and the Battalion was in Palestine for a short and uneventful three months, returning to Aldershot on New Year's Eve.

Less than twelve months later the 3rd Battalion returned to the region. In November 1937 it embarked on HMT *Dunera* for service in Egypt as part of the Canal Brigade. On arrival, it occupied barracks in Alexandria and on 9 June 1938 trooped the Regimental Colour in celebration of the King's Birthday. The security of the Suez Canal was seen to be particularly vulnerable to the strategic bomber and the Battalion found itself preparing large numbers of sand-bagged emplacements and participating in anti-aircraft exercises. However, in October these tasks were put to one side for more pressing security duties in Palestine.

Continuing erosion of their interests caused the Arab population to rebel, barricading the streets of the Arab City of Jerusalem and raising an armed insurrection. In haste, and under conditions of tight security, the 3rd Battalion made the short sea voyage to Haifa aboard SS *Vasna* to assist in an operation to cordon and search the City of Jerusalem. Elaborate plans, which took account of the sensitivity of the Holy Places and the magnitude of the task of searching every house within the Old City, had been made for this operation which was to start on 19 October.

The first part of the cordon was to be provided by the 1st Battalion Royal Northumberland Fusiliers who picketed the city walls with machine-gun posts. The 3rd Battalion then drove a wedge between the Temple area, which was not to be entered by British troops, and the Arab City. Operating under the pseudonym 'Monck's Regiment' for security reasons, Guardsmen entered Jerusalem wearing canvas shoes instead of nailed boots. Battalion Headquarters, guarded by the Pioneer Section carrying their rifles at the high port, took up a position just outside the Damascus Gate, where a wire cage was erected for prisoners. Three companies occupied the narrow streets of the city, from the Dung Gate to the Damascus Gate and thence along the Via Dolorosa to St Stephen's Gate. During the four days that it took to complete the search, some sniping was encountered and Guardsman Patfield was killed. Large numbers of Arabs were detained as a result of which much useful information about the rebels was gained, enabling a number of mined barricades to be safely removed and forty-seven Arab prisoners to be taken away in chains.

During the next month the Battalion carried out cordon and search operations in Gaza, Jericho, Haifa, Acre, Salama and Kafr Ana, Hebron and the adjoining villages. In mid-November a detachment of two platoons with No 2 Company's mortar detachments, under the command of Lieutenant R.G.V.FitzGeorge-Balfour, was engaged by a large band of rebels who had blocked the road between Bethlehem and Jerusalem. The platoons found themselves surrounded by rebels, some of whom crept to within thirty yards of the Guardsmen's hastily adopted defensive positions. When fire was returned by every available Lewis gun and rifle, the effect was such that the rebels were driven off, leaving numbers of dead and wounded. This incident resulted in the award of the Military Cross to Lieutenant FitzGeorge-Balfour, while Lance Corporal F.L.Karley and Guardsman W.Charlesworth were awarded the Military Medal.

The Battalion continued to assist with security operations for the next four months as the situation deteriorated. Further 'cordon and search' and security operations were conducted in Bani Naim, Kafar Sava and Taiyba. Weapons, ammunition and explosives in large quantities were found during operations and patrols were mounted against both Arabs and Jews. On Christmas Day 1938 a party from the Battalion went to Bethlehem, where they attended a carol service in the courtyard of the Church of the Holy Nativity. This period of intense activity concluded in April 1939 when the Battalion returned to Alexandria and resumed normal training.

Home Service, 1937–1939, 1st and 2nd Battalions

In England further changes in the equipment and organization of the Army were taking place in an effort to increase the operational capability of units. Carrier and Pioneer Platoons were formed and the Mortar Platoon's equipment was now carried in the Carden Loyd carrier. New weapons were introduced, including the 2" mortar, the Bren gun and the Boys anti-tank rifle. An appreciation of

1st Battalion's first ever move by air, Hendon to Catterick, 1937.

1st Battalion; King's Birthday Parade 1937. Captain of the Escort is Major I.N.McC. Tubbs, the Subaltern is Lieutenant the Lord Gilford and the Ensign Second Lieutenant R.J.V. Crichton.

the significance of air power, not only for strategic bombing but also for air transport, is to be seen from the first operational move of a British infantry battalion by air during the summer of 1937, when the 1st Battalion moved from Croydon to Catterick during a brigade exercise. Events such as these reflected developments in military tactics and capability which had had their genesis during the 1914–18 War, but which only became affordable as the priority for defence increased in response to the deteriorating international situation.

In March 1938 the German Army entered Austria. Three months later Hitler demanded the annexation of the western part of Czechoslovakia to the German Reich. In a fruitless attempt to forestall German action, a British force was warned for service in the Sudetenland, to provide security for a plebiscite on the acceptance of German sovereignty. This force was to include the 2nd Battalion. However, despite the 1st Battalion's successful air move during the previous summer, such an operation was considered impractical, since the force would have to be supported by surface routes which lay through Germany.

The 1st and 2nd Battalions were both training in the south of England during August 1939 when news was received of German moves against Poland. Both battalions were therefore at full strength when, early in September, they received orders to move to France as part of the British Expeditionary Force.

Note on Author

Major Robin Alderson was commissioned into the Coldstream Guards from Mons Officer Cadet School in 1965. He was posted to 2nd Battalion in Aden and served in Germany and Belize. He also served with 1st Battalion in Germany and was appointed Regimental Adjutant in 1981. He retired from the Army in 1986.

CHAPTER SEVEN

THE SECOND WORLD WAR

by Hugh Boscawen

When war was declared on 3 September 1939 the **1st Coldstream** was training at Pirbright, while the **2nd Battalion** was at Albuhera Barracks, Aldershot. The **3rd Battalion** was in Egypt, serving in the Canal Brigade, and based in Mustapha Barracks, Alexandria.

The outbreak of war was greeted (in 1st and 2nd Coldstream) by some with relief, even celebration; war, long anticipated, was now a reality and provided a degree of certainty. Some felt that it would be like the manoeuvres that the Battalions had done during the summer. A feeling of inevitability prevailed, however, among the many sons of those who had fought the Germans only twenty years before. Orders to mobilize had arrived on 1 September and, within hours, Reservists joined both Battalions.

Mechanization of the Army at home was completed in 1938 and battalions (twenty-three officers and 753 men in four Rifle Companies) had the .303" Bren light machine-gun, ten lightly armoured Bren Carriers, and a 3" Mortar Platoon. Anti-tank defence was provided by the Boys .55" anti-tank rifle, regarded as infamous for its savage kick. Battalions were expected to march (they lacked troop transport) and were equipped only to company level with radio. Tactics were based on the mobile warfare of 1918 with some emphasis on positional defence. The British Expeditionary Force (BEF) was partly organized for a war of manoeuvre, but it lacked armour and all arms training.

THE BRITISH EXPEDITIONARY FORCE, 1939–40[1]

The **2nd Battalion** was in 1st Guards Brigade (with 3rd Grenadiers and 2nd Hampshire Regiment, under Brigadier Merton Beckwith-Smith) in Major General the Hon Harold Alexander's[2] 1st 'Strategic Reserve' Division (I Corps). Commanded by Lieutenant Colonel Lionel Bootle-Wilbraham, the Battalion moved to Southampton on 19 September and sailed for Cherbourg, continuing by rail (as in 1914) in '*Hommes 40, Chevaux 8*' trucks to Sillé-le-Guillaume (near Le Mans) then marching on *pavé* (cobbles) to Conlie and later Arras.

The **1st Battalion** under Lieutenant Colonel Arnold Cazenove in 7th Guards Brigade (with 1st and 2nd Grenadiers, under Brigadier Sir John Whitaker, a Coldstreamer) was in Major General Bernard Montgomery's 3rd Division (II Corps) and arrived in Cherbourg on 30 September. They followed the same route, arriving near Roubaix on 12 October.

[1] Theatre Blazon, **North-West Europe 1940.**

[2] General Alexander was known throughout the Brigade of Guards, and later more widely, as General 'Alex'.

In 1938 plans had been made to deploy the BEF to Northern France which was unprotected by the much-vaunted Maginot Line. A few pillboxes and an incomplete anti-tank ditch existed along the border with neutral Belgium, and so the BEF had to construct a twenty-mile defensive line from Halluin (near Menin) to Maulde, south of Tournai.

The battalions spent the winter of 1939–40 constructing trenches, pillboxes and wire entanglements. The single battledress issued was inadequate for the cold and Guardsmen were mostly quartered in unheated barns. Little training was done in the Regular divisions, except 3rd Division where General Montgomery anticipated that battles would be fought on each river line. Bachy station platform was used for Adjutant's Drill Parades by 2nd Coldstream, and in December His Majesty the King visited the Battalion on one of the coldest days of the winter. Efforts were made to maintain morale and concerts by George Formby, Gracie Fields and others were popular. Morale was high and the Guardsmen, despite the most arduous conditions, complained little during this 'Phoney War'.

Lord Gort, Commander-in-Chief of the BEF, attended the Paris conference in November at which it was decided that if Belgian neutrality was violated the Allies would move forward sixty miles from the River Escaut to the River Dyle, east of Brussels. This – Plan 'D' – would shorten the Allied line, preserve Brussels, deny the Channel ports to Germany and might bring the Belgian Army on to the Allied side. No reconnaissance of Belgium was allowed, however, and the wisdom of moving forward was much debated.

In February 1940 the 2nd Battalion served in the Maginot Line near Lorry-lès-Metz and the companies were, for the first time, in sight of the enemy. Useful battle lessons were learned, particularly about dominating no-man's-land. Some Guardsmen acquired '*On ne passe pas*' Maginot badges; after Dunkirk many Coldstreamers felt that, unlike the Maginot defences, no one had passed *them*!

1st Battalion

The German invasion of the Low Countries on 10 May was followed by the advance into Belgium. 1st Coldstream moved to Vilvorde outside Brussels, then to Louvain and Herent, on the Mechelen-Louvain canal, where Coldstreamers first engaged German troops (14 May). An assault crossing in the Battalion area was repulsed next day, but during the action Lord Frederick Cambridge, commanding No 2 Company, was killed. The loss of this popular figure, the first Coldstream officer killed in the campaign, was a shock. The Battalion counter-attacked to the canal, but on 16 May the Germans crossed in the Belgian sector. Worse news followed; German tanks had broken through over the River Meuse eighty miles further south, outflanking the Maginot Line and threatening the BEF's flank.[3]

The 1st Battalion withdrew that night to the Escaut (temporarily beside the 2nd Battalion) and later into reserve. Refugees hindered movement and everyone witnessed terrible sights where civilians had been dive-bombed. On 22 May the 1st Battalion moved again to Wattrelos, east of Roubaix. The discipline and bearing of the Guardsmen on the march made a strong impression on many observers.

[3] Battle Honour **Dyle.**

2nd Battalion

The 2nd Coldstream received news of the attack on 10 May at Pont-à-Marcq, south of Lille. The Battalion marched twenty-one miles to Tournai next day before being lifted to Brussels, but had to march a further twelve miles to Duisburg village, and later Leefdaal, on the Brussels-Louvain road. Similar scenes of refugees choking the roads and rumours of 'Fifth Columnists' were encountered. No.3 Company's cookhouse in Leefdaal was bombed and the CQMS and a cook were killed, the first casualties suffered by the Battalion.

On 15 May, following the German crossing of the Dyle, the Battalion prepared to move amid order and counter-order. That night it withdrew, marching seventeen miles back to Zuun on the Brussels-Charleroi canal; two days later it completed another twenty miles to the Dendre at Ninove. The Commanding Officer commented that the Guardsmen marched well and were cheerful despite little sleep in the past forty-eight hours. The boots stood the test, but many felt that they had 'slept on the march'. On 19 May 2nd Coldstream had to withdraw in daylight in contact, under shellfire, from its positions forward of the Dendre.

The twenty-seven miles to Pecq on the Escaut were completed mostly on foot, fortunately without air attack, and the Battalion arrived late on 20 May. The Escaut was "as wide as the Basingstoke canal", but shallow; it gave Lord Gort the chance to deploy the BEF in the defence of a major

Guardsmen of No 1 Company 2nd Battalion about to eat at Bachy Station, winter 1939.

obstacle, although he had troops committed around Arras, thirty-five miles to the south-west. The BEF defences ran for thirty-two miles with 1st Guards Brigade in the centre.

The Guardsmen were tired – "over everybody there was a heavy air of fatigue and depression" one Company Commander wrote – but two platoons per company immediately began to dig in along an 1800 yard frontage, overlooked by the Mont St Aubert feature, 430 feet high, less than two miles away. No 3 Company guarded the bridge, demolished that night (20/21 May), while No 1 Company was behind the canal bank. During the dark night it was realized that there was a gap between the Coldstream and 3rd Grenadiers on the right, and a limited re-deployment took place. The Royal Artillery shelled movement on the far bank, but before dawn German mortaring started and heavy shellfire later hit both Battalions.

A determined river crossing by *31st Infantry Division* against the Coldstream-Grenadier boundary followed. Despite heavy fire, several German companies crossed and advanced towards the Pecq-Tournai road, digging in on rising ground ('Poplar Ridge'). Attempts by Coldstream Bren carriers to support No 1 Company, forced out of position, were only partially successful, several carriers being lost to assault guns. The attack towards Pecq was halted.

The situation was unclear; communications were difficult. Brigadier Beckwith-Smith, the Brigade Commander, ordered the Commanding Officers to restore the situation as best they could. No 3 Company of the Grenadiers counter-attacked, but, when this faltered, Lance Corporal Harry Nicholls of the Grenadiers (Imperial Forces Heavyweight Boxing Champion) charged the positions on Poplar Ridge firing his Bren, destroying the machine guns and causing numerous casualties, despite several wounds. This superb act of gallantry wrested the initiative from the Germans and Lance Corporal Nicholls was later awarded the Victoria Cross.

The Coldstream re-established their forward positions and by nightfall reported their front clear of enemy. The Battalion had suffered thirty casualties (fifteen killed) including several officers and seniors. In 1st Guards Brigade sector a Corps river crossing had been defeated and only one small penetration had been made down the whole Escaut Line.[4]

In the south, tanks from *Panzer Gruppe von Kleist*, the German main effort, reached the Channel late on 20/21 May. The BEF's resolute defence of the Escaut caused General von Bock to switch the effort of *Army Group B* (a subsidiary to the attack in the south) to the Courtrai-Ypres axis, the BEF boundary with the Belgians, in order to outflank the Escaut position. A salient began to develop around Lille.

Lord Gort saw the trap and decided, despite Allied pressure, to save the BEF. After several confused meetings in Ypres on 22 May Lord Gort ordered the BEF to withdraw to the 'Gort Line' constructed during the winter. This released divisions to attack south into *Panzer Gruppe von Kleist* (the offensive never materialized), to secure Dunkirk and to strengthen the northern flank with the Belgians.

The Dunkirk Perimeter. 1st and 2nd Battalions

The **2nd Battalion** withdrew from Pecq on 22 May to ill-prepared positions near Leers (east of Roubaix) but it was well supplied from the Lille NAAFI. On the 27th the Commanding Officer announced that 1st Division was to move to the Dunkirk perimeter. The intention "to march 55 miles back to the coast" produced misgivings!

[4] Battle Honour **Defence of Escaut**.

On 26 May **1st Coldstream** received orders regarding evacuation from Dunkirk, but with *Army Group B* attacking the BEF flank near Menin, the Battalion moved to Roncq (south of Menin). The German *VI Armee* broke through 5th Division at Houthem (near Ypres) and the position was only restored by a determined attack by 3rd Grenadiers, whose defence prevented *Army Group B* encircling the BEF. The 1st Coldstream withdrew (28 May) over Messines Ridge to Reninge, on the Yser, twelve miles from Dunkirk, down roads clogged with French, British and Belgian troops. (Belgium surrendered on 28 May). The Yser was the last significant obstacle south of the Dunkirk perimeter. The Battalion moved to Furnes, destroying its transport and keeping only the fighting vehicles. Dunkirk lay under a pall of smoke.

During 30 May German pressure increased north of Furnes; their *56th Division* attempted to cross the Bergues-Furnes canal. 1st Coldstream was ordered to relieve a battalion on the canal, but No.1 Company, reaching the position in the dark, found Germans on the near bank. An immediate counter-attack was mounted, but the situation remained confused. The Adjutant, Captain George Burns, took over No 1 Company and the Transport Officer No 3. At first light mortars and artillery opened fire and the crossing was defeated.

Pressure on 1st Coldstream increased on 31 May; the 3rd Division was ordered to embark that night and No 4 Company formed the Battalion rearguard. By 0300 hours the Guardsmen – and thousands of other troops – were on the beach at La Panne waiting for the tide. On 1 June 1st Coldstream, each man with his rifle and equipment, returned to England.

The **2nd Coldstream** had also been moving on 27 May from Roubaix, past Ploegsteert and Kemmelberg, to Locre, between Ypres and Bailleul, where it rested after marching thirty-two miles, and a thunderstorm soaked everyone. The Battalion marched a further fifteen miles, passing chaos in Poperinghe, to the Bergues-Furnes canal (with only a few miles in transport) before setting about the defence of a wide frontage astride a main route into the Dunkirk Perimeter. By late on 29 May 2nd Coldstream was dug in, but its strength was only 200 men. A detachment, 120 strong, later rejoined the Battalion from Houthem (near Hondschoote).

Troops, including wounded, straggled across the bridges all day, only ambulances being allowed to drive across. Two platoons of the Welsh Guards "marched across in formation, looking like Guardsmen and remarkably . . . well turned out compared with the rabble which was shuffling along the roads. It did us good to see them," wrote the Commanding Officer. On the 30th the Coldstream was ordered to form the rearguard for the BEF, fighting until receiving orders to evacuate. Rations were scanty and ammunition short.

Shelling increased, but it was not until 1 June that the position became precarious. German tanks crossed the canal, forcing No 1 Company back onto No 3, both Company Commanders being killed; but the Battalion held on, before withdrawing to the beaches that night. The Guardsmen spent 2 June hiding from *Stukas* in dunes near Dunkirk until evening before leaving in various craft. Colonel Bootle-Wilbraham (now commanding the Brigade) and Major W.S. ('Bunty') Stewart Brown, Acting Commanding Officer, were picked up by HMS *Sabre*. No Coldstreamer was allowed to board without his weapon; but once aboard, cocoa was served in galvanized buckets, and most Guardsmen slept until reaching Dover.[5]

The achievements of the Royal Navy and the 'Little Ships' of Dunkirk are well known. Dispersion to Reception Areas was another feat of improvisation; 545 trains were used to move the 338,226 men evacuated. Hundreds of volunteers produced tea and sandwiches. The 1st Battalion

[5] Blazon **Dunkirk 1940**.

re-assembled at Aldershot, while the 2nd collected at Walton, near Wakefield. Reorganization and training against an invasion was the priority.

The recovery of the BEF was a major success, but it was not a victory. Almost all heavy equipment was lost: over 84,400 vehicles were abandoned, including 98% of the tanks. Winston Churchill, Prime Minister since 10 May, inspired the nation, but stated that "wars are not won by evacuations". Britain had, however, recovered a third of a million trained Servicemen, and Dunkirk veterans went on to fight in every theatre of war. "Being evacuated," wrote one, "was the start of the road back."

The War Office Report later concluded that "without question the British soldier is at least as good as the German," but it was clear how ill-equipped the BEF had been for the campaign. The BEF and RAF had gained valuable exerience, but there was much to learn.[6]

Months later the 1st Battalion Commanding Officer's Bunting, battle-scarred and bloodied, arrived at Regimental Headquarters from HMS *Winchelsea* which had carried Colonel Cazenove back from the beaches. It now hangs in the 1st Battalion Sergeants' Mess, a symbol of the Coldstreamers who maintained traditional standards and discipline under very difficult circumstances during the Dunkirk campaign.[7]

The Home Front, 1939–41

Regimental Headquarters played a key role in posting officers, keeping battalions up to strength, and administering the Regiment. Successive Regimental Lieutenant Colonels – Guy Edwards, John Wynne Finch, Maurice Trew and Sandy Stratheden – were active in interviewing officer candidates, visiting battalions and keeping in touch with those employed outside battalions, or in hospital.

The Guards Depot remained at Caterham and turned recruits, including the Officers' Brigade Squad, into Guardsmen. Further training was done at the Guards Training Battalion, formed at Pirbright in August 1939. Pirbright was overcrowded and in late 1939 companies moved to Sandown Park. The regime at Caterham and Pirbright was described by Gerald Kersh in *They Died With Their Boots Clean* which immortalized the (fictitious) Coldstream Sergeant Nelson and gave an idea of what basic training, and fighting a campaign, was like.[8]

Although recent battle experience was at a premium, much was owed to the officers and seniors with First War experience who rejoined the Colours 'for the duration'. Although often regarded as 'dugouts', they offered valuable experience; they knew how to keep Guardsmen going in battle for extended periods and ran establishments in 'proper fashion', releasing younger men to Service Battalions.

A Holding Battalion was formed at Regent's Park Barracks from the Sandown companies; it provided guards and detachments, including the Coats Mission (see Chapter Eight) and protection for Churchill at Chequers. When, in June 1940, Lord Suffolk, the eminent scientist, brought 'heavy water' vital for nuclear research back from Paris a Coldstream platoon from the Holding Battalion

[6] Numbers evacuated: see *The Second World War: Their Finest Hour* by W.S.Churchill, London, 1949, vol.II, page 102. Over 112,500 of the total were Allied troops. "Road back": Mr Joe Nixon. *Lessons to be Learned from the Operations in Flanders*, Secret War Office Report of the Bartholomew Committee, 1940.

[7] Bunting: the Commanding Officer's small Captain's Colour, which denotes the position of Battalion Headquarters in the field, made of bunting material. The Bunting was presented to the Sergeants' Mess by Major Robert Cazenove, son of the Commanding Officer, when 1st Battalion Adjutant 1973–75.

[8] *They Died With Their Boots Clean*. G.Kersh, 1940. The author served in the Regiment.

was sent to Falmouth to collect it; rather than leave it in Barracks it was stored overnight in Pentonville Prison!

The Holding Battalion found Public Duties, and King's Guards in battledress marched behind the Corps of Drums from Regent's Park Barracks. Duties were drilled by Regimental Sergeant Major 'Tibby' Brittain, reputed to have the loudest voice in the Army, and later by Regimental Sergeant Major Yardley. In 1943 the Holding Battalions were amalgamated into the Westminster Garrison Battalion at Wellington Barracks.

Raising the 4th, 5th and 6th Battalions

The **4th Battalion** was raised in October 1940 at Elstree School by Lieutenant Colonel Norman Gwatkin, and later joined the new 30th Guards Brigade in the defence of London and Fighter Command Headquarters at Stanmore. The **5th Battalion** was also raised at Elstree by Lieutenant Colonel the Lord Stratheden, in October 1941, as part of 32nd Guards Brigade. At the same time a **6th Battalion** was raised at Harrow-on-the-Hill under Lieutenant Colonel Bunty Stewart Brown, but although it took part in several exercises, it became a holding battalion and disbanded in October 1943.

NORTH AFRICA 1940–43[9]

The Western Desert, 1940–42. 3rd Battalion

Italy entered the war in June 1940, and the campaign in the Western Desert started with 7th Armoured Division (Major General O'Moore Creagh) including 3rd Coldstream, under Lieutenant Colonel John Moubray, patrolling the Egyptian-Libyan border in July. On 13 September the Italians attacked and delaying actions were fought before the Coldstream (organized as a Motor Battalion and still wearing their solar topees) returned to Mersa Matruh.

General Sir Archibald Wavell, Commander-in-Chief Middle East Forces, planned to defeat the Italians at Sidi Barrani, between Mersa Matruh and Sollum. The Battalion took part in the diversionary attack on the Italian-Libyan force at Maktilla, although most of the enemy escaped to Sidi Barrani, where 4th Indian Division attacked from the south and 3rd Coldstream from the east. Some 6500 prisoners were taken (11 December 1940); "there were about five acres of officers and two hundred acres of other ranks"[10]. Wavell's offensive evicted the Italians from Bardia, Tobruk and Benghazi. The Guardsmen returned to Kasr-el-Nil Barracks (Cairo) before training for a landing on Rhodes.

Wavell's success prompted Hitler to create the *Deutsches Afrika Korps* under General Rommel. On 31 March 1941 Rommel attacked Northern Cyrenaica, lightly held since most British troops had been sent to Greece. 22nd Guards Brigade, under Brigadier Ian Erskine, rushed to Sidi Barrani, Sollum and Halfaya Pass. On 15 April the barracks above Sollum was raided, but, despite great gallantry, the Battalion suffered thirty-seven casualties for some seventy Germans killed.

[9] Theatre Blazon **North Africa 1940–43.**

[10] Battle Honour **Egyptian Frontier 1940** and Blazon **Sidi Barrani**. Acres: *Their Finest Hour op cit* Vol.II, page 539.

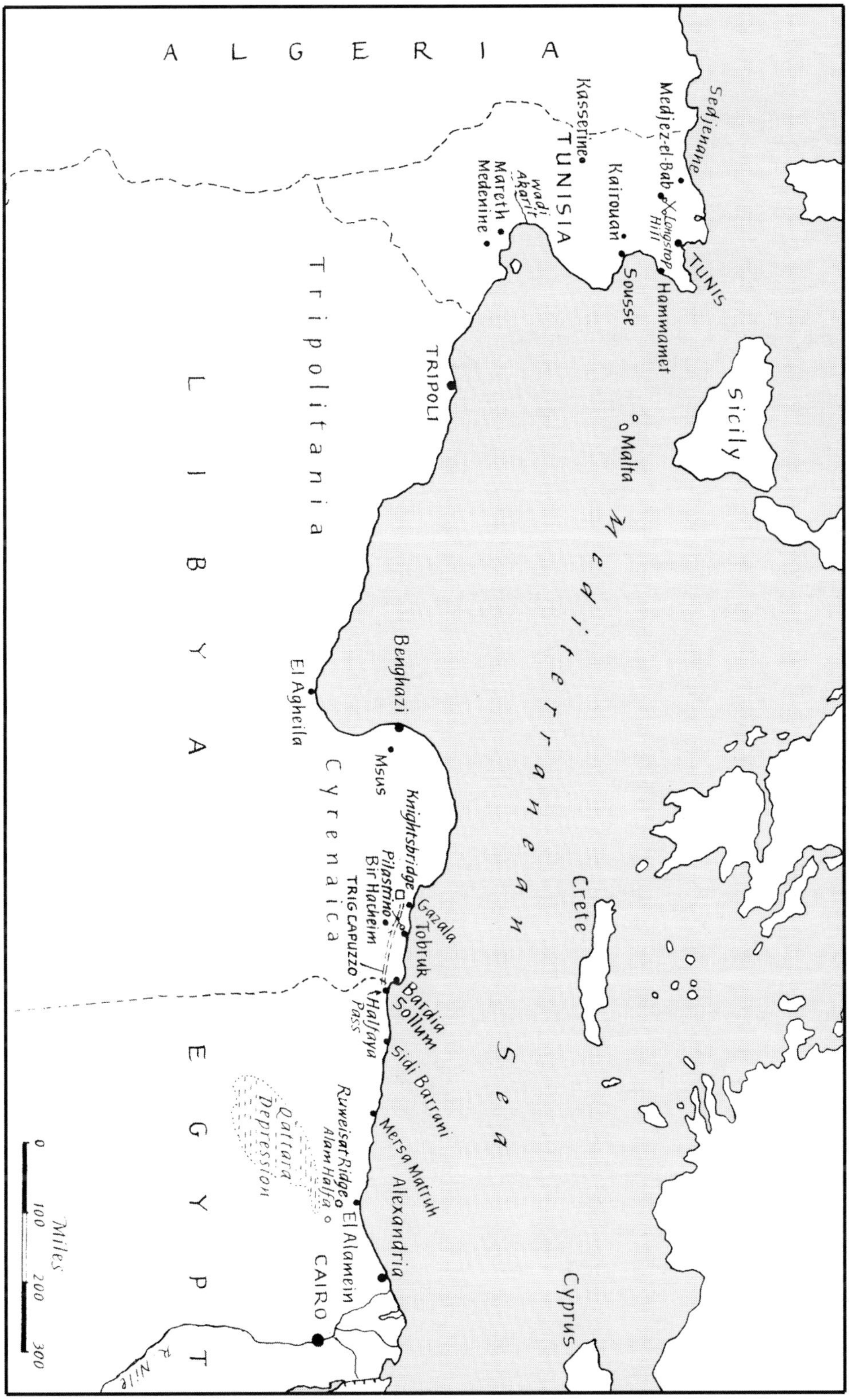
ALGERIA
TUNISIA
Kasserine
Medjez-el-Bab
Sedjenane
Longstop Hill
TUNIS
Kairouan
Sousse
Hammamet
Mareth
Medenine
wadi Akarit
Tripolitania
TRIPOLI
Malta
Sicily
LIBYA
Mediterranean Sea
El Agheila
Benghazi
Msus
Cyrenaica
Knightsbridge
Pilastrino
Bir Hacheim
TRIG CAPUZZO
Gazala
Tobruk
Bardia
Sollum
Halfaya Pass
Sidi Barrani
Crete
EGYPT
Qattara Depression
Mersa Matruh
Ruweisat Ridge
Alam Halfa
El Alamein
Alexandria
CAIRO
Nile
Cyprus
Miles
0
100
200
300

3rd Battalion. Company Administration at Sollum, September 1940.

A month later 22nd Guards Brigade again attacked Sollum, but faced German Mark III and IV tanks, and 88mm 'Flak' guns in the anti-tank role: all outclassed British tanks. The 3rd Coldstream defended Halfaya Pass, but was attacked by *Kampfgruppe von Herff* on 26 May. The Germans took a key hill at the top of the Pass (known as Point 190) and then assaulted Battalion positions in the defile itself, forcing the Guardsmen to fight a rearguard action. The *Afrika Korps* was a very different proposition from the Italians, but the dust storms, all-pervasive sand and myriad flies remained an unchanging feature of the campaign.[11]

After a brief respite 3rd Coldstream took part in Wavell's offensive in Cyrenaica. 22nd Guards Brigade again attacked Sollum barracks. The objectives, except for Halfaya Pass, were taken (15–16 June) but the *Afrika Korps* reacted quickly and 7th Armoured Division suffered heavily. The Coldstream narrowly escaped being trapped in the withdrawal; they were ordered to hold a 'box' (strongpoint) near Mersa Matruh – eighty-five miles from Alexandria.

From July to September the Battalion trained and patrolled. General Sir Claude Auchinleck replaced Wavell as Commander-in-Chief Middle East Forces in August, and the Eighth Army was formed under General Alan Cunningham. The CRUSADER offensive was mounted on 18 November, but 3rd Coldstream, in company columns with artillery, was not initially involved. No 1 Company later beat off a German force raiding the lines of communication. The Sidi Rezegh escarpment, south-west of Tobruk, was fiercely contested and 3rd Coldstream drove off a strong armoured column, inflicting casualties, including wounding Major General Neumann-Silkow, commanding *15th Panzer Division*.[12]

On 10 December 22nd Guards Brigade, now under Brigadier John Marriott, crossed the desert

[11] Battle Honour **Halfaya 1941**. Flak: from *Flugzeug-Abwehrkanone* – anti-aircraft gun.

[12] Blazon **Tobruk 1941**.

3rd Battalion Officers at Sidi Barrani, December 1940. Left to right: Tim Sainthill (2 Coy), David Forbes (3 Coy), Willie Forbes (HQ Coy), Victor FitzGeorge-Balfour (Int Offr).

to Antellat and Agedabia, occasionally encountering German and Italian tanks, but ran up against the German strongpoints near El Agheila. Rommel was close to his Tripoli bases; Eighth Army supply lines were over-extended and the brigade halted.

Rommel's counter-offensive started on 21 January. 22nd Guards Brigade now had to fight rear-guard actions back to Msus, harried by tanks and dive-bombers. The columns intermixed with friendly, and occasionally enemy, vehicles, and fought their way to Charuba. The outstanding leadership of Lieutenant Colonel Moubray resulted in the Battalion suffering only nine casualties with twenty-three missing; he received the DSO.[13]

Knightsbridge, Tobruk and the Alamein Line. May–July 1942, 3rd Battalion

The Eighth Army now created the Gazala Line from Tobruk to Bir Hacheim, a series of 'Boxes' with artillery round which armour could manoeuvre. The 3rd Coldstream, with a Scots Guards company and guns from 2nd Royal Horse Artillery and the Northumberland Hussars, occupied the vital Knightsbridge Box – flat desert two miles square – on the Trigh Capuzzo road south-west of Tobruk on 17 May. German tanks attacked ten days later, but were repulsed and their supply column was shelled. Patrols went out each day from the Box, which was shelled for seventeen days and roasted in the sun, with respite only during dust-storms.

[13] Battle Honour **Msus**.

Rommel found outflanking the Gazala Line achieved little since British armour was supplied from the Boxes, and switched his attacks onto the Boxes themselves. On 7 June *Kampfgruppe Wolz* and *15th Panzer Division* attacked Knightsbridge, but 4th Armoured Brigade forced a German withdrawal. Knightsbridge remained under shellfire for four more days while Rommel attacked the Free French at Bir Hacheim.

Orders for withdrawal from Knightsbridge were given on 11 June, but the Box could not be abandoned in daylight. On 12 June the Germans again attacked, in a dust-storm, but the air cleared at the crucial moment and every weapon opened fire. The attack was defeated, with seventy enemy dead. That night the defenders of Knightsbridge withdrew. "We marched in threes as in the old days, with the transport in rear, all our guns and equipment with us." 22nd Armoured Brigade, harried by two *Panzer Divisions*, protected the column. Rommel recorded: "The Guards Brigade [sic] evacuated Knightsbridge . . . after it had been subjected all morning to the combined fire of every gun we could bring to bear. This brigade was almost a living embodiment of the virtues and faults of the British soldier – tremendous courage and tenacity combined with a rigid lack of mobility." The column reached Acroma at dawn and dug in.

The defence of the Knightsbridge Box was a considerable feat. The efforts of the Medical Officer, Captain Charles Weir, and Padre Ronald Lunt who ran the Regimental Aid Post (RAP) in a trench were remarkable. The Battalion's losses – the much-liked Commanding Officer, Lieutenant Colonel Tom Bevan, and fourteen killed, twenty-three wounded, and seven prisoners – appeared light compared with the achievement, although the success was short-lived.[14]

The 3rd Coldstream now joined the South Africans and Indians in Tobruk. The Eighth Army relied on Tobruk for supplies, but the defences were neglected and plans had to be hastily improvised. The (renamed) 200th Guards Brigade and seventy tanks were designated as the reserve. Confusion reigned; two battalions joined the brigade and Coldstream anti-tank guns were detached. The 3rd Battalion, at Pilastrino, the south-western key to the inner perimeter, had three days' preparation before Rommel attacked on 20 June.

15th and *21st Panzer Divisions* and *Stukas* attacked 4th Indian Division fiercely and soon orders came for 3rd Coldstream and 4th Royal Tank Regiment to counter-attack. 4 RTR was already in action; Lieutenant Colonel Willie Forbes, the Coldstream Commanding Officer, set out with two companies. Garrison Headquarters was not in control: Rommel's attack had penetrated deep into the defences. The Battalion returned to Pilastrino and on the new Brigade Commander, Brigadier George Johnson's, initiative, redeployed to face the threat. The attack then burst on 3rd Coldstream and, despite considerable gallantry, the forward platoons and Brigade Headquarters were overrun. The Germans halted.

With Colonel Forbes a prisoner, Major Tim Sainthill assumed command and decided to withdraw to continue the defence. That night the Coldstream, with some 1st Worcesters and 1st Sherwood Foresters and South Africans, moved to new positions. Despite gloomy prospects, Regimental Sergeant Major Len Rowlands' "efforts to keep the men cheered were absolutely invaluable . . . telling them . . . that everything would be all right, that rather than surrender we would fight our way out on foot". A dawn attack was defeated but then huge explosions were heard. The South

[14] Battle Honour **Knightsbridge**. The achievement was celebrated in Sergeant Burton's ballad "*'Twas in the Box at Knightsbridge*" during many subsequent Sergeants' Mess parties. *The Rommel Papers* edited by Captain B.H.Liddell Hart, 1953, page 222. The situation was so confused that Guardsman 'Cod' Ayre, (Master Tailor of the 1st Battalion in 1964) was captured when he tried to fill his water bottle from a German water bowser.

Africans started destroying their guns, apparently on the Garrison Commander's orders. Tobruk had surrendered.

"Among all ranks one sensed a silent yet spontaneous refusal to accept surrender," wrote the Adjutant, Captain Mervyn Griffith-Jones. At that moment a Gunner officer who knew his way through the minefields appeared. Maps were examined and Major Sainthill decided to try to break out without delay, despite the dangers of daylight movement. Orders were simple: "Drive hard, shoot straight and go right through in a confusion of dust and bullets".

The column drove flat out, scattering surprised Italians, and headed for the RV twenty-five miles south, where sixty vehicles collected, including armoured cars and Coldstream carriers. A route was found onto the El Adem escarpment, but the appearance of armoured cars caused alarm, until they were identified as South African.

Two days later the column reached Daaba. No.1 Company (Captain David Watts-Russell) was already there, having lifted mines to find a way through. They had been overtaken by a Coldstream truck driven by Padre Lunt, held at gunpoint by an Italian. The guard was disarmed and the Company bluffed its way past more Italians, crossing the Tobruk by-pass while enemy vehicles waited for them. Others, including Lance Sergeants J.H.Brown and C.A.Turner in their unreliable Bren carriers, arrived later.

Major Sainthill brought seventeen Coldstream officers and 183 other ranks (and 200 South Africans) out of Tobruk; 388 Coldstreamers were captured. Tim Sainthill is reputed to have sent a signal to Headquarters stating that "Surrender is not an operation the Battalion has practised in peacetime and we do not intend to start now." He was awarded the DSO for what The King described as a "splendid exploit".[15]

The situation in the Western Desert following the Tobruk disaster was critical. General Auchinleck took personal command of Eighth Army on 25 June and prepared to defend Cairo. A Composite Guards Battalion, from 3rd Coldstream and 2nd Scots Guards, deployed to the Alamein Line on 9 July, where, for a fortnight, weary Guardsmen patrolled north of the Qattara Depression and Coldstream anti-tank guns fought gallantly on Ruweisat Ridge. Rommel described this part of the first El Alamein: "The enemy is using his superiority, especially in infantry, to destroy the Italian formations one by one and the German formations are too weak to stand alone." The Composite Battalion was relieved on 29 July and 3rd Coldstream moved to Mena, by the Pyramids.[16]

From September 1942 to February 1943 the Battalion trained in Syria. General Alexander meanwhile replaced Auchinleck as Commander-in-Chief Middle East and General Montgomery took command of Eighth Army in August; Rommel was held at Alam Halfa in early September. The Eighth Army was reinforced and re-equipped and Montgomery prepared to grind Rommel down at El Alamein.

[15] Blazon **Tobruk 1942**. Letter from Captain Roddie Faure Walker 25 Sep 42. RSM Rowlands was Mentioned in Despatches and later awarded the MBE. Another escaper from Tobruk was 'Kipper', a small Alexandria pi-dog, who was mascot to No 4 Company, and the 3rd Battalion generally; Kipper later retired to Yorkshire. Brigadier Johnson was captured, and escaped from prison after the invasion of Italy in Sep 43. Shortly afterwards he again succeeded Brigadier Marriott as Brigade Commander, this time of 32nd Guards Brigade in the Guards Armoured Division.

[16] Battle Honour **Defence of Alamein Line**. *The Rommel Papers* page 257.

THE TUNISIAN CAMPAIGN, 1942–43

2nd Battalion, Longstop Hill, December 1942

In November 1942 the Allies launched Operation TORCH, landing Task Forces at Casablanca, Oran and Algiers. The Eastern Task Force advanced on Tunis, Rommel's supply depot, and Allied troops were fifteen miles from the city when they were attacked by General Nehring (28 November). General Von Arnim rapidly established strong defensive positions.

1st Guards Brigade (3rd Grenadiers, 2nd Coldstream and 2nd Hampshires under Brigadier 'Cop' Copland-Griffiths, in 78th Division) landed at Algiers on 22 November, complete with denim uniforms and solar topees (soon returned to store) and moved to Medjez-el-Bab, thirty miles west-south-west of Tunis on 10 December. One 2nd Coldstream tradition started there – the *Medjez Mail*, a Roneo'd sheet informing the Guardsmen of campaign and Battalion news.

Medjez lay on the central route to Tunis from the west. A significant hill, Djebel Ahmera (800 feet high and two miles long) better known as Longstop Hill, lay astride the route to Tunis; a gap at the eastern end allowed the road and railway to skirt the Medjerda River. 2nd Coldstream, after halting German tanks in Medjez within hours of arrival, learned that it was to attack Longstop Hill to open the route to Tunis.

2nd Battalion advancing up Longstop Hill with American mortars in support, 25 December 1942.

The attack on Longstop started on 22 December in faint moonlight with a short artillery bombardment, and No 4 Company took the Col at the western end, which was unoccupied. No 1 Company passed through to attack the ridge, as planned by Lieutenant Colonel Stewart Brown, but met fierce resistance. Despite the loss of the Company Commander, Major Paddy Chichester, and Company Sergeant Major Callaghan, the platoons reached the summit and were reinforced by No 4 Company. At the same time No 2 Company crossed a minefield and captured the railway 'Halt' strongpoint east of Longstop, only to lose it to a German counter-attack during the planned relief by the US 18th Combat Team. Reconnaissance had not revealed a high spur, Djebel el Rhara, extending north-east from Longstop: this was not cleared by the Battalion.

With the relief complete the Battalion marched back the twelve miles to Medjez-el-Bab in pouring rain, only to hear that the Americans were in trouble. No 4 Company, with mortars and carriers, marched back to reinforce them. The Americans had been attacked from Djebel el Rhara by *754th Regiment* and driven back to the south-western slopes of Longstop. The remaining Coldstream companies, depleted, soaked and exhausted, marched back to Longstop that night.

On 24 December the Battalion was ordered to re-take Longstop. Owing to the muddy tracks, the plan was again to assault from the west two hours before last light. The rain was unrelenting. No.4 Company reached the crest after hand-to-hand fighting and sent a platoon to attack Djebel el Rhara, but it proved too strongly held. No 4 Company pulled back to scrape positions into the rocky hillside. No 2 Company carried supplies up from the Col and the wounded back, an exhausting task in the sodden undergrowth. The positions were mortared throughout the night and communications were very difficult. Ammunition ran short. A company of Algerian Tirailleurs arrived and was sent forward.

The German riposte on Christmas Day started with four armoured cars that drove the Tirailleurs back, but the counter-attack came from an unexpected direction. German troops worked their way round to attack the Americans from the rear. Shelling intensified and carrying parties found their task almost impossible. Losses among Coldstream commanders were serious: the Commanding Officer, Adjutant, three Company Commanders, three Company Sergeant Majors and eleven out of twelve Platoon Sergeants were killed or wounded. Major Roddy Hill, Second-in-Command, assumed command and went from post to post encouraging the Guardsmen. It was clear, however, that the Battalion would not be able to hold Longstop and at 1000 hours a withdrawal was ordered. It was "infantryman's war. No glamour, just simply a grim, deadly battle where boys quickly became veterans. We scrambled from boulder to boulder to escape the withering fire of the Spandaus."

Longstop Hill, a double battle, was not a success. The experience remained deeply etched in the minds of the survivors. Losses were heavy: ten officers and 200 men killed or wounded. Lessons were learned about operations at night and in hilly country, carrying parties and working with Allies. Of the quality of the Guardsmen and the leadership of their commanders there was no doubt. After a poignant memorial service, the Battalion set about reorganization and on 29 December was again ready for action.[17]

For the next month the Battalion occupied positions behind Medjez. General von Arnim mounted several operations to disrupt the widely spread First Army and to prevent it linking up with Eighth Army. 1st Guards Brigade was the mobile reserve, earning the nickname 'the Plumbers' owing to its great work in sealing breaches in First Army's line.

[17] Battle Honour **Longstop Hill 1942.** "No glamour": quoted from article by Mr Bill Fitness (No 2 Company). Lieutenant Colonel Stewart Brown was awarded the DSO for his gallant leadership on Longstop Hill.

Kasserine, February–March 1943. 2nd Battalion

In February 1943 the Brigade saw action south of Medjez near Bou Arada, supporting the Grenadiers' attack on Djebel Mansour and further south in 'Sunshine Valley'. On 14 February Rommel launched the veteran *21st Panzer* and some of *10th Panzer Division* towards the Kasserine Pass, mauling US 2nd Armoured Division, in order to prevent First Army reaching the Mediterranean. *21st Panzer* took Sbeitla and its road junction on 17 February.

1st Guards Brigade joined 6th Armoured Division and rushed to Sbiba, north of Sbeitla, to block the wide rocky valley. On 19 February concealed Coldstream 2-pounder anti-tank guns successfully engaged thirty tanks from *21st Panzer*; the tanks veered off to neighbouring American positions and were repulsed. Infantry attacked next morning but were driven back by the Guardsmen and the Ayrshire Yeomanry 25-pounders. No 1 Company Headquarters was shelled next day and several men, including Guardsman George Fairbairn, a talented professional Fulham FC footballer, were killed. A 'recce in force' with Guardsman riding on the new Churchill 'infantry tanks' was attempted, but was unsuccessful.[18]

Rommel, critical of *21st Panzer's* frontal attack, shifted his effort to the Kasserine Pass. The 'Plumbers' therefore rushed to the Thala valley on the 22nd and dug in. Rommel had visited Thala earlier that day and concluded that the Allied defences were too strong. The subsequent German withdrawal was harassed by Allied ground and air forces.

General von Arnim now threatened the Allies near El Aroussa (south of Longstop). 2nd Coldstream drove 100 miles and on 28 February No 3 Company, supported by 51st RTR Churchills, attacked a strongpoint held by the *Hermann Goering Division* with tanks and an 88mm gun at 'Steamroller Farm'. Despite some success, and *Stukas* dive-bombing with ration canisters, the Company was pinned down and No 2 Company advanced in support; the Germans withdrew that night.[19]

For the next three weeks the Battalion mounted mobile defensive operations without respite north of Medjez and in the Sedjenane area on the northern approach to Tunis. At last, on 23 March, the Battalion could rest, re-equip and train with 6th Armoured Division.

Medenine, Mareth and Tunis, March–May 1943.
2nd and 3rd Battalions

The **3rd Coldstream** had been in Syria while the 2nd Battalion had been fighting in Tunisia. Drafts arriving in the 3rd Battalion met all forms of dress, including the corduroys and Hebron coats depicted in Jon's 'Two Types'.[20] After re-equipping in February 1943, the renumbered 201st Guards Brigade (known – and renowned – as 'Two-O-One', and comprising 6th Grenadiers, 3rd Coldstream and 2nd Scots Guards under Brigadier Julian Gascoigne) set out to rejoin Eighth Army 1500 miles away.

The brigade moved straight from Tripoli to reinforce Medenine following Rommel's Kasserine

[18] Battle Honour **Sbiba**.

[19] Battle Honour **Steamroller Farm**. Diary of Mr John Elliott.

[20] 'Jon' – Captain W.J.P.Jones – volunteered in 1940 and was a Coldstream recruit at Caterham and Pirbright, before being commissioned into the Welch Regiment. Of his two famous creations in *Eighth Army News* and *Union Jack*, the officer with the dark moustache appeared to wear a Coldstream Star in his battered SD cap.

Jon's 'Two Types': "Careful, careful, old man; it will mean sending to Cairo for a new pair."

offensive. On 6 March three *Panzer Divisions* attacked Eighth Army, *21st Panzer* Division converging on 201st Guards Brigade covering Tadjera Chir hill; they were diverted by a dummy minefield and lost some fifty tanks to Coldstream and Scots Guards anti-tank guns. Infantry attacked later, but were met by Coldstream machine guns and New Zealand artillery. Rommel's attempt to disrupt Eighth Army's attack on Mareth failed with heavy losses.[21]

The Mareth Line, along the Wadi Zigzaou, was protected by the 600-foot 'Horseshoe' feature further south. 201st Guards Brigade was ordered to capture the Horseshoe, said to be "lightly held", in a preliminary to the main attack. 3rd Coldstream, and, on the right, 6th Grenadiers attacked at night on 14 March following a heavy artillery barrage. The companies advanced across the deep Wadi Zess, only to meet dense minefields and heavy fire. The leading Coldstream companies achieved some success, No 1 Company driving *III/47th Panzergrenadier Regiment* off Sidi-el-Guelaa (Point 153) and taking fifty prisoners, but at considerable cost. German troops then started to infiltrate behind them and counter-attacked. Carriers were sent forward in support, but were destroyed by mines. A similar fate befell the Grenadiers. Neither Battalion could get heavy weapons forward and Brigadier Gascoigne ordered a withdrawal. The forward troops were extricated with great difficulty, but most of the casualties were evacuated, some on the following night.

The 3rd Coldstream suffered heavily, losing ten officers and 126 other ranks. The Grenadiers lost over twice as many. It was discovered that the enemy had prior information on the attack from a captured map and the Horseshoe was held by three battalions from the veteran *90th Light Division* (who also lost heavily). Although General Montgomery and Lieutenant General Oliver Leese, XXX Corps Commander (and a distinguished Coldstreamer who had been awarded the DSO as a subaltern in the First War) were complimentary, the Battalions were depressed following the reverse.[22]

[21] Battle Honour **Medenine**.

[22] Battle Honour **Mareth**.

New Zealand troops outflanked the Mareth Line and on 20 March XXX Corps attacked on the coastal plain. 201 Guards Brigade provided fighting patrols. The Germans withdrew from Mareth, losing heavily to air attack. The Brigade joined 51st Highland Division for the operation against the Wadi Akarit position on 6 April, but the Guardsmen's role was again limited to patrolling. Rommel's Italian Divisions were effectively destroyed at Wadi Akarit and the Axis forces withdrew to Enfidaville 170 miles north.

General Alexander now attempted to cut off the Axis withdrawal and sent the Anglo-American IX Corps, including 1st Guards Brigade, through the mountains to Fondouk (taken by 3rd Welsh Guards) and Kairouan on the coast. IX Corps armour swung north, but failed to trap the Germans. **2nd Coldstream** returned to Kessera to rest, but Major Charles Harford, Second-in-Command, drove to Sfax to see the 3rd Battalion for the first time in the campaign.

An offensive was now planned by General Alexander to dislodge the Germans from the western approaches to Tunis. The 2nd Coldstream took part in IX Corps operations to outflank Longstop Hill from the south, advancing at night on to the Djebel Bou Kournine (25/26 April). At first light, as the mist cleared, the Battalion found itself overlooked and shelled by German positions. A hasty withdrawal started and some vehicles escaped, but No 1 Company's forward platoon was pinned down. Guardsman Andy Reading walked forward through a "murderous barrage" and carried the wounded driver of a blazing truck, Guardsman Thompson, back to safety. Colonel Stewart Brown crawled forward to see the platoon; Major Bill Harris, the Company Commander, stayed with them until nightfall to extricate his men. The Battalion suffered eighty casualties and was shaken by this 'Blunder Valley' disaster. The IX Corps operations ceased. Shortly afterwards Lieutenant Colonel Stewart Brown left to command 24th Guards Brigade, and Major Roddy Hill took over.[23]

After the capture of Longstop Hill by 78th Division, General Alexander ordered 7th Armoured Division to drive for Tunis while 6th Armoured (including 1st Guards Brigade and 2nd Coldstream) reinforced by 201st Guards Brigade (and 3rd Coldstream) attacked the hills south of the city. The attack started with heavy bombing on 6 May, and 201st Guards Brigade's first objective, Djebel Mengoub, was unoccupied. On 7 May fifty men from the *Hermann Goering Division* approached 3rd Coldstream with white flags, only to fire on their captors. After a robust response the perpetrators were taken to Divisional Headquarters. The Corps Commander, Lieutenant General Brian Horrocks, was visiting and told the Germans that he would stand no more of such behaviour and that they would be shot. The effect was salutary (although the threat was not enforced)! Tunis, regarded by Hitler as "a strategic position of the first order", fell on 7 May and the Axis forces retreated in confusion to the Cape Bon peninsula.[24]

Hamman Lif and Hammamet, May 1943. 2nd and 3rd Battalions

General Alexander ordered 6th Armoured Division to attack Cape Bon on 8 May, starting with the strong natural positions at Hamman Lif held by the *Hermann Goering Division*. 1st Guards Brigade attacked the five (600 foot) hills of Djebel-el-Rorouf in succession. The Welsh Guards carried the

[23] Guardsman Thompson had been mortally wounded and died later that day. Guardsman Reading was Mentioned in Despatches for his most gallant act.

[24] Blazon **Tunis**. White flags incident: *The Coldstream Guards 1920–46* by Michael Howard and John Sparrow, Oxford, 1951, pages 139, 141.

first hill in daylight, before No 1 Company (**2nd Coldstream**) assaulted the next summit against intense fire after dark, with light casualties. Other companies captured the remaining hills (and an 88mm gun that had sunk a destroyer at Tobruk). By first light 2nd Coldstream dominated Hamman Lif, although German tanks were in the town. Major Bill Anstruther-Gray, a Coldstreamer seconded to the Lothian and Border Horse, led his squadron down the beach and into the sea to reach the town, destroying an 88mm and forcing the German tanks to withdraw. Hamman Lif, and the Bey of Tunis's Palace, was in Allied hands.[25]

201st Guards Brigade now moved to Grombalia to secure the Potinville Hills. Early on 10 May the **3rd Battalion** overran German 75mm and 88mm anti-tank guns. The extent of the success became staggering; the Guardsmen captured twenty-five guns and 5000 prisoners by 0800 hours. 1st Guards Brigade now took the lead, passing thousands of surrendering troops, but a sharp fight ensued in Grombalia. Enemy positions were cleared and 2nd Coldstream set up a prisoner of war cage into which hundreds of Axis troops were collected overnight. 201 Guards Brigade and the 17th/21st Lancers pushed on that night, despite obstacles, for Hammamet before swinging south for Bou Ficha to confront *90th Light Division* again. German artillery was still firing, but following explosions, at 1700 hours 3rd Coldstream signallers heard that *90th Light* had surrendered. Drummer Archie Reeves therefore sounded 'Cease Fire'.

On 12 May the Axis forces in Africa capitulated and General Alexander signalled the Prime Minister "We are masters of the North African shores".[26] Churchill rated the victory at Tunis, where 250,415 German and Italian troops surrendered, on a par with that at Stalingrad. Many tasks faced the Allies in preparation for the next campaign, but there was also relief and rest, and on 14 May 200 Foot Guards officers from the 1st, 24th and 201st Guards Brigades met for a celebration dinner at Nabeul.

THE HOME FRONT 1941–44

In May 1941 General Sir Alan Brooke, Commander-in-Chief Home Forces, needed two more armoured divisions, and, after consulting the Major General Commanding the Brigade of Guards and His Majesty The King, the War Office ordered the Brigade to form an armoured division with two Guards brigades. The **1st Coldstream** was selected for conversion to an Armoured Battalion with officers and men drawn from the whole Regiment.

The Guards Armoured Division Headquarters formed in June 1941 under Major General Oliver Leese who inspired Guardsmen in their new role until being sent to command XXX Corps in the Desert in October 1942. Major General Allan Adair, who had led 3rd Grenadiers in the Dunkirk campaign, succeeded him.

In September 1941 the Headquarters moved to Wincanton in Somerset as the Division (5th and 6th Guards Armoured Brigades and the Support Group) formed in the Warminster-Shaftesbury-Midsomer Norton area. The Army's armoured experience was derived from the Western Desert and the Division was disproportionately strong in tanks, with few infantry. The arrival of 32nd Guards Brigade (including **5th Coldstream**) redressed the balance and allowed 'grouping' of infantry with tanks for fighting in close country.

[25] Battle Honour **Hamman Lif.** Major Anstruther-Gray was awarded the MC for this action.
[26] Quoted from *The Second World War: The Hinge of Fate* by W.S. Churchill *op cit* vol.IV, page 698.

There was reluctance to adopt the Guards Division 'Eye' sign from the First World War, but no one could produce a better idea, and senior officers were happy to see it resurrected. The distinguished artist Rex Whistler, serving in the Welsh Guards, painted twelve vehicles with different versions of the Eye and a choice was made. Before long every vehicle, and every Guardsmen, proudly bore the Eye.[27]

In June 1941 1st Coldstream marched from Poole to Yeovil, and later to Longbridge Deverill (near Warminster) for conversion training. The Battalion joined 2nd Grenadiers and 2nd Irish Guards as 'Armoured' Battalions, with 1st Grenadiers as the (infantry) Motor Battalion, in 5th Guards Armoured Brigade. Cruiser and then Covenanter tanks (2-pounder gun) arrived and gunnery, driving and maintenance (D&M) and the black beret became the order of the day.

Early tactical training was rudimentary, with groups of men on bicycles representing tank crews in the lanes of the Wylye Valley engaging bemused infantry armed with flags! In 1942 the 1st Battalion trained on Salisbury Plain and in Pembrokeshire. Morale was high, although there was much to learn: the Brigade Commander mentioned "loud singing from the Coldstream harbour areas" in one debrief! Later in 1942 the 1st Battalion, under Lieutenant Colonel Ririd Myddelton, a shy but most dedicated officer, moved into the barracks at Warminster alongside the Irish Guards and Divisional Staff.[28] Soon afterwards the Division received the Crusader tank.

30th Guards Brigade became 6th Guards Armoured Brigade, with **4th Coldstream** as Motor Battalion. The Battalion moved to Marston Bigot (near Frome in Somerset) in October 1941 and trained; a year later 6th Guards Armoured Brigade was reassigned to 15th (Scottish) Division in the Borders as 6th Guards Tank Brigade. The Battalions (4th Grenadiers, 4th Coldstream and 3rd Scots Guards) converted to Churchill tanks in record time and in the spring of 1943 moved to Bekenby Moor (Yorkshire) to join 15th Scottish. Shortly afterwards Lieutenant Colonel Sir Walter Barttelot, a great trainer, assumed command of the Battalion and the Guardsmen frequently exercised. In September 1943 the Battalion took part in VIII Corps' Exercise BLACKCOCK, before training with the new 51st (Highland) Division. In 1944, 4th Coldstream moved to Charing in Kent. Training with and getting to know the Scots infantry was to prove invaluable when both were committed to battle together in Normandy.

ITALY 1943–45[29]

Salerno, Point 270 (Cappezano) and Volturno. September–October 1943, 3rd Battalion

His Majesty The King and Winston Churchill visited Eighth Army in Tunisia after the Axis surrender and Coldstreamers found themselves on parades as well as training. The 3rd Battalion then received

[27] The idea for the 'Eye' came from General Sir Andrew Thorne, a Grenadier serving in the Guards Divisional Headquarters in 1915–16. He was told to produce ideas for a Divisional sign when he returned from leave in the United Kingdom and suggested the Eye from the current music hall hit song "Give Her the Glad Eye Now". The First World War 'Eye' sign was designed by Major Sir Eric Avery Bt in 1916.

[28] The Hore-Belisha period barracks at Warminster has, since 1945, been the School of Infantry.

[29] Theatre Blazon **Italy 1943–45**.

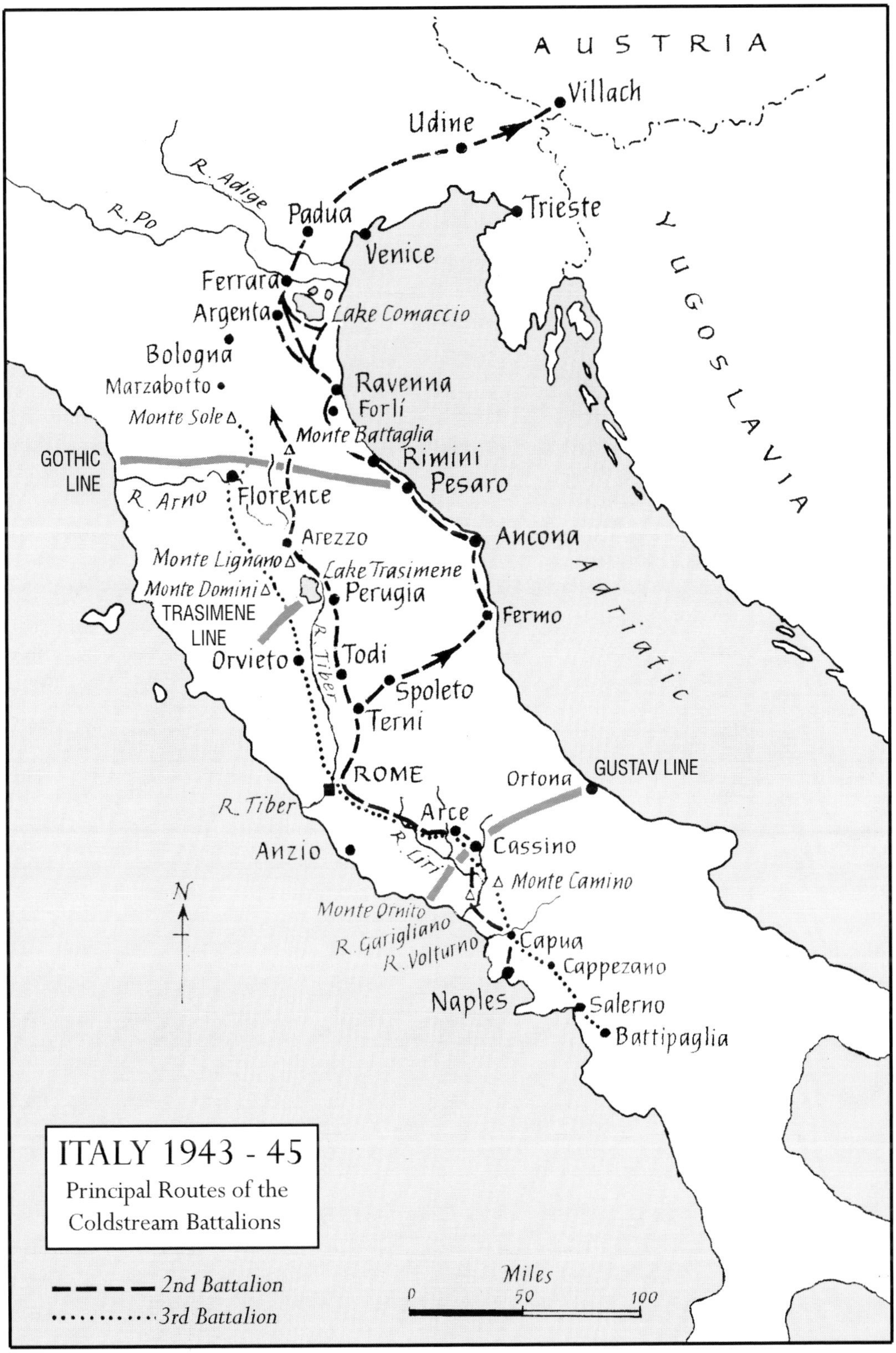
AUSTRIA
Villach
Udine
Trieste
YUGOSLAVIA
R. Adige
R. Po
Padua
Venice
Ferrara
Argenta
Lake Comaccio
Bologna
Marzabotto
Ravenna
Forlí
Monte Sole
Monte Battaglia
Rimini
Pesaro
GOTHIC LINE
R. Arno
Florence
Arezzo
Ancona
Monte Lignano
Lake Trasimene
Perugia
Monte Domini
TRASIMENE LINE
Adriatic
Fermo
R. Tiber
Todi
Orvieto
Spoleto
Terni
ROME
GUSTAV LINE
Ortona
R. Tiber
Arce
Cassino
Anzio
R. Liri
Monte Camino
N
Monte Ornito
R. Garigliano
R. Volturno
Capua
Cappezano
Naples
Salerno
Battipaglia
ITALY 1943 - 45
Principal Routes of the Coldstream Battalions
2nd Battalion
3rd Battalion
Miles
0
50
100

orders to secure Pantellaria, an island supply base fifty miles from Cape Bon, which had been bombed for twenty-five days before the Italian garrison surrendered (11 June). The Battalion arrived on 24 June and spent a month clearing up, guarding 11,000 prisoners and fighting fleas! On 14 July reinforcements arrived, together, unfortunately, with orders for the Battalion to revert from the motor to the infantry role – and companies lost their support platoons. A week later they returned to Tunisia and 201st Guards Brigade joined 56th Division (in General Horrocks' X Corps) training for the landings in Italy.

Sicily was invaded on 10/11 July and after a month's hard fighting the Allies occupied Messina. The Axis lost 164,000 men, but 100,000 men and 10,000 vehicles escaped across the Straits. The Armistice with Italy and Allied landings in Calabria took place on 3 September, but the main attack was mounted 170 miles away.

201st Guards Brigade landed at Salerno on 9 September. The German commander, Field Marshal Kesselring, was well prepared. 201st Brigade went into action on 10 September against the experienced *16th Schützstaffel (SS) Panzer Division* and, although 3rd Coldstream captured part of Monte Corvino airfield, 2nd Scots Guards could not take their objective, a tobacco factory. Brigadier Gascoigne consolidated the position, with 6th Grenadiers (and two Coldstream companies) around Battipaglia and Coldstreamers in depth on the Fosso Canal. The battalions were overlooked and shelled; a counter-attack on 11 September was fought off, but a further attack on the factory was unsuccessful. German artillery was very well employed in Italy, almost certainly as a result of the personal interest of Kesselring – a gunner by origin. Both sides strove to build up forces and on 13 September a battalion from *64th Panzergrenadier Regiment* (*16th SS Panzer Division*) attacked 3rd Coldstream with self-propelled guns and half-tracks. The attack was broken up by a huge artillery barrage. Coldstream mortars and the companies joined in, and thirty bodies and eight destroyed half-tracks were later found.

Further attacks by *16th SS Panzer* followed, but General Alexander launched his reserves, with support from the battleships *Warspite* and *Valiant*, and bombers. Another attack was mounted against the Coldstream on the canal before Kesselring ordered a withdrawal; three days later 201st Guards Brigade secured the tobacco factory and Battipaglia.[30]

General Alexander's priorities were to enlarge the Salerno bridgehead and to capture Naples. While 46th Division advanced on Nocera, 56th Division (including 201st Guards Brigade) was to mount a feint attack towards Avellino. The 3rd Coldstream was soon fighting (22 September) on precipitous hills above Salerno, harassed by shellfire, and when the Grenadiers tried to advance down the defile they were delayed by demolitions and mortaring from the heights. On 24 September the Grenadiers changed tack, assaulting the 600-foot Capella Ridge, and the Coldstream received orders to secure the next wooded hill, rising 500 feet above the road. Lieutenant Colonel Sir Terence Falkiner was wounded while on reconnaissance and Major David Forbes, Second-in-Command, took over.

Company Sergeant Major Peter Wright VC

Point 270 – Cappezano – had been held briefly by the Grenadiers, but they had had to withdraw and overnight 120 men from *29th Panzergrenadier Regiment* re-occupied the hill. The Coldstream attacked at noon on 25 September, Nos 1 and 3 Companies leading. German machine guns opened

[30] Battle Honour **Battipaglia.**

fire but the Guardsmen soon reached the brushwood and started to climb the very steep hill, despite close-range fire and grenades thrown down onto them. Burning brushwood added to the difficulties. No 3 Company under Major Griffith-Jones reached the crest after hand-to-hand fighting, but No 1 Company on the right was pinned down by three well-sited machine-gun posts.

Company Sergeant Major Peter Wright sensed that the Company was held up and came forward. He found that all the officers were casualties and took command. After a quick reconnaissance, he collected a section and positioned them for covering fire.

> "Single-handed he then attacked each post in turn with hand-grenade and bayonet, and silenced each one. He then led his Company on to the crest, but realized that the enemy fire made this position untenable. He therefore led them a short way down the hill again and up on to the objective from a different direction. Entirely regardless of enemy fire, which was very heavy, he then reorganized what was left of the company and placed them in position to consolidate the objective."[31]

Captain Christopher Bulteel went over to No 1 Company, and found "no officers were left and that CSM 'Misty' Wright was running the Company with his broad grin and slow speech". The forward companies, reinforced by No 2, later repulsed a hasty German counter-attack. The night was unpleasant, with mortaring and German sniping, which made casualty evacuation and water and ammunition resupply very difficult. Peter Wright continued to inspire his men, and for his "superb disregard of the enemy's fire, his magnificent leadership and his outstanding heroism throughout the action" he was awarded the Distinguished Conduct Medal. He received this from King George VI nine months later, but The King directed that the award should be replaced by the Victoria Cross.

The Battalion was relieved on 26 September and returned to Salerno in the first winter rainstorm. The first three weeks of the Italian campaign had been costly; 3rd Coldstream had lost eighteen officer and 223 other rank casualties, half of them in the attack on Point 270.

Naples surrendered on 1 October and Fifth Army advanced to the German defensive line that ran from the Abruzzi Mountains to the Volturno and Garigliano Rivers. In October 201 Guards Brigade moved to Capua; the Americans crossed the swollen Volturno River on 12 October and the brigade began to clear the Abruzzi ridges overlooking the plain, starting with Monte Grande. After a gallant platoon attack and patrolling, Nos 2 and 4 Companies assaulted the mountain in rain and darkness on 17 October, finding at first light that the Germans had withdrawn. Two days later 3rd Coldstream attacked the mountain village of Pozzillo, where No 4 Company came under intense fire. With help from No 2 Company, and Battalion suppressive fire, the platoons assaulted. Twelve machine-gun posts were later found.[32]

Monte Camino, November–December 1943. 3rd Battalion

The Grenadiers and Scots Guards secured the precipitous Rochetta heights, the Coldstream, with many others, carrying supplies up the 2000-foot slopes, and the division advanced on Monte Camino. This 3000-foot mountain dominated the Garigliano and the road to Rome, and was an

[31] Citation for WOII (Company Sergeant Major) P.Wright, quoted in *The Coldstream Guards 1920–46* page 456. Blazon **Salerno** and Battle Honour **Cappezano**.
[32] Battle Honour **Volturno Crossing**.

outpost of the German defensive 'Gustav Line' in the Liri valley, the key to which was Monte Cassino. Little was known about the enemy and Monte Camino was assessed as "lightly held"; Mareth veterans were sceptical!

From the summit of Monte Camino, Monastery Hill (Point 963, with its chapel) Razor Back Ridge ran southwards to Mieli village; further west, and parallel, the infamous 'Barearse Ridge' ran from a subsidiary peak (869) past 'the Saucer' to Point 727 and down to the hamlet of Calabritto. Another parallel ridge further west ran from Point 683 to 615 and was flanked by Acquapendola Ridge, which guarded the German supply route to the Garigliano River. The mountain had some scrub, but was mostly shale and rock. 3rd Coldstream opened the attack, advancing on Calabritto on 6 November. No 3 Company ran into a minefield, but a German soldier was captured and forced at bayonet point to lead the company through. No 4 Company established itself on Barearse Ridge without fighting, while No 3 followed a circuitous route, dealing with various machine guns, and attacked Calabritto at first light.

During the night the Grenadiers scaled Barearse Ridge, reaching the top (Point 727) despite heavy opposition from *129th Panzergrenadier Regiment (15th Division)*. The Grenadiers held on precariously on Point 819 for three days in sangars (stone breastworks) on the mountainside, with two companies cut off and casualties lying in the open. Frostbite struck. Calabritto was incessantly mortared and Lieutenant Colonel David Forbes, commanding 3rd Coldstream and a respected veteran of the Battalion since the outbreak of war, was mortally wounded; Major the Hon Ronnie Strutt assumed command. The Battalion relieved the Grenadiers at night on 10 November, but found the lodgement only sufficient for two companies. 3rd Coldstream held the position under almost continuous shellfire in appalling weather for five days, supplied up a mule track that took three hours to climb. The Scots Guards and others attacked to expand the lodgement without success. A senior officer arrived and was rebuked sharply by a Coldstreamer for precipitating a 'stonk': "You and your bloody red hat; you've gone and got my Guardsmen killed." The cap disappeared.

It was clear that more troops were required to take the mountain and, with the Division

3rd Battalion stretcher-bearers at Monte Camino, December 1943.

committed elsewhere, the Divisional Commander, Major General Gerald Templer, took the hard decision to withdraw. The new Commanding Officer, Lieutenant Colonel George Burns, arrived and his infectious enthusiasm lifted morale on the hillside, but on 14/15 November the Battalion destroyed its supplies and withdrew. German shelling continued for three days. Two officers and nineteen other ranks were killed on Barearse Ridge; sixty-eight were wounded.

The Battalion withdrew to Pugliano, near Naples, to rest and assimilate reinforcements. Regimental Sergeant Major Joel, who had organized the carrying parties on Camino so well, now drilled the Battalion while a new attack was planned. General Templer summoned the officers of the brigades and was both exacting in his criticism and fulsome in his praise. Many officers resented being lectured after such a dreadful ordeal with such losses, but Templer had great admiration for Guardsmen and wanted to restore their fighting efficiency.[33]

One 'misappropriation' from 3rd Coldstream at Camino was repaid 46 years later. A case of rum arrived at Regimental Headquarters in 1989 from former Lance Bombardier Spike Milligan of Goon Show fame, formerly of 56th Heavy Regiment RA. He unburdened his conscience:

> "On 5 November Lieutenant W.MC and myself . . . were in an OP [Observation Post] . . . overlooking . . . Calabritto. It was an appalling night . . . the position was heavily stonked by 88mm guns firing airbursts over our trenches. Somewhere about 3.00 in the morning it was my duty . . . to gather our rations . . . There were many units collecting various rations, and then . . . in the darkness a voice called out, 'Coldstream Guards rum ration', and in that split moment I shouted out, 'Here', and I was given a glass/carton container with rum in it. I got safely back to my OP trench where Lieutenant W and I drank it, all the while toasting the Brigade of Guards. . . . At dawn the next day . . . the relief party officer said, 'That was a nasty German attack last night', whereupon I replied in all innocence, 'What attack?'"[34]

X Corps now prepared to dislodge the six *Panzergrenadier* battalions on Monte Camino. On 2 December Army Groups Royal Artillery, American guns, X Corps Artillery and Bofors guns opened fire on the mountain. Major Griffith-Jones described it as "an awe-inspiring sight, more than 600 guns burst into action . . . the sides of Camino sparkled as thousands of shells burst upon its rocks". 167th Brigade took Barearse Ridge on 2/3 December, but 'LANCE FORCE' (mainly Major Roger Beck's No 4 Company of 3rd Coldstream) were unable owing to daylight to advance from Point 727 to seize Points 683 and 615 on the next ridge. At 2300 hours on 3 December the Battalion moved off, but it was "a desperate march", taking eight hours scrambling over boulders to advance 1000 yards. The column was shelled and the Medical Officer, Captain David Forgan, and Padre Levens were killed. The objectives were not occupied, but next morning sniping and mortaring against the reverse slope started and getting supplies forward proved almost impossible. The Guardsmen stayed on the mountain, without ration or water resupply.

> "After the first couple of days we had to stretch groundsheets and gas-capes out to catch rainwater for drinking," wrote Lieutenant David Helme. "No chance of shaving, as any

[33] Battle Honours **Calabritto** and **Monte Camino**. *Templer: Tiger of Malaya* by J.Cloake, London, 1985 pages 109–118.

[34] Letter from a "repentant but now sober" Spike Milligan to Regimental Headquarters Coldstream Guards 17 Jan 89, now in the 1st Battalion scrapbook.

cut would have become infected; but I had a good wash in a shell hole. . . . Very few rations arrived. . . . Rum rations more than welcome. Colonel George was a tremendous source of encouragement and cheer."

On 5 December the Grenadiers and Scots Guards advanced on Acquapendola village and the Durham Light Infantry used the Coldstream position to attack Calabritto from the rear. The attack on Acquapendola threatened the German supply line and the defenders withdrew on the 6th. However, the Acquapendola rearguard defied the Grenadiers until the 9th. The Coldstream left Camino next day after an ordeal later regarded by many as one of the toughest tests of endurance of the war; and the Allies advanced to the Garigliano and Cassino.

201st Guards Brigade stayed in the Garigliano valley for three months as General Alexander lacked the strength to force his way to Rome through mountainous country "ideally suited to defence" (the Staff description) in winter weather. On the Adriatic coast, on 30 December, General Montgomery left Eighth Army (which was also making slow progress) to prepare 21st Army Group for Operation OVERLORD, the invasion of Normandy. General Sir Oliver Leese, who had commanded XXX Corps since before Alamein, succeeded him.

X Corps' attack across the Garigliano and against the western Gustav Line started on 17 January. 201st Guards Brigade took over the left flank around Trimonsuoli (in the foothills of the Aurunci Mountains) on the 13th. A German counter-attack on the 21st retook Monte Natale and 3rd Coldstream was overlooked and heavily shelled. The Guardsmen held on for eight days in dreadful weather before the brigade successfully attacked Monte Natale. Over 100 men were lost to shell-fire and sickness, and the Battalion was allowed a rest before returning to Trimonsuoli and Tufo until 7 March.[35]

The plan to outflank the Gustav Line by an American assault across the Rapido River followed by an attack on Cassino, while VI Corps landed at Anzio further north (22 January) to cut German supply routes, and X Corps advanced from the Garigliano, was a compromise. II US Corps lost heavily on the Rapido and VI Corps' delayed attempt to break out of the Anzio bridgehead met strong German reserves. X Corps had to reinforce Anzio, hold Monte Natale and attack around Castelforte further east. The Allies were desperately short of troops; 1st Guards Brigade was summoned from North Africa.

Arrival in Italy and Monte Ornito, February 1944. 2nd Battalion

After the Axis surrender **2nd Coldstream** trained in Tunisia. On 12 June a detachment under Major Bill Harris joined the operation to capture Lampedusa, 100 miles west of Malta. Following a naval bombardment Major Harris and Drill Sergeant Knight went ashore and demanded an unconditional surrender. The Governor prevaricated in French, whereupon Major Harris threatened a ceaseless raid by 1000 bombers and bombardment by the Mediterranean Fleet. "The Drill Sergeant, with bayonet appropriately pointed at the backside of the Governor, shouted, 'Shall I kill him, Sir?'," whereupon the Governor asked for a pen, the Drill Sergeant held out his rifle-butt and the

[35] Battle Honour **Garigliano Crossing**. Trimonsuoli (1943) is now called Tremensuoli. Major Griffith-Jones, *The Coldstream Guards, 1920–46*, pages 168–9; Lieutenant Helme, *No Dishonourable Name*, edited by D.C. Quilter, London, 1947 (1972 Edition) page 195.

capitulation was signed! The 4600-strong garrison piled their weapons in 'Coldstream Square' and the White Ensign was then hoisted. The rest of the Battalion arrived for a week on Lampedusa before returning to Sousse.[36]

In December 1943 2nd Coldstream guarded President Roosevelt, General Eisenhower and Churchill. Orders to move to Italy at short notice arrived on 30 January 1944 and the Battalion, under Lieutenant Colonel Hugh Norman, landed at Naples on 5 February. 1st Guards Brigade (Brigadier Charles Haydon) joined 46th Division on the Garigliano. When X Corps sent a division to Anzio the planned attack on Castelforte was cancelled and the brigade was ordered to the salient in the eastern Aurunci Mountains. The forward position was Monte Ornito; Monte Faito, a higher peak, had been captured, but abandoned.

On 8 February the Guardsmen climbed for five hours in darkness and rain to 'sangars' on the steep reverse slopes of Monte Ornito, arriving during an attack. The companies were within a few hundred yards of each other; No 4 Company (Major the Hon Robert Palmer) on the Ornito peak, No 3 Company (Major Henry Green) on Point 711 on the left and No 2 Company (Major Ian Skimming) on Point 719 in between. Digging was impossible and near-continuous freezing rain, sleet or snow made it impossible to keep dry or warm; mist, noise and echoes were disorientating. Sickness, exposure and gangrene took their toll. Porters climbed for an hour to bring supplies to Battalion Headquarters from the supply dump. Water was scarce; many brewed tea with rainwater from shellholes. Rum was a lifeblood.

There was little time to settle in. At first light on 9 February No 2 Company took several prisoners close to its forward posts, but shellfire killed or wounded the Guardsmen and their captives. Next day fifty enemy from *III/71st Panzergrenadier Regiment* (*29th Division*) assaulted Point 711 and No 3 Company, and Captain Tom Jackson (from No 1 Company in reserve) was sent round the enemy flank. Hearing German voices, Major Green called down artillery fire on his position and Lieutenant Michael Hollings later charged the German remnants with the bayonet, "in a truly Pirbright-trained action", taking fifteen prisoners.

> "On Major Green's orders we ran and stumbled towards the crest, then down the other side screaming our heads off like some half-demented sub-humans," wrote Lance Sergeant John Elliott. "This side of the hill was littered with dead and wounded Germans. They had paid a very heavy price."

The Germans withdrew, but Captain Jackson and six Guardsmen were dead. Captain Elston Grey-Turner, Medical Officer since before Tunisia, and Padre George Forbes, with stretcher-bearers under Lance Corporal Gordon Spencer, managed with great difficulty in icy sleet to evacuate the forty-three wounded Coldstreamers – and many Germans. In these extreme conditions Guardsman 'Cockney Joe' Soper, of No 1 Company, 6'6" tall, of legendary smartness and a great Geordie morale-raiser, gave his greatcoat to a badly wounded *panzergrenadier* saying, "I'm all right, Sarge, that's so that the little bleeder doesn't die of cold!"

Enemy positions were only 400 yards away and the German tactic was to send large patrols creeping up the forward slopes at night. Days of constant alarms, sniping, grenading and short-range ambush among the crags were followed by night-fighting patrols as the Guardsmen strove to dominate no-man's-land. Battalion mortars 'cleared' the forward slopes before dawn. Patrols from

[36] Letter from Major Bill Harris 24 Oct 99.

No 1 Company (Captain Petre Crowder) located German positions, which were also mortared, but enemy shell and machine-gun fire was almost continuous, and a self-propelled gun was often in action. British artillery replied, but some rounds failed to clear the crests and landed short. German prisoners said that they knew they were facing a Guards Battalion; they noticed that empty bully beef tins had been picked up!

The companies rotated positions to allow some relief and sleep, and No 4 Company took over Point 711. At dawn on 17 February No 7 Platoon (No 1 Company) attacked to clear *II/104th Panzergrenadier* troops from the left flank of Point 711, but encountered enemy and lost most of its forward sections in seconds; the third section then ambushed the *panzergrenadiers* coming forward to mop up at 25 yards' range. Six German survivors were taken prisoner, but, sadly, among the dead was Guardsman Joe Soper. Shortly afterwards the Germans attacked No 4 Company on Point 711 in strength. The Guardsmen, with mortar support and enfilade fire from Point 719, held the attack, Lance Sergeant Joe Kidd and Guardsman Lesley Jenkins showing most determined leadership.

By 0800 hours a stalemate had been reached. No 4 Company called for smoke and, led by Lieutenant Stephen Whitwell, charged, bayonets fixed, taking an officer and twenty-six prisoners and leaving at least eighteen German casualties. That evening the Germans attacked Points 711 and 719 again. Platoons from Nos 1 and 3 Company went forward, but suffered heavily; companies from 3rd Grenadiers and 1/4th Hampshires followed, the latter taking over the Ornito peak where the Germans were now very close. After a tense night Colonel Norman adopted similar tactics, calling for artillery and mortar HE and smoke, and Captain David Toler led No 4 Company charging over the crest with the bayonet. Only ten prisoners were taken.

At dawn on the 19th a heavier 'stonk' descended and was followed by 4–500 enemy from *104th* and *129th Panzergrenadiers* attacking the Welsh Guards on the neighbouring Monte Cerasola and Ornito itself. Enfilading fire from Cerasola, artillery and a bayonet charge by the Hampshire company decisively defeated the attack and sixty-five prisoners were taken on Ornito; similar numbers lay dead. German shelling continued all day, but no new attack materialized.

2nd Coldstream was relieved from its ordeal on 20 February. "The dreadful conditions of mountain warfare, near Arctic weather, the mental and physical strains," Sergeant Elliott wrote, were "deeply etched in our faces"; the experience, like that of Longstop, also remained indelibly in the minds of the survivors. Coldstream casualties included two officers and thirty-one other ranks killed, seven officers and 150 wounded and missing – and fifty exposure and frostbite cases. Some platoons were reduced to five men. The Press described Monte Ornito as 'Misery Mount', or, in Cockney, ''Ell's 'Illside', but the result was a significant defensive victory; the Germans could not reduce the eastern salient of the Garigliano bridgehead. One *panzergrenadier* wrote of generous treatment from the Commanding Officer on 17 February; prisoners were told, "You have fought bravely, as hardly any enemy else. If you are now without arms, you are not without honour." Lieutenant Colonel Norman was awarded the DSO for his gallant leadership.[37]

After Ornito 2nd Coldstream trained at Casale, served in the Garigliano bridgehead, now a secondary sector, and rested at San Potito.

[37] Blazon **Monte Ornito**. Major Bob Palmer, Lieutenant Stephen Whitwell, Captain Elston Grey-Turner RAMC and Captain the Rev George Forbes RAChD were awarded the MC; and Lance Sergeant Kidd, Lance Corporal Spencer and Guardsman Jenkins were awarded Military Medals. Letter from Otto Stuchrmann 20 Apr 48 in 1948 *Coldstream Gazette* pages 11–12. 'Joe' Soper: Mr Joe Nixon. Bayonet charge and "dreadful conditions": *Diary of Mr John Elliott.*

Monte Cassino and Monte Piccolo, March–May 1944. 2nd Battalion

The Anzio landings and attacks on Cassino by 34th US Division and New Zealanders (12 and 15–18 February) failed to break the Gustav Line. General Alexander faced not only the German *1st Parachute Division* – whose tenacity at Cassino he described as "quite remarkable" – but also Italian geography, mud, the eruption of Mount Vesuvius (which slowed the landing of supplies) and pressure from London to release troops and shipping for the Second Front.

Mounting casualties from the winter fighting also faced the Allies and affected both Coldstream Battalions. During the reorganization in March–April 1944 201st Guards Brigade was ordered home as three Guards Brigades could not be sustained in Italy. **3rd Coldstream** received reinforcements and replaced 1st Irish Guards (who had lost heavily at Anzio) in 24th Guards Brigade (Brigadier Archer Clive) and the brigade joined 6th South African Armoured Division in Eighth Army. 1st Guards Brigade returned to 6th (UK) Armoured Division.

The assault on Monte Cassino was prepared in great secrecy. 1st Guards Brigade joined 4th Division (XIII Corps) to hold the 'town' below Monastery Hill. After the bombing (15 March) the Monastery and town were largely rubble with waterlogged craters, battered trees and section posts. These

> "were mere holes in the rubble . . . looking forward over stagnant water and scattered ruins to another wall or to the shapeless remains of a building only a few yards away in the ruins. . . . The forward sections felt themselves entirely isolated – seeing nothing but devastation, hearing nothing but the sigh of an occasional shell . . . visited only at night when porters came up with their rations."

On 5 April **2nd Coldstream**, reinforced by 'S' Company Scots Guards, occupied its sector, with two companies forward for eight-day spells. Supplies were brought up at night with extreme difficulty along the 'Mad Mile', blanketed by artillery smoke. Enemy outposts (some only fifty yards away) were engaged with mortars and guns rather than reveal section positions, which often had little protection, and were mortared frequently. A "repugnant stench" from dead bodies and no sanitation, swarms of flies and pervasive dust were ever present. Sleep was near impossible. Snipers predominated. Battalion Headquarters shared the 'Crypt' with 3rd Grenadiers, the RAPs and cookhouses; from here the Drill Sergeant in Waiting marshalled porters and the *Medjez Mail* kept people in touch. On St George's Day the Battalion was relieved, and trained, but returned to Cassino and Castle Hill on 5 May.

At 2300 hours on 11 May 1700 guns, even more than at Alamein, opened fire on the German positions, including Monastery Hill. "The noise was so terrific – even if one shouted in the ears of one's neighbour, he could not hear." 8th Indian and 4th Division crossed the River Gari and, with 78th Division, fought for three days to break through south of Cassino. 1st Guards Brigade's task was to hold the town, "to make faces" at the enemy (with machine guns and mortaring) and protect loudspeakers calling on the Germans to surrender, a role that involved continuation of the desperate close-range battle and mortaring in the rubble.

The 2nd Polish Corps assaulted the Cassino heights and, after gallant attacks, took the Monastery on 18 May; General Anders' men joined 78th Division on Highway 6 below. Success was indicated to the Guardsmen when war correspondents and military sightseers arrived in the ruins of Cassino.

Later that day 2nd Coldstream left Cassino; many Guardsmen were close to exhaustion after the unceasing noise, concussion, smell, smoke and dust, in addition to constant mortaring and machine-gun fire.[38]

On 25 May 2nd Coldstream advanced up the Liri Valley on 17/21st Lancer tanks, meeting rear-guards, snipers and hilltop artillery observers. Twelve miles beyond Cassino the Coldstream encountered *1st Parachute Regiment* on Monte Grande and Monte Piccolo, overlooking the defile. 1st Guards Brigade was ordered to take the hills on the night of 27 May. After rapid preparation and a night approach, No 4 Company took the first knoll of Monte Piccolo; and S and No 3 Company attacked the summit. The Grenadiers took Monte Grande, but a counter-attack forced them off the crest, exposing the Coldstream flank. Major Bob Coates took a scratch force of 'Left Out of Battle' men and others to the flank. Piccolo was counter-attacked and, while S and No 3 Company held on, they could not clear the forward slope. Supplies were brought up with difficulty. The Coldstream were again attacked, but, with artillery and tank support, the position held. The Germans withdrew, leaving forty bodies on the hill. 78th Division moved up the Sacco Valley towards Rome on 30 May.[39]

1st Guards Brigade stayed near Piccolo for three days. Denim trousers and camouflage smocks suited to the countryside and summer weather were issued. The Guardsmen witnessed the problem of "traffic in the narrow, over-crowded, mined and cratered valley [which] had been difficult from the moment after our dogged infantry had broken the bloody door and entered. Now traffic became impossible, . . . crowded vehicles and idle guns stood nose to petrol-smelling tail in helpless confusion."[40]

Rome to Florence and Arezzo, June–August 1944. 2nd and 3rd Battalions

On 1 June **2nd Coldstream** advanced on the northern side of the Sacco Valley, while Fifth Army entered Rome on 4 June; two days later the Battalion camped in sight of St Peter's Basilica. Eighth Army swung towards Tivoli to pursue the German *X Armee*. 6th South African Division moved up for the pursuit, exacerbating the traffic problem. The **3rd Coldstream** had spent May in the mountains near Rionero, twenty miles north-east of Cassino, overlooking the River Sangro, and patrolling no-man's-land. On 29 May 24th Guards Brigade moved towards Rome.

Kesselring had five weak divisions west of the Tiber facing Fifth and Eighth Armies, and thirteen east of the Apennines. General Alexander planned to breach the German defences in the Apennines – the 'Gothic Line' (Pisa to Rimini) – before they could be strengthened. On 6 June General Leese's Eighth Army was ordered to seize Florence and Arezzo, while Fifth Army advanced up the coast. 6th South African Division (XIII Corps) was to advance up the west bank of the Tiber while 6th Armoured Division (X Corps) cleared the east side.

[38] "Holes in the rubble": *The Coldstream Guards 1920–46* page 218. Noise: letter from Major Bill Harris 24 Oct 99. Diary of Mr John Elliott: "no one has experienced Hell if they had not been inside Cassino in World War Two."

[39] Battle Honour **Monte Piccolo**. 'Left Out of Battle': each Company selected a proportion of each rank to be LOB for a period so that a cadre remained in case of heavy casualties. This derived from First World War experience when units which had lost heavily in officers and seniors found it difficult to reorganize themselves.

[40] *The Campaign in Italy* by E.Linklater, HMSO, London, 1951, page 267.

3rd Battalion

On 6 June 3rd Coldstream crossed the Maximillo Bridge in Rome at night. As the column drove through the streets towards Highway 3 the electricity was restored and the lights came on. Hundreds of Roman citizens appeared, throwing flowers to welcome the Guardsmen.

Having captured groups of by-passed Germans near Civita Castellana, Colonel George Burns issued his great order on 8 June that "The 3rd Battalion Coldstream Guards will capture Florence". The Battalion drove over mountain roads to Viterbo and Orvieto, but was checked by enemy positions at Bagniero. These were attacked on 12 June, but the South African tanks encountered difficulties in close country. Most of the enemy (*Hermann Goering* and *4th Parachute Divisions*) had withdrawn when 3rd Coldstream assaulted, but mines caused casualties. The Guardsmen reached Orvieto on 15 June and enjoyed the local wines, but the weather broke and heavy rain brought back mud that severely hampered movement. The South Africans took Cetona on 22 June, but the *Hermann Goering Division* on Monte Cetona (the 'Trasimene Line') halted their advance of over eighty miles in sixteen days.

While the South Africans and 4th Division attacked the Trasimene Line the Coldstream and Scots Guards advanced on Sarteano in mist (23/24 June), supported by Pretoria Regiment tanks, and took their objectives. Mortaring, sniping and rain made life unpleasant later, even for the Echelon and RAP in Cetona. The Battalion left Sarteano on 28 June, 5th Grenadiers and 1st Scots Guards having cleared Chiusi. With the Trasimene Line broken, better weather and local information on German positions, a quicker advance was possible. On 29 June, after a brisk fight, the Battalion occupied Chianciano and was welcomed by its citizens.

No 2 Company relieved the Scots Guards in Montepulciano and 3rd Coldstream advanced to Trequanda in hot weather (1 July). Tiger tanks and 88mm guns surprised it next day and proved difficult to outflank. No 1 Company sustained nineteen casualties, but patrols later found no enemy. The advance continued until 5 July when Germans in Castel di Brolio stopped the Grenadiers; by-passing attempts were met by resistance from the Arezzo defences.

3rd Coldstream spent ten days around Brolio, patrolling, resting – and trying Chianti wines. The advance through the wooded Chianti countryside was a frustrating slog at infantry pace due to the tenacious defence, demolitions and mines, and the steep hills. All movement in the hills attracted shellfire. On 15 July a set-piece attack was mounted on Castel di Brolio, which proved abandoned. The Coldstream attacked another hilltop castle near Gaioli two days later, supported by Pretoria Regiment tanks, but it was steep and well-defended, and the Guardsmen could not take the summit. During the night, however, the Germans withdrew.

By 20 July the Brigade had reached Monte Domini, strongly held by the German *356th Division*. Attempts to infiltrate companies through the vineyards were unsuccessful and 3rd Coldstream therefore launched a deliberate attack in daylight on 23 July, 'two companies up' with Pretoria Regiment and Divisional artillery support. The Germans reacted to the smokescreen by donning respirators! The Guardsmen and tanks advanced through heavy defensive fire, but could not take the second crest. The companies dug in; a night patrol found the Germans gone. The attack on Domini was, the Commanding Officer wrote, "a most spirited affair, and a classic example of excellent teamwork between the infantry, the armour and artillery"; it had cost fourteen killed and twenty wounded.[41]

The Guardsmen advanced on Pretoria Regiment tanks to Strada (27 July) but were stopped by

[41] Battle Honour **Monte Domini**.

minefields, Tiger tanks and self-propelled guns. The companies climbed the hills overlooking the minefields and dug in under fire, but the Brigade could not move until other features in the 'Paula Line' had been taken. The Brigade advanced on 1 August, and two days later No 4 Company surprised the defenders of San Gersole, three miles from Florence. That night it heard the Florentine bridges being demolished.

3rd Coldstream consolidated around San Gersole on the 4th and Scots Guards patrols entered Florence. The advance to Florence – 270 miles – had taken ten weeks of almost daily fighting on steep hillsides and marching along dusty roads. It had cost three officers and fifty other ranks killed, and thirteen officers and 143 other ranks wounded, losses that grieved all ranks. The Battalion drove to Siena, and for three weeks the Guardsmen trained and drilled, assimilated drafts, went sightseeing and attended parties. "A large quantity of South African brandy became available," wrote Lord Andrew Cavendish, commanding No 4 Company. "Taken in moderation it was a good tonic, but too much left one feeling extremely ill!"[42]

2nd Battalion

On 6 June 6th Armoured Division pursued the Germans up the Tiber valley. On the 9th 2nd Coldstream and 17/21st Lancers reached the Poggio Mirteto defile and the companies moved onto the hills that night. No 3 Company, pushing forward into unknown country, found itself surrounded and under fire for much of the following day. The defile was shelled and Battalion Headquarters was hit; Lieutenant Colonel Hugh Norman and the Adjutant, Captain Dick Chaplin, with several others, were severely wounded. Major Bob Coates took command.

Attacks by 3rd Grenadiers and 3rd Welsh Guards forced a German withdrawal and 1st Guards Brigade followed up the advance until 17 June, when they halted near Perugia. On the 18th No 4 Company climbed steep terraces in heavy rain, and were close to the railway station on the south-western outskirts around dawn; patrols were sent towards the town centre. A counter-attack on the Grenadiers suggested a determined defence and Colonel Coates ordered Nos 2 and 3 Companies to take the station that night. Despite poor communications, success was achieved.

The capture of Monte Malfe, dominating Perugia from the west, at the same time, forced a German withdrawal, although Malfe and San Marco, held by the Welsh Guards, were strongly counter-attacked. 2nd Coldstream was ordered to take Monte Pacciano. S Company reached positions close to the summit on 22 June, but, although reinforced by No 4 Company, could not take the hill. The Battalion was on Pacciano for four days patrolling aggressively, but the Germans were still able to overlook Perugia. On 26 June the Coldstream, with a Welsh Guards Company, and the Grenadiers, assaulted, forcing the defenders off the Monte Pacciano crest.[43] No 3 Company suffered heavily and was disbanded. The Battalion spent two days patrolling to re-establish contact with the enemy before resting near Castiglione Fosco.

The next objective, Arezzo, was protected by mountains, including Monte Lignano (2750 feet) aslant Highway 71 and dominating the approaches. *15th Panzergrenadier Division* held Lignano; dust immediately brought German shells. 2nd New Zealand Division and 1st Guards Brigade (in XIII Corps again) were ordered to take the feature. After a heavy bombardment – and a thunder-storm – the Grenadiers attacked Lignano late on 14 July. At dawn No 4 Company (2nd Coldstream)

[42] Battle Honour **Advance to Florence**. Letter from Andrew Cavendish, 11th Duke of Devonshire, 4 Nov 98.

[43] Battle Honour **Capture of Perugia**.

assaulted along the ridge, meeting ferocious mortaring and a counter-attack against the Grenadiers on Point 575. No 4 Company helped restore the position and took its own objective, and S Company continued the attack. S Company took Point 501 under intense fire despite losing its Company Commander (Captain Andrew Neilson DSO): this was later felt to be the hardest attack S Company had done. S Company could not get beyond the crest, but No 2 Company, attacking later, found the enemy gone. New Zealanders took the summit, overlooking Arezzo and German gun positions. 1st Guards Brigade had driven a wedge into the defences; armour exploited the success. 2nd Coldstream lost ten killed and twenty wounded on Lignano. On 16 July Arezzo fell to the Allies.[44]

After ten days in Arezzo, and a visit by His Majesty The King, 1st Guards Brigade (now under Brigadier Andrew Montagu-Douglas-Scott) moved up the Arno valley. No 2 Company protected 6th Armoured Division's flank against attacks from the Prato Magno massif. 1st Guards Brigade led the advance, the Coldstream providing the 'point' on 2 August, but progress was slow in countryside pitted with demolitions, booby traps and 'stonks'. By 5 August 2nd Coldstream had reached Santa Agata, where shelling was intense, but next day La Torre was taken, although it was exposed to enemy fire. The advance halted on 7 August and the Battalion was later allowed a brief rest.

Advance to the Gothic Line. 2nd and 3rd Battalions

The Allies made great strides during the summer, but the Apennine Mountains and the 'Gothic Line' lay across the line of advance. Bologna, on the plain north of the Apennines, was the objective and General Alexander moved Eighth Army to the Adriatic coast to unhinge the Gothic Line from the east. Both Coldstream Battalions remained west of the Apennines.

2nd Coldstream followed the German withdrawal up the valley north of Pontassieve. 1st Guards Brigade again watched Prato Magno and the Guardsmen patrolled, and occasionally skirmished, before occupying Dicomano, devastated by the Germans, on 10 September. The advance continued up the mountain road on 11 September; 24 hours later, almost at the highest point of the Apennines, the Guardsmen could overlook the German defences. Kesselring had evidently abandoned the Gothic Line to release troops to hold Eighth Army. On 15 September the Brigade passed through the Line to Villore, finding, as so often, mines the greatest threat.

3rd Coldstream and 6th South African Armoured Division joined IV US Corps and moved up the Elsa valley on 22 August to Empoli, a sector away from the main attack. The positions were overlooked and mortared. The Guardsmen, supplied by night, patrolled in strength and with success. Patrols crossed the Arno on 31 August, followed by the brigade. The division advanced to Monsummano, opposed only by patrols, and entered the mountains near Montecatini (8 September). 3rd Coldstream was ordered to engage German attention while II US Corps attacked the key Futa Pass. On 22 September No 2 Company, with artillery and Pretoria Regiment tanks, took Serra, part of the Gothic Line, capturing twenty-one prisoners for no loss. Despite shellfire, patrols found the adjacent Femminamorta ridge unoccupied and the Battalion was able to return to Montecatini. The Guardsmen rested and re-equipped, and, departing from 3rd Battalion tradition, sewed the green and yellow triangular 6th South African Division flash onto their battledress as well as their Roman III.

[44] Battle Honour **Arezzo**.

The Setta Valley: Catarelto Ridge to Monte Sole. September 1944–January 1945, 3rd Battalion

24th Guards Brigade covered II US Corps' flank on Route 6620, running up the pass to Castiglione dei Pepoli and the Setta valley. **3rd Coldstream** moved up in autumnal rain on 29 September. Next day a patrol under Major David Helme discovered evidence of a dreadful massacre in San Martino. The Battalion Intelligence patrol (Sergeants Philip Gourd and Percy Phillips) found *16th SS Panzergrenadier Division* troops near Casaglia: on the previous day, led by the notorious Major Reder, the *SS* had killed some 1830 old men, women and children and burned their villages in reprisals against the 'Stella Rosa' partisans. Padre Theo Franklin and Guardsman Reg Turner carefully collected and buried many of the victims. The 'Marzabotto' massacre was one of the worst Nazi atrocities of the whole war.

On 1 October 3rd Coldstream advanced over the high ground opposite the Grenadiers and Scots Guards who had been fighting *16th SS Panzergrenadiers* on the 2000-foot Catarelto Ridge. Nos 3 and 4 Companies and a Pretoria Regiment squadron set off, but the tanks bogged down, enemy fire increased and the advance halted. Cold and rain increased the Guardsmen's discomfort, but on 3 October patrols found no enemy and the Battalion advanced to the Bucciagni Ridge. Colonel Burns tried 'ferreting' tactics, shelling outposts and picking off withdrawing enemy. Companies assisted the South Africans and when Monte Stanco fell the Guardsmen rested in Castiglione.[45]

The Setta valley was constricted by the formidable Monte Sole (2200 feet) which dominated the route to Bologna and gave excellent observation. In mid-October 24th Guards Brigade was ordered to capture Sole, and while the Scots Guards took the outlying Monte Alcino and Termine, the Coldstream patrolled and supported the Grenadiers' attack across the Setta near Gardaletta. Patrols from the Gardaletta bridgehead identified enemy strongpoints, but floods destroyed the bridges and made the use of tanks almost impossible. General Mark Clark cancelled all US Fifth Army attacks pending the arrival of frost, and so the brigade established a system of reliefs between forward positions and patrolling, and time in reserve at Prato. On 6 November Lieutenant Colonel George Burns, who had led the Battalion with such energy and cheerfulness, handed over to Lieutenant Colonel Billy Steele.

For the next six weeks the Guardsmen continued the rotation between Point 501 above La Quercia and Gardaletta and billets, while preparations were made to attack Monte Sole.

> "The Guardsmen, dishevelled and gigantic in their crumpled greatcoats and stocking caps," Lieutenant Michael Howard MC wrote, "seemed more content here, if the weather was fine, than in billets further back. . . . Sentry rosters were arranged amicably within the sections and were fulfilled without fuss; and for the rest of the time they

[45] Battle Honour **Catarelto Ridge**. Marzabotto Massacre: Kesselring bore responsibility for the massacres at Marzabotto, the Ardeatine Caves and elsewhere. In 1947 he was tried by a British Court Martial for "commanding German troops to kill Italian civilians as reprisals" [for partisan actions]. Reder was also tried. Both received death sentences, commuted to life imprisonment. Kesselring was released on health grounds in 1952. The massacre was commemorated in 1994 in Marzabotto, with Coldstreamers present, and throughout Italy. Monte Sole is "still a silent mountain, now uninhabited, with the ruins of houses and churches bearing unspoken witness to the horrible fate of the occupants": *Monte Sole, Italy: September 1944 and 1994* by Philip Gourd, 1995 *Coldstream Gazette*, pages 155–157, and 1999 *Gazette* pages 116–117. *War in Italy 1943–45: A Brutal Story* by R.Lamb, London, 1993 pages 64–79, 323–325.

contentedly slept, wrote letters, read the *Daily Mirror* and drank gallons of sweet tea."[46]

Deserters reported German supply difficulties; but Sole was held by two battalions protected by wire, mines and mortars. On 7 December the Coldstream were ordered to assault the mountain, but an outlying feature captured by the South Africans could not be held. The Germans responded by patrolling in large numbers; on 27 December a major attack on the Carrier Platoon was repulsed (an action for which Lieutenant John Lloyd was awarded the MC). The planned Christmas Day assault was postponed when heavy snow fell; on 28 December it was cancelled. The Gardaletta positions were close to enemy outposts, but although snow slowed movement, fighting patrols scored some successes. This existence continued until 18 January 1945 when 3rd Coldstream was relieved and, having said farewell to 6th South African Armoured Division, drove to Spoleto to reorganize with the 2nd Battalion.

"Has anybody got a match?" Lieutenant Colonel George Burns, Commanding Officer 3rd Battalion, 1944.

Monte Battaglia and Penzola, September 1944–February 1945. 2nd Battalion

1st Guards Brigade joined X Corps briefly, occupying positions on Monte Penna, east of the Upper Arno, on 22 September, but **2nd Coldstream** soon returned to Arezzo. No 3 Company was reformed and the Battalion rejoined 6th Division at Pontassieve, only to find the brigade again sent to XIII Corps in the Santerno valley. The American offensive had been checked by General Schlemm's *1st Parachute Korps*.

On 4 October 2nd Coldstream took over positions on Monte Battaglia, a 2400-foot ridge, from the Americans who had captured it. The *715th Infantry Division* overlooked the companies from adjoining ridges and the Guardsmen suffered ceaseless rain and harassing fire for four days and nights, an experience many considered as bad as Ornito. The Guardsmen (and their blankets) were constantly soaked and baled water from their trenches with mess-tins. Cooking was almost impossible. The positions were improved and the dead from earlier attacks buried. Patrols fought occasional close-range actions with Thompson sub-machine guns and Mills grenades. 150 mules working sixteen-hour nightly round-trips up a narrow, frequently shelled track brought up supplies; casualty evacuation was a lengthy process. The Battalion was relieved on 8 October, but on the 14th returned to the ridge for four more days, to positions yet more dangerous and difficult to supply.

46 *No Dishonourable Name* page 237.

Preparations were made to capture the adjoining Cornezzano feature. Patrols went out, but lost several men to mines. Poor weather forced postponement of the attack, but a patrol on 23 October found Cornezzano abandoned.

The Brigade reoccupied Battaglia and Cornezzano on 3 November in colder but drier weather after a six-hour climb, holding the heights for a week before a longer rest near Florence. 2nd Coldstream was to spend the winter alternating between the Sieve valley and forward positions in the mountains south-west of Imola, and west of Battaglia between Monte Maggiore and Monte Verro. On 19 November the Battalion occupied defences on Monte dell' Acqua Salata, adjacent to Monte Verro, observing by day and patrolling at night. The Germans shelled these positions with leaflets depicting the Alps, visible eighty miles away, with "next winter you will be fighting here". The Guardsmen were unconvinced! Mule-trains organized by RSM Ramsden (awarded the MC for his untiring efforts) brought up supplies; the Quartermasters' arrangements were invariably impressive.

The German positions between Monte Verro and Imola were based on the Vena del Gesso escarpment and, in order to outflank this, 2nd Coldstream was ordered to capture Monte Penzola (1300 feet). The companies moved up on 3 and 4 December and S Company forced the Germans from the summit in a courageous night attack, but clearing the mines and the ridge could not be achieved for several days. No 2 Company suffered from mortaring while on Penzola; but, as a renewed attack on the ridge was prepared, patrols found the German positions empty. Next day 2nd Coldstream left the mountain, taking eight hours down muddy tracks to reach basic billets. The Coldstream held Monte Penzola (alternating with the Welsh Guards) patrolling in winter weather, and occasional blizzards, against *754th Infantry Regiment*, their opponents on Longstop Hill two years before, until 14 February 1945.

Reorganization of the 2nd and 3rd Battalions, and Argenta to the River Po, February–May 1945.

Shortage of infantry was apparent throughout 1944 and by autumn General Alexander was again faced with under-strength battalions. Casualties, PYTHON (repatriation of Servicemen with lengthy overseas service) and desertions were a constant drain on the Army. In October battalions were reduced to 700 men and the War Office approved plans to disband units. **3rd Coldstream**, a Regular Battalion, was to be reduced to a cadre and returned to England. Having left the Apennines, the 2nd and 3rd Battalions met in Spoleto. Many in 3rd Coldstream had the requisite four and a half years' Service overseas and were chosen to go home.[47]

On 31 March Lieutenant Colonel Bob Coates and the 3rd Coldstream cadre arrived in Britain after eight years away. They moved to Hawick and rebuilt the Battalion, training for the Far East, although they eventually embarked for Palestine in October 1945. Many Guardsmen meanwhile joined the **4th and 5th Battalions** in the British Army on the Rhine.

The 'new' **2nd Battalion**, under Lieutenant Colonel Billy Steele, with four rifle (and two reserve) companies left for Forlì on 9 March and faced the challenge of campaigning on the flat plains of the Po. 2nd Coldstream (24th Guards Brigade, now under Brigadier Malcolm Erskine) joined 56th London Division with its Black Cat badge in V Corps and trained with Wasp

[47] [Official] History of the Second World War *The Mediterranean and Middle East*, vol.VI Part II, HMSO, 1987 page 372.

flamethrowers, turretless Sherman 'Kangaroo' troop carriers and amphibious vehicles.

V Corps was to operate on the Adriatic coast to distract German attention before Eighth Army attacked across the River Senio towards Bologna. The German flank rested on Lake Comacchio, and V Corps planned operations both up the sand spit that divided the lake from the sea and towards Argenta. On 1 April 2nd Coldstream left Forlì and relieved 2 Commando Brigade on the sand spit. On the 5th the Coldstream were ordered to raid across the Valletta Canal, but an alert enemy and the difficulty of launching boats meant that a deliberate operation was required. Colonel Steele therefore cancelled the operation.

56th Division was ordered to force the gap between the flooded areas east of Argenta. The 1st Buffs landed north of the 'Gap', seizing a vital bridge despite heavy casualties. On 14 April 2nd Coldstream attacked over flat country east of La Pioppa to join them. No 4 Company (Major David Toler) found its start line occupied by a German company. Accurate fire from supporting tanks and an outflanking movement by a platoon who charged with the bayonet led to the taking of ninety-seven prisoners from *15th Panzergrenadier Division*, at the cost of one killed and two wounded; the Company then captured a further strongpoint. Major Toler was awarded the MC for his leadership. The Battalion relieved the Buffs that night.

Early on 18 April 2nd Coldstream attacked across the Val d'Albero canal, one of many water obstacles running into Lake Comacchio, and the Guardsmen advanced behind a smokescreen and barrage to enter Chiesa del Banda. Prisoners were taken, but a Mk IV tank opened fire. The companies engaged it with small arms; fortunately it withdrew having wounded only three Guardsmen. The companies, unable to cross the Fossa Benvignante in daylight, took what cover they could, but lost thirteen killed and twenty-five wounded, mostly from airburst shelling, although 100 prisoners were taken. An attempt to rush the bridge was stopped by a minefield, and when, at dawn on 19 April, the road was cleared, the bridges were demolished. No 3 Company was able to scramble across the rubble and marched for five miles through closer country to Portoverrara on the Scolo Bolognese canal.

No 4 Company crossed the first waterway, but the Canale Diverso, 300 yards away, was strongly held. The leading platoon took cover in the canal, under accurate defensive mortaring. No 3 Company arrived in support but could make no progress; two officers and nine men were killed, and fifteen were wounded, but night patrols found the Germans gone. Next day No 1 Company advanced without opposition, until it was north-east of Portomaggiore where the Scots Guards took the lead. 2nd Coldstream had played a key part in forcing the Argenta Gap and the German defences were crumbling. Bologna fell on 21 April.[48]

The Scots Guards crossed the Po di Volano that day and Colonel Steele was ordered to take an armoured column comprising the Battalion, 27th Lancers, artillery and sappers – 'STEELFORCE' – in a dash to the Po. STEELFORCE advanced by moonlight on 22 April, and No 1 Company went via Formignano to bypass demolitions. By daybreak the companies were near Copparo, seven miles on, but No 2 Company was missing. That afternoon Nos 1 and 3 Companies crossed the Naviglio canal, and No 4 Company attacked Sesta; by dusk STEELFORCE had reached Canale Bianco, which the Scots Guards were to cross.

No 2 Company (Captain George Gidney MC) had become separated from the column in the darkness and ran into German positions. It occupied a farmhouse and some nearby trenches and these positions were held against infantry and tank attack all day until ammunition ran out. Much

[48] Battle Honour **Argenta Gap**.

of the Company was captured, but Lieutenant Charles Darley escaped with sixteen men and found the Battalion; the Company was released a week later.

On 25 April 2nd Coldstream advanced to the Po, passing masses of equipment abandoned by the Germans. A Divisional crossing was planned, but Colonel Steele was told "not to take any notice of the obstacle" and that the riverline was not occupied. A patrol crossed the Po, but Crespino was held and the patrol was captured. That night No 4 and No 3 Companies crossed; elsewhere the armour was pursuing the Germans towards the Alps. On 30 April the Battalion crossed the Po and drove forty miles to Campomagara, east of Padua, where, on 1 May, in sight of Venice, 2nd Coldstream heard of the surrender of the German Armies in Italy. There was little time for celebration for, four days later, the Battalion was ordered to join 91st US Division in Gorizia, which Yugoslavia was attempting to annex. 2nd Coldstream, based near Trieste, thus became involved in the opening confrontation of the Cold War.

NORTH-WEST EUROPE 1944–45[49]

The Landing in Normandy and Operation GOODWOOD, June–July 1944. 1st (Armoured) and 5th Battalions

In March 1943 the Guards Armoured Division, under General Allan Adair, took part in Exercise SPARTAN in which the new Armoured Divisions were 'shaken out'. The **5th Coldstream** finished up after the exercise at Hunstanton, while the 1st moved to near Thetford,[50] where it converted to the American Sherman tank with a 75mm gun. Although reliable, the Sherman's disadvantages were to be very apparent in Normandy, where it was out-gunned and under-armoured compared with the German Mk V 'Panther' with its "devilishly good" long-barrelled 75mm gun. At Easter 1944 one Sherman 'Firefly' armed with the superior 17-pounder gun was added to each troop to help redress the imbalance.

In July 1943 the Division moved to Helmsley and the Yorkshire Wolds, where in March 1944 it was reviewed by Winston Churchill. A month later the 1st, 4th and 5th Battalions held a St George's Day Parade Service in York Minster after which Colonel Maurice Trew (Regimental Lieutenant Colonel) took the salute.

Plans for the invasion of Europe were shrouded in secrecy despite the concentration of troops in Southern England. Thus, after loading the Division onto trains for an 'unknown destination', the **1st Battalion** was amazed when an ancient Yorkshire stationmaster solemnly chalked 'HOVE' on a carriage! On 29 April the Battalion duly arrived at Hove as part of Operation PHANTOM – to make the Germans believe that the invasion would be in the Pas de Calais. General Eisenhower visited 1st Coldstream there, impressing all he met. The 5th Battalion was nearby in Eastbourne. BBC reports of the landings in Northern France on 6 June were greeted with excitement and many felt that they were about to take part in great events.

While Allied air superiority prevented attacks by German aircraft, a new aerial threat, the V1 flying bomb, appeared. Five days after the first V1 landed on London, a flying bomb hit the Guards

[49] Theatre Blazon **North-West Europe 1944–45.**

[50] Not far from Stanford Training Area.

Chapel in Wellington Barracks, spiritual home of Guardsmen, collapsing the roof during morning service on 18 June. The King's Guard, just dismissed on the Square, ran to help, but Captain Windram, Coldstream Director of Music, five Musicians from the Regimental Band, sixteen other Coldstreamers and 100 members of the congregation were killed.

Elsewhere on 18 June, the Guards Armoured Division infantry, including 5th Coldstream under Lieutenant Colonel the Lord Stratheden, embarked at Tilbury and Southampton. Part of the Battalion landed at Arromanches on 23 June; two days later the remainder sighted the thousands of vessels, including HMS *Rodney*, and barrage balloons off Ver-sur-Mer (GOLD Beach); closer in, the battered houses and beach debris were evident. The Battalion moved inland to St Loup Hors near Bayeux.

On D + 19 General Montgomery's 21st Army Group held a bridgehead from the Orne, north round Caen, to Caumont and Carentan. US 1st Army had liberated most of the Cotentin peninsula. Montgomery's intention was to grind down German armoured reserves around Caen so that US 1st Army could attack south and then south-east, while awaiting the twenty-six American divisions due to arrive in Cherbourg (captured on 27 June).

On 26 June Montgomery opened a major offensive, Operation EPSOM, towards the River Odon, south-west of Caen. 32nd Guards Brigade (Brigadier George Johnson) joined 43rd (Wessex) Division, and 5th Coldstream held defensive positions at St Manvieu and Marcelet, west of Caen, a mile from Carpiquet airfield (held by *12th SS Panzer Division 'Hitlerjugend'*). The Guardsmen patrolled the devastated countryside and learned to live with the frequent shelling, which, with the stench of dead cattle, made the period most unpleasant. On 4 July 3rd Canadian Division assaulted Carpiquet with 5th Coldstream securing the start-line, while I Corps attacked Caen; the Canadians fought for four days to clear the airfield.

The 1st Coldstream embarked at Gosport on 29 June and, passing "hundreds of craft of all descriptions, the battleship *Ramillies*, cruisers and masses of landing craft" in Spithead, many wondered "if any of us will ever see England again". On 1 July it disembarked on GOLD Beach (Le Hamel) and drove to Esquay-sur-Seuilles, near Bayeux.

After EPSOM General Montgomery, determined to break out of the bridgehead, planned operations towards Falaise on his eastern flank. The fighting in Normandy had cost the inexperienced Allies many casualties: 4000 during EPSOM alone. Montgomery, like Alexander, was short of infantry, but, with tanks in reserve, he was determined to use his armoured divisions, strategic bombers and massed artillery. Operation GOODWOOD envisaged the 11th, 7th and Guards Armoured Divisions attacking south-east of Caen on the plain towards Bourguébus Ridge (five miles south) following raids by 2000 bombers.

The Guards Armoured Division was on the left. 5th Guards Armoured Brigade (three armoured battalions each with a Grenadier Motor Company under Brigadier Norman Gwatkin) was to attack Cagny, from where 32nd Guards Brigade (three infantry battalions) would seize Vimont. The intelligence picture was inaccurate. The 1st Coldstream Orders Group heard that feeble opposition was expected after the bombing, with perhaps thirty German tanks (against 700 in the armoured divisions); the only thing in Vimont would be the 'Tailor's Shop' of *21st Panzer Division*.

At 0600 hours on 18 July two hours of aerial bombardment started. Ominously, the 88mm Flak was undiminished as 11th Armoured Division advanced. 5th Guards Brigade crossed the Caen Canal at Pegasus Bridge but was shelled in its Assembly Area. Eventually 1st Coldstream tanks moved forward to the Caen–Troarn light railway. This attracted shellfire and Lieutenant Rex Whistler of

2nd Welsh Guards, the artist, was killed. Soon afterwards a Panther tank was destroyed by the first shot from Lieutenant Malcolm Lock's 'Firefly' Sherman. The Grenadiers were in action, but it was difficult to gain a clear picture. Major Bill Anstruther-Gray's No 2 Squadron of 1st Coldstream was then ordered to sweep round Cagny from the south-west.

German infantry screened the well-organized 75mm self-propelled guns from Major Becker's *200 Assault Gun Battalion* which were sited in considerable depth. In Cagny itself Colonel von Luck, commanding *125th Panzergrenadier Regiment*, saw 29th Armoured Brigade and hastily deployed his one tank, one 88mm anti-tank gun and his Headquarters. Finding an 88mm Flak battery, he told the *Luftwaffe* subaltern at gunpoint "either you're a dead man or you can earn yourself a medal"; the officer engaged the tanks with devastating effect. Around 1800 hours the King's Company 1st Grenadiers forced von Luck out of Cagny, while No 2 Squadron of the Coldstream reached the station at the far end of the village.

The prospect further south, across the Caen–Vimont railway, was frightening: burning Shermans from 11th Armoured Division, 'unhorsed' crews, some wounded, with armour-piercing shot and sniping from Frénouville. No 2 Squadron advanced towards Vimont, but met fire from self-propelled guns and enemy tanks behind the railway embankment and lost several tanks. Colonel Myddelton decided not to add to the confusion and Coldstream tanks remained on the forward edge of Cagny. Without infantry or artillery there was reluctance to advance against the anti-tank screen. Fortunately the concussion of the bombing had knocked most German tank gunsights out of alignment, but craters round Cagny made movement hazardous.

5th Coldstream came forward and dug in at 2300 hours after a frustrating day trying to edge forward from the mass of vehicles by the Orne crossings and holding positions north-east of Cagny. It had been shelled in Démouville where the Second-in-Command, the ubiquitous 'Bunty' Stewart Brown, was wounded: he died ten days later. Cagny was under direct fire, and during the night shelling and fire from multiple *nebelwerfer* mortars continued.

The 1st Coldstream spent next day in reserve behind Cagny, receiving occasional armour-piercing rounds from the left flank. The 5th Battalion mounted a successful dawn assault on Frénouville, a mile south-east of Cagny, on the 20th, although the Germans only retired a few hundred yards to rising ground, and both sides settled down to sniping. The rain descended that evening, effectively ending Operation GOODWOOD. The 5th Coldstream was again shelled and Lord Stratheden was wounded, a bitter disappointment since he had raised and trained the Battalion so well. Major Michael Adeane took command of the Battalion.

The Guards Armoured Division's first battle had been confusing and dispiriting. Confidence in the Sherman was badly knocked. The prospect of success had been widely written up and Montgomery attracted criticism. Lack of infantry and field artillery support for the tanks was clearly wrong. Controversy continues over the results of GOODWOOD: tank losses were heavy on both sides and the German loss of half the invaluable German anti-tank guns deployed was serious. German armoured reserves from as far west as Caumont had been drawn in; but 2nd (British) Army had not broken through.[51]

[51] Battle Honour **Cagny**.

Operation BLUECOAT, 1st (Armoured) and 5th, and 4th (Tank) Battalions

Both Coldstream Battalions withdrew to Giberville, a grimy suburb of Caen. The presence of the Division was intended to keep German reserves near Caen and the Guardsmen were subject to periodic 'stonks' and bombing until 30 July, when the 1st Battalion returned to Bayeux; the 1st Battalion Echelon in particular suffered from the bombing. The Americans reached Avranches, at the base of the Cotentin peninsula, that day and General Montgomery planned to support the US breakout with Operation BLUECOAT, an offensive in the *bocage* south of Caumont towards the high ground round Vire and Mont Pinçon, one of the highest parts of Normandy. He ordered Lieutenant General Dempsey (commanding 2nd (British) Army) to "step on the gas for Vire!" With German reserves still near Caen, BLUECOAT was intended to unhinge the German defence by denying them a firm flank and the Vire–Vassy–Condé-sur-Noireau road for reinforcement.[52]

Caumont: Hill 309 (Quarry Hill), 30 July–1 August 1944. 4th (Tank) Battalion

During BLUECOAT the Guards Armoured Division fought in General O'Connor's VIII Corps alongside 11th Armoured and 15th (Scottish) Divisions; the Scotsmen were supported by 6th Guards Tank Brigade. The **4th (Tank) Battalion** Coldstream Guards, under Lieutenant Colonel Sir Walter Barttelot, had landed on JUNO Beach on 20 and 21 July.

On 30 July 4th Coldstream went into action for the first time in the attack on Hill 309 (Quarry Hill), an outcrop of the Mont Pinçon massif near St Martin-des-Besaces. This was in the Normandy *bocage:* close, hilly country with very small fields, orchards, high hedges or banks and narrow winding lanes, interspersed with farms and hamlets – ideal defensive country.

After a bombardment by Lancasters and artillery, 15th (Scottish) Division advanced, but the tanks were slowed by the banks, mines and wire, the infantry by hedgerows, traffic blockages and mortaring. Brigadier Gerald Verney, commanding 6th Guards Brigade, ordered the Coldstream to follow the barrage, and the squadrons advanced at 0930 hours without infantry, machine-gunning the hedgerows and houses to dislodge snipers. Numerous enemy from *326th Infantry Division* surrendered as they passed. By noon the Battalion had captured Hervieux crossroads, three miles from Caumont, and, in the heat, awaited the infantry. The ride had been bruising and tank crews had been showered by small hard apples in the orchards.

Four hours later, still without infantry, but with information from prisoners, Colonel Barttelot was told to continue towards St Martin-des-Besaces, a most significant decision. Marauder aircraft bombed Hill 309; No 3 Squadron ran into a *Jagdpanther* in La Morichèse, but bypassed it. The ground became steeper and the country closer, but the only resistance was from machine guns; the Germans had not thought that tanks could climb the hill. The Commanding Officer urged his commanders on, and over another obstacle – a railway. Coldstream tanks reached the summit of Hill 309 around 1800 hours to find the defenders gone. Around midnight the Glasgow Highlanders appeared and the tanks pulled back a short distance into 'close leaguer'; however, Bois du Homme

[52] "Step on the gas . . .": quoted in the [Official] History of the Second World War *Victory in the West: the Battle for Normandy*, vol.I, HMSO, 1974 Edition, page 386.

and La Ferrière-au-Doyen village (a mile further east) were still in German hands. Hill 309 was shelled and sniped at by a *Jagdpanther*; at dawn on 1 August infantry and King Tiger tanks from *21st Panzer Division* counter-attacked from La Ferrière. General von Kluge (*Commander-in-Chief West)* had wasted no time in moving armour from Caen.

The *panzergrenadiers* suffered heavily, but the Churchills made little impression on the Tigers. RAF Typhoons and lack of automotive power, however, hindered the German tanks. Lieutenant Christopher Schofield and his troop bore the brunt of the defence. He called down medium artillery onto the Tigers, forcing their withdrawal around 1600 hours, when they were caught from a flank by the rest of Major Jocelyn Hambro's No 1 Squadron, who inflicted 200 casualties. Artillery broke up a later attack, but Hill 309 – 'Coldstream Hill' – was firmly in British hands and Coldstream Churchills supported an attack on La Mancellière, a mile south.

The capture of Hill 309 by a tank battalion without infantry was remarkable. General O'Connor praised them highly: "No tank unit," he said, "has ever been handled with greater dash and determination." The Guardsmen were impressed by the nickname given them by the Germans: 'Churchill's Butchers'. As infantrymen by nature, the Guardsmen understood foot soldiers' problems. 4th Coldstream had pressed on without concern for its flanks; Colonel Barttelot had hit on the tactics the Germans were using so successfully and had spearheaded the VIII Corps breakthrough. *21st Panzer* and *326th Divisions* suffered heavily, but there were few Coldstream casualties. Two days later Sir Walter Barttelot (awarded the DSO) was promoted to command 6th Guards Brigade and Major Billy Smith took over the Battalion.[52]

The *Bocage*: St Charles-de-Percy, La Marvindière, Montchamp, Le Busq, Estry, Chênedolle and Sourdeval, 31 July–15 August 1944. 1st (Armoured) and 5th, and 4th (Tank) Battalions

The capture of Hill 309 opened the way for the Guards Armoured Division, which, following GOODWOOD, had been formed into 'groups' of infantry and armour. Squadrons from 1st (Armoured) Coldstream were to support the 3rd Irish Guards and 1st Welsh Guards in 32nd Guards Brigade while the 5th Battalion joined the 2nd (Armoured) Irish (5th Guards Brigade). The Division (with 11th Armoured on its right) was to advance from Caumont, seize the key defile at Cathéolles on the main Caen–Vire road, cut the Vire–Vassy road seven miles further south and then swing east to Condé-sur-Noireau.

This area of close *bocage*, seven miles square, was bounded by the Caen–Vire road in the west, the River Souleuvre in the north (running east–west, with the wooded Montchauvet Ridge (280 metres) on its south bank) and by the Vire–Vassy road (dominated from the north by the Pavée-Perrier Ridge) in the south. Cathéolles, with its bridge over the Souleuvre and defile through Montchauvet Ridge, lay at the north-west corner, and from La Ferronière (a mile nearer Vire) a secondary road ran south-east to Estry and Vassy. From Vire another secondary road ran north-east along Estry Ridge to Estry, La Caverie and Aunay-sur-Odon. Several ridges crossed the line of advance and visibility was often limited. Unmetalled roads made 'DUST BRINGS

[52] Battle Honour **Quarry Hill**. A memorial was placed by the local Commune on 'Coldstream Hill' in 1994. Modern French maps record this as Point 308, and the *Bois du Homme* as Bois de Brimbois. A leaguer (or *laager*) was a tight formation with all-round defence, which tanks adopted at night often just behind a defensive position, since with limited night vision they were otherwise vulnerable to infantry attack.

SHELLS' warnings very real and many anti-tank *tellermines* were concealed in ditches and gateways.[54]

BLUECOAT lasted for thirteen days of bitter and confused fighting. Few people had much idea of what was going on outside their immediate area: there was no 'front line' for most of the time, and divisions – British and German – intermingled. After the Hill 309 battle 15th (Scottish) Division identified *21st Panzer* reconnaissance troops; the Germans were racing to deploy *ad hoc* groups across the Allied advance. Rumours that *9th SS Panzer Division 'Hohenstaufen'* was on the way proved true, but *21st Panzer* and *9th SS Panzer* had been significantly depleted by two months in action. The former had forty-two Mk IV tanks on 1 August, the latter seventy-six tanks (thirty-one Panthers) and assault guns on the 2nd, plus a heavy tank (Tiger) battalion. German commanders realized that their best tactic was a delaying battle and deployed small groups of infantry with two or three tanks or assault guns, supported by *nebelwerfers* or artillery.

The common experience in NW Europe (and elsewhere) was that:

> "Both in defence and in the attack the [German] tactic was to keep us at arm's length. When we attacked a German position the problem . . . was very difficult to overcome. Vastly superior infantry firepower, both small arms and anti-tank, was their trump card. A German infantry platoon could produce about five times our own firepower. There was just no way through the curtain of fire from the MG 42s. Sometimes, by stealth, we were able to by-pass it; otherwise, artillery or armoured support was necessary – sometimes both. But due to their excellent anti-tank guns, the 75mm and the 88mm, the use of armour could prove costly."[55]

On 31 July 5th Coldstream, with 2nd (Armoured) Irish Guards tanks, advanced from St Martin-des-Besaces to seize Point 238, two miles south, and crossings over the River Souleuvre. Initial progress was good, but the Shermans could not climb some slopes and the infantry were stopped short of Point 238 by machine guns. The companies dug in on Point 192 (west of 238) but found, in daylight, a Panther tank between them: *21st Panzer* had arrived!

Efforts to outflank Point 238 on 1 August failed and Lieutenant Colonel Adeane was wounded. Major the Marquess of Hartington assumed command. Brigadier Norman Gwatkin, 5th Guards Brigade Commander, decided to infiltrate No 4 Company and a squadron to St Denis-Maisoncelles to threaten the German rear, which proved successful, and Point 238 was secured. 32nd Guards Brigade passed through to Le Tourneur and the route to Cathéolles.

11th Armoured Division meanwhile captured Le Bény-Bocage (further south-west) and the bridge at Cathéolles, and elements were two miles south of Ferronière crossroads by nightfall. German commanders identified Caumont as the decisive sector and General von Kluge ordered *II SS Panzer Korps* to the area: *9th SS Panzer* to Bény Bocage-Le Tourneur, with *10th SS Panzer Division 'Frundsberg'* further east.

[54] The maps in use then were Ordnance Survey 1:100,000 scale (1943 edition) drawn from French 1:80,000 maps. Various place names were wrongly transcribed in the reprinting and thus, compared to modern maps, some villages appear to have 'moved': for *St Charles-de-Percy* (1944) read La Ferronière, *Montcharivel* read Montchauvet, *Courteil* read St Charles-de-Percy, *La Marvindière* read Le Bos (the 5th Coldstream Echelon was at La Marvindière itself).

[55] From *Close Combat, Arm's Length* by Sydney Jary and Colonel W.M.Crawshaw, British Army Review, no.122, Autumn 1999 page 53. Sydney Jary, of the Hampshire Regiment, commanded 18 Platoon in 4th Bn Somerset Light Infantry (43rd Wessex Division) from Jul 44 to Jun 45, and was awarded the MC.

On 2 August the Guards Armoured Division ordered an advance on Vassy. The 2nd Armoured Irish/5th Coldstream Group moved up the Cathéolles defile – 'Mortar Gulch' – to La Ferronière following Divisional Reconnaissance (2nd Welsh Guards), but the defile was overlooked and 5th Coldstream was shelled; Major B.E. 'Buster' Luard, Commanding Officer for twenty-seven hours, was wounded, and Lord Hartington again took over. The Irish/Coldstream Group encountered newly arrived *9th SS Panzer* assault guns in St Charles-de-Percy and veered off to the south. Coldstreamers perched on the Micks' Shermans had an uncomfortable, dusty and frightening experience as they seesawed over the hedgerows "like ships in a heavy sea". By evening the Group had advanced four miles to La Marvindière (less than two miles west of their objective – Estry – and close to the Estry–Vire Ridge). Moving supplies up was a major challenge and the Coldstreamers fed partly on the rations off the tanks.

With 5th Guards Brigade committed in two directions – the Grenadier Group on the Souleuvre, the 2nd Irish/5th Coldstream Group at La Marvindière – with *9th SS Panzer* in between, General Allan Adair ordered 32nd Guards Brigade to clear St Charles-de-Percy. Colonel Joe Vandeleur's 3rd Irish Guards approached the village supported by No 1 Squadron of 1st Coldstream. On 2 August Major Reggie Batt led his tanks to the north and the Micks gained a foothold in the village. Two miles further north, in the Souleuvre valley, a fighting patrol attacked No 3 Squadron that night, but was driven off with German losses.

11th Armoured reached Chênedolle on Pavée-Perrier Ridge, overlooking the Vire–Vassy road, that day, but was strongly attacked by *9th SS Panzer Division*. Chênedolle was abandoned, but 23rd Hussars/8th Rifle Brigade held Le Bas Perrier, while Presles was fought over extensively. By nightfall two other battalion groups had dug in south-west of La Marvindière and established liaison with the 2nd Irish/5th Coldstream Group.[56]

The 3rd Irish Guards Headquarters near La Ferronière was attacked on 3 August by a company from *326th Division*; Coldstream tanks helped defeat them. An advance was made towards Maisoncelles, south-east of St Charles-de-Percy, and later two Coldstream troops were sent south of La Ferronière towards Point 176 near Beaulieu (where Panthers had attacked 153rd Regiment RA (the Leicestershire Yeomanry)). Sadly, in the process, Major Batt of No 1 Squadron was shot by a sniper and three tanks were lost.

A mile further south, on 3 August, the 2nd (Armoured) Irish/5th Coldstream advanced towards Estry Ridge, believing Le Busq village and Estry to be lightly held. The Guardsmen met heavy fire from *9th SS Panzer* Tigers, Panthers and infantry as they crested the ridge and lost several tanks. The *Hohenstaufen Division* had reached Estry, although the road towards Vire was overlooked by the 2nd Irish/5th Coldstream Group, some Welsh Guards tanks and the battalion groups from 11th Armoured. The 2nd Irish/5th Coldstream Group, sensing isolation, withdrew to La Marvindière. Their losses over the past month had been serious; the Guardsmen were effectively cut off, frequently shelled and short of supplies. Unknown to them, the Germans had also suffered; that evening *9th SS Panzer* had only thirty-four tanks (eighteen of them Panthers), half its strength of the previous day.

The 3rd Irish/1st Coldstream Group renewed the attack on St Charles-de-Percy and Maisoncelles on 4 August. The 1st Welsh Guards cleared the lower slopes of Montchauvet Ridge with help from No 3 Squadron of the Coldstream and attacked Montchamp, east of St Charles-de-Percy. They took

[56] *The Black Bull: from Normandy to the Baltic with the 11th Armoured Division* by P.Delaforce, A.Sutton, Stroud, 1993 page 81.

the village but were counter-attacked by Panthers and *panzergrenadiers*; No 3 Squadron rushed to help them, stalking Panthers for several hours without success. The Welsh Guards later withdrew.

While the Welsh Guards were fighting in Montchamp, 15th (Scottish) Division battalions cleared Montchauvet Ridge, and **4th Coldstream** moved up to St Pierre Tarentaine (north of Cathéolles) as 15th (Scottish) prepared to extend the attack on the left flank of the Guards Armoured Division. At the same time Colonel Vandeleur sent 'X' Company Scots Guards (attached to 3rd Irish Guards) with a **1st Coldstream** (No 1 Squadron) troop towards Maisoncelles to protect the Micks' flank. At Point 192, south of Maisoncelles, was an 88mm Flak gun that had been harassing La Marvindière from the rear. Coming under fire as they reached the village, X Company and the tanks swung round to the west, catching the Germans unawares. Several German tanks were destroyed and 200 infantrymen withdrew hastily. X Company dug in but was attacked by Panthers and *panzergrenadiers* in the night; the Germans were driven off with considerable losses.

By morning on 5 August *9th SS Panzer*, now on the defensive, had abandoned Maisoncelles and Montchamp, and had withdrawn to Estry. This enabled La Marvindière to be relieved. Captain Jocelyn Pereira, **5th Coldstream** Intelligence Officer, wrote:

> "The position was not alarming, as we would have been fully capable of holding our own against anything that attacked us, but at the same time it was distinctly unpleasant to have to fight a battle on all four fronts at once, and we were sadly short of sleep. A great many factors combined together to bring this state of affairs to an end, but from the Battalion's point of view the chief event was the arrival of the new Commanding Officer . . . Colonel Roddy Hill. He seemed the very epitome of smart turnout; it was a revelation to us. . . . There was about him an air of unhurried disregard for the immediate *alarums* of the moment that was wonderful to see – we felt we'd never seen such imperturbability, and the effect on everyone was miraculous. Everything was going to be "*quite all right*", which was just as well, because the next day [6 August] we were ordered to attack Le Busq, a little village . . . on the same ridge as Estry."[57]

After the loss of three Commanding Officers in sixteen days Colonel Roddy's arrival "made all the difference": at every level morale picked up.

That morning No 2 Squadron of **4th Coldstream** (Major Mark Milbank) supported 2nd Gordons (15th (Scottish)) attacking the five-way crossroads near La Caverie on the Estry road two miles east of Montchamp to open an eastern approach to Estry, Vassy and Lassy. Minor opposition was encountered (*SS Panzer-Regiment 9* had withdrawn from Montchauvet overnight).

Both 4th and 5th Coldstream were to be heavily engaged on 6 August. Zero Hour for the 5th Battalion attack on Le Busq, the preliminary to an assault on Estry by 15th (Scottish), was 1400 hours and the leading companies were over the ridge and through the hamlet before they met serious resistance, including heavy defensive artillery fire. Colonel Roddy pulled them back behind the ridge and the Guardsmen dug in once again under shellfire.

[57] *A Distant Drum* by Captain J.Pereira, Aldershot, 1948 (1972 Edition) pages 49–50. The Battalion had lost, as Commanding Officer, Lord Stratheden (wounded 20 Jul), Michael Adeane (wounded 1 Aug), Buster Luard (wounded 2 Aug) and Majors Jack Hamilton, Kenneth Thornton (wounded 1 Aug) and Lord Hartington had also commanded the Battalion before Colonel Roddy Hill arrived on 3 Aug 44. Comments by Major Norman Duckworth MBE MM and Major Douglas Glisson MBE in Oct 99 refer.

Four miles to the north-east **4th Coldstream** Churchills supported the 15th (Scottish) attack against an enemy assessed to be 'in full retreat'. No 2 Squadron and 9th Cameronians advanced from La Chapelle au Cornu towards the Bois des Monts feature in close country. Intense artillery and machine-gun fire struck the infantry as they crossed the steep valley beyond the Bois (west of Gournay) and heavy casualties were sustained. A 'squadron shoot' followed, but the tanks could not get forward and the infantry remnants withdrew. Half a mile further south, Major Hambro's No 1 Squadron advanced from La Caverie towards Lassy, but as the tanks and carriers crested the Bois des Monts rise an 88mm gun destroyed the leading tank and machine guns and mortars again caused serious casualties. The enemy weapons were skilfully concealed and, despite several efforts, no progress could be made. Again the attackers withdrew.

Major Tollemache moved down the Vassy road at midday and broke up a counter-attack from Lassy; No 3 Squadron tanks caused the enemy to retire 'at the double', but hidden 88mm guns on Estry Ridge drove the Squadron back with three tanks destroyed. Captain Douglas Gascoigne and Lieutenant Anthony Coates courageously tried to stalk one gun in a tank destroyer, but their vehicle was hit and the crew killed. The *SS* troops and Tiger tanks, tenacious as ever, were certainly not 'on the run'.

The vigorous defence of Estry was no coincidence. On 6 August Hitler's offensive against the Americans at Mortain was launched. Estry protected the German right flank, but the week's operations had cost *9th SS* and *21st Panzer Divisions* much, for little gain; and these formations were fixed in close contact with the 11th, Guards Armoured and 15th (Scottish) Divisions. The Germans now had to commit another division against 11th Armoured's salient on Pavée-Perrier Ridge, further reducing the Mortain force; late on 6 August *10th SS Panzer* launched a ferocious attack against 11th Armoured's 'boxes' at Bas Perrier and La Pavée, two miles from Le Busq. The 1st Norfolks, relieving the 3rd Monmouths at Pavée, combined as the 'NorMons' to fight the onslaught. Meanwhile the Americans and Allied air power checked the German armour at Mortain. Estry was still held by *9th SS Panzer* and renewed attacks by 15th (Scottish) and 6th Guards Tank Brigade on 7 and 8 August were unsuccessful; 4th Coldstream was in reserve.[58]

On 9 August **5th Coldstream** moved forward to Bas Perrier and dug in under fire. 5th Guards Brigade replaced 11th Armoured on Pavée-Perrier Ridge and 3rd Irish Guards occupied Sourdeval and Pavée. These hamlets, fought over for a week, were littered with burnt-out tanks, dead cattle, splintered trees, shellholes and newly dug graves. No 2 Squadron of **1st Coldstream** was forward with the Micks among tiny fields on the crest of Pavée-Perrier Ridge; the rest of the Battalion was further back. This "dismal" position at Sourdeval/Pavée was overlooked from the east by Point 242 above Chênedolle, in German hands. On 10 August Panthers and infantry attacked the 3rd Irish Guards and were driven off; a new enemy formation, *5th Fallsturmjäger* [Parachute] *Regiment* of *3rd/5th Parachute Division*, was identified.

Operation GROUSE, an attack ostensibly to capture the high ground and the Vire–Vassy road, but in reality to ensure that the German formations did not move against the American breakout, was mounted on 11 August. The main effort was in the east where 1st Welsh Guards, 'shot in' by Scots Guards Churchills and Irish Guards Shermans, attacked Haut Perrier (including Point 242). Mist precluded bomber support, but after hard fighting against *9th SS Panzer Engineer Battalion*

[58] Blazon **Mont Pinçon** (covering all the actions south of Caumont) claimed for the 1st, 4th and 5th Battalions and Battle Honour **Estry** (4th Battalion). Corporal Sidney Bates of the Norfolks was later awarded a posthumous Victoria Cross for his gallantry at La Pavée.

(fighting as infantry) Haut Perrier fell around 1000 hours and **5th Coldstream** (with Scots Guards Churchills) attacked Chênedolle. By noon 5th Coldstream was digging in around the village; orders to cross the Vire–Vassy road were cancelled.

Although, on the right, the Grenadier Group captured Viessoix, the situation in the centre was very different. The 3rd Irish Guards, supported by No 2 Squadron of 1st Coldstream, was to attack to the line of the Vire–Vassy road. The Guardsmen, supported by one artillery battery, advanced over the forward slope at 0900 hours. Strongpoints in the valley and mortars (with good observation from the far hill) opened an intense fire, as did nine (or more) tanks and assault guns, and probably 88mm guns as well, with well-sited machine guns, enfilading the advance from Point 242 until the Welsh Guards cleared Haut Perrier. Panthers were reported on the right flank. "The men were splendid, advancing steadily in spite of the severe opposition," but the Micks lost very heavily, including many officers, and only six Coldstream Shermans were undamaged. The attack was called off about 1600 hours. General Adair later commented, in respect of the Sourdeval attack, that "we can't congratulate ourselves on some battles . . . with the benefit of hindsight, we can see that mistakes were made". The Guardsmen had the last word for Sourdeval: "Sod-valley."[59]

The Guards Armoured Division spent the next five days patrolling, monitoring German movements. **4th Coldstream** drove to Vire to join 3rd Division on 11 August, where, to some dismay, the Battalion was split, one squadron supporting each brigade. For the next three days Coldstream Churchills supported the attacks towards Tinchebray against minor opposition until late on the 13th when No 2 Squadron tanks did good work ferrying back wounded and No 1 Squadron carried out a most successful attack. The advance continued until 15 August when the Squadrons harboured near Flers, leaving others to pursue the Germans towards Falaise.

While the German armies in the Falaise 'pocket' were destroyed by Allied air power, the 1st and 5th Coldstream refitted near Estry. Reinforcements arrived and the Quartermasters, Sidney Middleditch (1st) and Sidney Cooper (5th Battalion), made good equipment losses. The Echelons, who had supported the squadrons and companies under difficult circumstances, came up; among them were old hands who had done much to sustain morale, including Majors Michael Fox and Billy Denbigh of the 1st Battalion and Cecil Feilden of the 5th. The Guardsmen rested and supplemented the rations with local produce while the Allied divisions raced for Paris and the Seine.

Liberation brought the occasional mixed blessing. A Coldstream tank entered one battered village and, as the citizens approached, the gunner inadvertently fired the 75mm gun, demolishing the church spire. The locals withdrew in trepidation and the tank commander tried to calm them – to the extent his minimal French would allow. "*Pardon,*" he said, "*Faux pas!*"

[59] "The men were splendid . . .": 3rd Bn Irish Guards War Diary, 11 Aug 44. The tanks on Hill 242: in 1991, Major (Retd) Tony Brady, late Irish Guards, found a USAF air photograph in the Keele University archives. Taken shortly after Zero Hour, it reveals clearly that, at 0930 hours, nine or more tanks and assault guns were deployed on Hill 242, dominating the left flank of the attack. *Guards General: Memoirs of Major General Sir Allan Adair* edited by O.J.M.Lindsay, London, 1986 page 148. *9th SS Panzer Division* had been ordered to send all its Mk.IV and V (Panther) tanks, and the attached Tigers, to the Falaise area on 8 Aug, and had very few tanks on Perrier Ridge; but seven Panthers and two assault guns were knocked out on 11 Aug. See *9th SS Panzer Division "Hohenstaufen"* by H.Furbinger, translated G.Bernage, Heimdal, 1985 pages 369–375.

The Advance to Brussels, 29 August–3 September 1944. 1st (Armoured) and 5th Battalions

The arrival of thousands of maps, and tank transporters, on 28 August heralded one of the greatest advances of the war. Lieutenant Colonel Ririd Myddelton, who had trained the 1st Battalion so well, was succeeded by Lieutenant Colonel Dick Gooch as Commanding Officer. Next day the Guards Armoured Division drove nearly 100 miles to join General Horrocks' XXX Corps. The Coldstream formed a Regimental Battle Group in 5th Guards Brigade. This historic decision led to a most harmonious and successful arrangement, which remained until the end of the war and contributed enormously to the morale of both battalions.

On 30 August the Division was ordered to advance seventy miles from Vernon (on the Seine) to seize crossings over the Somme, a momentous challenge! The Coldstream Group received a rapturous welcome in every village and reached Auneil that evening; it set off at 0200 hours next day for the Somme, sixty miles away, meeting little opposition. Captain Basil Sparrow, Reconnaissance Troop Commander, telephoned the Resistance in each village to discover enemy dispositions and many surprised Germans were captured. From Corbie, on the Somme, the Coldstream drove for Arras, thirty-five miles further on.

The momentum, and morale, was tremendous. As No 1 Squadron approached Arras, Captain Nico Collin:

> "remembering that it was 1 September [the first day of partridge shooting] . . . called our troop's tank commanders that there was a pound for anyone who downed a partridge. . . . A covey got up slap in front of my tank. I blazed away [with a machine gun] but sadly never disturbed a feather. Moreover, two very scared German soldiers arose from the kale with their hands up in surrender."[60]

At 1400 hours Captain Sparrow drove through Arras to seize the bridges on the far side and thousands of inhabitants appeared as Coldstream tanks entered the *Grand Place*, despite anti-tank and machine-gun fire (which sadly wounded several civilians). The infantry and *Maquis* rounded up Germans while the liberators were greeted with kisses, flowers and champagne, and encouragements chalked on the side of the tanks. The advance continued with little resistance, but the Division outran the RAF co-ordination line and during one halt two 'friendly' aircraft attacked the tanks. Amid burning bowsers, General Adair's ADC, Captain Aylmer Tryon, walked to the General's scout car and beside *"Vive le RAF"* chalked on the side he added *"less two Spitfires"*!

The Group leaguered north of Arras and moved to Douai airfield on 2 September, where the historic order was given to the Guards Armoured Division to capture Brussels ninety miles away! The advance started at 0600 hours on 3 September, with 2nd Welsh Guards (32nd Guards Brigade) on the main road, and the Grenadiers leading the Coldstream (5th Guards Brigade) via Lille, passing places familiar to 2nd Coldstream in 1940. Progress reports fuelled great enthusiasm and repairs on tanks normally taking hours were completed in minutes. 5th Coldstream discovered thirty Germans guarded by a small group of their Guardsmen who had been captured at Douai on 1 September.

The 2nd Welsh Guards won the race for Brussels by minutes and at nightfall Coldstreamers drove into the city to be swept up by crowds who, according to Captain Pereira,

[60] Partridges: letter from Major Nico Collin to *The Field*, May 1996.

> "cheered and sang and waved endlessly – a sea of faces that surged forward whenever there was a pause and clambered onto every vehicle they could get on to so that we were kissed and embraced and half-suffocated every ten minutes. They were deliriously happy, and we were happy too."[61]

The tanks moved slowly to the city centre, completing a Divisional advance of over ninety miles in a day, a record never equalled. The Resistance, the *Armée Blanche*, produced guides, intelligence – and hundreds of cases of champagne, labels overprinted "*Reservé à la Wehrmacht*", a windfall that sustained morale for weeks!

Heppen and the Road to Arnhem (Op MARKET GARDEN). September 1944, 1st (Armoured) and 5th Battalions

The liberators of Brussels were received magnificently. On 5 September the Coldstream Group resumed the advance northwards, with the challenge of crossing several major water obstacles, including the Rhine. The Welsh Guards secured a damaged bridge over the Albert Canal at Beeringen, forty miles north-east of Brussels, and the Division set about clearing Bourg Leopold and Hechtel on the far side.

Colonel Roddy Hill gave orders for the capture of Beverloo and Heppen, and then Bourg Leopold itself. On 8 September 5th Coldstream, with 1st Battalion tanks, advanced into the collieries beyond Beeringen. Assault guns were encountered but outflanked. Beverloo was captured and 100 veteran *SS* troops and recruits taken prisoner. A Panther at Heppen station led to another outflanking manoeuvre, but one *Jagdpanther* in Heppen itself destroyed several No 2 Squadron Shermans. Boggy ground and darkness compounded the difficulties. After an unpleasant night, the assault resumed; Germans in Bourg Leopold, further east, joined the battle.

Lord Hartington was killed leading No 3 Company into Heppen and, with the only Platoon Commander wounded, Company Sergeant Major Jim Cowley led the Company forward to clear the houses. He later reorganized the Company and from the church tower espied the German echelon; he then drove off a counter-attack. 5th Coldstream had ninety-five casualties (twenty-six killed) and the 1st nine killed and thirteen wounded at Heppen, and eleven tanks, but many dead Germans were found in addition to the prisoners taken. The Group's achievement was considerable and Colonel Roddy Hill was awarded the DSO. Company Sergeant Major Cowley received the DCM for "courage, leadership and initiative of a very high order".[62]

The advance continued, although the Welsh Guards were fighting hard in Hechtel. The seizure of 'Joe's Bridge' over the Meuse–Escaut Canal by Colonel Joe Vandeleur's 3rd Irish Guards opened the way for the next major advance – to Arnhem. Montgomery's intention in Operation MARKET GARDEN was to seize crossings over six major obstacles, including the Rivers Maas, Waal (at

[61] Tryon: *The Story of the Guards Armoured Division* by the Earl of Rosse and Colonel E.R.Hill, London, 1956 page 90. *A Distant Drum op cit* page 75.

[62] Battle Honour **Heppen**. The Heppen *Jagdpanther* was later knocked out in Hechtel by the Welsh Guards; it is on display in the Imperial War Museum in London. Supporting letter for Company Sergeant Major Cowley's citation: quoted in *A Distant Drum* page 204. *Bourg Leopold* has now been renamed Leopoldsburg. Company Sergeant Major Cowley became Drill Sergeant and was posted on the Start Line for various attacks to check on the officers' dress: Colonel Roddy Hill insisted on the officers being properly turned out with brass rank stars in the attack. Letter Major Jim Cowley 20 Sep 99.

Nijmegen) and Neder Rijn (Lower Rhine) at Arnhem so that the Allies could outflank the Siegfried Line (the German defensive 'West Wall') encircle the Ruhr and advance into Germany. The strategy, the dropping of airborne troops so far – up to sixty-five miles – ahead, the intelligence picture and the advance up one exposed route continue to be debated to this day.

The 5th Coldstream spent several days in the Escaut bridgehead, fighting a successful defensive battle. A surprise was to take prisoners from *9th SS Panzer Division*, not thought to be in the area. On 14 September Battalion Headquarters was shelled and an ammunition truck was hit; Regimental Sergeant Major Dusty Smith leaped into another burning ammunition vehicle and drove it away, saving many lives – and the Battalion's ammunition! He was awarded the DCM.

While the Airborne Corps landed on 17 September the Irish Guards Group led the way up the Arnhem Road. By coincidence Field Marshal Model (temporarily *Commander-in-Chief West*) was in Oosterbeek and when he saw the British airborne landings he quickly improvised a response. He realized that he had little to fear from 1st Airborne Division in Arnhem; the experienced *9th* and *10th SS Panzer Divisions* were refitting nearby and their tanks could outmatch the lightly armed airborne troops. Model saw that the priority was to guard against XXX Corps and 2nd Army advancing to link up with 1st Airborne. The *85th Division* was already in the area and Model ordered *59th Division* and *10th SS, 15th* and *41st Panzer Divisions* to converge on the routes in the Nijmegen–Arnhem area.[63]

The Coldstream Group was initially in reserve. It moved to Valkenswaard before joining 82nd US Airborne Division on 20 September and covering their eastern flank on the Maas-Waal Canal. No 3 Squadron took part in a counter-attack at Mook close to the German border. The Grenadiers cleared Nijmegen, seizing the Nijmegen road bridge on 20 September, but progress slowed thereafter. German strength on the 'Island' – between the Waal and the Neder Rijn – steadily increased, and the Arnhem road was, for much of its length, exposed on an embankment. Fighting on the Island was to show the limitations of tanks on waterlogged ground – they could often only move on roads – and their lack of vision at night.

On 22 September *59th Division* cut the road between Veghel and Uden, south of Nijmegen, and the Grenadiers and Coldstream were ordered back to re-open it. On 23 September No 1 Company, with No 1 Squadron, assaulted Vokel, encountering serious opposition. Company Sergeant Major Frank Farnhill took command of the Company when Major Viscount Long (who had arrived the previous day) was killed, and pressed home the attack; for his "presence of mind and personal example" he was awarded the DCM.[64] The road was re-opened, but on 25/26 September Montgomery withdrew the remnants of 1st Airborne Division across the Neder Rijn. As Lieutenant General 'Boy' Browning, commanding the Airborne Corps, had said to Montgomery, it was "a bridge too far". The Allies now faced a winter campaign: the last chance to end the war in 1944 was over.

While the Coldstream were at Vokel, Major Michael Willoughby took No 2 Company and tanks to secure the German food depot at Oss. An infantry counter-attack was driven off and several Germans arriving for rations were taken prisoner. On 30 September the Group returned to Mook to guard against attacks from the Reichswald Forest; next day the Coldstreamers crossed the Nijmegen bridge to relieve the Irish Guards on the 'Island', 5th Coldstream at Elst and 1st Battalion

[63] *Horrocks: The General Who Led From The Front* by P.Warner, London, 1984, page 113.

[64] Battle Honour **Nederrijn**. Citation: quoted in *A Distant Drum* page 204. "I just did what my training and wartime experience told me to do." Letter Mr Frank Farnhill 21 Sep 99.

Guards Armoured Division. Guardsmen of 5th Coldstream on the tanks of No 2 Troop, No 2 Squadron, 1st (Armoured) Coldstream at Oss, near Nijmegen, 23 September 1944. The crew of the 17-pounder Sherman 'Firefly' (left-hand tank) are: (left to right, dark berets): Lance Corporals G. Siddons and F. Snaith, Sergeant C. Shipley, and on the centre tank, standing, Lance Sergeant T. Fawcett.

tanks supporting 231st Brigade at Bemmel. Orchards, dykes and soft ground limited movement: the weather had broken. German artillery remained active and mud became an important factor.

Montgomery's priority was to open Antwerp for supplies; however, the eastern flank had to be guarded against attempts to recapture the Nijmegen bridge. A night attack by *9th SS Panzer* troops with heavy artillery support on 3 October was defeated by Lieutenant the Hon Robert Boscawen's troop (No.2 Squadron), an action for which he was awarded the MC. 231st Brigade capitalized on the success, capturing Heuvel next morning, 'shot in' by Coldstream tanks. The Brigadier, Sir Alexander Stanier (a Welsh Guardsman), was generous in his praise for the Coldstream.[65] Two days later they moved to Hatert to rest, train (and do some drill), but 5th Coldstream then joined 11th Armoured Division for a week south of Venraij, patrolling against *7th Parachute Division*.

On 12 November the Coldstream Group deployed alongside Ninth US Army as XXX Corps supported the US attack towards Aachen. 5th Coldstream occupied Wehr on the

[65] Diary of Lieutenant the Hon Robert Boscawen MC page 145–154. The attack on Heuvel secured the line of a canal that was to become the forward defensive line until the Rhine crossings six months later.

Sittard–Geilenkirchen road – in Germany – with the squadrons nearby, until 20 December. Apart from patrolling, the period was uneventful; an advance to the Roer was cancelled due to flooding.

Clearing the West Bank of the Maas (Venraij and Meijel), October–November 1944. 4th (Tank) Battalion

After the Tinchebray fighting in August, 4th Coldstream rested. On 18 August Brigadier Sir Walter Barttelot was killed when his scout-car struck *tellermines*, to the great sadness of the Regiment and 6th Guards Brigade. On 7 September his successor, Brigadier Douglas Greenacre, ordered the Tank Battalions forward to the Seine on their own tracks.

On 29 September 4th Coldstream moved to Eindhoven, and then Mook, before starting to clear the west bank of the Maas, an essential precursor to operations in the Rhineland. The attacks by 3rd Division and 4th Coldstream against Overloon and Venraij were delayed by appalling weather, inundated countryside and mud, but on 12 October the assault went in. Coldstream Headquarters tanks lost their infantry and entered Overloon by themselves, sustaining casualties to powerful *Riegel* bar-mines, anti-tank guns and Panthers, but the town was secured and the Grenadiers and Coldstream continued the attack towards Venraij.

After a day of maintenance the attack was resumed on 16 October, but the Molenbeek dyke proved a difficult obstacle. The infantry and some tanks, however, broke into Brabander on the edge of Venraij, and after thirty-six hours' fighting the town was secured. The Coldstream captured a monastery further east, only to hear BBC news announcing that 'American' tanks had taken Venraij! Progress had been slow in this most unpleasant battle: it had taken seven days to capture Venraij against a skilled enemy. 6th Guards Tank Brigade moved back on 20 October to Helmond, the Coldstream taking with them 'Cuckoo', a Panther tank captured in Overloon.[66]

On 24 October 6th Guards Brigade, supporting 15th (Scottish) Division again, advanced north from Eindhoven, but meeting no resistance, was diverted to capture Tilburg. Mines and floods hindered progress, but 4th Coldstream approached from the south-east and a squadron with 7th Seaforth Highlanders entered the town on the 26th, the 4th Battalion following next morning. The reception was ecstatic, but the chance to enjoy it was short-lived as 9th *Panzer* and *15th Panzergrenadier Divisions* attacked across the Deurne Canal, east of Helmond, and 15th Scottish with 6th Guards Tank Brigade were despatched to stop them.

The 4th Coldstream, supporting 9th Camerons, attacked southwards near Vreekwijk on 30 October and towards Liesel next day. Self-propelled guns delayed the advance; one was stalked to within fifty yards before it was destroyed. The Churchills helped to clear the hamlets of Slot and Huttern (1 November), but soft ground and mud brought the armour to a halt. The 4th Coldstream withdrew to Helmond to refit while 15th Scottish, and the Grenadiers, attacked Meijel.[67]

A fortnight later 4th Coldstream returned to Venraij to dislodge the remaining enemy west of the Maas. No Germans were found near Veulen (23 November), but mud and floods again proved a major factor. On the 27th the Battalion supported 8th Infantry Brigade attacking Geisteren Kasteel, a moated fortress held by Officer Cadets led by an individual nicknamed the 'Bad Baron'. An 'exhibition shoot' by 4th Coldstream followed an air and artillery bombardment, 'Cuckoo' the Panther proving particularly useful, but when the assault went in the enemy had disappeared.

[66] Battle Honour **Venraij**.
[67] Battle Honour **Meijel**.

Cuckoo, the Panther captured by the 4th Battalion at Overloon in October 1944.

The Ardennes Offensive, December 1944. 1st (Armoured) and 5th and 4th (Tank) Battalions

General von Rundstedt's counter-stroke was launched against the Americans in the Ardennes in poor weather on 16 December and achieved tactical surprise. Order and counter-order reigned until 20 December when the news blackout lifted, and, with German armour only twenty miles from Liège, Field Marshal Montgomery moved XXX Corps south to block the German advance. 32nd Guards Brigade drove to Tirlemont (now Tienen, twenty-five miles east of Brussels) and 1st and 5th Coldstream were billeted in Neerheylissem and Opheylissem.

A rapid move to Namur, junction of the Sambre and Maas (Meuse) Rivers, was ordered and the Coldstream Group drove there in bitterly cold weather on Christmas Day, to find the Americans withdrawing and the authorities trying to save antique trams. Nos 1 and 2 Companies, each with a troop from No 2 Squadron, guarded bridges below the citadel captured by their Coldstream forbears in 1695. German bombing detonated the charges on the railway bridge, causing great alarm and wild firing by the Americans. The damage to a nearby wine shop, however, allowed 'war stocks' to be appropriated for the Guardsmen's Christmas! Returning to the Heylissems on 27 December, the Battalions celebrated Christmas, complete with the Regimental Band. When, on 4 January 1945, eighty-one Coldstream officers dined in the Château d'Outremont each place had its bottle of champagne!

At the same time 6th Guards Tank Brigade had been assigned to the Canadian, 2nd British and Ninth US Armies in rapid succession. On 22 December the Battalions moved to Maastricht, joining 51st (Highland), and later 43rd (Wessex) Division between Maastricht and Sittard. The Allied counter-offensive started on 30 December and Allied air power came into play as the weather cleared. While near Maastricht 4th Coldstream heard that the Commanding Officer, Lieutenant Colonel Billy Smith, had been awarded the DSO. A most courageous act occurred at this time when Lance Sergeant Clifford Lowe noticed a grenade about to explode on the floor of the troop billet. He picked it up and rushed out; although severely wounded, his action saved the lives of his comrades and he was awarded the George Medal for his bravery.

The Roer: Operation BLACKCOCK, January 1945. 4th (Tank) Battalion

On 16 January XII Corps attacked in the 'Roermond Triangle' to eliminate the German salient west of the Maas (south of the River Roer) close to where the Coldstream had been in December. **4th Coldstream** moved to Schinveld (near Brunssum) where the tanks were whitewashed for camouflage, and the squadrons supported 43rd (Wessex) Division in attacks on Scheierwaldenrath on 21 January, and later Putt and Waldenrath. The battalions stayed in the positions they had captured in freezing weather, amid numerous minefields, before advancing on Dremmen (25 January). 6th Guards Tank Brigade returned to Tilburg a week later, and the first leave to England for the Guardsmen since the invasion started.[68]

The Reichswald and Rhineland: Operation VERITABLE, February–March 1945. 4th (Tank) and 5th Battalions

With the Ardennes counter-offensive under way, the Supreme Commander issued a directive to Field Marshal Montgomery on 31 December. Eisenhower envisaged Allied crossings of the Rhine north of the Ruhr, but Montgomery had to destroy the German forces west of the Rhine beforehand. General Schlemm's *1st Parachute Army* was deployed between the Maas and the Rhine/Waal Rivers, and in addition to natural obstacles (including the Reichswald Forest and Hochwald feature) and the towns of Cleve and Goch, there were the Siegfried Line defences, elaborate in places. The Germans were fighting on the soil of the Fatherland, for which Hitler ordered "no withdrawal"; the Rhine was a vital artery for barges supplying the Ruhr. Unfortunately a thaw and rain a week before the operations started turned the ground into mud.

Montgomery gave the task of clearing the Rhineland as far as the Xanten-Geldern line – Operation VERITABLE – to General Crerar's Canadian Army, with General Horrocks' XXX Corps (300,000 strong) under command. XXX Corps was to attack with five infantry divisions abreast and then the Guards Armoured Division would exploit towards Wesel, with "speed and extreme violence", as Eisenhower stressed. 6th Guards Tank Brigade would support 15th (Scottish) Division's assault down the Nijmegen–Cleve road to seize the Nutterden feature and 'gap' south of Cleve, vital ground for the Allied breakout – and for German reserves – and then capture Cleve itself. In early February the troops moved to Nijmegen in great secrecy at night.

On 8 February a massive aerial and artillery bombardment, significantly greater than at Alamein (by now the soldier's yardstick), started. 46th Brigade, in 'Kangaroo' troop-carriers, and **4th Coldstream** attacked in the rain south of Kranenburg, seven miles from Nijmegen, taking objectives on the outer belt of the Siegfried Line. Thick mud and mines delayed progress, but 9th Cameronians and No.1 Squadron skirted the north-west shoulder of the Reichswald before more mines halted them short of their objective, Frasselt, in front of the main Siegfried defences. With no Sappers or flail tanks available, Lieutenant Geoffrey Anson dismounted and energetically organized mine-clearing parties, helping the Cameronians to clear Frasselt before organizing the defence (which earned him an MC).

15th (Scottish) Division's attack had started well and the Grenadiers came forward to breach the main obstacles, but the Groesbeek–Frasselt road began to disintegrate. Coldstreamers threw timber

[68] Battle Honour **The Roer.**

and rubble onto this road and the Grenadiers managed to pass through before another hazard appeared. The Germans breached the dykes, submerging the Nijmegen–Cleve road (further north) by 18 inches. The Grenadiers crossed the Siegfried Line behind Frasselt and inched towards Cleve.

At this stage General Horrocks, hearing that 15th Scottish was almost in Cleve, unleashed his reserve, 43rd (Wessex) Division, towards the city. "This was one of the worst mistakes I made in the war," wrote Horrocks. The "Division caused one of the worst traffic jams of the whole war. The language heard that night has seldom if ever been equalled." Some of 43rd Wessex got through, but met considerable resistance in the rubble of Cleve resulting from Allied bombing. While neighbouring divisions fought through the forest in indescribable conditions, 4th Coldstream struggled to keep the Groesbeek–Frasselt road open, recovering over 100 bogged vehicles during the ensuing 36 hours. The surrender of *276th Magen Abteilung* – the 'Stomach' Battalion from their common ailment – to 4th Coldstream presented a new challenge, but the *Magen* was soon marching towards the prisoner of war cage! On 9 February 6th Guards Tank Brigade and 15th Scottish captured the Nutterden feature before enemy reserves – *7th Para Division* – arrived. Two days later 6th Guards and 44th (Lowland) Brigades moved into Cleve, the first major town in Germany to be captured.[69]

On 12 February 15th Scottish advanced towards Calcar (Kalkar) led by No 2 Squadron of 4th Coldstream. Fierce resistance was encountered in Qualberg, two miles from Cleve, where the leading 7th Seaforth's Kangaroos were destroyed. Lieutenant Michael Woodall of the Coldstream destroyed a self-propelled gun and led the Group into the village, which was cleared quickly, before setting out for Hasselt. Reports of a counter-attack further south led to consolidation in Qualberg; the Coldstream Churchills returned to Cleve.

Two days later, in clearer weather, 2nd Glasgow Highlanders and No 3 Squadron advanced on Moyland, beyond Hasselt, but the 48-hour lull had allowed *15th Panzergrenadier Division*, Schlemm's reserve, to occupy the wooded hills south-west of Moyland. Shelling delayed the weary Scotsmen, although attacks supported by the other Coldstream Squadrons fared better. The assault on Moyland was renewed next day with 9th Seaforths and No 1 Squadron, but without success.[70]

The Attack on Mull, 16–22 February 1945. 5th Battalion

It became clear early on that the battle would not be characterized by 'speed and violence'. The prospect of the infantry, supported by Churchill tanks, flails and flamethrowers, having to eradicate a tenacious enemy from every village and wood, in terrible weather and mud, was now reality. Montgomery was again short of infantry. On 11 February the Guards Armoured Division received orders, not for exploitation but for the infantry to join 51st (Highland) Division south of the Reichswald. The task was to expand the bridgehead over the swollen River Gennep at Niers to give XXX Corps room for manoeuvre towards Goch.

On 14 February Colonel Roddy Hill led **5th Coldstream** into an area of sand dunes, before attacking the farms at Mull, south of Hommersum (recently taken by 3rd Irish Guards). Two days later No 4 Company (Major Jack Hamilton) advanced on Mull, crossing a causeway and fighting through the farm against *1222nd Grenadier Regiment* (*180th Infantry Division*) with No 1

[69] Horrocks: *A Full Life* by Lieutenant General Sir Brian Horrocks, London, 1960 page 250. Battle Honours **The Reichswald** and **Cleve**.

[70] Battle Honour **Moyland**. Lieutenant Woodall was awarded the MC for his actions.

Company (Major David Kennard) on the right, straddling the Dutch-German border. A deep anti-tank ditch delayed the attackers and they 'lost the barrage', but many German strongpoints, concrete 'haystacks' camouflaged with straw, were unoccupied. Most of the supporting Welsh Guards tanks bogged down, but No 3 Company (Captain Derek Eastman) proceeded to take two more farms. Colonel Roddy congratulated the Battalion in the *Brussels Sprout* – 5th Coldstream equivalent of *Medjez Mail* – "for having fought such a fine battle". The Battalion took 154 prisoners ("our third best bag") at a cost of thirteen dead and twenty-eight wounded, and remained at Mull for five days, supplied by amphibious vehicles. One Guardsman found a draught horse and cart, and returned to his platoon "laughing like mad" having been asked for a lift by the Commanding Officer. During this period a Coldstreamer was hit by machine-gun fire:

> "My Army torch held at the exit wound lit up the whole of his thoracic cavity most beautifully as seen through the entrance," Captain John Ingram RAMC later wrote, "but the heart was still beating. I thought that he would be bound to die, but we got to work on him and I heard he was out riding horses in England quite soon."[71]

Goch and the Hochwald, February–March 1945. 4th (Tank) Battalion

Five miles further east, on 18 February, XXX Corps attacked Goch with three divisions, 6th Guards Tank Brigade again supporting 15th Scottish. Two days later 227th Highland Brigade and **4th Coldstream** attacked German Paras at Buchholt (east of Goch) capturing 150 prisoners, despite heavy shelling. The tanks moved into woods near Schloss Kalbeck, but three soon 'bogged' in drainage ditches. Captain Ralph Tennyson-d'Eyncourt, the ever-cheerful Technical Adjutant affectionately known as 'Uncle Tinker', who had worked tirelessly on the Groesbeek–Frasselt road, came up, was wounded twice, but continued to direct operations. He died of wounds shortly afterwards; Colonel Billy Smith described him as "one of the best officers the Regiment ever had".[72]

German counter-attacks on the 23rd brought Coldstream Churchills forward again and No 3 Squadron advanced towards the Goch–Wesel railway. After close-quarter fighting, the tanks returned to Cleve; sadly 'Cuckoo' the Panther had to be abandoned as beyond repair.

By 22 February the Allies had taken the Cleve–Goch area and Montgomery launched the American offensive towards Wesel (Operation GRENADE). General Crerar's Canadians attacked the Hochwald-Balbergerwald feature – the 'Layback' – while XXX Corps advanced further south. 3rd Division replaced the weary 15th Scottish and on 27 February advanced towards the Udem–Weeze road. The Grenadiers and Scots Guards fought *7th Para Division* at close range in the woods before securing the road, and 4th Coldstream advanced on 28 February to attack Kervenheim, between Kevelaer and Udem. Resolute Paras with self-propelled guns and shelling slowed the attack, which continued next day against strong opposition. No 2 Squadron supported 2nd King's Shropshire Light Infantry in the north. Lieutenant Alec Foucard dismounted several times to lead his tanks and infantry on foot under fire, enabling them to take the crossroads

[71] Letter from Dr John Ingram dated 12 Dec 95.
[72] Battle Honour **Goch**.

north of the town. Although Lieutenant Prince Melikoff's troop (No 3 Squadron) and some of 1st Norfolks entered Kervenheim from the west, *panzerfausts* and mortaring forced a withdrawal. The enemy main body departed overnight, abandoning three self-propelled guns. On 2 March the attack resumed and once again Lieutenant Foucard dismounted to locate enemy machine guns for destruction. For his outstanding gallantry and initiative he was awarded an immediate MC.[73]

The Coldstream tanks had just leaguered on 3 March when they were ordered to exploit the Scots Guards' capture of Winnekendonk (south of Kervenheim) by attacking Kappellen, to widen the gap south of the Hochwald. The Commanding Officer "imposed his personality" for two hours to shift a traffic jam, and No 2 Squadron and the King's Shropshire Light Infantry advanced. An intermediate position caused delay, but No 1 Squadron and 2nd Royal Warwicks entered Kappellen next day. General Horrocks was determined to exploit further and on 4 March passed the Irish Guards (5th Guards Brigade) through 4th Coldstream, who refitted near Winnekendonk having been in action for twenty out of twenty-six days – a remarkable feat. It had lost five killed and forty-four wounded, but had given great service to many battalions in this hard-fought battle.[74]

Bonninghardt Ridge and the Xanten–Rheinberg Road (Haus Loo), March 1945 No.1 Squadron 1st (Armoured) and 5th Battalion

The Grenadier and Irish Groups (5th Guards Brigade) encountered similar resistance to that met by 3rd Division. Two miles from Kappellen lay the wooded Bonninghardt Ridge, running from the Hochwald almost to Rheinberg. This protected General Schlemm's withdrawal route to Wesel and his 'key lateral' road for reinforcement (the Xanten–Rheinberg road). On 5 March **5th Coldstream** advanced to seize the German post at Metxekath crossroads on the Bonninghardt Ridge.

Colonel Hill led the companies through fir woods after a heavy bombardment (some of which fell short), but when the Guardsmen reached the clearing in which Metxekath – two farms – lay self-propelled and anti-tank guns from *8th Para Division* opened fire. The Guardsmen destroyed these one by one and then cleared the buildings; 105 prisoners were counted. The Battalion dug in while 32nd Guards Brigade prepared to clear Bonninghardt.

II Parachute Corps contested almost every village, but by 5 March the Canadians were closing on Veen; the Guards Armoured Division was poised to attack off Bonninghardt Ridge; their neighbour 52nd (Lowland) Division was set to assault Alpen, on the Geldern–Wesel road; and the Americans had reached Rheinberg. On 7 March the Scots-Welsh Guards Group advanced from Bonninghardt towards the railway line which ran parallel to the Xanten–Rheinberg road. 5th Coldstream, with No 1 Squadron of the 1st Battalion under Major Jeffrey Darell, was to pass through to cut the Xanten–Rheinberg road. On the right, north of Alpen, lay Haus Loo, a large farm

73 Private James Stokes of the 2nd Bn King's Shropshire Light Infantry, which, supported by No 2 Squadron, attacked Kervenheim from the north, was posthumously awarded the Victoria Cross for his gallantry in this battle. The *Panzerfaust* was a simple, hand-held, short-range (up to 80 yards) anti-tank rocket with a shaped charge warhead which could penetrate the frontal armour of Churchill and Sherman tanks. Lieutenant Foucard's citation states: ". . . as a result of his great energy, determination and personal example, he was solely responsible for the success of the operation".

74 Battle Honour **Hochwald**.

defended by a company from *19th Para Regiment* (*7th Para Division*) with self-propelled guns, and a moated earthwork, which dominated the vital Xanten–Rheinberg Geldern–Wesel crossroads.

General Adair told Colonel Hill that:

> "There was no question of the 5th Battalion being asked to attack until Haus Loo had been attacked by a neighbouring [52nd Lowland] Division. A few hours later [Colonel Hill] was told that [that] was taking too long and other formations on the left and right could be delayed no longer. We had to go that afternoon."

H Hour was set at 1430 hours on 9 March and the Coldstream Group descended the escarpment concealed by dust and haze. As always, Bob Tomlinson, long-time Padre to 5th Coldstream, was on the start line, encouraging the troops and prepared for his tireless bravery with the stretcher-bearers: his calling was an example and comfort to all. A heavy bombardment was fired with Haus Loo being 'smoked off', and Nos 1 and 2 Companies crossed the start line, a railway embankment. The tanks had difficulty crossing this but they were able to catch up with the infantry. Mines and heavy fire from Haus Loo caused casualties to the tanks and to No 2 Company on the right.

The 4th King's Own Scottish Borders had been fighting towards Haus Loo for some hours under heavy fire. One wrote: "The Guards came up on the left and attacked magnificently, taking very heavy punishment. However, with tank support they managed to get forward and clear up some houses on the left." Coldstream tanks 'softened up' various machine-gun posts, allowing the Borderers to assault Haus Loo itself. The Coldstream met considerable resistance from the Xanten road, but the Guardsmen fought through the houses before going firm on a track beyond, under heavy artillery fire for over three hours, thought by many to be the heaviest shelling the Battalions experienced during the campaign. The other companies came up; Colonel Roddy went round the positions oblivious to the shellfire, impressing everyone who saw him. That night the Group returned to Bonninghardt: they had lost thirteen killed and thirty-eight wounded, but had taken 128 prisoners.

Around midnight two huge explosions were heard as the Wesel bridges were demolished. The battle was witnessed and described by several War Correspondents and *The Times* mentioned in a leading article a Regiment by name for the first time in the war (as censorship was lifted):

> "The Coldstream Guards advanced under a hail of fire from front and flanks, some of it directed from houses not 100 yards distant. . . . The men who met and beat the Parachutists were nurtured on drill and discipline, minor tactics, and the honour and duty of a guardsman. They have carried their courage and efficiency into many campaigns of the war, but they have borne along with it their good behaviour and friendliness. Their pride is a wholesome tonic, devoid of arrogance."[75]

The Coldstream Group had cut General Schlemm's 'key lateral' and rendered the remaining German defence west of the Rhine untenable; the Rhineland battle, fought in terrible conditions – sometimes resembling Passchendaele – was over.

[75] Blazon **Rhineland.** Letter from Colonel E.R.Hill DSO 27 Apr 95. *War History of the 4th (Border) Battalion The King's Own Scottish Borderers* by Captain F.H.Coutts, Minden, 1945 page 143. *The Times* 23 Mar 45. Major Darell and Lieutenant the Hon Peter Strutt (No 2 Company) received the MC; Major Kennard (No 1 Company) was awarded a bar to his MC (won leading the 3rd Coldstream anti-tank platoon on Ruweisat Ridge in Jul 42). Sergeant F.Onions of No 1 Squadron was awarded the MM.

1. Coldstreamers at sea (from a painting by R. Wymer).

2. Watermanship training, 1794 (from a painting by R. Wymer).

3. Coldstreamers on Horse Guards Parade in 1821 (from a painting by Denis Dighton).

4. Her Majesty The Queen and Prince Philip attending the Bicentenary Dinner of the Nulli Secundus Club in 1983. In the centre is the Regimental Lieutenant Colonel, Colonel M.W.F. Maxse. To the right is the Colonel of the Regiment, Major General Sir George Burns.

5. An early Bank Picquet.

6. Drum Major in State Dress 1893.

7. Coldstream Musicians circa 1830.

8. Guard Mounting at St James's Palace, 1840 (from a painting by R. Wymer).

9. Coldstream Guardsmen at Waterloo Barracks, Tower of London, 1905 (from a painting by R. Wymer).

10. Lieutenant Colonel J. V. Campbell, Commanding Officer of the 3rd Battalion, winning the Victoria Cross at the Battle of the Somme on 15 September, 1916 (from a painting by R. Caton-Woodville).

11. Company Sergeant Major Peter Wright winning the Victoria Cross, Salerno, 25 September 1943.

12. Captain Ian Liddell winning the Victoria Cross on the bridge at Altenlingen, 3 April 1945.

13. May 1990. Colonel E. R. Hill, Commanding Officer 5th Battalion 1944/45, describing the action of Captain Ian Liddell winning the Victoria Cross. On Colonel Hill's left is Captain R. P. Laurie, who was a Platoon Commander in Captain Liddell's Company at the time.

14. 2nd Battalion Recce Platoon picketing Khuraibah Pass up to Dhala, Aden 1964-65.

15. 2nd Battalion Company Camp at Dhala, Aden 1964-65.

16. The Officers of the 2nd Battalion on the occasion of Their Majesties' visit to Wellington Barracks on 9 May 1985. Back Row; left to right: 2nd Lieutenants F. R. Batt, J. E. J. N. Giles, Lieutenants A. W. Fortescue, N. C. Deterding, R. F. Allhusen, Captain R. Watson, Lieutenants R. G. Drax, R. L. W. Frisby, C. E. Perry, 2nd Lieutenants C. J. C. Henty, W. J. Tower, B. R. Osborn-Smith. Middle Row; left to right: Rev. J. N. Thomas, Lieutenant Colonel R. D. George, R.A.M.C., Captains E. T. Nicholls, A. J. B. Johnston, H. R. L. Parker, B. B. Smart, H. C. Barratt, (Q.M.), C. J. Louch, J. J. C. Bucknall, J. J. S. Bourne-May, B. Mather, Major G. A. Fyfe R. A. P. C. Seated; left to right: Majors A. F. Matheson, J. M. Turner-Bridger, Sir Ralph Anstruther Bt., E. M. Crofton, Her Majesty The Queen, Lieutenant Colonel R. J. Heywood, Her Majesty Queen Elizabeth The Queen Mother, Majors R. N. F. Sweeting, I. H. McNeil, D. D. S. A. Vandeleur.

The Rhine Battles and Advance on Münster, March–April 1945. 4th (Armoured) Battalion

Operation VARSITY was launched on 23 March with assault crossings of the Rhine and airborne drops north of Wesel. General optimism and a feeling that the war could not last much longer followed. One Coldstream Officer in the Guards Armoured Division wrote, "We are keen to be flung in, so as to race across Germany. Lead on. It is a terrific feeling. Really after six years it is coming to an end. Roll on victory."[76]

The retitled 6th Guards (Armoured) Brigade was to link up with the airborne forces. **4th Coldstream** teamed up with 3rd Bn US 513th Parachute Regiment in 17th US Airborne Division. The landings were successful and 4th Coldstream was not called forward until 26 March; next day orders were given to capture Münster, fifty miles away. On the 28th the Coldstream took the lead and, with American parachutists on their Churchills, drove from Dorsten, along the River Lippe towards Haltern. Infantry with 88mm guns were encountered at Lippramsdorf, but Colonel Billy Smith sent No 2 Squadron round to the north, where Sergeant S.K.Wheeler destroyed several 88s, and the squadrons made for Haltern, which No 1 Squadron reached round 2100 hours.

The Lippe bridges had been demolished and the Commanding Officer ordered No 3 Squadron to advance on Dülmen, seven miles away; "Münster or bust" was the cry. Finding the way out of Haltern was difficult and Lieutenant Peter Stannard found himself behind a Panther; he destroyed it from the rear, but this blocked the road! Despite isolated shooting, Dülmen, in ruins from bombing, was reached at 0800 hours. The American Paras cleared the town and the tank crews snatched some sleep. At 0300 hours on 30 March No 2 Squadron left for Buldern, where the tanks were ambushed at close range. Once again the Americans and Coldstream tanks cleared the village, a process that took eight hours. At 1700 hours Colonel Smith ordered No 1 Squadron, and the fresh 1st Bn 513th Para, to carry on, but a Panther and self-propelled guns blocked the route. After a 'stonk' the Squadron pressed on to Appelhülsen and took the defenders by surprise.

With the Scots Guards moving parallel further north, Colonel Smith pushed forward on 31 March to Albachten. Numerous Germans, many *Volksturm* (troops too young or too old for regular service), defending roadblocks were encountered. Albachten was shelled and No 3 Squadron drove in, spending 1 April (Easter Day) there. The Group continued that evening, but, meeting serious resistance from 88mm Flak batteries, Colonel Smith halted to plan an assault on Münster.

Next day a messenger arrived from a German battery offering to surrender and Captain Graham Montague Jones negotiated the capitulation of the garrison; but the Commandant received a *Führerbefehl* – Hitler's order – to fight to the last round. It was agreed that the "massive" planned attack should be delayed; the Coldstream later entered Münster from the south-west, while the Scots Guards, both with their American Parachutists, advanced from the north. The Coldstream cleared southern Münster without a casualty. Colonel Billy Smith was talking to Captain Christopher Schofield, the Adjutant, when several Germans in unfamiliar uniforms approached with their hands up, before pleading for mercy on their knees. They proved to be postal workers who believed that the Allies would shoot everyone in uniform on sight!

6th Guards Brigade Group had achieved a tremendous advance in six days, 4th Coldstream losing only three men killed, twenty-six wounded and eleven missing. Co-operation with 513th Regiment

[76] Diary of Lieutenant the Hon Robert Boscawen MC 28 Mar 45.

had been excellent: the Guardsmen were sad to see them go. The Coldstream occupied Hermann Goering Barracks and enjoyed the contents of a nearby brewery, between tank maintenance periods, for three days.[77]

The Rhine to the Ems, and Lingen, March–April 1945. 1st (Armoured) and 5th Battalions

The **1st Battalion** waited near Tilburg, Nijmegen and Goch during the Reichswald battles, but, apart from No.1 Squadron, was not committed. One Battalion innovation was to add RAF Typhoon rockets to their Shermans to increase firepower. **5th Coldstream** had meanwhile provided a guard for Queen Wilhelmina of the Netherlands. On 29 March the Guards Armoured Division was ordered to advance from Rees through Groenlo to Enschede and on to Bremen and Hamburg. Next day 1st/5th Coldstream crossed the Bailey pontoon bridge at Rees and reached Dinxperloo, before moving to Lictenvoorde and Neede, where they met resistance.

The next obstacle was the Twente Canal linking Hengelo and Enschede, which was thought to be strongly held. When the Household Cavalry Regiment reported an intact bridge between the towns Lieutenant Colonel Gooch ordered No 2 Squadron under Major Jimmy Priestley to seize the crossing. The squadron found itself on the canal bank under heavy fire and Lieutenant Ian Jardine's troop rushed the Lonneker bridge, only to be engaged by four 105mm Flak guns to their rear; the bridge exploded and tanks were hit on both sides of the canal. Dutch Resistance men had earlier counted some 200–250 Germans there, many from *7th Para Division*. 5th Coldstream and No 1 Squadron (Major Darell) later attacked western Enschede, advancing in battle order through a town among civilians in their best clothes going to Easter Services. The citizens cheered their liberators; the occupied Netherlands had almost starved since Arnhem and in Enschede people had been summarily executed in the street only minutes before the Guardsmen attacked. No 1 Squadron destroyed resistance at Twente Airfield and cut the Rotterdam–Bremen road, taking twenty-eight prisoners.[78]

Captain Ian Liddell VC

The Scots-Welsh Group reached Lingen on 2 April, finding the bridges destroyed. The Coldstream were north of the town while 3rd Division prepared to cross the River Ems and Dortmund–Ems canal; an undamaged bridge over the river was then discovered. Reconnaissance revealed a road-block with 500lb bombs for demolition on the bridge, three 88s with smaller guns and an infantry company on the far bank. After careful planning, at 1630 hours a sudden, unadjusted artillery barrage burst on the enemy and Major Peter Hunt's No 3 Squadron opened fire with tank guns, Typhoon rockets and machine guns from a wooded rise 500 yards from the Ems, covering No 3 Company's advance. The defenders were queuing for food when the shells landed.

Captain Ian Liddell, the Company Commander, rushed forward, climbed the ten-foot roadblock and, despite intense fire, cut the wires to the charges both on top of the bridge and underneath. The Germans were completely taken by surprise as Captain Liddell charged, leading his whole company;

[77] Battle Honour **The Rhine**. The Hermann Goering Barracks was renamed Oxford Barracks and was home to the 1st Bn Coldstream Guards from 1991–98. Postal workers: letter from Captain Christopher Schofield 5 Oct 99.

[78] *De Bevrijding van Enschede* by A.M.Roding, Enschede, 1990. Lieutenant Jardine was awarded an immediate MC.

having lost his Thompson submachine gun, he hurled the wire-cutters at a nearby German. The platoons were clearing the far bank when Captain Nico Collin brought his tank up and, encouraging it as he might a racehorse, charged the roadblock, which eventually gave way. The tanks then crossed the bridge. As Guardsman Laws said:

> "All the time [Captain Liddell] was on the bridge Jerry was firing everything he had. How he came through all that firepower unhurt was a miracle. At one time he was a sitting target about twenty yards from the nearest gun and the same from a bazooka, whom we finished off when we crossed. His heroic act inspired all of us that saw it."

Captain Ian Liddell and Sergeants in the street at Lingen, April 1945.

After this magnificent gallantry, fifty prisoners were taken, and forty Germans lay dead. Coldstream casualties were one killed and four wounded. General Adair appeared and said to Captain Liddell that he could be awarded an immediate DSO, or his name could be forwarded to the King for a Victoria Cross; he replied, "The latter, Sir". General Horrocks visited 'Ian's Bridge' next day. Ian Liddell was awarded the Victoria Cross for his outstanding action, although, tragically, he was killed eighteen days later, before the award was announced. Lieutenant Colonel Gooch received the DSO.

Lingen was still occupied and, as 3rd Division crossed the Dortmund–Ems canal, 5th Coldstream cleared the town. A large barracks was attacked, but the tanks were held up and Sergeant Norman Duckworth fought his platoon resolutely among the blocks against heavy machine-gun fire. He personally took command of a section before outflanking a strongpoint and forcing its surrender, courage that resulted in the award of a Military Medal. Over 200 prisoners were taken.[79]

[79] Battle Honour **Lingen**. Citation: *A Distant Drum* pages 197–8. Viscount Ridley (former No 3 Squadron Troop Commander) letter Apr 95. Captain Liddell and Sergeant Duckworth tried to roll the bombs, which had no tail-fins, into the river, but were unable to do so. The bridge at Altenlingen (three miles from the centre of Lingen) was rebuilt in 1993 higher and with a slightly different alignment, but the line of the old bridge and its eastern approach (parallel to the river) are easily discernible.

On 3 Apr 1995 a commemoration and TEWT was held at Ian's Bridge, attended by several Coldstreamers who had fought there 50 years before; the German positions, and Coldstream tank track marks, were evident, and ammunition boxes were found in the undergrowth. Newsreel film of Coldstream tanks crossing the bridge in 1945 and of Ian Liddell with his Platoon Commanders and Sergeants in the street in Lingen exists in the Imperial War Museum.

Lingen to Stade, April–May 1945. 1st (Armoured) and 5th Battalions

On 6 April the Coldstream Group cleared resistance at Remsel and advanced on Thuine, Guardsmen riding on 1st Battalion tanks. A strike by Typhoons shattered the defence at Thuine. The Coldstream were then sent to assist the Scots/Welsh Group in Lengerich. Moving across country, they liberated a prisoner of war camp, including some Guardsmen, before cutting off the town. The infantry cleared some woods; by evening Lengerich had fallen, with 111 prisoners.

Roadblocks delayed progress on 9 April and the next village, Berge, proved strongly held. Colonel Hill again arranged for Typhoons, artillery and mortars, and No 2 Squadron (Major Priestley) attacked using Typhoon rockets, only to lose tanks to *panzerfausts*. The tanks withdrew, but 'shot in' the infantry, who cleared the village house by house, although tracer rounds set the buildings and strongpoints alight. The defenders, *7th Para* again, had orders to defend Berge to the last round; when it fell 100 were dead and a similar number were marched away to captivity.

On 11 April the Coldstream Group was ordered to seize crossings over the River Hase at Boen. The companies were very exposed in the flat landscape and Colonel Hill therefore planned an assault crossing. News came of a damaged footbridge a mile further east and No 4 Company crossed this before advancing to Boen on the far bank. Despite resistance in the woods, the other companies followed and the attack on Boen was launched that evening. The Parachutists defended with determination and two hours of heavy fighting followed. Snipers remained active for some time. The capture of Boen was a notable success; the Coldstream took 200 prisoners, but at a cost of forty men.

Several days were spent 'mopping up' around Emstek before the Division joined XII Corps, clearing between the Elbe and the Weser. The Coldstream drove ninety miles to Eilsdorf, south-east of Bremen, on 17 April and next day attacked Neuenkirchen, before joining the Scots-Welsh Group in action at Visselhovede two days later. The Coldstream Group cleared Tewel and Deepden, north of Neuenkirchen, but at Westersede the Burgomeister surrendered his town, and at Scheesel the Burgomeister agreed to capitulate and sat on the leading Coldstream tank clutching a white flag.

Rotenburg was more resolutely defended. On 21 April No 3 Squadron and No 3 Company attacked a level crossing to secure the brigade start line. Although successful, as the Company advanced Captain Ian Liddell was fatally wounded by a sniper's bullet and died shortly afterwards. The Brigade took Rotenburg next day, 5th Coldstream and No 1 Squadron entering from the north.

The Coldstream then supported 5th Guards Brigade, who had met strong opposition from *15th Panzergrenadier Division* at Zeven fifteen miles further north. The Coldstream were shelled while forming up for the attack and several officers were wounded. The infantry were supported by 'Wasp' flamethrowers (the only occasion the 5th Battalion used them) and once a *Jagdpanther* and defended houses on the outskirts were destroyed there was little resistance. The Coldstream 'mopped up' around Zeven for some days before cutting withdrawal routes north-east of Bremen.

As VIII Corps neared Hamburg the Guards Armoured Division was directed to clear the west bank of the Elbe. On 30 April the Coldstream moved to Hellenburg, twenty miles west of Hamburg. The Guardsmen were warned to take no undue risks and the Group advanced, hindered by mines, including large sea mines, clearing Stade on 1 May and Himmelpforten next day. The 1st and 5th Coldstream were near Stade when, at 2300 hours on 3 May, news of the capitulation arrived; the following day 5th Battalion undertook its last action, taking the village of Hechthausen. At 0800 hours on 5 May the unconditional surrender of Germany and the ceasefire took effect.

Münster to Hamburg, April–May 1945.
4th (Armoured) Battalion

On 6 April **4th Coldstream** left Münster to rejoin 15th Scottish and, after an awful five-day journey, joined 46th Brigade advancing on Celle. They reached Ramlingen at dusk and attacked a group of fanatical officer cadets, who destroyed some tanks with *panzerfausts*. The Scots Guards, on another route, occupied Celle, a historic and largely undamaged town. 15th Scottish advanced north through extensive woods, 4th Coldstream becoming involved in a sharp fight with *SS* troops at Unterluss. The advance continued on 14 April and many Germans were captured; several prisoner of war and forced labour camps were liberated in this area of munitions factories and dumps.

That night No 3 Squadron, 2nd Glasgow Highlanders, and two artillery batteries harboured in Stadensen, near Uelzen. Around 0200 hours German half-tracks and self-propelled guns from *Panzerdivision Clausewitz* drove in and close-quarter fighting followed, with the 25-pounders firing over open sights. Two Churchills were destroyed and trucks and houses were ablaze before the defenders gained the upper hand; hours of house clearing followed. Around dawn, 0600 hours, the Germans withdrew. Their vehicles were picked off by tanks and anti-tank guns; they lost twelve self-propelled guns, seven half-tracks, fifty dead and 150 prisoners. The Coldstream had three dead and three wounded, while the Highlanders lost forty killed and sixty missing – and their transport.

Coldstream squadrons found several abandoned half-tracks as they cleared Nettelcamp before attacking Uelzen on 17 April. The initial break-in was successful and next day Typhoons and

"The Special Relationship". 4th Battalion and US 513th Parachute Regiment near Dülmen in March 1945.

artillery preceded 46th Brigade. Coldstream Churchills destroyed self-propelled guns and strongpoints as the Scotsmen cleared the town house by house until 1730 hours. On 20 April the Coldstream escorted 46th Brigade to the Elbe before concentrating at Altenmedingen.[80]

15th Scottish assaulted across the Elbe on 29 April. The river was bridged, despite attacks from heavy railway guns and jet aircraft. The Coldstream crossed the bridge next day, but 'A' Echelon was hit by shells and, amid burning trucks, Padre Tony Tremlett, affectionately known as Trubshaw, tended the wounded. On 1 May 15th Scottish moved into the Sachsenwald and Fahren Hills east of Hamburg, clearing Fahrendorf, Dassendorf and Hohenhorn of marines and U-boat crews; resistance was brief. Next day emissaries of the German Commander-in-Chief approached Lieutenant Peter Revell-Smith asking to see Field Marshal Montgomery to arrange surrender terms.

On 3 May the Army was ordered to stand fast, but the 4th Coldstream Second-in-Command, Major Arthur Pilkington, took a 'patrol' into Hamburg to find wine for the Officers' Mess. With Padre Tremlett and Reconnaissance Troop vehicles the patrol reached Hamburg and a War Correspondent took them to the Stadthaus where General Kehrle and the Burgomeister were waiting to hand over the city. After discussions and photographs with the German officers, the patrol continued (finding some wine); later the Press published pictures of Hamburg being liberated by "Major Polkington [sic] of the Guards Armoured Division"!

Victory in Europe, May–June 1945. 1st, 4th and 5th Battalions

The reactions of many to the ceasefire and victory were muted. This overwhelming news – the successful conclusion of six years of total war in Europe – and all that had meant for people – took time to sink in. It was uncertain whether all German troops would stop fighting. The Guards Armoured Division arranged the surrender of *Corps Ems* but found *7th Parachute Division* moving through to fight the Russians. Eventually *7th Para* agreed to surrender, but only to the Guards Armoured Division. **5th Coldstream**, who had met *7th Para* at Venraij and fought them from Wesel to the Elbe, went to Cuxhaven airfield where Colonel Menzel reviewed his men before Colonel Roddy Hill marched the officers and then the soldiers – some of the *Wehrmacht's* finest – into captivity.

On 6 May **4th Coldstream** moved "to impress the German Navy and the people of Kiel with a display of smartness and of armoured might". Two days later – Victory in Europe (VE) Day – the Battalion drove "majestically" through devastated Kiel, watched in "awed silence". Soon afterwards the Battalion, manning a prisoner reception area, saw 2000 well-disciplined Germans approaching, led by a striking figure. On meeting Coldstreamers, Colonel Hubner addressed *24th Para Regiment* (*8th Para Division*), "We are proud to be able to surrender to the *Sexte Britische Guards Panzerbrigade*, worthy opponents on several occasions," before marching them into captivity too.[81]

Farewell to Armour

It was appreciated, soon after the surrender, that the Guardsmen would revert to the infantry role before long and a 'Farewell to Armour' parade was held on 7 June at Rotenburg airfield. The Battalions, with detachments from 6th Guards Armoured Brigade (about to lose their Churchills)

[80] Battle Honour **Uelzen**.
[81] War Diary 4th Bn Coldstream Guards May 1945. Major General Ronnie Buckland 25 Oct 99.

Farewell to Armour Parade, 7 June 1945. In the foreground are the crews of the 1st Battalion. Field Marshal Montgomery is in the inspecting vehicle.

were reviewed by Field Marshal Montgomery. The tanks drove off and their crews rejoined their comrades before the new 'Guards Division' came to Attention. The Field Marshal then addressed the parade, paying the Guardsmen, and General Allan Adair, a great tribute:

> "In modern war it is the co-operation of all Arms, armoured and unarmoured, that wins the battle, and in this respect you have achieved great results. In fact, the Guards have shown that whatever they are asked to do, whatever they take on, they do well; they maintain always the highest standards and give a lead to all others. Now you are to return to your traditional role of infantry. The infantry arm . . . is the most versatile of all the arms; nothing can be done without infantry and there is never enough for the tasks that have to be done. We need you in the infantry; we need your high standards, your great efficiency in all matters and your old traditions of duty and service. . . . You can look back with pride on your excursion into the realms of armoured warfare, and the experience . . . gained will always be valuable to you."[82]

Before 4th Coldstream handed over its Churchills it joined the King's Birthday drive through Kiel in June. The Royal Navy had taken possession of the *Luftwaffe* 100 square-metre yachts in Kiel,

[82] *The Story of the Guards Armoured Division op cit* page 302–303.

but had to turn to 6th Guards Brigade and the Royal Air Force for crews to sail them to England! The Household Brigade named its 'windfall' yacht *Gladeye* after the Eye sign.

6th Guards Tank Brigade held its final parade as an independent formation near Cologne in June, and on 10 July **5th Coldstream** paraded for the last time before General Allan Adair, although it did not disband until November 1945. **4th Coldstream** returned to the United Kingdom in July 1946 and was disbanded; the Guards Division remained until late 1946.

As well as training as infantrymen, running classes for those awaiting demobilization, guarding German prisoners, mine clearance and assisting the Customs, officers and Guardsmen undertook myriad duties. Coldstreamers worked in the Allied Military Government, the prosecution staff of the Nuremburg Trials, Civilian Relief Overseas (running hospitals for German wounded, re-patriating displaced persons and feeding children) and other organizations. Captain Michael Bendix found himself escorting a consignment of postage stamps bearing the head of Himmler rather than Hitler!

ROLL OF HONOUR 1939–45

The Regiment in 1945 numbered some 600 Officers and 11,000 Other Ranks; 17,470 men had worn a Coldstream capstar since 1939. It had lost 112 Officers and 1320 Other Ranks killed, and 200 Officers and 2538 Other Ranks wounded; some 800 of all ranks had been taken prisoner. Fifteen Officers had been awarded the DSO and 75 Officers and Warrant Officers the MC. Fourteen Distinguished Conduct Medals were won and 114 Military Medals; 332 Coldstreamers were Mentioned in Despatches. Sergeant Clifford Lowe was awarded the George Medal and Brigadier Arthur Nicholls the George Cross for leading the Military Mission in Albania. Captain Ian Liddell and Company Sergeant Major Peter Wright both received the Victoria Cross for their outstanding gallantry. The Regiment was awarded fifty-five Battle Honours for the Second World War, ten of them emblazoned on the Colours.[83]

Note on Author

Lieutenant Colonel Hugh Boscawen was commissioned into the Regiment in 1976, following a long and distinguished line of his family into the Regiment. He commanded the 1st Battalion from 1994–1996. He is co-author of *Design for Military Operations: the British Military Doctrine* and is currently MA to the United Nations Secretary General's Special Representative in Kosovo.

[83] For the detailed Roll of Honour and statistics see *The Coldstream Guards 1920–46 op cit* page 381 *et seq.*

CHAPTER EIGHT

SPECIAL FORCES

by Peter Stewart-Richardson

Introduction

The Second World War saw the birth of many new and varied 'special forces'. Most of them survived only 'for the duration', while others, such as the SAS and the Parachute Regiment, continued as part of the post-war army. Most of them were instigated initially by Winston Churchill as Prime Minister and Minister of Defence in the dark days of 1940 when we were in no position to take any significant offensive action against the enemy. Small-scale operations by specially trained troops were the only way in which we could hit back.

The 'special forces' created during the war all proved their worth to varying degrees, but the principle always aroused controversy, as to whether it really paid off to attract the best officers and men away from their units to join such forces, as opposed to using Regular units to do the tasks required. It is an argument that continues today. It should also be remembered that, brave as the men of the 'special forces' were, the soldiers in conventional units who crossed the Start Line time and time again on standard operations were just as gallant, but they tend to receive less publicity.

The Coldstream Guards contributed to ten of the 'special forces' in 1940–45, which were:

1. The Ski Battalion for Finland
2. The Coats Mission
3. Chequers Guard
4. Commando Forces
5. The Glider Pilot Regiment
6. The Special Air Service (SAS)
7. The Long Range Desert Group (LRDG)
8. The Special Boat Squadron (SBS)
9. Special Operations Executive (SOE)
10. Military Intelligence 9 (MI9)
11. The Parachute Regiment

THE SKI BATTALION FOR FINLAND, 1940

In August 1939 the Soviet Union signed an 'unholy alliance' with Nazi Germany and soon threatened the Baltic States. Finland defiantly refused to meet the Russian demands and was

promptly invaded. The small Finnish Army put up a most gallant defence, but was totally outnumbered and the Allies decided to send them military aid. France offered her Chasseurs Alpins and Britain earmarked two infantry divisions; but it was felt that a unit trained in winter warfare was essential, however small, and so was formed the 5th (Special Reserve) Battalion Scots Guards.

This was a supreme example of improvisation, for it was decided that, rather than employ a conventional, trained infantry battalion, the War Office would form a unit from already experienced skiers. So during January and February 1940 volunteers with ski experience were called for from units worldwide, while a headquarters and advance party was set up by the Brigade of Guards at Quebec Barracks, Bordon.

Command of the Battalion, (which soon became known as 'The Snowballers') was given to a Coldstreamer, Major Jimmy Coats MC[1]. He was told to have his battalion ready and equipped for overseas service by 1 March, twenty-three days in which to assemble, organize, equip, inoculate and train a body of men not only from all ranks of the Army, but from civilian life as well, who had never served together before.

Around 1000 individuals volunteered, 600 of whom were officers; many were weeded out early on as unsuitable, and the difficult task then began of selecting the officers and NCOs for the unit. One problem was that there were many more officers among the volunteers than there were officers appointments in the battalion and, once the few vacancies had been filled, the remainder had to be invited to relinquish their commissioned rank and serve in the ranks.

Many declined the terms and left, and of the 167 officers who remained five were Coldstreamers, ie Lieutenant Colonel Coats, Lieutenants Bridge, Thorny and Waken, and 2nd Lieutenant the Earl Jellicoe.

[1] Although promoted to Lieutenant Colonel for this appointment, he had to revert to his substantive rank of Major when he subsequently commanded the Coats Mission (see page 154) He won his MC in 1917.

(This page and opposite) Ski Battalion 1940.

The Battalion trained frantically to prepare itself for the strange skills of winter warfare. They were among the first troops to receive the new No 4 Rifle with the short bayonet, but it then emerged that many of the volunteers had never before handled, let alone fired, any Service rifle! Skis and boots were requisitioned from Lillywhites and other sports stores, and it was pot luck whether any of the equipment fitted!

On 2 March 1940 the Battalion embarked in the greatest secrecy for a destination supposedly known only to the Commanding Officer. Rumours as to where this was ranged from Scandinavia to the Caucasus, but they actually arrived at Chamonix in the French Alps, only to have Lord Haw Haw[2] announce the fact the next day!

The companies were billeted in local hotels awaiting the arrival of their kit which eventually appeared three days later and it was during this time that it was discovered that cooks are seldom found amongst a party of volunteer skiers. Hardly a man had ever been inside a kitchen for a useful purpose in his life and the food was inedible; indeed some of the cooks even failed to strip the hair off the horse meat issued by the French! Almost everyone ate out in Chamonix, much to the joy of the local 'patrons' whose restaurants were still open.[3]

Training continued under the 199th Battalion of the Chasseurs Alpins and great progress was made. Then on 10 March Lord Haw-Haw announced that "the 5th Battalion Scots Guards will leave Chamonix by train at 7 o'clock on the morning of the 11th".[4] It was an uncomfortable

[2] 'Lord Haw Haw' was an Irishman called William Joyce, who had some Nazi sympathies and moved from England to Germany in 1939. He broadcast propaganda over the German radio throughout the war, but was treated by the British as a national joke.

[3] The Army 'rations' included a weekly issue of two tins of fifty Gold Flake cigarettes which were worth their weight in gold. An Alpini told 270005 'Guardsman X' of the Battalion (who was in fact an officer in the Norfolk Regiment), that he could get a woman and upwards for one tin; even today, he is a chocoholic and he chose chocolates – "*chacun à son gout*".

[4] On 9 March a most secret conversation took place in Hindustani between the War Office in London and the Battalion at Chamonix concerning the departure of the Battalion – 'Lord Haw-Haw' had got it right again.

journey but made easier for some by 'Guardsman' W. Rothschild of the Scots Guards who kindly arranged for the delivery of a hamper from his family during the stop in Paris!

On 14 March the Battalion embarked on a Polish Liner, MS *Batory*, in Glasgow docks, but that same afternoon came the order to disembark and return to Bordon as the Finns had been forced to surrender; two days later the Major General visited Quebec Barracks to say that he had been ordered to disband the Battalion. The news was received with intense disappointment, but it was perhaps just as well that such a concentration of leadership material never went to war, particularly in a situation where the odds were very heavily weighed against them.

THE COATS MISSION, 1940–1942

One 'special force' that was almost entirely run by the Coldstream Guards was the Coats Mission, established in June 1940 as a personal bodyguard to the Royal Family. It was given the title because it was formed and commanded by Major Jimmy Coats of the Regiment, who had just three months earlier formed and commanded the short-lived Ski Battalion. He was a man of outstanding drive and determination, and was well suited to the task.

The need for such a force had become clear in June 1940 as Hitler's armies swept across Europe, occupying one country after another. The Royal Families of Norway and the Netherlands arrived in Britain in some disarray, having only just managed to escape capture by the Germans, and, with invasion threatened, the Coats Mission was formed. Its role was to guard our Royal Family at Windsor and Sandringham, escort them to and from their public engagements and, in the event of invasion, to move them to a 'safe house'. This last task was known only to the officers, and the houses selected were Newby Hall in Yorkshire, the home of a Coldstreamer, Robin Compton; Pitchford Hall in Shropshire, the home of General Sir Charles Grant, also a Coldstreamer; and Madresfield Court in Worcestershire, owned by the Beauchamp family. A secondary role was to reinforce Headquarters Fighter Command at Bentley Priory.

The force consisted of a Coldstream company with a War Establishment of five officers and 124 men, each of whom was personally interviewed by the Commanding Officer before being selected. It was formed officially on 9 October 1940 and was billeted initially at Elstree School, moving in November 1940 to Bushey. The officers were Major Coats, Captain W.G.Tatham[5], an Eton housemaster, and three subalterns, Lieutenant W.S.Thompson, Lieutenant J.L.Darell[6] and Lieutenant I.O.Liddell.[7]

Attached to the Coats Mission was an armoured car troop from the 12th Lancers, equipped with four 1920 Rolls-Royce armoured cars that were kept at the Royal Mews; but they were replaced within a week by more up-to-date vehicles. The troop was commanded by Lieutenant W.A. Morris with Sergeant Thurston MM and became known as 'the Morris Detachment'; they lived initially in Wellington Barracks and, when The King and Queen moved to Windsor, they were put into the Household Cavalry Barracks there. Their primary task was to escort The King and Queen whenever they moved by road.

[5] He won the MC in the First World War

[6] He later won a MC

[7] He later won a Victoria Cross.

A second troop, from the 2nd Northamptonshire Yeomanry, was quartered in the stables at Windsor Castle, under Lieutenant Michael Tomkin, who later won the MC, and Lieutenant Michael Humble-Crofts. Their role was to escort Princess Elizabeth and Princess Margaret to the chosen 'safe house' in an emergency. Two of the armoured cars in each troop were converted to 'passenger-carrying' vehicles by removing the gun, installing a slightly more comfortable seat and putting linoleum on the floor.

Transport for the Coldstream element was provided by a Royal Army Service Corps section of twelve men under Sergeant Pritchard RASC; they drove four Leyland single-decker buses and were stationed at Bushey Golf Club near Watford. Six military policemen (among them Corporal Crofts and Corporal Day, who later won a MM in Italy) were posted for traffic control during moves and for carrying important messages. They came from the Provost Company of the 1st London Territorial Division and were commanded by Sir Malcolm Campbell who had in September 1935 achieved the world land speed record of 301 mph in his car 'Bluebird'. As a result they soon became known as 'the Bluebirds'.

Major Coats soon found that the 'Army issue' motorcycles were not up to the task and he therefore acquired by 'local purchase' some 500 cc Norton machines. The vehicle sign of a white 101 on a red background, together with a blue light on the bonnet of every vehicle, ensured that the convoys of the Coats Mission were probably the fastest and the safest in the country.

The training for the company was basic infantry training, with the mobile element practising convoy movement and emergency drills in the event of an attack; exercises were carried out frequently, concentrating on night driving and immediate reaction drills. The order of march for the Royal Escort convoys was:

Leading armoured car with the Troop Commander.
No 2 Car. The Royal Person
No 3 Car. The Equerry and a detective.
A petrol/food lorry.
Rear armoured car – Lieutenant M.Humble-Crofts and Sergeant Thurston.

The plan was that, while the armoured escort groups moved independently, the Coldstream company was to move at top speed to the designated 'safe house' to prepare it for their arrival. The nearest that this came to being put into effect was on 7 September 1940 when the codeword 'Cromwell' was received. This meant that invasion was imminent and the Coats Mission immediately loaded up and stood by for further orders. But within hours it proved to be a false alarm.

In November 1940 the first armoured limousines were delivered to replace the 'passenger-carrying' armoured cars in each troop; they were a great improvement, with bullet-proof glass, armoured side plates and special Dunlop tyres for the extra weight.

The training and fitness of the Mission was brought to a very high standard; 'Gussie' Tatham was an Olympic runner and both subalterns were high-class cricketers, while Jim Thompson was an exceptional rugby player. Captain Tatham excelled at arranging highly imaginative exercises, several of which were planned in cooperation with the American Home Guard Detachment in London, raised and commanded by Charles Sweeny. One involved 'capturing' the actress Merle Oberon, and this was entirely successful. Another one had a less happy ending!

The task this time was to 'capture' Major General Bertram Sergison-Brooke, the General Officer Commanding London District. He was known to be lunching one Sunday at Ascot and would have

Coats Mission. Coldstream Officers in the rear are: (left to right) Lieutenant W.S. Thompson, Captain M.E. Hancock, Major W.G. Tatham, Lieutenant The Hon J.T. Holland-Hibbert and Lieutenant I.O. Liddell.

an escort provided by the Americans. The Company knew his route and duly laid an ambush. No trains ran on Sunday during the war and the signalman at Datchet was persuaded to play his part by closing the gates at the level crossing at the crucial moment. The Company was concealed round the crossing and one of the Military Policemen placed an 'Unexploded Bomb' sign on one road to ensure that the General had to use the crossing.

The leading cars were allowed through and, as the General approached, the gates were shut, smoke bombs were thrown, wire was placed across the road and the escort vehicles were 'shot up'. It was a successful ambush, but as the General got out of his car choking from the smoke, he made it clear with a few well chosen words that he was not amused!

When the Royal Family stayed at Sandringham,[8] they lived at Appleton House, where there was a large bunker constructed for their safety, and the Company lived in York Cottage. By day an Observation Post was manned on the Water Tower, with a standing patrol below ready to move at a moment's notice. At night a platoon was dug in round the house, the area was patrolled, and a second platoon slept fully clothed for immediate reaction to counter any airborne attack or raid to capture the Sovereign.

[8] This occurred on five occasions: 8–13 April 1941; 1–8 July 1941; 26 September – 8 October 1941; 28 December 1941 – 4 February 1942 and 1–13 October 1942.

During the winter months of 1941 the officers enjoyed the privilege of shooting with The King and there was no shortage of volunteers from the Guardsmen to beat. On one occasion one of the guns, a senior general, jokingly ventured to suggest to The King that Army Orders forbade the employment of soldiers for beating. To which he received the reply, "General, I seem to have to remind you who owns and is Commander-in-Chief of the Army".

Everyone appreciated that The King and Queen took a great interest in the welfare of the Company and, during their visit to Sandringham over Christmas 1941, they attended the Company Pantomime produced by Ian Liddell, who was an accomplished musician.[9]

The King used also to inspect the Company before the Sunday Church Service and on one occasion had drinks with the officers and NCOs afterwards in York Cottage, when he referred to Coats Mission as "my private Army". On one inspection he 'took the name' of all those on whose capstar the cross of St George was no longer visible, due to persistent polishing!

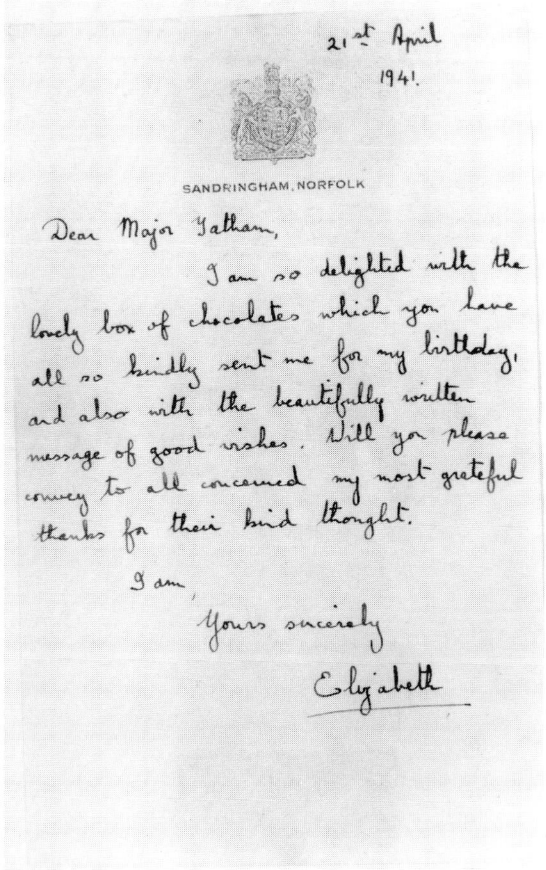

21st April
1941.

SANDRINGHAM, NORFOLK

Dear Major Yatham,

I am so delighted with the lovely box of chocolates which you have all so kindly sent me for my birthday, and also with the beautifully written message of good wishes. Will you please convey to all concerned my most grateful thanks for their kind thought.

I am,

Yours sincerely

Elizabeth

Letter to members of the Coats Mission from HRH Princess Elizabeth.

The Coats Mission continued until the threat of invasion had faded in 1942 and the Household Cavalry then took over what was after all their traditional role of providing the Sovereign's Escort. At 1000 on 10 May 1942 the Coats Mission formed up in the inner quadrangle of Windsor Castle and was inspected for the last time by The King and Queen with Princess Elizabeth and Princess Margaret present; all ranks then returned to duty with the Regiment and the official disbandment followed in a few days.

It was regarded as a very real privilege to be the personal bodyguard of the Sovereign and the Royal Family in time of war and in particular when the country was threatened with invasion. The Coats Mission was indeed a very special force, also very much 'a happy family'; it was with considerable sadness that it finally disbanded.

[9] A programme was signed by all four members of the Royal Family and is now at Regimental Headquarters. Princess Elizabeth on her fifteenth birthday received a box of chocolates with a card from all ranks of the Company and her letter of thanks is also at Regimental Headquarters.

CHEQUERS GUARD

The Coats Mission was not, however, the only VIP guard carried out by the Coldstream, for the Regiment also provided a company to protect the Prime Minister at his country residence, Chequers.[10]

There is a tale that the sentry one night saw a light blazing in one of the windows when there was a strict blackout. He shouted up, "Put out that . . . . . . light," and it was promptly extinguished. The next morning a memo from the Prime Minister was delivered to the Company Commander which read:

> "The Prime Minister presents his compliments and wishes the sentry on the garden post last night to be commended for his vigilance. The culprits were the Prime Minister and the Commander-in-Chief, Anti-Aircraft Command. The offence will not occur again."[11]

COMMANDO FORCES

Winston Churchill wrote on 18 June 1940 that "there ought to be at least 20,000 Storm Troops or Leopards drawn from existing units to spring at the throats of any small landings or descents"[12]. The 'Leopards' were planned as 'Striking Companies' and eventually emerged from the discussions as 'Commandos', ten of which were to be formed from the Regular Army and the Royal Marines. Most Commanding Officers were loath to lose their better men in this way, but Churchill insisted that there was a waiting list of volunteers to join the Commandos.

8 (Guards) Commando

8 (Guards) Commando was formed in June 1940 commanded by Lieutenant Colonel Bob Laycock with around eighty-five per cent Guardsmen, a few Royal Marines and some men from the Light Infantry. No 2 Troop, consisting mostly of Coldstreamers, was commanded by Captain Mervyn Griffith-Jones with Lieutenant the Earl Jellicoe and Second Lieutenant Ian Collins. Four Coldstreamers in the Troop, who would later be founder members of the SAS, were Jim Almonds, Pat Riley, Bob Lilley and James Blakeney.[13]

8 (Guards) Commando sailed from Glasgow on 31 January 1941 in the *Glenroy* and the *Glengyle*, together with 7 and 11 Commandos, so making up 'Z' Force. On arrival in Egypt in March 1941 they were joined by 50 and 52 Commandos, which had been in East Africa, and became Layforce. 8 (Guards) Commando did not take part in the battle for Crete, but carried out some small raids on the North African coast including a number of local operations whilst in the Tobruk Garrison where the four Coldstreamers above gained a reputation for successful special tasks and became known as the 'Tobruk Four'.

[10] The word 'Chequers' was forbidden on security grounds, and it was always referred to as the 'Special Area'.

[11] A letter to the *Daily Telegraph* dated 30 January 1965 from Captain Richard McDougall ERD who was in the company on guard at that time. As he commented, "Only a really great man could have written a letter like that." The Guardsman concerned was shown the letter and duly commended.

[12] *The Second World War* Winston Churchill, Page 147

[13] Captain Griffith-Jones later won a MC, Jim Almonds a MM and Bar, Pat Riley a DCM and Bob Lilley a BEM and MM.

2 Troop 8 (Guards) Commando. Commanded by Captain Mervyn Griffith-Jones, seen here seated between Lieutenant the Earl Jellicoe (with stick) and 2nd Lieutenant Ian Collins. The 'Tobruk Four' are numbered: 1. Jim Almonds, 2. Jim Blakeney, 3. Bob Lilley, 4. Pat Riley.

Layforce was disbanded in July 1941, as was 8 (Guards) Commando, as no suitable task could be found for them, due to lack of equipment and suitable landing craft.

Operation MUSKETOON, 1942

A most successful Commando undertaking was Operation 'MUSKETOON' in September 1942, aimed at destroying the Norwegian hydro-electric power station at Glomfjord which was supplying the power for a factory that produced much-needed aluminium for Germany's war effort. The task was carried out in such a way that the factory never again went into production.

The raiding party of twelve men included CSM Miller Smith of the Regiment, who was captured as a result of returning to the area of the engagement to give a wounded comrade morphine. Five men escaped into Sweden, but of the remaining seven, one Norwegian Commando died of wounds, six, including CSM Miller Smith, were captured and, after interrogation, were sent to Colditz where they tried unsuccessfully to escape. They were then handed over to the Gestapo in Berlin for further interrogation. After torture they were executed on 23 October 1942, in accordance with Hitler's Top Secret Commando Order to execute "all enemies on commando missions". This was despite the fact that the order was issued after the commandos were captured.

Commando Actions in the Balkans

Major Michael Stilwell CBE MC served as a Troop Commander with No 2 Commando based on the island of Vis. The aim was to retake the Dalmatian Islands and deny them to the enemy; the Commando task consisted of raids and boarding parties. On the night of 3 February 1944 Lieutenant Stilwell and six men were travelling in a Motor Torpedo Boat when they closed with a schooner that had been impressed into service with the Germans. His party lay low on the deck as the MTB drew alongside. He leapt aboard with his men, accompanied by two sailors, each armed with a cutlass. After a roughhouse seventeen disconsolate Germans surrendered; they were on their way home for leave!

He also took part in six major raids in 1944, notably on the island of Solta, capturing many prisoners, and later at Spilje in Albania. As they were waiting to withdraw with their prisoners from the former an irate woman appeared from her house. She demanded to know why the English from London and the Germans from Berlin had to come and fight over her garden and who was going to repair the wall they had knocked down.

D Day

On 3 September 1942 Guardsman Cyril Chew joined the Coldstream in which his father had served. In November 1943 he volunteered for the Commandos together with Guardsman Nicklin. On 1 January 1944 they marched in pouring rain the seven miles to Achnacarry Castle from the railway station expecting 'no bull'. They were soon disillusioned, for when they passed through the very smart entrance into the Commando Depot, they were met by RSM James and Drill Sergeant Williams, both from the disbanded 6th Battalion; the Commandant, Lieutenant Colonel Charles Vaughan, was also of the Regiment. When training was complete they were posted to No 3 Commando, commanded by Lieutenant Colonel Peter Young DSO MC, who wrote of this draft in his book, *Invasion from the Sea*; "Once again we were lucky, for among them were fifty well-trained Guardsmen".

Chew joined No 5 Troop together with six other Coldstreamers – Sergeant Crick and Guardsmen Jackson, Griffiths, Kevin, Nicklin and Paterson, but his war was to be brief. He landed on D Day with No 1 Special Service Brigade in the second wave of the assault force and described their departure from Warsash as "a most inspiring sight. There were so many ships present it felt as if the whole fleet was there, especially when each ship gave a mighty cheer as the LCIs passed, which was answered in a similar fashion". But within thirty-six hours Chew was wounded by a mine, captured and ended up in a German hospital in Paris.

Airborne Forces

After the success of the German invasion of the Low Countries in 1940 using parachutists and glider-borne troops, Churchill saw the potential of such a force, but little could be done in Britain at the time, primarily because of the serious lack of aircraft. Nevertheless, in June 1940 the Central Landing School was set up at the RAF Station, Ringway, and put under the command of the Director of Combined Operations with the task of investigating the use of parachutists and gliders in war.

Three experimental units were formed: Technical Development, a Parachute School and a Glider Training Squadron. In September 1940 it was decided to recruit glider pilots from the Army. Volunteers were called for and sent to the Training Depot at Tilshead Camp on Salisbury Plain, where they were trained to the highest standards by Regimental Sergeant Major Jim Cowley[14] of the Coldstream and Michael Briody of the Irish Guards, whose names are recorded for posterity in the Museum at Nether Wallop.

Cowley is remembered for the great work he did for the Glider Pilot Regiment in its early days and also for the story of how he took his troops on a route march one day and allowed them to fall out for a rest by a farmyard. When the time came to fall in again he gave the cautionary word of command "Battalion–nn–nn . . .". At that moment a sheepdog in the yard gave a bark and the Battalion, as one man, sprang smartly to Attention!

In May 1941, following the German seizure of Crete by airborne forces, Churchill acted and formed 1st Airborne Division, consisting of one parachute brigade and an air-landing brigade carried in gliders.

Wing Commander G.H.Briggs DFC

On 1 January 1938 Second Lieutenant Geoffrey Briggs joined the 1st Battalion at Wellington Barracks and, as a young officer, became a member of the Household Brigade Flying Club; he learned to fly a glider at the London Gliding Club at Dunstable, for which he soon showed an aptitude.

His flights started with his soldier servant, Guardsman Lock, securing the hood of his glider, seeing him airborne and then towing the trailer to the agreed RV, usually an inn; there he

'Buster' Briggs DFC and his orderly, Guardsman Lock.

[14] He later won a DCM with the 5th Battalion. He became a Major as a Quartermaster, was appointed a Military Knight of Windsor, and was awarded the OBE.

would be joined by 'Buster', as he was known, who would have given some local lad half a crown (12½ pence) to look after the glider until he returned to collect it.

When war was declared 'Buster' went to France with the 1st Battalion and returned with them via Dunkirk. The Glider Pilot Regiment was being formed in 1940 and the Air Ministry asked the Regiment to loan them Lieutenant Briggs due to his skill and experience as a glider pilot. This was agreed and he reported to Army Cooperation Command, dressed in light blue as a Pilot Officer. Here he trained soldiers to fly Tiger Moths and Hotspur gliders towed by Hector aircraft.

One day the station was visited by Air Vice Marshal 'Ugly' Barratt, who asked Briggs why he was not wearing 'wings'. On being told that he was not 'Royal Air Force qualified', he ordered him to put them up the following day. Briggs thus joined Winston Churchill as the only other 'unqualified' person to have this honour.[15]

In December 1941 RAF Training took over Army flying training and Briggs became a member of 295 Squadron as a Flying Officer. He was closely involved in Operation 'HUSKY' in July 1943, the first major British airborne operation as part of the invasion of Sicily. Briggs flew the leading aircraft towing a Horsa glider from Britain to the RAF staging post at Rabat, a distance of 1300 miles, the longest operational glider tow in history. The actual invasion called for an airlift during the period 9–15 July, and aircraft casualties were heavy, 295 Squadron ending up with only four planes intact out of twelve.[16]

Once home, Briggs commanded 298 Squadron of twenty aircraft, based at Tarrant Rushton, and trained hard for D Day, when his planes released the four gliders that had the task of seizing Pegasus Bridge, while the remainder took part in the attack on the Merville coastal battery. This was followed by Operation MARKET GARDEN at Arnhem, in which his squadron was again involved.

After three and a half years of operational flying, Briggs was now ordered to rest and went to teach at the School of Air Support at Old Sarum, and then to command 190 Squadron engaged on SOE operations. He contracted polio which affected an arm and hence his ability to fly. In 1945 he was a Wing Commander, had been awarded the Distinguished Flying Cross and had been twice mentioned in despatches. He now returned to the Coldstream Guards, with the seniority of Captain, and was invalided out of the Service, but retained his rank as a Wing Commander.

THE SPECIAL AIR SERVICE

Formation

The Special Air Service (SAS) was formed in November 1941 from the Commandos of Layforce and in particular from 8 (Guards) Commando. They were initially stationed at Kabrit on the Suez Canal, awaiting the decision on what to do with them, when Lieutenant Jock Lewes, Welsh Guards, obtained some parachutes which had been off-loaded in error at Suez. The RAF were persuaded to allow them to parachute from a Vickers Valencia, but Lieutenant David Stirling, Scots Guards, had a hard landing and spent the next two months in hospital temporarily paralysed from the waist

[15] Winston was in 1939 granted the rank of Honorary Air Commodore of 615 Squadron RAF (VR).

[16] The Chairman of the Glider Pilot Association described Briggs as "an illustrious tug pilot who behaved with considerable courage and consideration for his passengers on the 'run in' over Sicily – in stark contrast to some of the other Allied pilots – of course we knew he was in the Coldstream Guards."

down. During this time he considered how the unsuccessful raiding by the Commandos could be improved and came to the conclusion that the enemy bases and airfields the length of the North African coastline behind the lines provided ideal targets. He wrote a paper in which he advocated the use of four-to-five-men parties infiltrating from the sea by submarine and small craft or from the south in vehicles or by parachute.

As soon as he was able to walk, Stirling managed to get his paper laid before the C-in-C Middle East, General Auchinleck, who, after an interview and discussion of the plan, promoted him to Captain and told him to raise a force of sixty-five men which was to be known as 'L' Detachment 1st Special Air Service Brigade. They were tasked to drop from Bombay aircraft behind the enemy lines to attack airfields two days before the start of the 8th Army offensive, Operation CRUSADER in four months time. Stirling recruited most of his men from Layforce who were at Tobruk, knowing that they had operational experience and had trained a lot after dark. The 'Tobruk Four', Coldstreamers Jim Almonds, Pat Riley, Bob Lilley and James Blakeney, were members of 'L' Detachment from the start (see illustration p.159).

At the end of 1942 David Stirling was summoned to meet the Prime Minister, who was visiting the Middle East, and General Sir Harold Alexander, who had replaced Auchinleck as Commander-in-Chief. After this meeting 'L' Detachment was officially recognized as 1st Special Air Service Regiment with Lieutenant Colonel David Stirling as the Commanding Officer. At this time the decision was also taken to raise a second regiment.

The two SAS Regiments took part in the invasion of Italy and the fighting thereafter, until prior to the invasion of Normandy they returned to the United Kingdom and were dropped into France to arm and train the French Resistance and also to carry out offensive operations in the enemy rear areas. Between D Day and November 1944 members of the SAS (only 2000 strong) killed or seriously wounded 7753 of the enemy and took 4764 prisoners. In addition 7600 vehicles, twenty-nine locomotives and eighty-nine goods wagons were destroyed and the railway lines cut in 164 places.[17]

The Earl Jellicoe

Captain the Earl Jellicoe DSO MC

Several Coldstreamers served with distinction in the SAS and some of their exploits make impressive reading. One of the outstanding members was Captain the Earl Jellicoe of the Regiment. He spoke French fluently and was recruited into 'L' Detachment SAS as Second-in-Command by Major David Stirling to improve the administration of the unit and to liaise with the Free French unit under his command. He

[17] *This is the SAS* by Tony Geraghty – Page 30

soon joined in on operations, his first action with Stirling being to attack the German airfield at Heraklion on Crete in June 1942 together with Major Bergé and three men from the Free French Detachment attached to the SAS. They landed by submarine, sank the rubber dinghies and set off for the airfield; but there was no time for reconnaissance and they bumped into a German patrol who shot at them.

The following day they observed the target which was surrounded by a twenty-foot-wide wire fence and that night, as they were cutting their way through, they again met a German patrol. The French Sergeant was inspired – he rolled over on his back and snored; the Germans took them for drunken Cretans and moved on. They then attacked the airfield, placing Lewes bombs in about twenty-three aircraft.

It took three days to cross the island and when they were lying up at the end of the trek they were discovered by a Cretan who pretended to be friendly, but proved to be one of the very few quislings on the island and informed the Germans of their presence. Meanwhile Bergé had sent Jellicoe to recce the evacuation beach, and a little later found himself surrounded; he fought it out, losing a man killed and another wounded before he surrendered. Jellicoe was evacuated three nights later by boat to Mersa Matruh, and for this operation he was awarded the DSO.

He later took part in a number of raids of which the most effective was on the airfield at Sidi Haneish. Stirling, with seventeen jeeps, was guided to the airfield by the LRDG. Once inside the perimeter wire, he led two columns of eight jeeps, one led by Lord Jellicoe, between two rows of parked aircraft each firing at the planes on their flank, destroying between thirty and thirty-five.

Major John Edward Almonds MM and Bar

2655648 Guardsman 'Jim' Almonds, later nicknamed 'Gentleman Jim', joined the Regiment in 1932 at the age of 18 and served with the 2nd Battalion in London. On completion of his engagement he joined the Police in Bristol, but returned to the Colours in 1939 and in September 1940 volunteered for 8 (Guards) Commando, where he won his spurs operating with 'The Tobruk Four' before joining 'L' Detachment SAS.

He took part in a number of raids, which included a successful 'beat up' on the coastal road and the destruction of aircraft on the Nofilia airstrip where Lieutenant Lewes was

Sergeant 'Gentleman Jim' Almonds, 'L' Detachment, 1 SAS Cairo, 1941.

killed. Almonds had fortunately camouflaged a vehicle and had conserved some water, so he led the party back to Jalo. He then took part in raids on the Fuka area and on Sidi Haneish airfield, whereupon Stirling recommended him for the Military Medal and an Emergency Commission.

He next took part in an SAS attack on Benghazi and Tobruk, led by David Stirling. Almonds' task was to seize a ship in Benghazi harbour and sink it in the harbour mouth. Stirling ran into a manned road block and summoned Sergeant Almonds to the front. Under heavy fire Almonds broke through to reach their objectives, enabling Stirling to withdraw. The following day Almonds was captured and towed through the town in a cart manacled in chains – both wrists to a leg – and a rifle at his head to an intense interrogation. After a stretch in solitary confinement when he designed a sailing boat in his head he was moved to a camp at Altimura in Italy; following an unsuccessful escape attempt, he was moved to Ancona.

When Mussolini was deposed and the King of Italy sued for peace, the Camp Commandant gave Jim a set of civilian clothes and asked him if he would go out to report where the Germans were in the area. He did not have to be asked twice and, after a walk around, telephoned the Commandant to report that there were no Germans in the area. On being told to return to camp he declined, saying that he was going home, and made for the mountains. After travelling south for thirty-one days, he met up with an American pilot who had been shot down and they made off that night, passing through a minefield; Jim led, telling the airman to walk in his footsteps. In daylight he memorized the details of the obstacle and, when they were eventually picked up by some American soldiers at Benevento, he gave the information to their commander which undoubtedly saved lives. He was awarded a Bar to the MM and rejoined Lieutenant Colonel Paddy Mayne who had taken over 1st SAS Regiment after Stirling was captured.

Both SAS Regiments returned to England in January 1944 and Sergeant Almonds, after a spell on the Chequers Guard, rejoined 1st SAS in Scotland. Promoted to Squadron Sergeant Major (under the well known cartoonist Major Ian Fenwick), he parachuted into France in June 1944 to carry out several sabotage operations.

Once his task was complete, Almonds withdrew, but ran into the 3rd United States Army commanded by General Patton, who greeted him with the threat that if he turned out not to be British he would be shot. Before he returned home he visited Field Marshal Montgomery with Colonel Paddy Mayne, who recommended that he should be commissioned, and this was agreed on the steps of the Field-Marshal's caravan. He finished the war as a Captain with a MM and Bar and also a Croix de Guerre (Metropolitan) avec Étoile d'Argent.

When demobilized he returned to the Bristol Police, but after a short time rejoined the SAS in 1949 to serve in Malaya. He then went to train the soldiers in Ethiopia, in Eritrea and finally in West Africa under Nkrumah where he built the boat designed during 'solitary' and sailed home to live in Lincolnshire.

Major Pat Riley DCM

Guardsman Pat Riley joined the Regiment on 15 January 1934 aged 17, completed his Colour Service, was mobilized in 1939 and then joined 8 (Guards) Commando as a Sergeant. He was a member of the 'Tobruk Four' and joined the SAS as a Company Sergeant Major, to become the Regimental Sergeant Major in September 1940. Riley had a very considerable reputation in 1 SAS. He took part in the first disastrous SAS parachute operation and was one of the twenty-two men who returned to base to carry out a number of raids later, winning the DCM at Buerat. He took part with 1 SAS in the Sicily invasion when they captured a coastal battery at Marro di Porco and ended up with two other batteries under their control, capturing 600 prisoners and freeing a number of glider pilots. He fought up Italy until 1 SAS went home for D-Day when he was commissioned.

On demobilization he rejoined the Cambridgeshire Constabulary until the SAS was re-formed to operate in the jungle during the Malayan Emergency; he was promoted to Major and finally retired to the Dolphin Hotel in Colchester.

2658672 Sergeant William Duffy MM and Bar

Guardsman W.Duffy, a member of the TA, joined the Regiment in 1939. He volunteered for 8 (Guards) Commando and served with it in Tobruk. He was in 2 Troop when it destroyed the heavy gun which was causing considerable annoyance to the garrison. He joined the Special Boat Section and was in a raid against Catania airport in Sicily. He was captured, finally getting away when the Italian Government collapsed, trekking 200 miles to freedom to re-join 1 SAS.

He returned to England prior to D-Day and landed on the night 16/17 June in France. In the same D Squadron where Almonds was Squadron Sergeant Major, Duffy was in the Squadron Commander's jeep when it was ambushed. He had multiple injuries – a broken leg, jaw and fingers, a lacerated hand and blindness in his right eye for three weeks.

Sergeant W Duffy then and later.

He was taken to a hospital at Fontainebleau and, hearing of his imminent transfer to Germany, managed with the help of French nurses and cleaners to procure a German Medical Officer's uniform and cap and walked out of camp acknowledging the salutes of the sentries. He eventually found some Resistance men who took him to a doctor who attended his injuries. When the Americans reached the area he was sent to the 5th American Base Hospital where he immediately underwent surgery and was awarded the Purple Heart. He recovered completely, returned to 1 SAS and transferred to the Army Air Corps in April 1945.

26560915 WO2 Ernest Lilley BEM. MM

Guardsman Lilley joined the Regiment in 1940 aged 25, volunteering for 8 (Guards) Commando in October that year as a Guardsman. When it was disbanded he transferred to 'L' Detachment, SAS Brigade and was promoted to Lance Sergeant. He distinguished himself in a number of raids, but when returning from the raid on Beria aerodrome he was captured. Although completely unarmed he subsequently surprised and strangled his guard returning on his own to the RV. He was awarded the MM and later Mentioned in Despatches in January 1944 before 1 SAS returned to England from Italy when he was transferred to the Army Air Corps.

WO1 John Alcock

2657449 Guardsman Alcock joined the Coldstream Guards on 30 July 1936, went to France in 1939 with the 2nd Battalion and was evacuated from Dunkirk. He later joined 2 SAS and returned with them to England from Italy on 14 March 1944, where they prepared for the invasion of France.

Now an SQMS, he took part in Operation PISTOL, landing in the area south-west of Saarburg as commander of C2 patrol. They took off on the night 15/16 September 1944 and were dropped from a height of 800 feet at a place fifteen miles from the planned DZ. The following night they laid a charge which destroyed an engine with its tender and a goods truck.

The weather was appalling and one of the patrol developed malaria, so they returned to a farm where they had been welcomed previously and met a Frenchman who was on the run from the Gestapo. They left him on the 26th and met two Polish civilians who took them to a farm. The Poles left the house at midday and at one o'clock a truckload of Germans appeared, two of whom covered the rear of the building. These men soon joined their comrades at the front and the SAS party moved swiftly to a wood from which they could observe what was going on. The SQMS realized to his horror that he had left a glove and a carbine magazine at the house, which must have been found, as the Germans came out of the house towards their hiding place. They engaged them and all were seen to drop bar one, who ran for the house. They heard more transport arrive, so moved off, and to their distress heard two shots which they guessed was German retribution on the householders.

Alcock operated behind the enemy lines for over two weeks, disrupting German troop movement and gathering important information. For this operation SQMS Alcock was awarded the French Croix de Guerre.[18]

On 31 March 1946 he joined the Parachute Regiment and returned to the Coldstream Guards in February 1951. He became Regimental Sergeant Major to 3 PARA and left the Colours on 31 March 1958, but rejoined the SAS with whom he served in Borneo until his final retirement in 1960.

[18] Told by his son who has followed the route of his father's action.

The activities of Coldstreamers in the SAS since 1945 are not covered as current SAS security restrictions (as at 2000) ban any mention of SAS operations post-war, even if the information has already been published.

LONG RANGE DESERT GROUP

Napoleon is reputed to have said that deserts are the most formidable of military obstacles, but the men of the Long Range Desert Group (LRDG) proved that the North African desert could be mastered and even used to advantage. In July 1939 General Sir Archibald Wavell took over command in the Middle East with responsibility for operations in East Africa, Egypt, Palestine and the Near East. When Italy entered the war on 10 June 1940 the threat to the Middle East increased significantly and he needed to know the enemy's intentions, particularly in the Western Desert.

One answer was provided by Major Ralph Bagnold, Royal Signals, who had spent years before 1939 exploring the Libyan Desert and had imaginative ideas about long range desert operations. Wavell believed in this too and appreciated that a small body of bold men operating behind the enemy lines could influence events out of all proportion to their numbers. He interviewed Bagnold and was convinced by his proposals for a small scouting force that would penetrate deep into the

'G' Patrol at Khanga, 1941, composed of Coldstreamers and Scots Guardsmen. The Coldstreamers are:-
1. Gdsm Griffiths; 2. Gdsm Chapman; 3. Ben Waiting; 4. Jack Dennis; 5. Sid Webb;
6. Gdsm McDiarmid; 7. George Herd; 8. Ron Scoury; 9. Gdsm Stacey; 10. Bill Rogers;
11. 'Jess' Matthews; 12. Lt 'Maggie' Gibbs; 13. Jim Roberts.

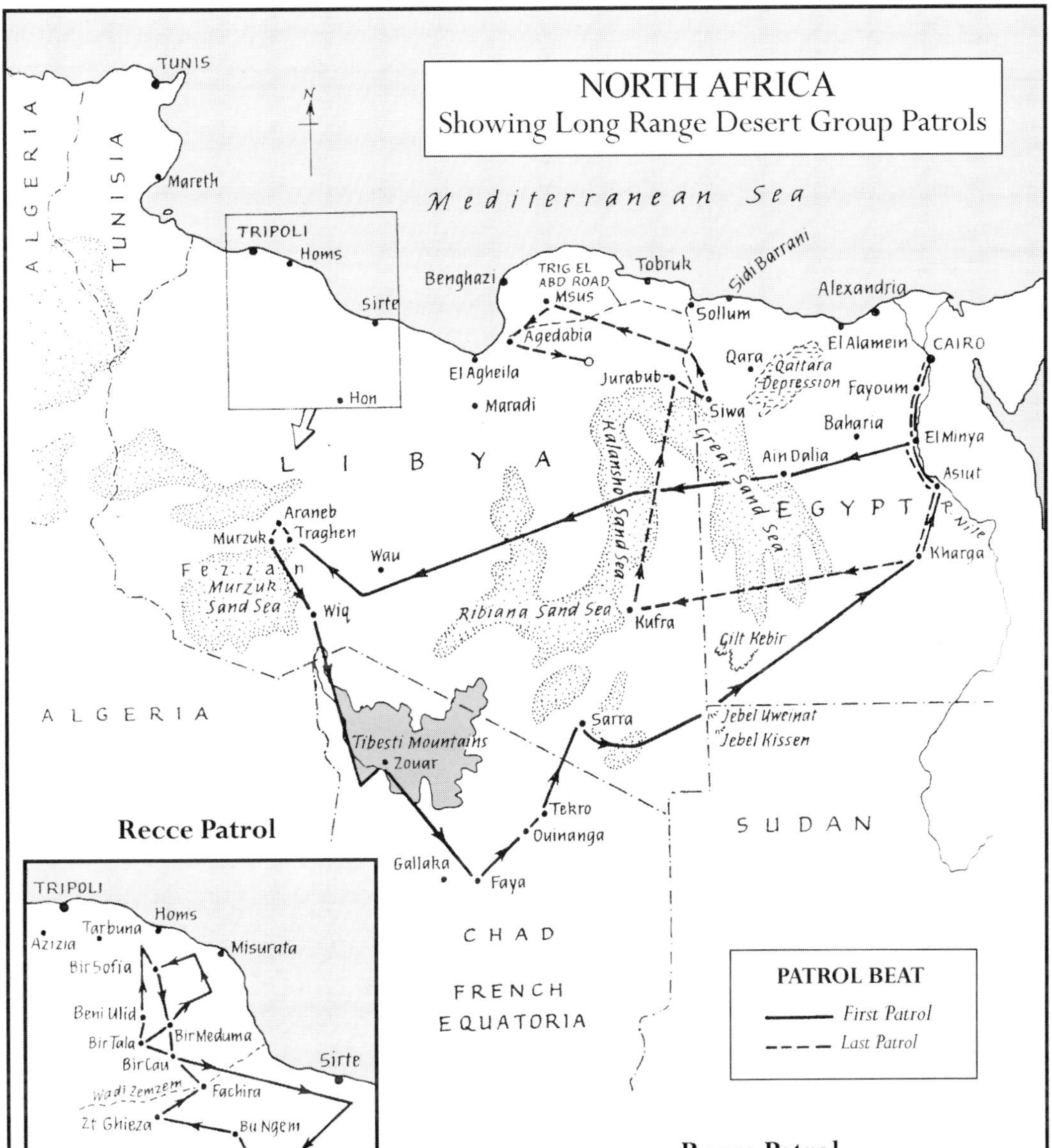

First Patrol

26 December 1940 to
9 February 1941
G Patrol (Guards) and
T Patrol (New Zealand)

11 Jan 41 *Attack Murzuk*
15 Jan *Arrive Zouar*
24 Jan *Meet Col. Leclerc at Faya Patrol attacked. Col Clayton wounded and captured*

Last Patrol

10 October to
18 December 1941

19 Oct *Arrive Kufra*
6 Nov *Leave Kufra*
18 Nov *Roadwatch Triq el Abd Road*
24-27 Nov *Join G2. Attacked by aircraft*
28 Nov *Beat up 'Roadhouse'. Return to Siwa*
10 Dec *G1 leave to raid coastal road*
14/15 Dec *Successful attacks*
16 Dec *Captured*

Recce Patrol

25 Dec 42 - 12 Feb 43
G Patrol (Guards)

26 Dec *Hon area - refuel with Indian Squadron*
1 Jan 43 *Wadi Zem Zem - chased by enemy armoured cars*
2 Jan *Bir Cau. Patrol split with Bruce to Bir Tala / Homs area Major Player to Bir Meduma / Misurata area. Both a close recce of Homs and back to Bir Cau by different routes*
6 Jan *Both RV at Bir Sofia.*

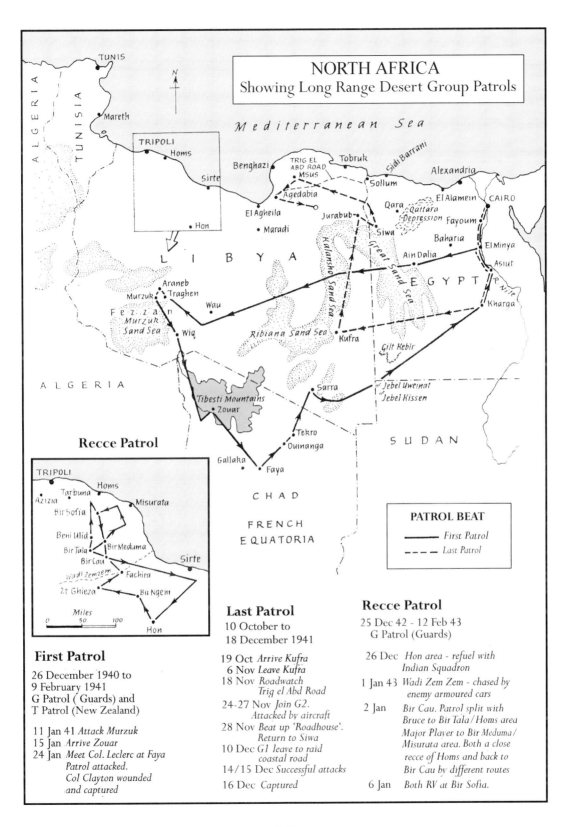

desert and provide information. He gave Bagnold six weeks to set it up, summoned his Chief of Staff, Major General Arthur Smith, a Coldstreamer, and told him to ensure that Major Bagnold got immediate and absolute support from the staff, which he did.

On time, three New Zealand teams were ready ('R', 'T' and 'W' Patrols); they not only carried out a successful reconnaissance, but went on to the offensive laying mines and destroying enemy stores. Wavell was convinced and decided to raise more patrols, so on 7 December 1940 'G' Patrol was formed from 3rd Battalion Coldstream Guards and 2nd Battalion Scots Guards, both in the Middle East.

The Patrol was commanded by Captain Michael Crichton-Stuart, Scots Guards, and his Second-in-Command was Lieutenant Martin Gibbs of the Regiment. There were eighteen volunteers from the 3rd Battalion, all Regular soldiers, mostly townsmen, young and highly disciplined; their first loyalty remained to their Battalion and they regarded themselves as being on temporary duty only with the LRDG. Major General David Lloyd Owen CB DSO OBE MC wrote, "Even the worst of Guardsmen are good and yet suffice to say that we were fortunate in that we had the best."[19]

The role of the LRDG was to dominate the southern flank of the battlefield, to be a nuisance to the Italians and to provide information on the terrain and enemy forces by means of organized vehicle patrols and road-watch operations. Later it developed to offensive action against specific targets and carrying and recovering agents, as well as guiding SAS units to and from their target area.

'G' Patrol had just ten days before they set off on their first operational journey that would last no less than forty days, but they were lucky to take over from the New Zealanders who willingly passed on all the knowledge they could. The plan was for two patrols – 'G' and New Zealand 'T' – to join up with a small French force from the Fezzan in order to raid Muzurk; depending on the outcome, they were then to attack further Italian-held forts as well as producing a detailed report on the terrain.

The force set off from Cairo on Boxing Day 1940, totalling seventy-six men and twenty-four vehicles, and heading towards the desert. They met up with the French party, who re-supplied them with fuel, and together they made plans to attack Muzurk, a town of some 2500 inhabitants with a garrison of 2–300 Italian troops. The operation was highly successful, resulting in forty prisoners and around thirty enemy casualties, together with several aircraft and a fuel dump destroyed.

The next objective was Kufra, an important prize, as whoever occupied Kufra controlled the innermost desert; it had a garrison of around 1200 with artillery and air support. On 24 January 'G' and 'T' Patrols entered Faya and linked up with the Free French force under Colonel Leclerc[20] who planned the attack on Kufra. However, surprise was lost and the assault had to be cancelled. 'G' Patrol was ordered back to Cairo where they arrived on 9 February, the 45th day of the operation, during which they had covered 4300 miles, a record at that time.

Kufra was later captured by the French on 1 March and 'A' Squadron of the LRDG, made up of 'G' Patrol and the newly formed Yeomanry 'Y' Patrol, moved on 25 March to establish a base there for further action. When the Germans attacked 8th Army in the north the Squadron was tasked to observe the routes around Jarabub. It was, however, grounded by a khamseen and ran out of water; many of them, including Lieutenant Gibbs, were in a bad way and were evacuated to Cairo.

[19] *The Desert My Dwelling Place*, p.58.

[20] – Alias, Colonel Vicomte de Haute Cloque, who changed his name to protect his family who were still in France. As General Leclerc he later led the Free French Armoured Division to liberate Paris.

Gibbs wrote, "When I got back to the hospital I had a fairly good beard and, for some reason, probably not unconnected with my mad state of mind, was wearing a double-thickness Hebron coat. I was met by an orderly who said, 'Do you speak English?' and was then passed to the Matron who said, 'Indian Officers this way, please'." It was two months before he recovered and 'G' Patrol commander wrote that, "to the Patrol's loss, he was returned to his battalion".

On 13 May a new 'H' Patrol was formed which started with a successful foray that scored "twelve certainties and four probables" out of a convoy of sixteen Italian vehicles; Sergeant Dennis of the Regiment was the Patrol Sergeant.

The LRDG now had a change of tactics and each patrol was halved in size; 'G' Patrol became 'G'1 and 'G'2, making ten LRDG Patrols altogether, of which eight were always in action. They also established a close liaison with the SAS. On 19 June Lieutenant Tony Hay from the Regiment joined 'G'1 Patrol and led them on several operations.

In November 1941 General Auchinleck was planning his offensive aimed at relieving Tobruk and advancing into Tripolitania. 'G'1 was ordered to watch the southern flank of the advance and they had some good shoots. But the Germans were now taking strong action against the LRDG and Lord Haw-Haw promised stern reprisals against these "Dick Turpins of the desert".

After a successful shoot on the coastal road on 28 November the patrol withdrew to meet up with an Indian column. Very tired, they saw a group of soldiers with British trucks and Lieutenant Hay went forward to meet them. They were, however, German troops, who cut off most of the patrol, capturing its commander and ten men.

In December 1942 8th Army was at Buerat with 7th Armoured, the New Zealand and the Highland Divisions waiting for re-supply. The Army Commander, General Montgomery, wished to know the suitability of the terrain for all arms around his left flank, and Lieutenant Bruce, Scots Guards, was given instructions to carry out this reconnaissance. 'G' Patrol left on Christmas Day 1942 (with Major Player from Army Headquarters to advise on the going for armour); after contacts with and sightings of enemy forces, he returned to Headquarters 8th Army on 12 January. On the 13th he had a long interview with General Montgomery which closed with the blessing "Just what I wanted". He was instructed to detail experienced men to act as guides to the leading formations in the advance, and he chose the Patrol navigator, Guardsman Crossley of the Regiment, to lead 7th Armoured Division, and a Coldstream Reservist, Guardsman Murphy, to lead the New Zealanders. Thus two Coldstreamers led Montgomery's famous 'left hook' which resulted in the capture of Tripoli.

The last task of 'G' Patrol, led by Lieutenant Bruce was to report on the 'going' round the south flank of the Mareth Line and, in particular, whether there was a way round Chott Djerid. They set out on 3 February 1943, consisting of three Grenadiers (since 3rd Coldstream, due to heavy casualties, could no longer reinforce the Patrol), five Coldstreamers and seven Scots Guardsmen. They crossed into Morocco, were the first of the 8th Army to contact 1st Army and finally ended up at General Alexander's Headquarters at Constantine. When they finally got back they had covered 3015 miles in thirty-seven days which made a total of over 9000 miles of desert travel since they left Cairo four and a half months before.

The Grenadiers and Coldstream had suffered heavy casualties at Mareth and badly needed reinforcements, so 'G' Patrol was disbanded. Squadron Sergeant Major Penfold of the Regiment remained with the LRDG to operate in the Aegean and the remainder returned to their regiments. As they left the desert on the road to Cairo for the last time, Coldstreamer Crossley, the navigator, summed up the thoughts of them all when he said, "It's like saying goodbye to an old schoolmaster who was very severe and frightening, but whom one knew one was very fond of in the end".[21]

Some people were surprised that Guardsmen of 'G' Patrol, the only Regular Army Patrol in the LRDG, excelled at such a game as long range desert work, which obviously called for the greatest initiative, self-reliance and independence. But, in fact, operations of this type demanded just the self-discipline and self-confidence to which all Guardsmen are trained. "It was no accident," wrote Michael Crichton-Stuart later, "that the man whose gun was always ready for action, despite the dust, the driver whose truck tyres were always at the right pressure, the reliable guard on solitary night watch was, in barracks, among the smartest on the square."[22]

THE SPECIAL BOAT SQUADRON

A Special Boat Section was originally part of 1 SAS, and in May 1943 when the campaign in North Africa ended, it became an independent unit called the Special Boat Squadron (SBS), and command of it was given to Major the Earl Jellicoe.[23] It consisted of three Detachments ('L', 'M' and 'S'), each of five patrols of one officer and twelve men with the role of beach reconnaissance and raiding.

Two Coldstream officers were involved in these operations. Lieutenant Michael Bolitho was given the task of blowing up the boom covering the mouth of Oran harbour, but as he was swimming towards his target, a bullet hit the explosive charge he was carrying with the inevitable result. Captain Edward Imbert-Terry attacked an airfield in Sardinia, blowing up three aircraft, but was then captured; he escaped, was re-captured, escaped again and spent five months with the partisans in the hills in Italy before rejoining the 8th Army in December 1943. He was awarded a Military Cross.

At the time that Jellicoe took over SBS, Churchill was set on launching a Dodecanese Campaign to secure Rhodes with its vital airfields and to gain control of the Aegean. The strategic aim was to bring Turkey with its forty divisions into the Allied camp as well as opening up a supply route to Russia through the Dardanelles (much as he had planned in 1915 with his Gallipoli Campaign!) With this in mind, an organization was set up called Raiding Forces Middle East, with its headquarters at Azzib in Palestine. It consisted of the Special Boat Squadron, the Greek Sacred Squadron and the Levant Schooner Flotilla of the Royal Navy.

The first move was to gain control of Rhodes which was held by 35,000 Italians and some 7,000 Germans with seventy tanks under an Italian C-in-C, Admiral Campioni. It was thought that the Admiral might be persuaded to co-operate, as Italy was on the verge of breaking with Germany. Jellicoe, with the Senior SOE officer Major Dolbey (in fact Count Dobrski) as interpreter and Sergeant Kesterton as Wireless Operator, was parachuted inaccurately into Rhodes; Major Dolbey broke his leg on landing, while enemy small arms fire in their direction led to the consumption by Jellicoe of General Wilson's letter to Campioni. Eventually Jellicoe was taken to meet the Admiral, who, although sympathetic, did not feel able to take any positive action and they had to leave Rhodes empty-handed. He did, however, provide a seaplane to take Major Dolbey with his broken leg to Cyprus and a motor torpedo boat to take Jellicoe and Kesterton, together with the Italian Chief of

[21] *War Behind Enemy Lines*, J.Thompson, p.110
[22] 'G' Patrol, page 27
[23] An appropriate appointment for the son of Admiral of the Fleet Earl Jellicoe who commanded the British naval force at the Battle of Jutland in May 1916.

Staff, to Castelrosso which by then had been occupied by an SBS squadron under Captain David Sutherland. He also gave them a chart of the Axis minefields in the Aegean. Campioni was later handed over by the Germans to the Italian Republic of the North and executed. Jellicoe was decorated with the Military Cross.

Plans were then made to occupy some of the other key Dodecanese islands. Jellicoe, together with Sutherland and his SBS detachment, sailed for Simi where the Italian garrison came over to our side. Jellicoe then sailed on in an Italian MTB to Leros where the Italian Commander, Admiral Mascherpa, also agreed to co-operate. Cos was then taken over by a Battalion Group and Leros by 234 Brigade, supported by SBS, LRDG and the Greek Sacred Squadron.

Cos, however, was recaptured by the Germans some six weeks later and they then launched a powerful attack on Leros. After three days of heavy fighting Jellicoe was asked to report to Brigadier Tilney at his Headquarters on the island. But when he reached the HQ at night it was to be met not by Brigadier Tilney but by a German Colonel who had commanded the successful assault on the HQ. Jellicoe had to surrender, but gave his parole to the Colonel in order to look for a close friend, Lieutenant Alan Phipps RN, who had commanded the final fortress defence. After searching unsuccessfully for Phipps he surrendered his parole, but managed to escape soon after being marched down to the harbour. He collected his soldiers, commandeered a caique and made his way back to Cairo.

The loss of Leros effectively ended the Dodecanese Campaign, and responsibility for the Aegean was split into two: north of Leros was allotted to the Greek Sacred Squadron under Colonel Tsigantes, while the south became the responsibility of the SBS. They continued to be extremely active, attacking Axis shipping, destroying communications and killing Germans at every opportunity. 'S' Detachment, for example, under Captain David Sutherland of the Black Watch, managed in two months to capture and destroy fifteen caiques, fourteen radio stations and three cable stations as well as killing or capturing 110 enemy. The aim of the operation was achieved in that it drove the enemy to reinforce the area with 4,000 troops which they could ill afford.

In July 1944 it was decided that the Special Boat Squadron, now a Regiment (SBR), was no longer needed in the Aegean and they were sent to operate in the Adriatic, based on Bari in Italy which was now on our side. Here they happily joined up with the LRDG and, together with 2 Commando, became Land Forces Adriatic.

When the Germans began to withdraw from Greece, Jellicoe, now a Lieutenant Colonel, was put in command of 'Bucketforce', consisting of 'L' Squadron of the SBR under Major Patterson, a LRDG Troop, a section of the Royal Marine Commando, an RAF Armoured Car Detachment and supporting arms; later two companies of the Highland Light Infantry joined him. In September 1944 'Bucketforce' landed at Araxos airfield and at Katakalon in the north-west Peloponnese and invested Patras, the main city, which was held by some 900 Germans and 1600 members of a Greek Security Battalion. The latter soon surrendered and the Germans evacuated the city on 3 October. Jellicoe was appointed Military Governor of the North-West Peloponnese, with orders to do everything possible to prevent the outbreak of civil war in the area and also to establish a military presence in Athens as quickly as possible.

On 12 October 4th Parachute Battalion landed at Megara and two days later Jellicoe (now temporarily promoted to Brigadier) was ordered to enter Athens with the least possible delay. He and Major Patterson landed by caique near Scaramanga, east of Eleusis, and that night bicycled into Athens as the last of the German rearguard withdrew.

Jellicoe was now put in command of 'Pompforce', consisting of the original members of

'Bucketforce' plus 4th Parachute Battalion and some supporting arms, and told to harry the retreating Germans. He did so most effectively until they reached the Yugoslav frontier where they were ordered to halt.

In December 1994 Jellicoe was nominated for the Staff College in Haifa with a view to a posting to Special Forces in the Far East (which never materialized) and he handed over command of the Special Boat Regiment after eighteen months of most distinguished service. He had been awarded a DSO, MC, Legion d'Honneur, a Croix de Guerre, Greek War Cross and three times Mentioned in Despatches.[24]

SPECIAL OPERATIONS EXECUTIVE

Introduction

Special Operations Executive (better known as SOE) was created immediately after the fall of France in 1940, with the aim of stirring up Resistance movements against the Germans in Occupied Europe and anywhere else an opportunity offered. Winston Churchill's instructions to the Minister responsible were simply "and now set Europe ablaze".

This was easier said than done, for Britain's dogged fight against Hitler did not at that moment look like a cause worth backing. It was only when the Soviet Union and the United States joined the struggle that the Resistance movements really got going. Also it took time to organize and train a completely new and secret organization covering the whole of Europe and much of the Middle East. Key figures such as agents, local resistance groups and radio operators had to be identified, screened, recruited and trained, and tasks for them to carry out had to be selected and planned.

The first chief of SOE was Sir Frank Nelson, who played a most important part in the initial stages; when he retired early in 1942 due to ill health and overwork he was succeeded by his Second-in-Command, a Coldstreamer, Colonel Sir Charles Hambro. He had won a MC in the First World War and was a highly respected figure in the City; he remained at the head of SOE until August 1943. By the end of the war SOE employed some 13,000 people *excluding* those who worked in the many Resistance Movements; they parachuted no less than 40,000 tons of arms and equipments into Europe and made a considerable contribution to the Allied war effort.

The Coldstream in turn made a contribution to SOE, not only in the shape of Charles Hambro, but also two gallant individuals who earned a George Cross and a Military Cross.

Brigadier Arthur Nicholls GC

Arthur Nicholls joined the Coldstream Guards as a Lieutenant in the Supplementary Reserve on 19 May 1937 and in 1939 went to France with the 2nd Battalion. He became ADC to General Alexander, commanding 1st Division, and in June 1941 attended a Junior War Staff Course before joining the Special Operations Executive in the War Office.

In August 1943 he was posted to Cairo as a Lieutenant Colonel and was dropped into Albania on 10 October as GSOI to a Brigadier Davies, whose task was to coordinate the partisans fighting

[24] He left the Coldstream in August 1946, and became, alongside other appointments, Minister of Defence for the Royal Navy, Leader of the House of Lords and a Privy Councillor. He was also appointed a KBE.

behind the lines in the Balkans. He was met by two experienced guerrilla leaders, Major David Smiley and Major Fitzroy Maclean, who apparently regarded him initially as not really suited to guerrilla warfare. Their view was reinforced when Nicholls declared that the camp needed cleaning up and ordered all the Partisans – Vlachs, Albanians and Italians – to line up and pick up all the litter. Rather surprisingly they did so, but when he congratulated them they all dropped the litter at their feet and moved off! But in the end Nicholls had his way and camp administration improved considerably.

Arthur Nicholls GC.

Soon afterwards Smiley and Maclean, who had been in the country some time, were sent home on leave, but within a week were summoned to SOE Headquarters to be told that the Mission in Albania had been attacked, Brigadier Davies had been wounded and captured, and the remainder had had to disperse. It was, however, known that Colonel Nicholls had survived and had taken charge. He had made the difficult decision that some of the wounded who could not be evacuated must be abandoned to the enemy and had organized the others to move north in order to reach a radio and report on the situation. He appreciated that important questions of Allied strategy and policy in the Balkans depended on getting the information that only he possessed through to Headquarters without delay and he determined to achieve just that at all costs.

Gathering together the survivors of the Headquarters, Nicholls led the party off in search of an Allied radio set that was thought to be in working order in the north. It was the depths of a Balkan winter and the enemy were close on their heels. Before long he and the only other officer, Lieutenant Alan Hare of The Life Guards, were suffering from frostbite in both feet and Nicholls also had a badly dislocated shoulder. Then his feet turned gangrenous and there was no medical treatment available.

When he found that he could no longer walk, Nicholls ordered Hare to head south to another Allied post, while he continued northwards with two Albanian partisans. For fifteen days they struggled on, with Nicholls being pulled through the snow on his greatcoat and sometimes riding on a mule. Finally he arrived at the post and passed on his message. But so serious was his condition that he was put in the hands of an Albanian patriot called Ihsan Toptani[25] who bravely took him into his house and called a doctor, who promptly amputated all Nicholls' toes. But the gangrene, shock and suffering of his journey proved too much and he died within a week.

[25] He is still alive in London and has confirmed this story.

His Albanian comrades reported that the Partisans were filled with admiration for his gallant behaviour under such incredible suffering and that his reputation for courage stood high with them and will long be remembered. He was awarded a posthumous George Cross in 1946, the citation stating "He set an example of heroism, fortitude, courage, leadership, the will to win and devotion to duty which has seldom been equalled and never surpassed. He carried on far longer than could normally be considered possible and this undoubtedly caused his death."[26]

Captain I.W.S. Moss MC

Bill Moss was commissioned into the Coldstream Guards in 1941 and served with the 3rd Battalion in North Africa until he joined Force 133 of the SOE in Cairo in September 1943. At that time plans were afoot to carry out a daring operation in German-occupied Crete aimed at capturing General Kreipe who commanded the 22nd Sebastopol (Bremen) Division in Crete. Those involved were Major Patrick Leigh Fermor, Irish Guards, and Bill Moss, together with two Cretan guerrillas. After seven abortive attempts due to bad weather, Bill Moss finally parachuted into Soutsouro on 4 April 1944.

Bill Moss

Several days of observation revealed that the General usually left his headquarters at Archanes for his residence at Knossos every night between dusk and 2100, and the plan was to 'lift' him on this journey. Three uncertainties were a cause for concern:

a. To be sure to get the right car. An agent was detailed to find out all necessary details.
b. How to dispose of any other vehicles and individuals who might pass by during the operation. A good Cretan, Athanasios Bourdzalis, and fifteen Andartes (partisans) undertook to capture the passengers and drivers and ditch the vehicles, so that was left to them.
c. How to avoid reprisals against the local population. For this Bill Moss prepared a plan which he hoped would solve the matter.

On the night of 16 April the ambush was set up, but could not be activated that evening or on the next three nights because the General passed by before dark. Then on the 20th he was delayed, the signal was passed to the snatch party and Moss and Leigh Fermor, dressed as German Military Policemen, stood in the road waving red lamps as the car approached. In the ditches on either side of the road were nine picked men of the Andartes.

[26] *London Gazette* 1 March 1946. He was also Mentioned in Despatches in 1944.

The General was sitting next to the driver and, when Leigh Fermor asked for his papers, he began an explanation. As this was going on, Moss opened the driver's door, struck the driver with a 'life preserver' and threw the unconscious man on to the road. Leigh Fermor then put on the General's hat and, with two Cretans, pushed him into the rear seat, handcuffed and bound. A Cretan sat on either side of the General, each with a knife against his body, and within sixty seconds they were away, with Moss at the wheel.

They drove through Heraklion, where the German HQ was located, to Yeni up in the hills, passing through no less than twenty-two road blocks on the way, with the sentries saluting or coming to attention when they saw the General's pennant. The General had given his word that he would not escape or draw attention to himself and seemed to accept his capture as a *fait accompli.*

Moss and the Cretans took him to a large, patriotic village in the hills, while Patrick Leigh Fermor drove the car to a possible submarine landing beach at Amyra, where they hoped to be collected. Here they left the car, with a note pointing out that the General was an honourable prisoner of war who had been captured by a British raiding party without the help of the Cretans. The party had used members of His Majesty's Hellenic Forces in the Middle East as guides and reprisals against the local population would be wholly unwarranted. The explanation was accepted by the Germans and they did not take punitive action on this occasion.

But now things started to go seriously wrong. The British Liaison Officer who should have arranged for them to be picked up went down with malaria and his radio was not working; as a result they had to remain in the mountains for the next eighteen days. Runners were sent many miles to reach three other known radio sets to arrange a pick-up point, but without success, and all the time the Germans were tightening their control of the beaches on the south coast and continuing their search for the kidnappers of their general.

One pick-up party arranged by Earl Jellicoe's Special Boat Squadron had to be cancelled because the Germans had the beach covered, so the party moved westwards to a less heavily guarded area. On the night of 10/11 May they suggested an evacuation on 14/15 May, which was agreed by Force 133; it was successfully completed, and the two officers, with their prisoner, thankfully set sail for Mersa Matruh.

The General's behaviour was friendly and helpful throughout, and his only complaint was that he had lost his Knight's Cross of the Iron Cross. Leigh Fermor was awarded a DSO and Moss a Military Cross. The story of their exploit was later written up as a book called *Ill Met by Moonlight*, which was then made into a film with the same title.

Captain Moss returned to Crete again with a plan to capture General Kreipe's successor, but this proved impossible, whereupon he carried out several successful guerrilla operations, supported by a number of escaped Russian prisoners of war, who had heard of his reputation. He then moved to Greece, but his activities there were frustrated by the activities of the ELAS Communists. When the war ended in Europe he went to the Far East, operating with Force 136 in Siam (now Thailand) until the surrender of the Japanese.

Major General Sir John Younger Bt CBE

Jack Younger joined the Regiment in October 1939 and was posted to the 3rd Battalion in Egypt. With the remnants of the Battalion he tried to break out from Tobruk in June 1942 by tagging on to the end of a German convoy travelling eastwards, but was 'rumbled' and captured when the Gurkhas ambushed the column.

He ended up in Camp 49 near Fontenallato and when the Italian Armistice was signed in September 1943 he and Captain Richard Broke, Scots Guards, made for the hills and spent four months at Pelegrino. Jack Younger joined a partisan group in January 1944 and formed an organization to send escaping and evading officers to Switzerland. Thanks to him, eighteen reached safety, (one escapee crossed the border as the 'fireman' on the footplate of a railway locomotive).

He gathered much useful 'military information' which he sent back via partisan sources and himself commanded a partisan group in a successful sabotage programme until, in October 1944, he was ordered to return to the 8th Army with a party of escaping prisoners.

For this successful period behind enemy lines he was awarded the MBE.

MILITARY INTELLIGENCE 9

MI 9 was a vital department set up and run by a Coldstreamer, Lieutenant Colonel J.M.Langley, with the aim of bringing Allied evaders from behind the enemy lines in Europe. The organization had few trained agents in the field and depended on several thousand volunteers known as 'helpers' to contact the men and hide them until they could be brought to safety. These volunteers considered their work to be a great human cause and it inspired doctors and nurses, artists and poets to risk their lives, but the majority came from lowly cafés, farms and working-class homes in all corners of North-West Europe.

It was a role particularly suited to women. Airmen were often wounded and needed nursing in secret, sometimes for weeks on end, and quite young girls also took on the responsibility of escorting parties of 'evaders' who spoke no French from Paris and Brussels by train to the Spanish frontier. Thanks to these remarkably brave, largely unknown volunteers, over 3000 Allied airmen and several hundred soldiers evaded capture, but 500 of these helpers were executed or died in concentration camps, and a far greater number succumbed to their ill treatment from the Gestapo. These patriots, unlike the men whom they rescued, were not protected by the Geneva Convention and so were exposed to the brutal treatment of the German Counter-Espionage Services.

Lieutenant Colonel J.M.Langley MBE MC

The Regiment can claim to have played a major part in this unusual organization for the escape routes were set up and run from 1940 onwards by Lieutenant Colonel Jimmy Langley, based on his own experience as an evader in 1940. He joined the 1st Battalion in 1936, reverted to the Officers' Reserve and was recalled to the 2nd Battalion in May 1939.[27] During the fighting at Dunkirk he was severely wounded in the shoulder, but was not evacuated because he was on a stretcher and the orders were "walking wounded only", on the basis that stretcher cases took the places of four men. He therefore returned to 12 Casualty Clearing Station, where he was looked after by Philip Newman, a surgeon who stayed behind to care for the more serious casualties.

During the following weeks Jimmy moved to various hospitals in the area, at one of which his

[27] He was in No 3 Company (otherwise known as the 'Coal Box Company' because it contained the shortest members of the Battalion, who were, it was said, short enough to be buried in coal boxes if there was a shortage of coffins); it was commanded by Major Angus McCorquodale. (*Fight Another Day* by J.M.Langley, page 26).

shoulder exploded, with a jet of blood hitting him in the face; but fortunately Philip Newman was in the ward, stopped the bleeding and amputated the arm within the hour! During this time there was precious little medical treatment and food was scarce, but the French civilians were magnificent in their generosity, bringing food for the wounded.

His final destination was at the Faculté Catholique at Lille where French women known as *Marraines de Guerre* (War Godmothers) each adopted a badly wounded soldier and gave them individual parcels. Madame Caron, wife of a gendarme and a cleaner in the hospital, adopted Jimmy, providing him with a substantial meal each day. Rumour started that the wounded were to be removed to Germany in the near future and so escape was urgent. Madame Caron passed him a 'safe address' and a French-speaking RAMC corporal helped push Jimmy through the window of the Porter's Lodge. He landed in the street and scuttled across when the sentry was talking to a friend. He found the 'safe house' and was welcomed in by a dentist, Monsieur Carpentier, whose wife and two attractive daughters were also dentists; he was given a hot meal, a glass of wine and a comfortable bed.

Guides took him by train to Paris where the 'safe house' belonged to a Madame Veuve who hated *les sales Boches* and made sure everyone knew; she also used to carry stick grenades under her skirt which she threw over railway bridges or rolled under enemy vehicles, so it was not surprising that she did not survive the war. She gladly produced a signed blank identity card; a photograph was taken and, to get the official stamp, a shelled hard-boiled egg was first rolled over the stamp on her card and then over Jimmy's to complete the new identity document.

Jimmy, now officially Monsieur Dupont, an inhabitant of Dunkirk, decided to go to Marseilles, travelling through the Non-Occupied Zone (NOZ) and then over the Pyrenees into Spain.

While waiting for the spring to make the journey possible, he investigated ways of escape; a number of like-minded officers discussed the escape problem with him and they all decided that someone was required to co-ordinate and control the escape efforts.

He managed to convince a French Medical Board that he was unfit for active service and arrived at Liverpool on a cold March morning; he immediately reported to Regimental Headquarters, still wearing his evading kit – no stiff white collar, bowler hat, gloves or rolled umbrella! He was given a month's leave, during which he gave a talk, arranged by his father, to the local 'open' Borstal; the audience were very attentive, but the governor was not amused when eight boys escaped that night.

After only five days' leave he was recalled for an interview over lunch at the Savoy with a Colonel Claude Dansey of MI 6[28], who told him to report to his office, where he was briefed on the task that he would carry out for the rest of the war, running MI 9, the Allied evading organization.

The system he set up consisted of four 'Evading Lines'[29] and it worked so well that after a while Hermann Goering, furious at the number of shot-down aircrew who were escaping, ordered the Luftwaffe Security Police, the Abwehr and the Gestapo to take ruthless action against 'evaders' and the 'evader' organizations. They did so with such ruthless efficiency (helped by some treachery) that all four of the 'evading lines' were destroyed; a few of the operators managed to escape, one of whom was a very gallant helper, Peggy van Lier, who was later to become his wife.

[28] He was instructed, in the best espionage tradition, to look for someone with a carnation and reading *The Times*.

[29] The O'Leary Line led by Ian Garrow (Seaforth Highlanders) and based in Marseilles; the Comet Line, led by Mlle Andreé de Jongh (Dedée) based in Brussels; the Line run by Mary Lidell, Countess de Milleville from Limoges; and Operation 'SHELBURNE' in Brittany led by Captain Lucien Demais (Canadian Army) after Vladimir Bourysch had been arrested.

Assisted by Major Airey Neave, who had just escaped from Colditz, Langley now set about resuscitating the 'Lines' and supported by the matchless courage of the survivors. By the autumn of 1943 they were ready to operate again. Langley was now given a new job as part of the invasion plans, which was to set up Intelligence School No.9 Western Europe Army (IS 9 (WEA)) and to hand over Room 900 to Airey Neave. Half the personnel of IS 9 (WEA) were American and half British and their role was to establish Centres as far forward as feasible behind the advancing Allied armies to collect, feed, clothe, interrogate and repatriate the several hundred 'evaders' believed still to be in France, Belgium and Holland. Secondly they were to implement the rescue of evaders and escapees in enemy territory. When the invasion was deemed successful, Langley was to take over the evading organizations.

In September 1944 the failure of the Arnhem airborne operation required IS 9 to rescue around 300 men in hiding in the area. Operation 'PEGASUS 1' was successful in evacuating 138 men, but a further 150 remained. Then a major breach of security occurred, when a journalist by devious means discovered the story of 'PEGASUS 1' and wrote a detailed article about it which somehow got through the censor and was published. Within days the enemy had copies of the papers from neutral countries and increased their riverbank patrols and house searches in the Arnhem area. Such a large number of men could not be hidden and fed for long, and so Operation 'PEGASUS 2' was brought forward to early November; but 120 evaders were ambushed on the Arnhem – Ede road and three men only crossed the Rhine that night.

When the Germans surrendered, the IS 9 teams and also MI 9 were disbanded, and Jimmy Langley, who had seven months to serve before his release date, accepted the post of Town Major in Antwerp. On his way to take up his post he visited the battlefields of his platoon in 1940 and was amused to find a white cross with his name on it at the 12 CCS site outside Dunkirk. The reunion with his 'war godmother', Madame Caron, was most moving; she still had two brass Coldstream badges of rank which he had given her, and asked with tears if she might keep them as they had meant so much to her during the years of German occupation. The Carpentier family of dentists gave him a warm welcome and prepared a special dinner to say "Thank you for liberation". The great leaders of his escape lines, together with those of their associates who survived, met him and they all undertook to continue to devote themselves to working for others.

There is little doubt that Jimmy Langley made a significant contribution to final victory by his work in a decidedly unusual organization. He not only repatriated many Allied Servicemen who could fight again, but he did much to keep alive the spirit of resistance in the Occupied Countries among the amazingly gallant 'helpers' who every day risked death or torture for the Allied cause.

THE PARACHUTE REGIMENT

1st (Guards) Parachute Battalion

In 1945 the 1st Airborne Division was disbanded, but 6th Airborne Division survived and was sent to Palestine in September 1945. Within a year it was reduced from three to two brigades and in November 1946 the 1st Parachute Battalion became the 1st (Guards) Parachute Battalion, commanded by Lieutenant Colonel John Nelson DSO MC, Grenadier Guards. By the end of 1947 there was a good percentage of Coldstreamers in the battalion including Captain R.D.Dobson, Captain G.Smith (who was Intelligence Officer), Lieutenant R.B.Barter, Lieutenant G.C.Middleton,

Lieutenant C.L.StH.Pelham-Burn, Lieutenant T.H.Stanley, RSM J.C.Cowley, DCM, CSM 'Tipper' Davies, Sergeant Pearson, Lance Corporals J.Lawton, J.Robinson and Nunn; there were also Guardsmen Cope, Forrester and Richards, to name but a few.

In August 1947 the Battalion was at Camp 260 near Nahariya and then moved to Mount Carmel in Haifa, where it was heavily involved in Internal Security duties. On 13 October of that year RSM Cowley was hit on the head by the 'hammer' during a battalion sports meeting and a Parachute Regiment Private was heard to comment "Just as we get a good Sergeant Major, some silly b . . . . . r has to hit him on the head with a hammer". He made a full recovery, however, and became RSM of the 1st Battalion in Egypt.

The Battalion had an exciting time keeping the peace between Arab and Jew, and defending itself against either or both, and when British troops left Palestine in May 1948, the GOC, General Sir Gordon MacMillan, asked especially for the Guards Parachute Battalion to remain until the last to maintain order in Jerusalem. This it did and finally had the honour of escorting the last British High Commissioner out of the city on 14 May 1948, after which it returned home to Cirencester in Wiltshire.

The Guards Parachute Company[30]

That summer 6th Airborne Division was disbanded and 16th Independent Parachute Brigade was formed to replace it. The Guards Parachute Battalion was allowed to keep its identity and became the Pathfinder Company of the brigade. This made it unique, in that it was the only all-Regular unit in a National Service Army. The Company Commander was Major R.Steele, Grenadier Guards, and two of the subalterns were Coldstreamers, Lieutenants G.Smith and T.Stanley. It was agreed that the Company would wear the Parachute Regiment red beret and their badge, but with a blue/red/blue flash behind it.

Before leaving England to join the Parachute Brigade in Germany, the Company, wearing the red beret, mounted King's Guard at Buckingham Palace. CSM Davies of the Regiment, one of only two members of the Company with pre-war service, ensured that the proper traditions of the Household Brigade were maintained on this first occasion on which the red beret was seen on Public Duties.

Once in BAOR it patrolled the border between East and West Germany and practised its pathfinder role, adapting wartime techniques to peacetime requirements. It also formed an outstanding Company rugby team that not only won the Prince of Wales Cup and the Eastern Command Challenge Cup, but became the smallest unit ever to reach the finals of the Army Rugby Cup, which it lost 6–9 to the Royal Corps of Signals. Coldstreamers in the team were the new Company Commander, Major Nevin Agnew, Lance Sergeants Sykes and Whitehorn, Lance Corporal Ryan and Guardsman Cope.

In June 1951 the Company was sent to Cyprus and also did a spell in the Canal Zone before returning to Pirbright in June 1954, when there were thirty-four Coldstreamers serving in it, including three Company officers. At that time the Regimental Sergeant Major of the 3rd Parachute Battalion was WOI 'Solly' Joel of the Regiment who won a MM and Bar in North Africa and Italy.

[30] On formation it was called 16th (Guards) Independent Parachute Company as the Pathfinders for 16 Independent Parachute Brigade. This was later changed to 1 (Guards) Independent Parachute Company, but it was known as The Guards Parachute Company, or 'The Pathfinders.'

1 (Guards) Independent Parachute Company. Coldstreamers All. **Back rows;** left to right: Guardsmen Lister, Mays, Teal, Matthews, Ward, Westerman, Haley, Jeffreys, Gallimord, Fisher, Child, Cowell, Seal, Cross, Lund, Ella, Wilson and Neighbour. **Seated:** Guardsmen Clay, Trigg, Lance Corporals Gibbons, Patterson, Captain H.F. Gibbs, Sergeant Cummings, Captain P.N.R. Stewart-Richardson, Lance Sergeant Longstaff, Captain C.W.B. Jacot de Boinod, Lance Corporals Finn, Painter, Moore and Guardsman Jordan.

June 1954 saw the unit in Cyprus once more, where it was involved in Internal Security duties against EOKA, while remaining poised to intervene in Egypt if necessary. The Colour Sergeant of the Guards Parachute Company was CQMS Arthur Channon of the Regiment, who became RSM of 3 PARA, Quartermaster of 10 PARA and finally a Lieutenant Colonel in the Parachute Regiment.

When Nasser nationalized the Suez Canal in October 1956 one stick of the Company, led by Captain Murray de Klee of the Scots Guards, with Coldstreamer Sergeant Longstaff as Stick Sergeant, took part in the airborne attack on Port Said and then patrolled south down the Canal road, where they were joined by the remainder of the Company. It took up a defensive position south of El Cap, and when relieved by the Royal West Kent Regiment returned to Cyprus. It remained there until February 1957 when it returned to Pirbright with the clasps 'Cyprus' and 'Near East' on the General Service Medal.

The role of the Company was now assumed to be that of reconnaissance and flank protection, and it was Major Peter Stewart-Richardson (known as 'Scrubber') who, when commanding the Company in 1957, pressed for quarter-ton vehicles and the necessary long-range communications for such a role. This was accepted and training began with the help of the Household Cavalry.

Major Stewart-Richardson later went on to command 10 PARA(V) in London, but he was not in fact the first Coldstreamer to do so, as it had been commanded in 1950–1951 by Lieutenant Colonel John Mogg DSO and Bar, who as 2656022 Guardsman H.J.Mogg joined the Regiment in

Coldstream Group 1933, showing second from left middle row, 2656022 Guardsman John Mogg. Next to him on the end of the row is 2655397 Guardsman 'Solly' Joel, who rose to the rank of Major (QM) and was awarded the MM and Bar.

May 1933. He served first with the 3rd Battalion and then the 1st in which he became a Lance Corporal. He then went to Sandhurst, won the Sword of Honour and was commissioned into the Oxfordshire and Buckinghamshire Light Infantry. He became Adjutant General and Deputy SACEUR, before retiring as General Sir John Mogg GCB CBE DSO DL. He is proud of his service in the Regiment and never fails to visit any Coldstream battalion when he is in the vicinity; he is a most popular and welcome visitor with all ranks.

A number of other Coldstreamers joined the Parachute Regiment, including Lieutenant Colonel Bill Corbould, who ran their Recruit Company in the 1950s on Guards Depot lines.

Another Coldstreamer to serve in 10 PARA(V) was Major Bernard Cazenove, who was first a private soldier in that battalion and later became a Company Commander and Second-in-Command. He is now the Honorary Colonel of 4 PARA(V), the only Coldstreamer to have been granted such an honour by the Parachute Regiment.

While commanding the Guards Parachute Company Major Stewart-Richardson initiated the idea of a Company Colour; he was not able to see it through at the time, but it was duly designed and was handed over to the Company on 21 June 1961 by General Sir Charles Loyd, the Colonel of the Regiment, acting on behalf of The Queen. It now rests in the Guards Chapel.

On 12 June 1958 the Company kept the ground for the Queen's Birthday Parade and two days later, with no warning, was in Cyprus on IS duties. The situation in the Middle East was on the boil and Jordan was threatened by the newly-formed United Arab Republic of Egypt and Syria. On 17 July it de-planed in Amman Airport and received a warm welcome from the Jordanian Army. The country was calm, but certain contingency plans had to be drawn up, including being ready to 'rescue' King Hussein (known as PLK or the 'Plucky Little King'). In the event no trouble developed and in November it returned to Pirbright, where it would remain for the next four years.

The emphasis was now on pathfinder training and the main role of the Company was confirmed as medium reconnaissance. Landrovers were not suitable for this and they were replaced by armoured Ferret scout cars, three for each stick and three for Company Headquarters. Training was strenuous but varied, involving exercises in the UK, Cyprus and Singapore. Captain J.Cadge, a Coldstream officer, was the first member to be sent on a free-fall course and was followed by many others.

Over New Year 1963 the Company was on leave when orders came to "Return in all haste" and within two days an Advance Party was flying to Cyprus. On 5 January 1964 the Company, as part of 1 PARA Group, was ordered to 'keep the peace' in an area that included Limassol, Ktimi, Paphos, Polis and the Troodos Mountains. On 2 February it handed over to 'A' Squadron, the Royal Dragoons, and was home within 48 hours. Three days later it was briefed on its next task, which was to operate in Borneo preventing incursions by the Indonesian Army over the Malaysian border. On 27 April 1964 it touched down at Singapore and within four days landed by helicopter far and wide in the jungle carrying out four-man patrols and receiving supplies every fortnight by air. It returned to England on 6 November; CQMS Smurthwaite was awarded the BEM for his outstanding performance in the re-supply of the many patrols and Guardsman Shepherd was Mentioned in Despatches for ambushing some terrorists who were tailing his patrol; he killed two of them. In December 1968 Captain 'Nick' Nicholas joined the Company as Administrative Officer, a much-needed addition to the establishment, taking a load off the shoulders of the Company Commander and CQMS.

1970 was the start of the Company involvement in Northern Ireland, and by mid-February it was patrolling the Shankill and the 'Peace Line' from a base at the Red Hart bottling factory; it returned home in June 1970. With Major Bill Coleridge in command, it returned in 1971; this time it operated in Co Armagh based in a school at Newry which was an improvement on the Shankill Road. It returned to Pirbright and took part in Exercise 'Battle Royal', an event proposed by The Duke of Edinburgh to make the public realize that the Household Division spent more time preparing for war than on ceremonial. The demonstration was impressive and pleased those who saw it.

In March 1972 the Company returned to Northern Ireland, operating in Antrim. It travelled by sea and it was no fault of the IRA that they arrived safely, as an unexploded 40lb bomb was found in the ferry after the passengers had disembarked.

In 1974 command passed to Major Robert Corbett, Irish Guards (later Major General Commanding The Household Division), and his Second-in-Command was Captain Nick Emson of the Regiment, who had won a Military Cross in Aden with 1 PARA.[31]

In November the Company spent several weeks in Gibraltar doing frontier guards and ceremonial duties – the first time since 1924 that a unit of the Household Division had mounted the Convent Guard on Government House.

After block leave in August it did a drop in the south of France where eleven members of the Company (including the Company Commander) suffered broken limbs. The wind was at twenty-three knots and they were dropped by French aircraft 1.5 kilometres short of the DZ.

But its days were numbered and on 24 October 1975 its Farewell Parade took place at Pirbright,

[31] 2nd Lieutenant Emson was serving with 1 PARA in Aden in June 1967 when he distinguished himself on two occasions, showing considerable gallantry and coolness under fire – the more so when on the second occasion his radio headset was shot off his head. (*The London Gazette*, 19 January 1968.)

with the Company and many Old Comrades marching past Field Marshal Sir Gerald Templer. In his speech the Field Marshal declared, "The secret of the Company's outstanding success lies, of course, in the fact that all of its members, of whatever rank, brought with the man intense pride in their parent Regiment and in their profession as the Household Troops of the Sovereign". It would not have been superfluous to have added that they found a strong measure of *amour propre* and healthy conceit in belonging to the finest little military fraternity in the world.[32]

The Company Colour was handed over for safe keeping in the Guards Chapel on Sunday 24 October 1976 by Major General Sir John Nelson, former Commanding Officer of the 1st (Guards) Parachute Battalion, and was received by the Reverend Robin Wood, Chaplain to the Household Division.

Also in the Guards Chapel there is a commemorative window commissioned by Major General Sir Robert Corbett and designed by Gordon Beningfold. It was dedicated at the same time as the Company Colour was handed over and it shows a pathfinder stick leaving a Hercules aircraft over a DZ in Sharjah. It is dedicated to all former members of the Guards Parachute Battalion and the Independent Company who served between 1946 and 1975.

Note on Author

Brigadier Peter (Scrubber) Stewart-Richardson enlisted in the Regiment as Guardsman 2666501 in 1943 and was commissioned in 1944. During his service he served in four Coldstream Battalions, the 1st, 2nd, 3rd and 5th. While serving with the 2nd Battalion in Malaya he arranged to spend his leave with the 1st Battalion of the Foreign Legion in French Indo-China. He was wounded in an ambush and was awarded the Croix de Guerre. He commanded the Guards Independent Parachute Company in 1957/58 and 10th (V) Battalion the Parachute Regiment in 1967/68. His final appointment in the Army before his retirement in 1981 was as Brigadier Infantry. He is President of the King's Lynn Branch of The Coldstream Guards Association.

[32] *Guardsmen of the Sky*, J.N.P.Watson, page 149.

CHAPTER NINE

THE COLD WAR, 1945–1989

by Alistair Horne

'Cold War' Begins Immediately 'Hot War' Ends

On 5 March 1946 Winston Churchill, then out of power, declared in a famous speech at Fulton, Missouri, USA, that Stalin's Soviet Russia had brought down an 'Iron Curtain' across Eastern Europe. This date is always held to mark the beginning of the 'Cold War', but from the British Army's point of view for all practical purposes there had been little, if any, gap between that and the ending of the 'Hot War' in Germany in May 1945.

As a wartime serving officer then on the staff of GHQ, Middle East, I remember well this fact being brought home to us, painfully, by Field Marshal Montgomery, then CIGS under Attlee's 1945 Labour Government. Summoning us all together at a base in the desert he announced that our demob would have to be deferred for six months on account of on-going British commitments across the globe.

Our forces were indeed heavily stretched, with the immediate post-war economy strained to breaking point in its efforts to meet Socialist targets of nationalization. At that time we had a large army of occupation in Germany and Austria. Its primary role was to maintain control over a war-shattered enemy, but, progressively as the Soviets in Eastern Europe became increasingly aggressive, it was to act as the West's forward line of defence against any Communist attack.

We also still had occupation troops in other areas of Europe over which the Second World War had been fought, such as Italy and Greece. In the Middle East there was a vast administrative headquarters in Cairo and residual troops left over from the Desert War. There were forces protecting the lifeline of the Suez Canal, with detachments of troops all the way from Tripoli in the west to Kenya in the south, from Syria in the north to Baghdad in the east.

As Jewish terrorism mounted from 1946 onwards, our forces had to expand vigorously in Palestine, a territory mandated from 1918 and considered strategically vital to protecting Suez and the British imperial lifeline to India and Australia.

In the Far East were British forces left over from the war against Japan, predominantly in Burma and Malaya, plus Britain's long-term presence in Imperial India. All these commitments required further troops to protect lines of communication.

The Years of Extreme Danger, 1945–1953

Galvanized by Churchill's 1946 warning, the United States President Harry S.Truman moved in 1947 to pick up the role that Britain could no longer afford in Greece (where a Communist-initiated civil war had broken out) and also in Turkey. Thus began a historic commitment for a US Government in peacetime. In 1948, following the Communist takeover in Czechoslovakia, America led the way in the creation of the North Atlantic Treaty Organization (NATO). The purpose of NATO, as it was whispered at the time in British officers' messes, was to "keep the US in, Russia out, and Germany down"!

At the same time the Labour Government was bent on terminating Britain's imperial legacy everywhere as swiftly as possible. 1947 saw the partitioning of India and the British decision to return the Palestine mandate to the United Nations. Independence was successively granted to Burma and to colonies in Africa, permitting a withdrawal and retrenchment of British forces.

It was upon divided Germany and its future, however, that the 'Cold War' was to focus over the next four decades. In June 1948 the Russians attempted to take over the three Western sectors of Berlin by imposing a blockade of the city, which lay inside their allotted zone. But the Allies rose to the challenge by mounting the massive Berlin Airlift which, after an anxious nine months in which Europe seemed to teeter on the brink of war again, finally forced Russia to back down. It was a first victory for Western technology, of the order that was to defeat 'The Evil Empire' forty years later.

In August 1949 Stalin stunned the West by exploding the first Soviet atomic bomb. The following year, egged on by the USSR, North Korea invaded South Korea, and UN forces, led by the US under General Douglas MacArthur, intervened. From near defeat MacArthur swept into the North, reaching the Yalu River frontier with Chinese Manchuria, thereby exceeding his UN brief. An alarmed Communist China now came into the war, inflicting a humiliating defeat upon MacArthur, who was then sacked by Truman. A stalemate ensued, with negotiations dragging on for three years.

In 1952 the United States elected General Dwight D.Eisenhower as President; in England Winston Churchill had been returned to power and in March of 1953 Stalin died, precipitating a period of extreme tension in Europe.

A New Threat, 1953–1964

Out of the power struggle inside the Kremlin Nikita Krushchev eventually emerged in control. Confusingly, one minute he talked about 'peaceful co-existence', the next he was threatening the West with challenges such as "We will bury you"! Aware of the West's acute inferiority in terms of manpower, US Secretary of State Dulles responded with the policy of 'massive (ie nuclear) retaliation'. This meant that NATO would respond to any conventional Soviet attack in Europe with nuclear weapons. It in turn was followed by the doctrine of 'Mutually Assured Destruction' (MAD) and the Nuclear Deterrent.

1956 was the year of Suez and Hungary. The US forced upon her British and French allies a humiliating withdrawal at Suez, thereby defining a new re-appraisal of the reality of British world power. It was the date when Britain was forced to abandon pretences, beyond her means, of continuing to be a Great Power. France, however, having been forced to abandon her colonial position in Indo-China, now became involved in a losing colonial war that was to last for eight years in Algeria. Meanwhile, Krushchev's tanks crushed the Hungarian revolt – and remained astride in Hungary.

In August 1961 Krushchev's construction of the Berlin Wall, designed not to keep West Germans out but the oppressed East Germans in, ushered in a new bout of maximum danger and confrontation in the Cold War. At one moment US and Soviet tanks faced each other, muzzle to muzzle, in Berlin. When Krushchev and Castro between them challenged Kennedy over the Cuban Missile Crisis in October 1962 it brought the whole world closer to the brink, and to the unthinkable horror of nuclear war, than at any time since 1945. Civilization held its breath; but Krushchev flinched and Kennedy won.

Soon thereafter Krushchev was toppled and replaced in the Kremlin by the dead hand of Leonid Brezhnev.

In retrospect Harold Macmillan, who was Prime Minister at the time, considered the Cuban Missile Crisis of October 1962 to have been "one of the great turning points in history". In realization of the extreme danger that had confronted civilization, a new era of détente began; the 'hot-line' to Moscow was installed, and in the summer of 1963 a first Nuclear Test Ban Treaty signed. Though only 'partial', it led to the series of negotiations arising from the Strategic Arms Limitation Treaty (SALT) that ran on into the Reagan-Gorbachev era of the 1980s.

Cold War Spills into Third World

Meanwhile, however, the Cold War had spilled over into the Third World in the 1960s and 1970s. With the collapse of the South Vietnam government, created in the aftermath of the French withdrawal from Indo-China, America became bogged down in the costly and futile ten-year Vietnam War. Britain, under Harold Wilson, refused to become involved. In 1973 President Nixon cut US losses and pulled out, leaving America's South Vietnamese allies to a dreadful Communist fate. It was a humiliating defeat for the US; though Vietnam today, since the collapse of Communism, now gives the impression of being more US than Marxist orientated.

One bonus of Vietnam was the Nixon-Kissinger diplomacy bringing the colossus of Communist China back into the comity of nations from the purdah in which it had glowered since the Korean War.

In the Middle East two fierce, brief wars fought between Israel and her Arab neighbours in 1968 and 1973 saw the biggest tank engagements since the Russian Front in World War II and resulted in a stand-off. Russia and the US stood on the sidelines as their client-states slugged it out, but (only just) avoided involvement.

Brezhnev to Gorbachev/Reagan 1964–1989

In Eastern Europe the oppressed Soviet satellites continued to grow restive. With the 'Prague Spring' of 1968, a liberalizing regime under Alexander Dubcek was crushed, once again, by Soviet tanks. But later the 'Solidarity' movement in Poland was allowed to survive and take root. In retrospect it now seems that 1968 was a kind of watershed in Soviet power; invisible to most Western eyes at the time was the remorseless stagnation of the Soviet economy.

In 1979 the fall of the Shah of Persia and the rise of Moslem Fundamentalism presented the West with a new foe. But that same year the invasion of Afghanistan, at least as disastrous to the Russians as Vietnam had been to the Americans, revealed the terrifying Red Army, which had held the West in thrall all those years, to be a giant with feet of clay.

Gorbachev succeeded Brezhnev after two ailing Soviet leaders (Yuri Andropov and Konstantin Chernenko) died in quick succession. In 1979 Margaret Thatcher took over a new and invigorated Tory Government in Britain, while the following year the arch-conservative Ronald

Reagan succeeded the enfeebled President Carter. His eight years in office heralded a new policy in the Cold War: on the one hand détente with a willing Gorbachev, on the other hand an economic, high-tech challenge to bankrupt the tottering Soviet military machine.

In the words of Douglas Hurd human rights provisions agreed with Gorbachev

> "gave the West a lever to prise open, slowly and with setbacks, some of the dark shutters of the Soviet system and let in light".[1]

America's Anti-Ballistic Missile (ABM) enterprise known as 'Star Wars' proved the last straw. The rickety USSR military economy collapsed trying to compete. After one last desperate attempt to save Communism, Gorbachev was overwhelmed by mounting discontent in the East European satellites, coupled with economic and social disarray at home.

November 1989 saw the fall of the Berlin Wall, the very symbol of Soviet Power in Europe. In swift succession the other East European countries rediscovered their independence. The Warsaw Pact simply fell apart, while at home the mighty Soviet Union split into its ethnic parts, leaving a much truncated and impoverished Russia militarily gelded. Germany was reunited, to become once more the most numerous and potentially most powerful component of Western Europe.

The Cold War was over; fought, and won, remarkably without the death in direct conflict of a single British, American or Soviet soldier. Considering the dangers that had been faced, it was nothing short of a miracle!

Colonialism and Post-Colonialism

From the 1950s onwards Britain had committed herself to maintaining in Germany four divisions, the bulk of the heavy armour, as her substantial contribution to NATO in the Cold War. Meanwhile, however, *pari passu* with this she had to shoulder the burdens of colonial and post-colonial commitments. No sooner was Palestine resolved than there was Communist terrorism in Malaya to deal with. Malaya was followed by Mau-Mau in Kenya and EOKA in Cyprus; in turn came Aden and the Borneo campaign.

Then, in 1982, Britain found herself committed to a full-scale war 7000 miles away, in the Falklands which was to tax particularly her naval capacity to the very limit. Yet at least it proved that Britain could still act, within limitations, as a global power. These limitations were seen in 1990, during the Gulf War, when, to meet the invasion of Kuwait by Iraq, a third-rate power, the US had to mount the biggest operations since D-Day. As her loyalest ally, Britain was only able to provide some ten percent of the troops and then only by draining the bottom of the barrel in Europe down almost to the last functioning tank. But, in quality, the contribution of 1st Armoured Division was to prove quite outstanding.

The ending of the Cold War and the Gulf War brought a whole range of new tasks to be faced by the West and Britain's Armed Forces. The disintegration of Yugoslavia and the brutal civil war in Bosnia invented a new word in the military vocabulary – peace-keeping.

[1] Hurd, Douglas, *The Search for Peace, a Century of Peace Diplomacy*, Little Brown, 1997.

Defence 'Streamlining' Cuts

Through all these trials and commitments since 1945, the true motto of the British Army might with justice be said to have been: ADAPTABILITY. In many ways successive chiefs of the Armed Forces proved to be more adaptable to each fresh crisis than their political bosses.

Ever since Attlee's Emmanuel Shinwell, Governments, whether Labour or Conservative, have imposed cut after cut on the Army, yet expected it to fulfil each new heavy task imposed on it. In 1951, for instance, British infantry battalions had already been reduced to 85; by 1957 the number had been further slashed to 77 and was soon to come down to 60.

Yet, typically, the Army (as Lord Carver points out in his comprehensive book *Britain's Army in the 20th Century)* "was almost as heavily involved as it had been before Suez".[2] Macmillan, Mountbatten and Sandys came along to end National Service and further 'streamline' the Army's effectives. Then followed Denis Healey and the withdrawal from East of Suez. In 1970 Heath inherited an army of only 41 infantry battalions.

Next came the cuts imposed by Defence Minister John Nott in 1981 which nearly left the Navy without a carrier at the time of the Falklands; then came 'Options for Change' in 1991, reducing Army effectives for the first time to a figure bordering on the 100,000 mark[3], and this was followed by further cuts under George Robertson and New Labour. The Territorial Army was cut to the bone; by year 2000 it was reckoned that, with a total of only some 450 main battle tanks, Britain would rank 44th in the world league of armour.

Yet Government planners still reckon on Britain's ability to "send abroad two complete Army Corps" (just as at the time of the Stanhope Memorandum of 1888 111 years ago!)

What Next?

And so it goes on. What kind of Army can Britain really be expected to field over the first decades of the twenty-first Century? What will its commitments be? Almost certainly peace-keeping will become a primary function.

Though the danger will continue to exist as long as small boys play with sling-shots and madmen emerge to seize power anywhere in the globe, the likelihood of major conflict on the scale of either World War looks happily more remote than at any time over the past century. As in the 1920s, planners designing the army of the future find themselves confronted by the question of who will be our enemy in ten years' time? But now the costs are infinitely higher, the expensiveness of a mistake equally so, but the resources available reduced to a mere fraction.

Conclusion

Finally, the historian might ask himself: was the Cold War a 'good war'? For the Soviets, piling up some seventy years of misery and deprivation ever since the 1917 Revolution, it was without question an unmitigated disaster. For the West, faced with fighting only 'brush-fire' wars along the periphery, but, as pointed out earlier, not losing a single man in a major confrontation in Europe, yes, undoubtedly this was a 'good war'. The fifty-year period of calm and relative stability which

[2] Macmillan 1998.

[3] As of April 1997, the Regular Army, excluding Gurkhas, totalled 111,572 soldiers, of whom 6932 were women.

the nuclear deadlock produced in Europe's turbulent twentieth century may well come to be regarded by future generations as indeed a kind of Golden Age.

Note on Author
Alistair Horne served in the Coldstream Guards from 1944–1947, retiring as a Captain, attached to Intelligence. He has written many books on military history and biography; for his contributions to History he has been awarded both the CBE and Légion d'Honneur, and he is a Doctor of Literature of Cambridge University.

COLD WAR CAMPAIGNING

by Philip Warner

In 1945, when Germany and Japan had both been well and truly beaten, the average Guardsman, if such a being exists, might naturally have assumed that the future of soldiering would be unexciting garrison duties and peacetime soldiering of 1930's style. Even the most imaginative could not have predicted what an enormous variety of experience lay ahead. There would, of course, be garrison duties in occupied territories while the mess of the Second World War was tidied up, but who would have guessed at the amount of anti-terrorist duties, and hard fighting in mountainous country, desert or dense jungle, sometimes a combination of all?

For nearly twenty years the Regiment would have a new type of recruit, the National Serviceman (peacetime conscript). It was made clear to these young men during their first few days at the Guards Depot, and frequently thereafter, that they were welcomed as members of the Regiment. They would be treated in the same manner and required to measure up to the same standards demanded of their fellow Coldstreamers who were on a Regular engagement. Good leadership and the Regimental Spirit insured that the majority of National Servicemen met the demands made on them admirably. Some in due course converted to a Regular engagement. Today many Coldstream National Servicemen, now middle-aged and retired, continue to serve the Regiment by their loyal and enthusiastic support of their local Branch of The Coldstream Guards Association.[4]

The good news was that when presented with new challenges in unfamiliar settings the Coldstream Guardsmen rose to the occasion in a way that silenced potential critics. This should not have surprised anyone. In the early days of World War II, when the proposal to form a Guards Armoured Division had been put forward, there had been a lot of people who had thought it was a mad idea. The Guardsmen, they said, were too tall and too thick (in both senses of the word) to fight in a tank. Long before 1945 nobody was saying that any more. The Armoured Division had its problems in the early stages, but it overcame them and became an élite formation.

The new challenges were not too long in coming, some through purely local reasons, while others would be the result of the subversive activities of our wartime ally, the Soviet Union. The Soviet

[4] Letter from Major General Colin Wallis-King, CBE. January 2000.

Union was the major player in the Cold War and necessitated Coldstreamers being stationed in Germany on continuous alert from time to time over a period of fifty years.

While Britain and America were rapidly reducing their forces, the Russians still kept four million men under arms; the atomic bomb deterred them from making a frontal attack, but they soon resorted to a different means of attack – subversion. Every possible method was used to soften the West's resistance to Communism. The first big Cold War confrontation would come in 1948, in Malaya, but long before that the 3rd Battalion Coldstream Guards was in action in Palestine in that most unpleasant and frustrating form of warfare – counter-terrorism.

Palestine 1945–1948, 3rd Battalion

Palestine had been part of the Turkish Empire until the First World War, but in the ensuing Peace Treaties was entrusted to Britain (in what was then described as a 'Mandate') to be groomed for self-government after thirty years. For centuries Palestine had been occupied by Arabs, although a few Jews had also settled there for sentimental reasons. However, during and after the Second World War, when Jews were fleeing from the Nazi extermination camps, the inflow became a flood, much resented by the Arabs, who felt that they alone were the rightful occupants of the country. Britain was blamed by the Arabs for allowing in too many Jews and by the Jews for not allowing in enough.

The Jews created an underground National Army, the Haganah, which included two terrorist groups, Irgun and the Stern Gang, with which they planned to take control of the country. The 3rd Battalion therefore sailed into a situation in which Jews were trying to drive out the Arabs and the Arabs were determined not to lose their homes to the Jewish immigrants. Both sides regarded the British as the enemy because each felt the British were responsible for the unfortunate state the country was in. It was the first post-war example of the role that the Army would come to know in Ireland and elsewhere for the rest of the century.

The Battalion set up road blocks, searched vehicles for arms and explosives, checked roads and railways for mines (one patrol even went out on horseback) and questioned endless suspects. They soon found out (what their fellow-Guardsmen would also encounter later in other countries) that terrorists are particularly skilled in concealing arms and vital documents. Arms caches were found in children's nurseries, under floors, even in sewers. There was often considerable resistance by men, women and children to any search operation, but it was not all bad news, for the Battalion's disciplined restraint under provocation, combined with courtesy and friendliness (where possible), produced a grudging admiration from the population and, possibly, less support for the terrorists. However, when walking out, Guardsmen still had to be in parties of four and to carry arms.

There were, of course, occasions when the local population felt a hatred for the Guardsmen and a large cordon and search operation in March 1947 was one of them. Designed to flush out terrorists, it lasted fifteen days, in which the occupants of the area had no communication with anyone outside the cordoned area which was ten miles long and five miles broad and contained some 300,000 people. There were casualties. A Jewish cyclist was challenged three times by a sentry but failed to respond and was shot dead; soon afterwards Guardsman Stocker was killed by a grenade when on sentry duty.

In July 1947 two Field Security Police Sergeants were kidnapped in Nathanya, and although the area was cordoned off and searched, they could not be found. Irgun had announced that the Sergeants were being held as hostages for three Jewish terrorists who had been convicted and were awaiting execution in Acre jail. Nevertheless the convicted terrorists were duly hanged on

Tel Aviv 1947. Citrus House housing most of the 3rd Battalion. (Note the anti-tank gun on the roof)

29 July and two days later the bodies of the Sergeants were found by the Battalion. They had been hanged in an orange grove near Nathanya and the ground underneath the bodies had also been mined.

In October 1947 the Battalion moved to Trans-Jordan for training, but here it found a new problem – the local Bedouin, who had turned pilfering into a fine art. The problem was solved by inviting the chief of the local Bedouin tribe, the Beni Hassan, into the camp for tea and Beating Retreat by the Corps of Drums. He was a splendid old man, said to be aged 137, and he so enjoyed the display that he asked if he could buy the Corps of Drums! It was all a great success and from that moment all pilfering ceased as if by magic in the Coldstream lines, while neighbouring units reported increased raids on their camps.

In December the Battalion was back in Lydda and a patrol investigating an Arab farm recovered four Bren guns, fifteen Stens, 160 rifles and 70,000 rounds of ammunition.

Towards the end of the tour the Band of the Irish Guards visited Palestine and No 2 Company, under Lieutenant R.R.Cooper, was sent to escort them on a sightseeing trip to Jerusalem and Bethlehem. The group was given wrong information by the Police about which roads were safe and ran into an Arab ambush intended for the Jews. They managed to extricate themselves, but one Bandsman was killed and three wounded, and one Coldstream Guardsman was wounded.

In March 1948 the 3rd Battalion was relieved by the 1st, which had been in London for two years. The Commanding Officer was Lieutenant Colonel John Chandos-Pole, but he was wounded early on during some fighting in Haifa, and when the Second-in-Command, Major B.E.Luard MC, arrived, he found himself a Lieutenant Colonel and in command of the Battalion.

The British Mandate for Palestine ended on 15 May and the country became the independent State of Israel. The 1st Battalion, which had seen considerable action in its three months there, left in the final incident-free evacuation on 30 June 1948 and headed for Tripoli.

Cold War Commitments

The Cold War led to the Regiment being deployed on operations of many types round the world from 1945 to 1990. All three Battalions served many times in Germany as part of BAOR (the British Army of the Rhine), which was the front line against the Soviet Army, with the accompanying threat of nuclear warfare.

The Middle East was another trouble spot where the Communists took every opportunity to stir up nationalist feeling against Britain, and the Regiment saw service in Egypt, South Arabia, North Africa, Kuwait, Kenya, Zanzibar and Mauritius. Further afield it played its part in the Emergency in Malaya in 1948, in Borneo and in Belize.

Keeping the Peace

In addition to these Cold War commitments, which were all part of the worldwide struggle against Communism, the Regiment was also committed to a series of peace-keeping operations, starting with Palestine (1945–1948), then in Cyprus and of course, Northern Ireland from 1969 onwards. Today it faces a new form of peace-keeping in the Balkans.

The Regiment's Cold War campaigns are dealt with in more detail in the following chapter, which in turn is followed by chapters on home service and peace-keeping commitments in Northern Ireland.

Note on Author

Philip Warner was formerly Senior Lecturer at RMA Sandhurst and Chief Examiner in Military History, Staff College Entrance and Promotion Examinations. He was the *Daily Telegraph* Military Obituaries correspondent and the author of various books, including histories of the First and Second World Wars. His cousin served in the Regiment. He died in September 2000.

CHAPTER TEN

THE COLDSTREAM IN THE COLD WAR

by Edward Crofton

MALAYA, 1948–1950

2nd Battalion

The 2nd Battalion returned to England in 1946 after four years in North Africa and Italy, and spent the next eighteen months on ceremonial duties (in battledress until the middle of 1948), when rumours began to circulate that it would move to the West Indies the following spring. However, events overtook that prognosis and in August (Friday the 13th in fact) the Battalion, under the command of Lieutenant Colonel Dick Gooch DSO MC was ordered to be ready to sail to Malaya at the beginning of September. Since 1945 the internal security situation in that country had deteriorated with the emergence of the Malayan Communist Party on to the political scene. Murders and acts of terrorism had increased in number and a State of Emergency had been declared. The Battalion was to form part of 2nd Guards Brigade, which also included 3rd Battalion Grenadier Guards and 2nd Battalion Scots Guards.

Home Service clothing was exchanged for jungle green. Cynics regarded the issue with some scepticism for on more than one occasion troops had been issued with tropical kit only to find at the last minute that they were switched to a decidedly untropical climate. The reverse process had also occurred: some soldiers (not Guardsmen) who were sent to the Falklands in 1982 arrived there kitted out for Belize. In the Second World War it was said that supplying the wrong weight of clothing was deliberate to deceive enemy spies, but in fact it was more likely because of last-minute changes of plan!

2nd Guards Brigade formation sign.

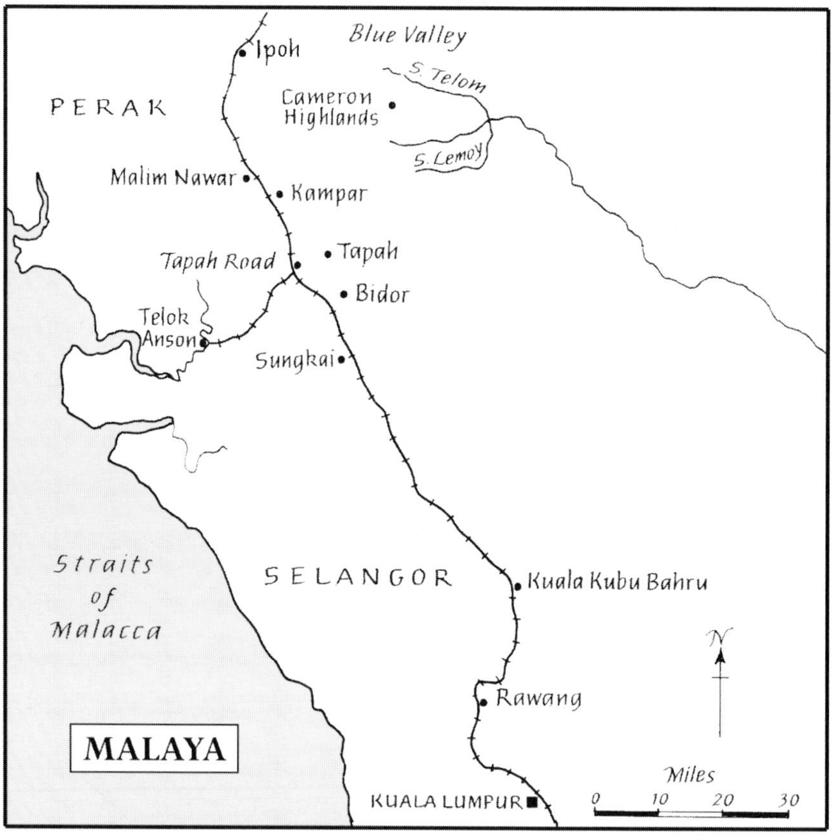

The Battalion duly arrived, correctly kitted out, in Singapore in October. As the Guardsmen soon discovered, Malaya is a very beautiful country but also very wet with rain falling every day, usually at about three o'clock in the afternoon, with dramatic thunder and lightning. It also contains scorpions, snakes and a variety of insects of which mosquitoes and leeches are the most persistently maddening. Acclimatization training took place in a temperature of 90°F in the shade. Platoon Commanders and Sergeants were sent to courses at the Jungle Warfare School in Johore and on the 21st the main body of the Battalion moved by train up to Tapah.

Temoh Hill Camp, Tapah, was a sea of mud and a pile of tents when the Battalion arrived. However, attap huts were rapidly constructed. They were roomy buildings with walls and roofs made of broad long leaves, and were ideal for a country which is blazingly hot in the day but cools considerably at night. The autumn also saw the appearance of the dreaded square, although it was hardly up to Wellington Barracks standards![1]

The Malayan population (excluding Singapore) was made up of 2½ million Malayans, a similar number of Chinese and about 300,000 Tamils from India, who worked as tappers on the rubber plantations. Some 5000 Communist terrorists (CTs) were also hiding out in jungle camps, with a number of sympathizers in the towns. It was these Communist terrorists, now calling themselves the Malayan Peoples' Anti-British Army (MPABA), who had been responsible for the enforced State

[1] *Clothed All in Green-O!*, an account of the activities of the 2nd Battalion in Malaya 1948–49.

of Emergency. Their aim was to take over the country by killing as many rubber planters and tin miners as possible, making forays from their jungle camps, intimidating and murdering rubber tappers and reducing the country to bankruptcy. However, they relied on obtaining food and other supplies from villages (kampongs) on the edge of the jungle.

Tapah Camp, Malaya, 1948–1950.

The task of the British troops was to protect the planters and mine-workers and to kill or capture as many CTs as possible; but they were highly skilled at operating from the jungle and when they emerged from it, if not obviously armed, looked much the same as any other Chinese labourer. To relieve the stress and monotony of terrorist hunting, Guardsmen would enjoy periods of leave in Penang, Kuala Lumpur, or similar towns where the standards of recreation often seemed to mimic a Hollywood film setting.

The Battalion soon set about its task of eliminating CTs and at the same time also began resettling villages, often occupied by squatters, away from areas where they could be intimidated into supplying the CTs.

Usually the Guardsmen carried a Sten (not always reliable), a Bren gun or a Lee-Enfield Mark V, which with ammunition, change of clothing and five days' rations, weighed 60 lbs: and seemed heavier in the heat.

During the first few months of 1949 it became evident that some success was being achieved, as bandit activity in the more civilized areas became much more restricted, with gangs being forced back into the hills and jungle, which meant for them not only difficulties in obtaining supplies, but also long and difficult marches to reach worthwhile targets for their activities, and therefore the very good chance of running into one of our patrols on the way. For the remainder of the Battalion's tour of duty its task fell roughly into two phases: firstly screening operations in villages and patrols deep into the jungle with the object of eradicating the bandits by military action, and, secondly, with

2nd Battalion No 3 Company; Kampar, Perak 1949. From right to left: Sergeant Riddick, Guardsmen Ormond, Roddis, Findley, Radford, Sergeants Willis and Baxter, Guardsmen Hill and Small.

2nd Battalion Corps of Drums marching through Kampar, Perak, 1949.

the same objective, to resettle the squatters, on whom the bandits lived to a very large extent.

However, by the beginning of 1950 it was clear that the incident rate had not decreased, and so renewed emphasis was placed on the second phase, the resettlement of the squatters. Lieutenant Colonel Victor FitzGeorge-Balfour CBE MC had taken over command of the Battalion from Colonel Gooch and he initiated a scheme which was to be copied throughout the country. This involved the concentration of some 7,000 squatter families (between 30,000 and 40,000 people) into about thirty new villages, each with an average population of 1200 and to an extent of approximately 25 acres. The density of houses was to be between ten and twelve to the acre; each village was to have a Police post, a well and a village hall, and was to be surrounded by an 8' perimeter fence which involved the use of some 350 miles of barbed wire. Each squatter family was to dismantle its own house and reassemble it on an allotted site in the new village, free transport being provided by the Army. As far as possible, squatters were to be left in possession of their existing plots of land and only be made to move their houses into the village. In the case of those squatter areas which were too remote and too exposed to bandit influence or too small to warrant a setting up of a new village, they would be moved right away into one of the other new villages and would be given new land in the surrounding area.

The scheme was undoubtedly a success and by the time that the Battalion handed over to 45 Royal Marine Commando in July 1950 seven new villages had been established and were well on their way to becoming orderly communities, while two more were ready for the squatters to move in. Two of these villages were named after the Battalion, becoming Kampong Coldstream and Kampong Balfour respectively.

There were occasional large jungle sweeps, but in general there were innumerable guard patrols. One of the more remarkable took place

2nd Battalion Number 3 Company with Police (in front) and Interpreters, Bidor area. Left to right: Two Interpreters, Guardsmen Harding, Findley, Andrews, Humber, Riley, Interpreter.

in April 1949. Intended to last three hours, it ran over seven and a half days. It began when Lance Sergeant Gulston and Guardsmen Crisp, Knowles, Ingles and Thorp set off to investigate a jungle track which looked as if it might lead to a CT camp. They soon had a brisk gunfight with some bandits who then melted away into the jungle, but when they themselves tried to return to their base they found a strong force blocking the way.

They decided to work their way back through the jungle, which also involved crossing streams and climbing steep ridges. Their rations were soon exhausted and opportunities for rest or sleep were very limited as the CTs were close on their heels waiting for an opportunity to make a surprise attack. On the first morning of their trek they encountered a CT whom Gulston promptly shot dead with his Sten: on the second they encountered another six, one of whom was killed by Knowles and a second wounded by Gulston, before they too faded away into the jungle. The following day their return route involved climbing to 5000 feet where the night was bitterly cold and where they were also soaking wet.

On the next day they saw no CTs, but they were fired on from the jungle and also encountered a large cobra on the track. On the seventh day they came across four Army biscuits which had been dropped by another patrol: they did not last long and equally important was the realization that they were getting close to their base. Later that day they met a patrol which was out looking for them.

Gulston was awarded an immediate Military Medal and Knowles was Mentioned in Despatches. Members of the general public, who only see Guardsmen when they are in full ceremonial order, seldom appreciate that they are soldiers first and performers of Public Duties second.

There were a number of other notable incidents in Malaya. During Operation RAMILLIES in April 1949 Major Sir Ralph Anstruther was

Building Kampong Coldstream 1950.

Number 3 Company Patrol 1948.

CT Camp – recently evacuated.

crossing a flooded river when he slipped on a stone and was carried away by the fast current. Guardsman Pratt plunged into the water, grabbed Major Anstruther with one hand and, after both had been carried down the river some distance, grabbed a rock with his other hand and held on until rescue came. Pratt was subsequently awarded the Bronze Medal of the Royal Humane Society.

Guardsmen Kenningham, Humber, Hobin with locals.

On another occasion, in July 1949, a patrol led by Lance Sergeant Brennan followed some fresh tracks and by maintaining complete silence got to within five yards of a camp holding 150 CTs, all of whom fled as the Guardsmen opened fire. Lance Sergeant Brennan's determination and example on this and other occasions earned him the Military Medal. In the same month Sergeant Howells was also awarded the MM for his part in an attack on a bandit camp in the hills near Kampar, following an earlier intimidatory attack on the local population, and Captain The Hon A.P.Harbord-Hamond was awarded the Military Cross for his courage and leadership when the platoon he was leading was ambushed while crossing a river at Kuala Kas. In March 1950 2nd Lieutenant J.A.McGougan and Lance Sergeant Butler were awarded the MC and MM respectively for their gallantry and determination in the follow-up to an ambush south of Tapah.

The Battalion returned to England in September 1950. It had been a highly successful operational tour, as was confirmed by the award of the DSO to the Commanding Officer, together with the award of two MCs, one MBE, five MMs, two BEMs and thirteen members of the Battalion Mentioned in Despatches. The Emergency continued until 1960, by which time over 6500 CTs had been killed and a further 4000 had either been captured or had surrendered, but at a cost of over 2400 civilians and over 1800 members of the Security Forces killed. The Regiment sadly lost Sergeant I.Lawson BEM, Guardsman S.Palfrey and Guardsman J.Parkin who died in action.

SUEZ, 1956

2nd and 3rd Battalions

In June 1956 the **3rd Battalion** under Lieutenant Colonel Claude Worrall moved to Moore Barracks at Shorncliffe and joined 1st Guards Brigade. Six weeks later Egypt decided to nationalize the Suez Canal. On 4 August orders to mobilize were received and Reservists began turning up the following week. A large proportion of these men were specialists.

Captain D.H.A.Lewey had recently assumed the appointment of Adjutant of the Battalion and he describes their arrival: "RSM D.Glisson and I set up a receiving office and together saw and posted each man individually as he arrived. Some of the Class B Specialist Reservists had been out for six or seven years, but every single man, and I think there were some 300 of them, came into that little office as though he had never left the Colours, 'pulling the feet in' and giving his name, service dates and qualifications. Of all the 3rd Battalion Reservists only two failed to appear at

Pirbright within the specified 24 hours; one was in Canada and the other seriously ill in hospital. I have seldom seen anything more heartening than these men's reactions to their sudden recall. They were splendid.

"The officer side was less successful. Perhaps because the only Regimental plans were for a general mobilization of officers, the partial recall at this time seemed to cause a nonsense. We received some ten captains and subalterns who had been 'asked' to return. Apparently they were the wrong ones, for most of them disappeared within a few days and others took their place. I am still uncertain on what basis these officers returned to us, but I believe that in the first instance they all did so voluntarily, in many cases at the cost of great disruption of their private and business lives."

The specialists were absorbed into Headquarters and Support Companies, with the remainder going to No 2 Company. The strength of the Battalion soon rose to around 800. Moore Barracks was not designed to accommodate that number and so the Battalion had to resort to double-tier bunks and two sittings for each meal. Captain Lewey continues: "We were mostly at 48 hours' notice. The first operation orders and loading plans lasted us some time. The fighting echelon of vehicles, loaded to breaking point with ammunition, was in a Landing Ship in Barry Docks, Glamorgan. We had painted these vehicles yellow with large white 'Hs' for recognition. Without vehicles we marched everywhere and became very fit. Unfortunately it was not only our vehicles but most of our radio equipment and support weapons which were embarked, and training began to become wearisome and unproductive without them. The authorities therefore issued us with a duplicate set, mostly produced from Territorial Army sources.

"Realistic information on what was happening was hard to come by and I used occasionally to take a boat out from the Household Brigade Yacht Club at Hamble to see if our Landing Ship was still there. Cowes roads were always full of hired transports loaded with 3rd Division vehicles. One day I sailed round to find our Landing Ship full of most unmilitary looking people; of our vital fighting echelon vehicles there was no sign. It transpired that the plans had been changed, our vehicles sent back to us and the War Correspondents embarked in our Landing Ship.

"One now knows that this marked the end of the plan to land on the beaches of Alexandria, a plan in which 1st Guards Brigade, to which we belonged, was to have been an assault brigade. With the change of plan to a Port Said landing we entered a prolonged period of chaos, passing through a dozen variations of orders and periods of notice including two recalls to immediate notice and a day when the Commanding Officer told the Battalion, 'This time it really is firm: we sail tomorrow'. The morale of the Battalion soared to dizzy heights and I fingered the sealed orders in the safe. Two days later we returned the orders unopened and reverted to seven days' notice.

"Once again, in mid-November, our transport went off, this time all to Welsh ports and we were brought to short notice once more. By now we were becoming veterans of false alarms and I was woken at one o'clock in the morning with a signal telling us to produce fresh loading plans for an amphibious exercise at Stranraer. 'I don't believe a word of it,' I remember saying. 'Do nothing.' The exercise was cancelled at noon next day.

"While we came down to 48 hours' notice once again, our transport and equipment actually set sail in two ships for the Mediterranean. Captain R.A.Q.Shuldham, the Transport Officer, and about 120 NCOs and men, mostly drivers, were aboard. As far as we were concerned they sailed into limbo: we had no idea where they were.

"The Parachute landings took place in Egypt. We followed the news anxiously, daily expecting orders to move ourselves. Suddenly in the early hours of a Monday morning we heard that the Anglo-French forces had halted. In due course the whole depressing truth became clear and the Reservists began to enquire about their future. A sudden order arrived to release them – all of them, wherever they were. A lot of ours were on the two transports, which we discovered had arrived, one at Malta and one at Gibraltar, and between them these Reservists had about a quarter of the Battalion's vehicles and equipment on their temporary charge. Released they were. We never even saw them. A Court of Inquiry on the inevitable losses was ordered, despite our objections, with Major Buckland, the Second-in-Command, as President. Halfway through his labours when he was still totalling the thousands of pounds worth of missing items, this crowning folly was cancelled; all losses were to be written off.

"It had been an instructive few weeks for a new Adjutant but it is hard to find any other kind words for the experience.

"Only one member of the Battalion actually landed in Egypt – Captain M.G.Willasey-Wilsey, attached as a Liaison Officer to Headquarters 3rd Division.

"The Battalion returned to peacetime activities, was told to learn Greek and a few weeks later was posted to Germany."[2]

The **2nd Battalion**, commanded by Lieutenant Colonel Henry Green, was training at Thetford when the crisis broke. The Reservists who were training with it were sent home and the Battalion, having been ordered to mobilize as part of 1st Guards Brigade, returned to Chelsea Barracks. Regular Army Reservists began to arrive on 9 August and the accommodation at Chelsea soon became inadequate. This, together with the need to train the Battalion, necessitated a move out of London, and, although the remainder of 1st Guards Brigade was at Shorncliffe, it was decided that a move to Pirbright would be practical, and so the Battalion duly moved there on 23 August. At Pirbright khaki drill was issued, vehicles were painted sand colour, anti-tank guns were exchanged due to a lack of appropriate ammunition. Orders and counter-orders followed, vehicles were packed and unpacked, and sailing dates were given, only to be postponed. In mid-November the vehicles, fully loaded, sailed and reached Malta and Gibraltar, only to be sent home again. The majority of the Battalion who had been involved in the merry-go-round were kept at various states of readiness to move. Three days before they were due to sail for Cyprus the ceasefire was blown. The Battalion returned to Lower Establishment, the Reservists went home to their civilian jobs and, after some leave, the Battalion returned to its normal routine.

KENYA, 1959–1962

2nd Battalion

In March 1959 the 2nd Battalion under Lieutenant Colonel Ken Sweeting was sent to Kenya to join 24th Infantry Brigade under Brigadier R.C.T.Miers DSO, OBE. The Battalion was based at Gilgil some seventy miles north of Nairobi with the role of flying to any trouble spot in the Middle East. The first eighteen months were spent in Alanbrooke Camp, which was tented, but in May 1961 the Battalion moved one mile into Slim Camp, which had huts and also married quarters.

It was an exceptionally enjoyable station, for the Mau Mau Emergency was over and it was possible to travel freely, be it to game parks (with no tourists around) to the coast at Mombasa and Malindi, and also to many other countries. The training facilities were excellent and there was scope

[2] *The Coldstream Guards 1946–70* R.J.V.Crichton, p.50–52.

too for unusual Adventure Training. This included two expeditions to climb Mount Kenya and Mount Kilimanjaro, which at 17,058 feet and 19,565 feet respectively are the two highest mountains in Africa. No less than 114 volunteers, led by the new Commanding Officer, Lieutenant Colonel Julian Paget, reached Gilman's Point, the accepted 'top' of Kilimanjaro, the previous largest group being seventy-six. A party of seventy-two then went on to Kaiser Wilhelm Spitze, the highest point of all, and this was more than twice as many as had ever got there in a group before.

Bahrain/Kuwait, 1961

But it was not all just training, and there was a serious operational role as well. 24th Brigade maintained a detachment of a half-battalion in Bahrain, due to the possibility of aggression by Iraq against its oil-rich neighbour, Kuwait. In February 1961 the 2nd Battalion was ordered to take over this commitment and so the Bahrain Detachment was formed. It consisted of Nos 1 and 3 Companies and part of Headquarter Company and was commanded by the Second-in-Command, Major Roy Dobson; it was 275 strong and included twenty-three married families.

Bahrain was considerably less attractive than Kenya, but, thanks to excellent relations with the Royal Navy and the RAF, a certain amount of training, travel and relaxation was possible.[3] But in June 1961 it suddenly became 'the real thing', when Iraq looked like invading Kuwait. The only troops immediately available were the Bahrain Detachment, 42 Royal Marine Commando and a squadron of 3rd Dragoon Guards. But they were able to move into Kuwait immediately and secure the airfield, hoping that they would not have to face the entire Iraqi Army. It turned out to be a perfect example of 'a stitch in time' and it was enough to deter the aggression.

Zanzibar, 1961

These commitments did, however, place a considerable strain on the Battalion and in July 1961 No 1 Company of the 1st Battalion was sent out to Kenya to reinforce it. It was just as well, for in September the Bahrain Detachment was ordered to Zanzibar, where impending elections had led to riots and sixty-eight deaths. It was a striking contrast to the bareness of the Gulf and daily patrolling was a welcome activity; in October an exercise was held to rehearse reinforcing the island and this brought the whole Battalion together for a few days. The only other event of interest was when a party from the Detachment, under Captain J.H.James, flew to Dar es Salaam to represent the British Army at the Tanganyika Independence Celebrations.

In February 1962 the Detachment rejoined the Battalion, now at Muthaiga Camp in Nairobi, and everyone returned home to Wellington Barracks in March.

BRITISH GUIANA, 1962

1st Battalion

British Guiana (now Guyana) was granted internal self-government in April 1953, but the Communists promptly stirred up trouble and it had to be suspended the next year. It was re-granted

[3] The Bahrain Detachment printed a news sheet entitled *Naha Bari Jundi*, which being translated from the Arabic means "Cold Water Soldiers".

again in 1962, but this led to more riots and 1st Battalion The Royal Anglian Regiment was sent out there on a nine-month tour.

In October 1962 the 1st Battalion of the Regiment, commanded by Lieutenant Colonel Ronnie Buckland MBE, took over on a six- to nine-month tour. The 2nd Battalion, mindful of the reinforcements received in Kenya, sent No 2 Company, commanded by Major E.I.Windsor Clive. The Battalion's arrival created a precedent in that it was the first Foot Guards unit to serve in South America.

The first six months were quiet, but in April 1963 serious riots broke out following the calling of a General Strike by the colony's Trade Union Council in protest against the Government's new Labour Relations Bill. A lighter touch came when rioters occupied a building near the camp. Smoke shells were fired to evict them and the smoke drifted into the Officers' Mess, waking an officer who was enjoying a siesta. Choking, he rang for a drink, whereupon a Mess waiter (who knew his taste) appeared carrying a glass of champagne on a silver salver, but wearing his respirator!

1st Battalion, vehicle patrol in Georgetown, British Guiana.

Foot patrol in Georgetown.

An unpleasant incident occurred on 6/7 July when a patrol was attacked and had to open fire. Guardsman Barker waded in with his bayonet and rifle butt, and ended up by arresting fifteen rioters, five of whom were wounded. He was awarded the British Empire Medal for Gallantry.

The General Strike ended on 8 July. By that time Lieutenant Colonel Alan Pemberton MBE had succeeded Lieutenant Colonel Buckland as Commanding Officer. Part of the Battalion was billeted at an American airbase, and the GIs watched in wonder as, while the Battalion was preparing to go home, part of their airfield was marked out in white lines representing the Forecourt of Buckingham Palace and the Guardsmen practised for guard mounting! The Battalion returned to Windsor in the latter part of July and undertook the real thing again.

ADEN AND MAURITIUS, 1964–1965
by Andrew Napier

2nd Battalion, 1964–1965

To understand why British troops were deployed in Aden and the Western Aden Protectorate it is necessary to look back in history. In 1839 this inhospitable spot at the mouth of the Red Sea was taken over by Britain because the large harbour there was valuable as a coaling station en route to India and the Far East. It became even more important when the Suez Canal opened in 1869.

In 1939 Aden State became a Crown Colony and the hinterland was made into the Western Aden Protectorate, composed of seventeen independent states, each with its own Sultan or Amir. Trouble began after World War II when the British Empire was being dismantled and particularly after the Suez fiasco in 1956; Arab nationalism increased and the Yemen, strongly supported by Egypt, laid claim to Aden.

To counter this the British Government set out in 1959 to convert the Western Aden Protectorate into a Federation with a view to eventual independence. This did not suit Egypt and the Yemen who, encouraged by Russia, promptly set about undermining the Federation and British influence in the area by every possible means. First, they launched guerrilla warfare in the mountainous interior of the Federation, and, second, they began a campaign of urban terrorism in Aden State.

The Federal rulers demanded support and protection from Britain, and from April–June 1964 the Radfan Campaign was fought by British and Federal troops against the Yemeni rebels in the hinterland. It was successful in that it drove the dissidents from their strongholds and re-established British control of the area, but spasmodic Egyptian-sponsored guerrilla warfare continued up-country for another two and a half years, reinforced by increasingly aggressive urban terrorism in Aden State. British troops therefore remained in Aden to support the Federal rulers against both threats.

The Regiment was not involved in the Radfan Campaign of 1964, but from October 1964 to October 1965 the 2nd Battalion operated up-country in South Arabia and also in Aden State, and was followed by the 1st Battalion which was involved in Internal Security duties in Aden State from October 1965 to May 1966.

The 2nd Battalion, under Lieutenant Colonel Sir Ian Jardine Bt MC, moved into Salerno Camp in Little Aden in October 1964 as part of 24th Infantry Brigade, commanded by Brigadier David Lloyd-Owen DSO MC. Within ten days of arrival the first incident had taken place, when a Land Rover containing Captain P.A.Fazil, the Adjutant, and Guardsman A.Norton was blown up on a mine. The blast took off Philip Fazil's leg, as well as inflicting other injuries on him, and burning

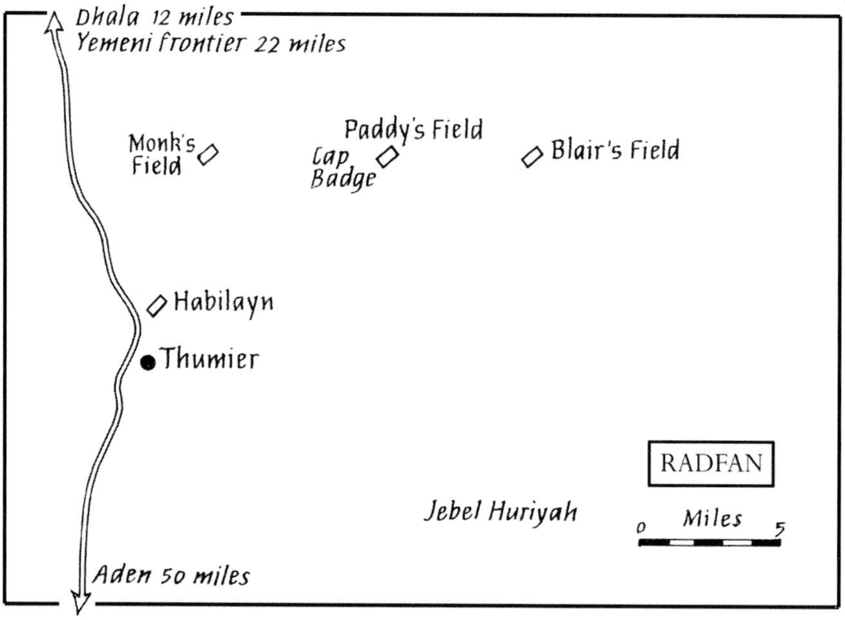
Dhala 12 miles
Yemeni frontier 22 miles
Monk's Field
Paddy's Field
Cap Badge
Blair's Field
Habilayn
Thumier
RADFAN
Jebel Huriyah
0 Miles 5
Aden 50 miles

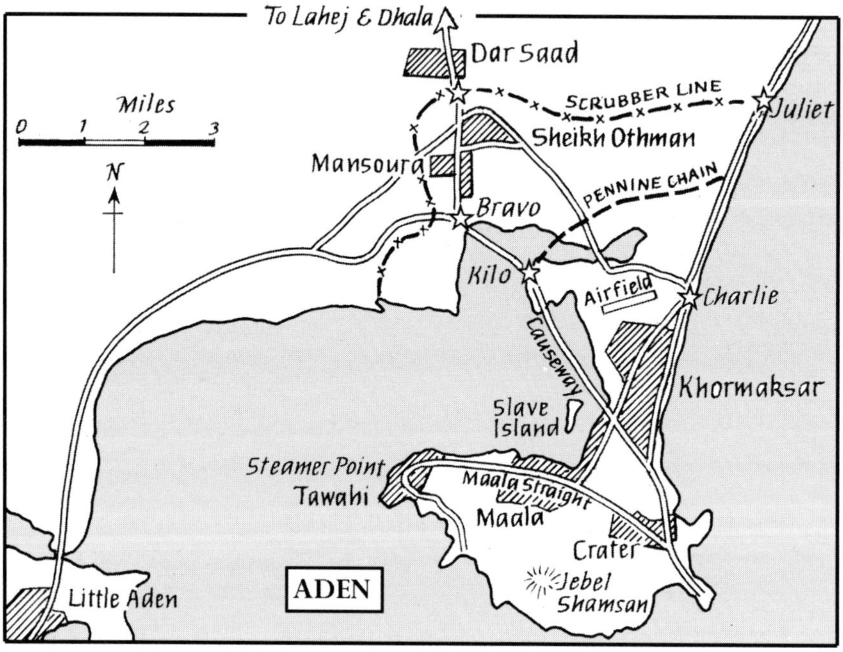
To Lahej & Dhala
Dar Saad
Miles
0 1 2 3
N
SCRUBBER LINE
Juliet
Sheikh Othman
Mansoura
PENNINE CHAIN
Bravo
Kilo
Airfield
Charlie
Causeway
Khormaksar
Slave Island
Steamer Point
Tawahi
Maala Straight
Maala
Crater
Jebel Shamsan
ADEN
Little Aden

Guardsman Norton, who temporarily lost the sight of one eye. Norton, ignoring his own injuries, applied a tourniquet to Philip Fazil's leg and put him in the shade. He then commandeered an Arab car and drove it back until he found another military vehicle, which he took as close as possible to Captain Fazil, despite the obvious danger of more mines. He then tended him on the twenty-mile drive to the hospital and by his actions undoubtedly saved Captain Fazil's life. He was awarded the George Medal.

On 9 November the Battalion moved up into Radfan and took over from the 1st Battalion Royal Anglian Regiment. Its role was to dominate the area, keep the roads open and enforce the curfew. At the start operations were mounted from four locations, each with its own airstrip, and companies changed round periodically:

Battalion Headquarters and Corps of Drums	-	Paddy's Field
No 1 Company (Major the Hon H.E.C.Willoughby)	-	Monk's Field
No 3 Company (Major P.R.Adair)	-	Blair's Field
No 4 Company (Major A.P.F.Napier)	-	Thumier

2nd Battalion Officers – Aden 1965. Back row; left to right: 2nd Lieutenant R.J. Heywood, Lieutenant N.G. Gold, 2nd Lieutenants P.L. Bell, P.M. Hare, C.P. Foord-Kelcey, R.M. Smith, R.J.S. Wardle, C.J.N. Felton. Middle row: Lieutenant P.W.D. de Sausmarez, Captain (QM) N. Duckworth, Captain G. Wolcough, Major P.J. Blackburn RAMC, Captain J.H. James, Captain S.E. Barnett, Lieutenants S.J. Davie, S.A.J. Blake. Seated: Major the Hon H.E.C. Willoughby, Major C.W.B. Jacot de Boinod, Captain G.A. Philippi, Lieutenant Colonel Sir Ian Jardine Bt, Majors E.I. Windsor Clive, P.R. Adair, and A.P.F. Napier.

A sangar position in Radfan.

Most of the company positions were at about 2–4000 feet. The rocky ground meant that stone 'sangars' and sandbags had to be used for protection against the all too frequent dissident attacks using 81mm mortars, rocket launchers, rifles and machine guns. The dissidents were organized in well-trained bands of forty to fifty men, spread round different areas, and they usually attacked company positions after dark, aiming to be well clear of the area by dawn.

The companies were widely scattered and it was a fine opportunity for the Company Commanders to be truly independent, but they were at the same time very much aware of how dependent they were on Battalion Headquarters and Headquarter Company. Administering the companies and many picquets was a major challenge and supplies were usually delivered by aircraft or helicopter, and thence by truck, donkeys and camels to some of the more inaccessible picquets.

Communications were always difficult and messages by day between Battalion Headquarters and companies had to be by Morse code, though by night voice was usually possible. The airstrips and every track that was in regular use had to be kept clear of mines and the Assault Pioneers under Sergeant E.C.Hilling did a remarkable job in achieving this.

The three Rifle Companies were all kept busy with continuous patrolling, laying ambushes, mine clearance and manning the various permanent picquet positions. Each company had many encounters with the dissidents and inflicted casualties on them, including the destruction of one of their 81mm mortars.

During the early part of 1965 the Radfan positions at Blair's and Paddy's Fields were abandoned, leaving the remaining positions at Monk's Field, Piccadilly and Cap Badge occupied by a single company, supported by a troop of the 10th Hussars and a troop of the Royal Artillery. As a result the Battalion became even more widely spread with companies based from time to time at Dhala, Monk's Field, Thumier, Ad Dimnah and Mukeiras.

On 1 December 1964 No 3 Company sent out a large fighting patrol, sixty strong, under Major

2nd Battalion; Major the Hon H.E.C. Willoughby and Second Lieutenant R.M. Smith of Number 1 Company.

P.R.Adair, and as part of the operation 2nd Lieutenant R.J.S.Wardle set up an ambush. This led to a brisk fire-fight with a strong party of dissidents and the men behind the two GPMGs were both wounded. One of the GPMGs rolled down a bank, but was recovered under heavy fire by Sergeant P.S.Goddard, who brought it into action again. The other was retrieved by Guardsman W.Nicholson, who, on his own initiative, ran across open ground, got it into action again and engaged the dissidents for ten minutes from a very exposed position, until they withdrew, leaving four killed and two wounded. Sergeant Goddard and Guardsman Nicholson were both awarded the Military Medal and 2nd Lieutenant Wardle received the Queen's Commendation.

The main danger of casualties came from the dissidents' 81mm mortars. On 21/22 December No 1 Company flew up to Mukeiras for a six-week tour. Mukeiras is on the Yemen frontier on top of a 7000-foot plateau where there was an RAF radar detachment and a battalion of the Federal Regular Army.

2nd Battalion typical sentry position in the Radfan.

On 14 January 1965 one of that Company's outlying picquets was attacked by dissidents who landed an 81mm mortar bomb on a sangar, killing Guardsman D.Millard and wounding Lance Sergeant Parker and Guardsman Tozer. Sergeant D.J.Fogarty, the acting Platoon Commander, drove a mile to the scene with a medical orderly, evacuated the casualties and quickly called down mortar fire on the dissidents. He received the Queen's Commendation for his gallant action.

On 20 March No 3 Company at Ad Dimnah also had the tragic misfortune to get a direct hit from a dissident mortar onto one of the 3" mortar pits, killing Guardsman A.C.Edge, Guardsman M.Reynolds and Guardsman D.M.Wilkins. It started a fire in the pit which contained a considerable number of HE and phosphorous bombs, some of which were smouldering. Captain S.E.Barnett, the Company Second-in-Command, and CQMS F.Pell ran to the scene and, although they realized that a large explosion might take place at any moment, they removed the casualties together with the bombs and put out the fire. CQMS Pell's hands were so covered with phosphorus that they were glowing six hours later. Even so he accompanied Captain Barnett across a stretch of open ground to fire at probable enemy positions with the Mobat. For their courage and initiative Captain Barnett was awarded the MBE and CQMS Pell the BEM.

In May 1965 the Battalion moved back to the Radfan for a further tour of duty. In June a patrol from No 3 Company at Dhala went out under 2nd Lieutenant C.P.Foord-Kelcey; it ambushed a group of dissidents on their way back from an attack on the company camp and killed four of them. For their gallantry in the action Lance Sergeant A.Connell and Guardsman C.Snape were both awarded the BEM.

No 4 Company spent some ten months up-country at Thumier, Monk's Field and Ad Dimnah, but mostly at Dhala. They also did three weeks' IS duty at Crater in Aden State. At Dhala the chief villain was called Antar who led a band of some fifty well-trained and well-armed dissidents; they had two 81mm mortars which outranged our 3" mortars by some 1000 yards and regularly opened up on our positions.

Dhala was probably the most interesting company position. The Emir of Dhala lived in a hilltop fort in the middle of Dhala Town, which was in turn overlooked by the massive Jebel Jihaf (7000 foot), which contained several small villages and a Federal National Guard fort at Assirir. The fort was often under attack and No 4 Company was required to visit it about once a week and to 'show the flag' round the villages. It was an eighteen-mile trek with a climb of some 3000 feet, so the Company was pretty fit and agile; various routes were used up and down the Jebel and mortar, artillery and aircraft support was always on call.

Come New Year's Eve 1964 it was planned that the Company would stand to at 2345 and welcome in the New Year with a *feu de joie*. Silently everyone got in to their positions, when at five minutes to midnight Antar and his band opened up on the camp with heavy small arms fire, obviously thinking that everyone would be asleep or drunk. There was an immediate and impressive response from the whole Company and the dissidents had a nasty shock. Every weapon opened up, including the Mobat, which killed one dissident by removing his leg (probably the first casualty inflicted by a Mobat); some four other dissidents were killed or wounded by the other weapons.

One evening when the Company was at Monk's Field a signal arrived from Battalion Headquarters saying that the DMO would be arriving at 0930 next morning by air. I briefed CSM Gulston and CQMS Pickles to see that the latrines, cookhouse and medical orderlies were in their usual good order, while I got on with other things. When I met the Beaver aircraft, out stepped a decidedly senior-looking General, who turned out to be the Director of Military Operations from the War Office.

He was fortunately much amused by the mix-up and relieved not to have to inspect the latrines. He took a great interest in what was going on and asked if he could do anything to help or if there was anything we lacked. I replied that we needed 81mm mortars, as our 3" mortars were out-ranged by those of the dissidents. I also asked for some 2" mortar high explosive bombs which had not been issued to the British Army for some ten years. We had borrowed a few HE bombs from the Federal Regular Army and they had proved very useful in covering the area up to 300 yards, which was not covered by our 3" mortars.

The DMO was most understanding and all that we required was delivered from England by Red Star indent within the week. That really was quite something and showed what could be achieved in an emergency. My view of Generals improved greatly!

In fact his action paid dividends within a few weeks, for, when we returned to Dhala, Antar and his gang were up to their usual tricks and shooting up the camp fairly frequently. One evening they made a more determined attack than usual, attempting to assault the machine-gun emplacement at the west end of the camp, and got right up to the perimeter wire. Lance Corporal I.Carr did excellent work with his 2" mortar HE and put paid to the dissident Bren-gun group that was giving covering fire from about 100 yards. We found a blood-stained magazine and head-dress full of brains the next morning. During the attack a dissident rocket launcher missile hit another GPMG emplacement in the middle of the camp, but no one in the Company was injured.

There was another success due to Lance Sergeant G.Monk who led an observation patrol one night to a fairly high hilltop some 3000 yards due east of our position, which covered an area from which the dissident mortars could shoot down the line of our long narrow camp. Sure enough Lance Sergeant Monk spotted movement and brief torchlight, way below, and then the flash of the dissident mortar opening fire. Our new 81mm mortars were laid on to the general area and he directed them with great skill on to the enemy mortar position. One of their mortar men was killed and others wounded, and their mortar damaged beyond repair.

In May 1965 trouble erupted on the island of Mauritius, which lies some 550 miles east of Madagascar in the Indian Ocean. It was a British Colony and was about to be granted Independence, which led to the usual violence between rival claimants to power. The population of 700,000 consisted of 70 per cent Indians and 30 per cent French Mauritians, Creoles, Chinese and a few British. The Indians favoured Independence, but the rest did not, and when this led to riots and murder, the Governor, Sir John Rennie, declared a State of Emergency and called for troops.

Mauritius came under Headquarters Middle East and on 23 May 1965 No 1 Company, under Major the Hon H.E.C.Willoughby,[4] was flown at short notice to Mauritius from Aden. On arrival the Company was divided into two groups; two platoons under Captain H.M.C.Havergal were based at the Royal Navy Leave Camp at Le Chaland, while the other two platoons under Major Willoughby moved thirty miles to the capital of Port Louis, where they were quartered in the Police Barracks. A welcome surprise was to find that the Chief Secretary to the Governor was Tom Vickers who had been a Captain in the 3rd Battalion during the Second World War.

For the first three weeks patrols were deployed round the island on foot and in vehicles to show the flag, but no shots were fired; demonstrations of riot drills were enough. They only operated by day and the police took over at night, leaving them to return to barracks while the police rested during the day. By the end of the month the situation had eased enough for the Company to be

[4] By a remarkable coincidence Major Willoughby was of the same family as Captain Nesbit Willoughby RN, who commanded a British frigate that was in action against the French before the island was seized from them in 1810.

concentrated at Le Chaland, though patrols were still sent round the island and one platoon lived 'on board' HMS *Mauritius*, the naval communications centre on the island, to ensure it had adequate protection.

The threat of disturbances soon died down and it was decided to mount a Queen's Birthday Parade on 12 June in the capital, Port Louis. Major Willoughby describes the occasion:

> "The Company played a leading part, together with the Mauritian Naval Volunteer Reserve, the Special (Mobile) Force, the Fire Brigade, two ancient saluting guns, Old Comrades of many kinds and hues, Boy Scouts, Girl Guides and Nurses on parade. A far cry from Horse Guards, but just as sincere. Any squabbles concerning precedence were forestalled when the Coldstream Company volunteered to parade on the left of the line and to march past last; even the Royal Navy could not object to this. The Guardsmen in khaki drill and forage caps swung past, each man eight foot tall, it seemed, and at the end of the Parade the spectators rose to their feet, cheering and applauding. 'Milanollo' never sounded better."[5]

The last weeks were devoted to training, various competitions and sports, and everyone also enjoyed the very generous hospitality of the people of Mauritius. It was a sad Company that flew back to Aden on 18 July.

By September 1965 the Battalion had completed four tours up-country in the Radfan and returned to Little Aden only to find itself heavily involved in Internal Security duties in Aden State. This included one successful incident when four men were foolish enough to throw a grenade at a Land Rover containing Captain S.E.Barnett, CSM Smurthwaite, CQMS Pell and Drum Major Kirk. All four gave chase and caught the four men thought to be responsible, who turned out to be leading NLF terrorists.

In October the Battalion returned to Elizabeth Barracks, Pirbright. During the operational tour five Guardsmen had been killed and eighteen wounded. Fourteen individuals received awards for gallantry.[6] It had been a hard and challenging year, but the Guardsmen rose to the occasion with great spirit and proved that there is naught wrong with the young men of Britain if they are properly trained, disciplined and motivated. Most members of the 2nd Battalion would reckon that their year's tour in South Arabia was a most rewarding part of their service.

Note on Author

Major Andrew Napier enlisted into the Coldstream Guards in 1950, was commissioned from RMA Sandhurst in 1952 and retired in 1971. He was seconded to the Aden Protectorate Levies 1958–60 and commanded No 4 Company, 2nd Battalion 1964–1966. He was Regimental Adjutant 1968–1971. He is President of the Suffolk Branch of The Coldstream Guards Association.

[5] *Guards Magazine*, Autumn 1965

[6] In addition to those already mentioned, Lieutenant Colonel Sir Ian Jardine Bt MC was awarded an OBE for his outstanding leadership and Sergeant T.Parris a BEM; a Queen's Commendation went to 2nd Lieutenant R.J.Heywood and Sergeant E.C.Hilling, and a C-in-C's Commendation to Lance Corporal E.Mavin.

ADEN, 1965–1966

1st Battalion

The 1st Battalion, commanded by Lieutenant Colonel Timmy Smyth-Osbourne, moved from Iserlohn in Germany to Aden at the end of October 1965 for a six-month unaccompanied tour just as the 2nd Battalion left. The Battalion took over from 1st Battalion The Royal Sussex Regiment and moved into Radfan Camp between Aden and Sheikh Othman, with one platoon detached to guard a Diplomatic Wireless Station on the Island of Perim, where some excellent fishing and swimming was enjoyed.

The Battalion's main duties were Internal Security in Aden Town, where terrorism was building up as the date for Independence drew near. A major task was to prevent the import of arms and ammunition to the terrorists, and it was far from easy, for the Battalion area ran from a mile or so north to Aden and Crater, up to Sheikh Othman, and included the airfield at Khormaksar, a very sensitive spot which the authorities feared might come under terrorist mortar fire. There were several miles of open desert which was impossible to control, so it was decided to build a barbed wire fence from coast to coast, a distance of eleven miles. This would at least funnel vehicles and animals through the various checkpoints and deter humans from avoiding them; it would also keep the airfield out of mortar range of any terrorists to the north of the area.

The chief architect of the line was the Second-in-Command, Major P.N.R.Stewart-Richardson, known to all and sundry as 'Scrubber', and so it became 'the Scrubber Line'. Almost everyone in the Battalion played a part in its construction, the leading lights being the Corps of Drums under Drum Major Hayler.

1st Battalion; construction of the Scrubber Line 1965. Left to right: Guardsmen Unsworth, Bowie, Peters, White, Alderman and Lance Sergeant Long.

With the completion of the 'Scrubber Line' there were three entry points into Aden area, each manned by a platoon living on the site in a few tents, with one section on duty at a time, stopping people and vehicles, and searching men, women and transport. Women presented a particular problem, as there were no female searchers available, so the Battalion Intelligence Officer, Lieutenant Sir Brian Barttelot, fitted chairs with mine detectors, and suspicious females were then invited to 'take a seat'. There is, however, no recorded instance of any contraband being discovered by this method!

In addition to manning checkpoints and hunting terrorists, the Battalion was also responsible for guarding Mansoura Prison. Most days produced an incident of some sort, even Christmas Day, when a rocket was fired at the prison. The most prevalent terrorist activity was throwing grenades at military vehicles and there were several casualties as a result, though luckily none was fatal.

By the end of April 1966 the Battalion's six-month tour was complete and, having handed over to 1st Battalion The Somerset and Cornwall Light Infantry, it left Aden and returned to Germany.

MALAYSIA, 1966–1967

Composite Platoon

The Borneo Confrontation with Indonesia erupted in 1960. A composite platoon from both Battalions, commanded by 2nd Lieutenant E.M.Crofton, was sent out in June 1966 to join No 9

Number 18 Platoon Coldstream Guards attached to 1st Battalion Scots Guards, Malaysia, 1966/67.

Coldstream Platoon training 1966. Guardsmen Bannister standing and Wright (left forefront) Front rear. Lance Sergeant Smith, Guardsmen Hunt and Yarde.

Company Irish Guards, in place of those members of the Irish Guards who were required for an operational tour in Aden with their 1st Battalion. No 9 Company in turn was attached to 1st Battalion Scots Guards as part of 28th Commonwealth Brigade which was based in Malacca; it had joined that Battalion in September 1964 at the start of its tour in the Far East. Another Coldstreamer, Captain A.J.M.Drake, had commanded the Battalion's Air Platoon in 1965.

The Battalion had already carried out two four-month operational tours in areas of Borneo. A third was due to start in September and so the Battalion disappeared into the jungle on the final warm-up exercise. On emerging five days later, news came through that hostilities had ended. The remaining six months of the tour were taken up with a mixture of training and savouring the delights of that part of the world, which included a visit to Kampong Coldstream, which had been built by the 2nd Battalion during the Malayan Emergency.

The attachment of the Coldstream platoon worked extremely well and highlighted the family

Kampong Coldstream February 1967. Coldstreamers from left to right: Lance Sergeant Dean, Guardsmen Wilcox (in rear), Hunt, Lance Sergeant Hodson.

Kampong Coldstream Town Hall 1967.

spirit and flexibility which have always existed in the Household Division. There have been numerous instances of attachments within Regiments of both formed units and individuals. Second Lieutenant A.S.H.Pollen commanded a Coldstream platoon with the Irish Guards in Aden in 1967 and over the last thirty years hardly an operational tour in Northern Ireland has gone by without some form of inter-regimental support.

BRITISH HONDURAS (BELIZE), 1967–1968

No 2 Company, 1st Battalion

In August 1967 the 1st Battalion was required to send a company on a six-month unaccompanied tour of duty to British Honduras, a Crown Colony on the east coast of Central America, which is bordered by Mexico and Guatemala. The latter had been casting envious eyes on the Colony, which did not wish to reciprocate, as it would undoubtedly have meant a lower standard of living, higher unemployment and a lessening of the political stability which was enjoyed as a British Colony.

No 2 Company, commanded by Major P.E.W.Gibbs (succeeded later by Major R.A.Q.Shuldham) arrived in British Honduras at the end of August to take over from 1st Battalion The King's Regiment. The Company was housed close to Belize International Airport in a well-appointed and modern camp, and was part of the small garrison which otherwise consisted of a commander, a small staff and a stockpile of stores and vehicles. The role of the garrison was fourfold: internal security, external defence, showing the flag and hurricane defence. Internal security was no problem, as the people were pro-British and had no wish for union with Guatemala. External defence meant defending the airport to allow the arrival of reinforcements. It was apparently felt that a company, even a Coldstream Company, could not be expected to carry out what was envisaged as a proper role of defending the frontiers of a country the size of Wales! 'Showing the flag' was a real necessity in a country of loyal members of the Commonwealth, to demonstrate to the more remote villages that there were British troops in the Colony and that the British Government cared for their defence.

Hurricane defence involved rescue and relief and the prevention of looting in the event of a hurricane. Although for a moment one of the latter became a possibility, it fortunately did not materialize.

For most of the time three out of the four platoons were out of camp, either on military training or expeditions. Places visited included Mexico and Panama, and some particularly fortunate members were able to get to San Salvador and the USA. The Company returned to England in February 1968.

AMF(L) TIDWORTH, 1968–1970

1st Battalion

In July 1968 the 1st Battalion, commanded by Lieutenant Colonel Pat MacLellan MBE, joined the NATO Allied Command Europe Mobile Force (Land Component), otherwise referred to as AMF(L). The Battalion, as part of 5th Brigade, moved to Assaye Barracks Tidworth in December. The role of the AMF(L) was deployment on the flanks of NATO as a declaration of intent that vulnerable areas would be defended against an incursion by Warsaw Pact forces. The AMF(L) at that time included both a Canadian and an Italian Alpini unit, together with a British Logistic Support Battalion as well as other supporting arms. All units participated on a rotation basis.

The area of Northern Norway required an AMF(L) unit to be specifically trained in winter warfare; this training took place annually, as part of a two-year cycle, with exercises in Northern Norway the following year. The Battalion's introduction to winter warfare was not long in coming. On 3 January 1969 No 2 Company left for the Cairngorms and the advance party from No 3 Company left for Canada. By the end of January No 3 Company was complete in Canada, experiencing the coldest winter conditions recorded there for sixty years, No 2 Company was at Voss in Norway and had been followed to the Cairngorms and Norway by Support Company and elements of Headquarter Company.

1st Battalion; Norway 1968/70.

The training in Norway lasted for three weeks, under the instruction of Norwegian officers, and in that time members of the Battalion learned how to fight and survive in conditions of extreme cold. Every man learned to move across country on either skis or snowshoes, carrying bergen rucksacks and pulling toboggans loaded with tents, cooking equipment and rations. They were also taught how to set up camp in the snow, how to live in crowded conditions in very low temperatures, all aspects of weapon handling in the cold, how to construct and live in a snow hole, to construct and lay out a defensive position in deep snow, to picquet high snow and to patrol by day and night on skis or snowshoes. In addition many members passed their 10-kilometre ski test.

Skis were put away for the summer during which time the Battalion returned to a period of conventional military training. The NATO training exercise season began in September with Exercise GREEN EXPRESS taking place on the islands of Falster and Zealand. The Battalion performed a remarkable number of military manoeuvres in a very short space of time. A moment of light relief was provided by a number of young Danish demonstrators who distributed anti-NATO and anti-Vietnam leaflets embellished with pornographic photographs! They came in useful when the Guardsmen were able to visit Copenhagen after the exercise.

Further Arctic training began in earnest at the end of December 1969, individuals departing for Norway in preparation for the major exercise of 1970, Exercise ARCTIC EXPRESS, which took place during March in the Bardufoss area of North Norway. It was designed to test the ability of the AMF(L) to work as a team and consisted of a series of simulated battles for the control of the many rugged fjords.

A highlight of the latter part of 1970 was the visit in October by a composite company, commanded by Major J.R.Macfarlane, to Fort Hood in Texas for a six-week training and cultural exchange with the American Army. The training was valuable and provided interesting comparisons with the American Army, which at the time was heavily involved in Vietnam. The Company returned to Tidworth in mid-November in time to move with the Battalion to Chelsea at the end of what had been a challenging but rewarding two years in the AMF(L).

These events are a brief summary of the worldwide activities of the Regiment during the Cold War outside of what has come to be regarded as the bread-and-butter circuit of the British Army, namely tours of duty in West Germany and Northern Ireland. The former are described in this chapter, while the details of Regimental tours in Ulster form part of Chapter 13.

GERMANY, 1949–1998

1st, 2nd and 3rd Battalions

Following the formation of NATO in 1949 the United Kingdom undertook to maintain a highly trained force in West Germany. Thus the British Army of the Rhine (BAOR) came into being. The **2nd Battalion** under Lieutenant Colonel Arthur Fortescue MBE MC moved to Krefeld in 1952 as part of 4th Guards Brigade, the formation in which all battalions of the Household Division served until its disbandment in 1976, following the 1974 Defence Review. In 1955 the Battalion handed over to the **1st Battalion**, commanded by Lieutenant Colonel Richard Crichton MC, whose tour of duty lasted for nearly three years. Towards the end of its tour, the Battalion moved to Hubbelrath, where it joined the **3rd Battalion**, under Lieutenant Colonel Bob Windsor Clive, during what

2nd Battalion; Krefeld 1952.

were to be the final two years of that Battalion's service abroad, before it was placed in suspended animation in 1959, after a life of some sixty-two years.

The **1st Battalion**, under Lieutenant Colonel Alan Pemberton MBE,[7] returned to West Germany and 4th Guards Brigade in 1965, becoming an Armoured Personnel Carrier (APC) Battalion for the first time. The APC was to dominate all aspects of a battalion's life in BAOR for the remainder of the twentieth century. Being an APC Battalion meant owning a significant number of extra vehicles and having to train the drivers for them. At the start of the Battalion's tour these included armoured Humber one-tonners which were subsequently exchanged for Saracens. In addition, as communications improved, large numbers of extra wireless operators had to be trained. A major difference from the Battalion's earlier tour in BAOR was that the training and duties were more varied and training had become worldwide. Early in 1965 the Battalion trained for three weeks in Libya, and in October of that year experienced a foretaste of what was to come in future years, namely an operational tour, this time to Aden for six months.

The **2nd Battalion**, commanded by Lieutenant Colonel 'Lump' Windsor Clive, moved to Münster in March 1969 and once again became part of 4th Guards Armoured Brigade. Like the 1st Battalion, it too became an APC Battalion, but the APC was now a tracked fighting vehicle (FV) 432 requiring trained drivers and signallers, and whose maintenance was the responsibility of the section as a whole. The first parade of the day was a servicing parade and every man had a job to do in his section or headquarters vehicle. The FV 432 strength of the Battalion was some eighty vehicles, quite apart from the old-established wheeled favourites such as landrovers, Ferret scout cars and 3-tonners.

4th Guards Armoured Brigade as a 'Square Brigade' comprised two armoured regiments and two Foot Guards battalions. These four major units were required to train and operate as All Arms Battle Groups, taking under command such squadrons and companies as were required to complete their missions. This philosophy was reflected at a lower level with squadrons and companies operating as Combat Teams, with armoured troops or platoons under command as circumstances dictated. The Battle Groups were supported by artillery units, retaining wherever possible the same battery throughout training, thereby ensuring a tightly knit team.

This concept demanded a very high standard of all arms training and cooperation, which, together with the improvements in equipment, ensured that the reputation of 1(BR) Corps as an operational force among our NATO Allies became second to none. This was all the more praiseworthy considering the severe disruption caused by emergency tours and the constant overstretch through other commitments.

Like the 1st Battalion previously, the **2nd Battalion** found itself on operations away from BAOR. Soon after its arrival trouble flared in Ulster and thus began the regular conveyor belt of operational

[7] Who was shortly to hand over to Lieutenant Colonel Timmy Smyth-Osbourne.

Major D.H.A. Lewey, Second-in-Command 2nd Battalion, on exercise, West Germany, 1969.

tours over there carried out by BAOR regiments. In 1970 the Battalion, now commanded by Lieutenant Colonel Colin Wallis-King, was earmarked for a four-month emergency tour in West Belfast.

An operational tour in Ulster to all intents and purposes wrote off a battalion's training cycle in Germany for the best part of a year. There was the pre-training followed by leave prior to embarkation, a period of approximately two months; the tour itself, which over the years has been extended from four to six months; followed by post-tour leave of some three weeks' duration. His ability to assimilate a disruption of such magnitude within a completely different requirement in Germany has highlighted the exceptional qualities of the British soldier over three decades.

2nd Battalion inspection by The Major General in Buller Barracks, Münster, 1971.

2nd Battalion 1969. Typical APC problems!

BERLIN, 1972–75

1st Battalion

In 1971 the 2nd Battalion departed from BAOR. It was succeeded in 1972 by the 1st Battalion, under Lieutenant Colonel Peter Tower, not in BAOR but as part of the 3000-strong Berlin Infantry Brigade. This was the Battalion's second tour of duty in Berlin, the first having been for four months in 1946. Based at Spandau, in the Central Allied Sector of West Berlin, its role was very different from battalions that were in 'the Zone'. Surrounded by Iron Curtain Countries, only a maximum of 10 per cent was allowed out of station at any one time, apart from two periods in the year when the Battalion was allowed out en bloc for training. There was little scope for military training other than at a low level, and as always ammunition was at an extreme premium. However, this did provide the opportunity for Corporals' Courses and other basic cadres to be organized, which had not happened for some time. There were six FV 432s on the Battalion MT Establishment, but they remained firmly in the rear of the MT Park! Because of the restrictions on movement allowed out of Berlin, the tour enabled the Battalion to

Guardsman Ragwort 1969, as seen by the Regimental cartoonist, Lance Sergeant S. Rutherford.

1st Battalion Farewell March through Spandau, West Berlin, 1975. The Commanding Officer, Lieutenant Colonel P.G.S. Tower, is followed by the Adjutant, Captain R. de L. Cazenove, who in turn is followed by the Regimental Sergeant Major, T.N. Storey. Major P.L. Bell is the Officer Commanding Number 1 Company.

settle down to Regimental soldiering after the turbulence of the previous twelve months, which had seen the Battalion twice in Ulster, the second occasion necessitating a recall from leave.

The Battalion's programme was nevertheless very full. In addition to seemingly endless Garrison tasks, operational duties included Border Patrols, Flag Tours in East Berlin, the daily Military Train Guard to and from Brunswick, and the Allied Kommandantura Guard.[8] The Battalion also took its turn, along with the three other major Occupying Powers, in providing the guard for the one remaining Nazi incarcerated in the notorious Spandau prison, Rudolph Hess. The tour ended in 1975.

However, two years later the **1st Battalion** was back in BAOR, this time in the mechanized role, and stationed in Fallingbostel as part of 1st Armoured Division. Wessex Barracks had previously been the barracks of an armoured regiment, but had been redesignated to the infantry as part of the

[8] Among activities in barracks pigs were kept on a commercial basis!

17. Presentation of Colours, Horse Guards, 22 May, 1985. March Off of the Old Colours. Left to right: Second Lieutenants J. M. Vernon, J. G. B. Gittings (1st Battalion), A. W. Fortescue, R. L. W. Frisby (2nd Battalion).

18. Presentation of Colours, Windsor Castle, 22 May 1999.

19. 2nd Battalion. Major J. R. Macfarlane, commanding No 4 Company, escorting Archbishop Makarios in Fort George Camp, Paphos, after the coup in 1974. In the background is Captain R. A. H. Greenly.

20. The Gulf 1991. Burning oil wells.

21. 1st Battalion, Germany 1991-98. Anti-tank training.

22. Warrior. The modern Infantry Armoured Fighting Vehicle.

23. 2nd Battalion Farewell Parade, 31 July 1993. The Colonel of the Regiment, Major General Sir George Burns, with the Commanding Officer, Lieutenant Colonel A. R. Biggs.

24. Her Majesty The Queen speaking to Company Sergeant Major and Mrs Carr at the Number 7 Company and The Coldstream Guards Association Garden Party on 1 June 2000. The two Number 7 Company Officers are 2nd Lieutenant W.G.L. Luther (centre) and Captain J.L.A. Scott.

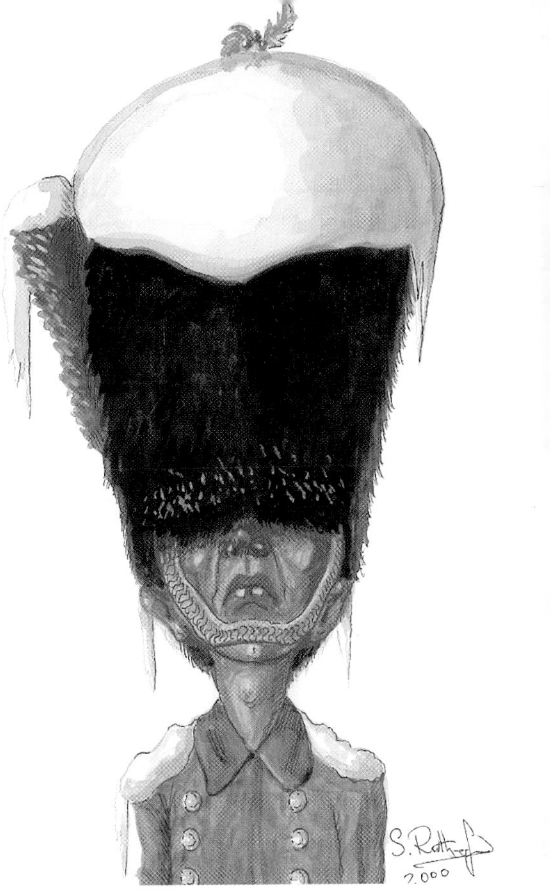

25. Warrant Officer – On the Square.

26. Officer – Winter Guard Order.

27. The Band at Sarajevo, 20 March 1994. As General Rose, Commander Bosnia/Herzegovina Command, said, "Another small step on the path to normal life in this beautiful land."

28. The victorious Coldstream golf teams in the Colonel-in-Chief's Cup 1999. The Winners: Back row; left to right: Brigadier M. R. Frisby, Brigadier R. J. Heywood, G. R. Pinto, Captain G. M. Pope, Major C. K. Macfarlane, D. J. Loveridge. The Runners-Up: Front row; left to right: Guardsman Leech, Company Sergeant Major Adams, Captain S. P. Tester, Regimental Sergeant Major D. P. Hall, Lance Sergeants Douglas and Wright.

29. The Queen's Birthday Parade, 17 June 2000. Number 7 Company finds the Escort, which is commanded by Major W. J. Tower. The Ensign is 2nd Lieutenant W. G. L. Luther and the subaltern (out of picture) is Captain J.L.A. Scott.

30. The March through the City of London, 21 June 2000. The Regiment marching past the Lord Mayor and the Colonel of the Regiment at the Mansion House.

31. The Regiment and members of The Coldstream Guards Association marching down Marygate past the Mayor and the Colonel of the Regiment after receiving the Freedom of the Borough of Berwick-upon-Tweed, 25 July 2000.

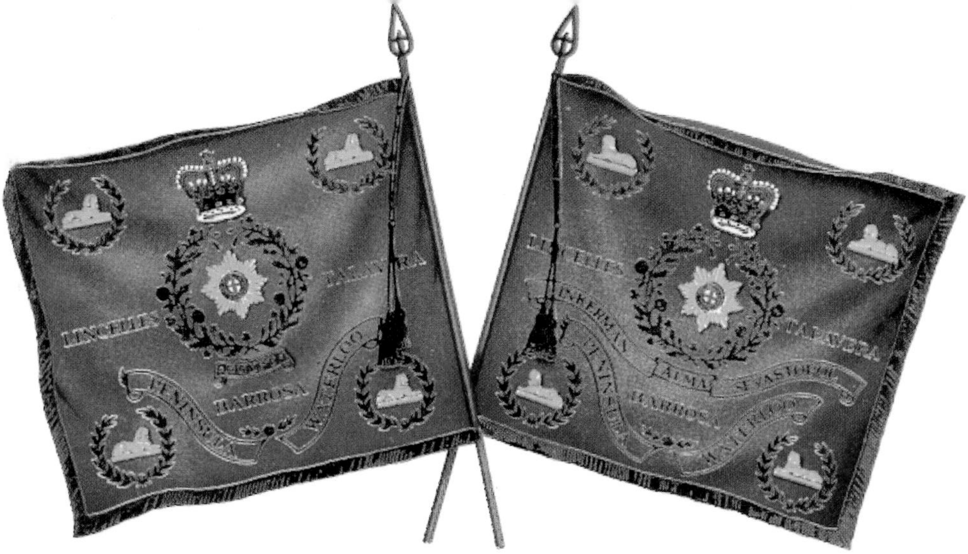

32. The State Colours. First State Colour on left; the second on right showing the additional Battle Honours Alma, Inkerman, Sevastopol.

33. 1st Battalion Queen's Colour.

2nd Battalion Queen's Colour held by Number 7 Company.

34. 1st Battalion Regimental Colour

2nd Battalion Regimental Colour held by Number 7 Company.

restructuring of BAOR.[9] The reorganization had seen the demise of brigades as formations, so that the Battalion found itself with two masters, being under the operational command of Headquarters 1st Armoured Division at Verden but administered by Headquarters Soltau Garrison. On operations it was part of the impersonally titled 'Task Force Alpha'. Command Post Exercises (CPXs) were a feature of military training, which invariably only involved the Battalion seniors, leaving the junior element behind in barracks. The principles of mechanized training had not greatly changed since the days of the 2nd Battalion and the FV 432 continued to have a major influence on Battalion life both in and out of barracks. However, the routine of life in BAOR was once again broken in 1978 by a four-month visit to Ulster and West Belfast. On its return the Battalion found itself spread widely, with Battle Group training in Suffield, Canada, for some and for others field firing in Germany and adventure training in various parts of the world. It is worth noting that the Battle Group in Canada comprised nearly 1000 men sporting between them some seventeen cap badges.

The autumn in Germany is the season for the Field Training Exercises (FTXs). Tactical doctrine is refreshed and the pace of training is increased. The annual FTX invariably seemed to be the "largest of its kind ever mounted" and provided enough discussion to last until the next season!

The Battalions changed over in Wessex Barracks in late 1980. The **2nd Battalion**, commanded by Lieutenant Colonel Richard MacFarlane, took up the BAOR mantle, this time as part of 7th Armoured Brigade at Soltau, brigades being back in fashion. Its training was once again interrupted with a tour, this time of six months' duration, to Ulster and West Belfast in 1982. The following year Battle Group Training in Canada was a major feature, with perhaps an even more diverse combination than previously described for the 1st Battalion, with both the attached armoured squadrons coming from different brigades. Fortunately for those who had been there with the 1st Battalion, little of the Alberta countryside had changed! The beginning of 1983 saw the Battalion coming under new management, that of 22nd Armoured Brigade at Hohne.

The next year brought a double handover, with Wessex Barracks reverting to armour and to 2nd Royal Tank Regiment, while the G1098 equipment went to 1st Battalion Welsh Guards who broke new ground for the Household Division by being the first Foot Guards Battalion to be stationed in Hohne.

GERMANY, 1991–98

1st Battalion

The **1st Battalion**, under Lieutenant Colonel Peter Williams, returned to Germany and Münster in October 1991, and to a very different scenario. The Cold War was over, the Berlin Wall had been dismantled and the Warsaw Pact had evaporated. At home, the 1991 reorganization of the Army, Options for Change, was to have far-reaching consequences for the Household Division. Future tours in Germany for the Household Division battalions would last for six years, a considerable change from what had gone before. It is a sobering thought that a battalion in future is likely to be posted to Germany only once in a generation. Perhaps the only members to have had previous

[9] The Barracks reverted to its original status in 1984, and so had the unique distinction of housing both Coldstream Battalions in succession, during its one period as an infantry station.

experience of soldiering in Germany will be the Commanding Officer and the Quartermaster when they were Ensign and Guardsman respectively.

The Battalion was stationed in Oxford Barracks which, as Hermann Goering Barracks, had briefly been the billet of the 4th Battalion in April 1945. It was now part of 4th Armoured Brigade and was one of the two battalions in the theatre to be issued with Warrior, the new infantry armoured fighting vehicle. In the early part of 1992 training followed the traditional preparation for conversion to mechanization, leading on to live firing and the various Divisional Concentrations. However, the Battalion was not far into the tour when yet again all the hard work and achievements were brought to a halt by the announcement of a six-month emergency tour to Northern Ireland, this time in East Tyrone. 1993 was seen in while on post-tour leave. This was just as well, as in May the Battalion was warned for a six-month deployment to Bosnia, which duly took place in November. It returned to Münster the following May and the remainder of 1994 was spent brushing up on mechanized training and working with the other Allied Armies.

1995 was notable for several events to mark the 50th Anniversary of the ending of the Second World War. Battle Group Training in Canada took place and the momentum continued with the Battalion being warned for an operational reinforcement to Bosnia. The Battalion departed on leave, only to return to find a completely different operational requirement, namely another six-month tour in Northern Ireland! Early in 1996 the Battalion, now under Lieutenant Colonel Hugh Boscawen, returned to South Armagh after an interval of some thirteen years. The next year saw 4th Armoured Brigade programmed as the Training Support Brigade, and so the Battalion was fully involved in that capacity. However, this did mean that individuals were able to get away from Münster on a variety of activities. Later in the year new ground was broken by the majority of the Battalion training in Poland. The woods and water of that country provided a significant contrast

Germany 1992/98. Members of No 2 Company 1st Battalion on Dorbaum Training Area.

to the open prairie of Canada, but were nevertheless equally challenging for navigators as the maps were overprinted with two separate grid systems!

The Battalion's activities during its final six months in Germany provided a comprehensive mix of training, ceremonial activities and handover preparations. Training support commitments for both 4th Armoured Brigade and 1st (UK) Armoured Division continued apace, thus prompting the Chief of the General Staff to declare that the Battalion was the most hard-worked Battalion in NATO. That comment has epitomized the contribution of all three Coldstream Battalions to soldiering in Germany over forty years. The Battalion returned to the United Kingdom in February 1998 after an absence of six and a quarter years. Whether a Coldstream Battalion will return to Germany again remains to be seen.

BRIXMIS

One of the phenomena of the Cold War was BRIXMIS, the full title of which was "The British Commanders'-in-Chief Mission to the Soviet Forces in Germany". It had been set up on 16 September 1946 to establish a reciprocal exchange of liaison missions between British and Soviet Forces in Germany during the occupation. The French and Americans had similar organizations, and the Russian equivalent was called 'SOXMIS'. This situation continued until 2 October 1990 when all the missions were de-activated.

BRIXMIS became known as the Cold War's 'Great Game', in which each side did its utmost to learn anything it could about the other's military secrets, while overtly carrying out purely liaison duties. The British players had to learn Russian of course, and also become skilled in equipment recognition, photography, reconnaissance, bluff and what was termed 'touring tradecraft'. They then travelled round the Soviet sector trying to shake off the inevitable Soviet 'tails' and at the same time pick up any useful information they could, preferably without getting caught. It was challenging and exciting work, and was carried out by Regular officers and NCOs seconded to BRIXMIS for around three years.

One of the top players on our side was acknowledged to be Captain Peter Williams of the Regiment, who did two tours, 1981–1983 and 1987–1989. He enjoyed it and also excelled at it, so much so that his performance was respectfully recognized by the Russians themselves. Indeed on one occasion when the British team were entertaining their Soviet opposite numbers at a party, the British Commander suggested that the Russians might like to watch the latest James Bond film. To which his counterpart replied, with a smile, "Thank you, Brigadier, but no. We have enough of your own James Bond, Captain Williams."

Note on Author

Major Edward Crofton was commissioned into the Regiment in 1965 and served with the 1st and 2nd Battalions. He was Regimental Adjutant in 1986 and then retired. He became a stockbroker with Brewin Dolphin and returned to the Regiment in 1995 to resume his former appointment as Regimental Adjutant, but now as a Retired Officer. He is President of the Dorset and West Hants Branch of The Coldstream Guards Association.

COLDSTREAM CAMPAIGNING (1945–2000)

Year	1st Battalion	2nd Battalion	3rd Battalion
1945	BAOR/Berlin	Yugoslavia/Trieste	Palestine
6	UK	UK	
7			
8	Palestine/Tripoli	Malaya	UK
9			
1950	UK	UK	Tripoli
1			Canal Zone
2	Canal Zone	BAOR	
3	UK		
4			UK
5	BAOR	UK	
6			
7			BAOR
8	UK		
9		Kenya	UK/Disbanded
1960			
1		Two Coys Bahrain and Zanzibar	
2	British Guiana	Zanzibar/UK	
3	UK	UK	
4	BAOR	UK/Aden	
5	Aden	Coy Mauritius	
6	UK	UK	
7	UK/Coy British Honduras		
8	AMF(L)		
9		BAOR	
1970	UK/Ulster	BAOR/Ulster	
1	UK/Ulster	BAOR	
2	UK/Ulster/Berlin	UK/Ulster	
3	Berlin	UK	
4		Cyprus	
5	UK/Ulster	UK	
6	UK	Ulster	
7	BAOR	Ulster	
8	BAOR/Ulster	Ulster/UK	
9	BAOR		
1980	UK	BAOR	
1			
2	UK/Ulster	BAOR/Ulster	
3	UK	BAOR	
4	Falklands	UK	
5	UK		
6	Hong Kong	UK/Ulster	
7		UK	

Year	1st Battalion	2nd Battalion
1988	UK/Ulster	Cyprus
9	UK	
1990		UK
1	BAOR/The Gulf	UK/Ulster
2	Ulster	UK
3	Bosnia	Disbanded
4		**Number 7 Company**
5		UK
6	Ulster	UK/Ulster
7		UK
8	UK	
9	Ulster	
2000	UK	

CHAPTER ELEVEN

KEEPING THE PEACE, 1945–2000

by Edward Crofton

CYPRUS, 1974 AND 1988–1990

2nd Battalion

If Palestine (1945–1948) is regarded as the first peace-keeping operation post-war, the next did not come, as far as the Regiment was concerned, until it became involved in Cyprus in 1974.

Cyprus has long been a potential problem for several reasons. First, it has a divided population. Some 78 per cent are Greek-Cypriots, though the island has never belonged to Greece. Eighteen per cent are Turkish-Cypriots and the island was ruled by Turkey for 300 years until Britain took over its administration in 1878. In 1914 Britain annexed Cyprus, following Turkey joining Germany as an ally in the First World War, and this was recognized by the Treaty of Lausanne in 1920.

In the 1950s the Greek-Cypriot majority began demanding union with Greece (Enosis) and stirred up such violence and antagonism against Britain that a State of Emergency was declared from 1955 to 1959. This was led by Archbishop Makarios as the political leader, supported by General Grivas as the military commander.

In 1960 Britain, Greece and Turkey agreed to give Cyprus independence, provided that it did not join either of those countries and also allowed Britain, for strategic reasons, to retain two Sovereign Base Areas (SBAs) on the island. Archbishop Makarios became President of Cyprus. But this arrangement did not work, with the Turks becoming increasingly resentful over the treatment they were receiving, and inter-communal trouble soon developed.[1]

In March 1964 the United Nations intervened and the Security Council authorized the establishment on a three-month basis of a United Nations Peacekeeping Force in Cyprus (UNFICYP).[2] Its initial strength was 6,400 men from nine countries, with the largest contingent coming from Britain, and its task was to keep the peace, while others sought to find a political solution. It met with some success and in April–May 1974 was able to implement a plan to reduce the strength of the force to 2,340 men deployed all round the island in small detachments manning some forty static observation posts supported by mobile patrols.

For the British contingent this meant that what had been a full battalion commitment was now reduced by half, the balance being stationed in the Sovereign Base Areas under British rather than United Nations command. Thus, when the 2nd Battalion, under Lieutenant Colonel The Hon

[1] Letter 19.1.00 from Brigadier F.Henn, CBE, Chief of Staff UNFICYP in 1974.

[2] The mandate was then renewed every six months, and by June 2000 UNFICYP is in its 37th year.

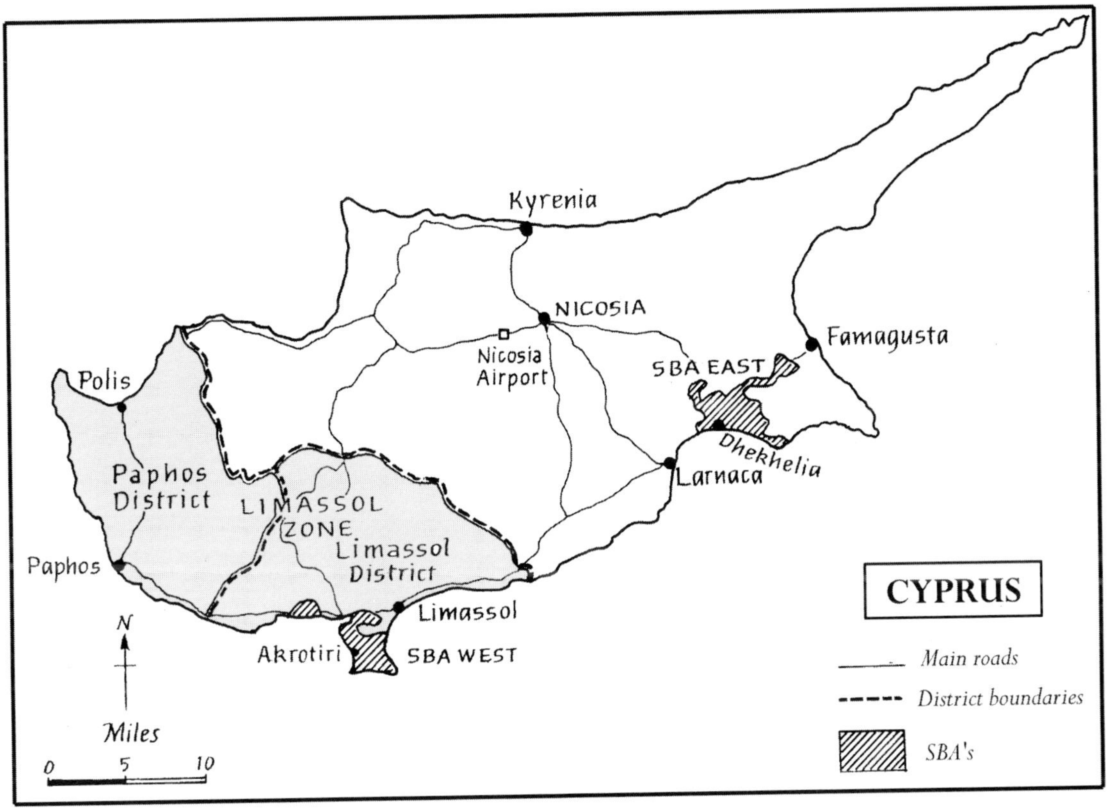

Christopher Willoughby, was posted to Cyprus in May 1974 it was immediately split into two. Battalion Headquarters with Nos 1 and 4 Companies and the Parachute Squadron RAC was under command of HQ UNFICYP and responsible for the Limassol Zone. The remainder of the Battalion, under the Second-in-Command, Major P.E.W Gibbs, was stationed in the Eastern SBA at Dhekelia under the command of HQ NEARELF, where it carried out garrison duties and training.

The UNFICYP Battalion was responsible in Limassol Zone for preventing a recurrence of the fighting and contributing to the restoration of law and order. The Zone was commanded by the Commanding Officer and was divided between Limassol and Paphos Districts. These were put under the command of No 1 Company, Major M.R.Frisby, and No 4 Company, Major J.R.Macfarlane, respectively, each with two troops of Ferret scout cars from the Parachute Squadron. OPs were established in areas of likely confrontation between the Greek Cypriots and the Turkish communities and mobile patrols regularly visited villages in the outlying areas.

A satisfactory routine was being followed by mid-July. The UN Battalion appeared to be carrying out its job; no fighting had broken out and law and order seemed generally to be observed. The SBA half was getting on with training. Several families had visited to see husbands and more were planning to come out for the summer holidays.

The summer lethargy was rudely shattered when, at 0930 on Monday 15 July, heavy firing broke out in Limassol in the areas of the main Police Stations, when the Police were attacked by the National Guard, the authorized Cypriot military force. News also came through from Nicosia that the National Guard had taken over the airport and that the Presidential Palace was being attacked.

Paphos, a stronghold of Makarios supporters, remained quiet and the National Guard remained loyal to the Archbishop, or to his memory; as reports of his death were given out during the morning by the National Guard-controlled radio in Nicosia. Larnaca was the scene of considerable shooting and several Coldstream wives had an unpleasant and worrying time until the following afternoon when their husbands were allowed to rejoin them.

The duties of the UN did not include participation in affairs involving only the Greek Cypriot community, but made it necessary to take all steps possible to prevent the fighting from spilling over into or from the Turkish Cypriot sectors of Limassol or Paphos Districts and to gain all information possible about the progress of the fighting.

In Paphos there was frenetic activity in the community when news came that there had been a coup in Nicosia, that President Makarios was dead and that Nicos Sampson had assumed power. The activity was particularly relevant for a number of reasons to Major Macfarlane and No 4 Company who were located in St Patrick's Camp about a mile north of the town. Firstly, it gave the Turkish Enclave the opportunity to improve its fortifications, thereby creating considerable inter-communal tension, something which had until then been an UNFICYP priority to prevent. The precarious situation was further exacerbated by the locking up of Greek National Guard officers by Makarios loyalists, thereby making any attempt at relieving inter-communal tension impossible. A further problem for Major Macfarlane was the loss of direct communications by both telephone and radio during 15 July.

Major Macfarlane goes on to describe the extraordinary events which followed during the ensuing twenty-four hours of 15/16 July:

"The only remaining communication for No 4 Company was through an insecure voice relay station on Mount Troodos through which any messages to HQ UNFICYP in Nicosia had to be repeated by the operator. This was a laborious and tentative link for the significant events which followed. The BBC World Service news bulletin became effectively the only source of intelligence available and continued to pronounce Makarios as dead throughout 15 July.

"It was particularly surprising when, in the late afternoon, Mr Stephanedes, the (Greek) District Officer, arrived at St Patrick's Camp and informed me that Makarios was safe and well and in the Paphos Bishopric. He also handed me a handwritten note allegedly from Makarios with a request for the message to be sent to HQ UN in New York. Thoroughly sceptical, I transmitted this news of Makarios and his message through the tenuous voice relay station. He also asked to meet Makarios in person to satisfy himself of the truth of this extraordinary turn of events.

"The meeting took place in the Bishopric at about 1930. Makarios was dignified, composed and recited the remarkable story of his escape from Nicosia and his journey to Paphos. He was particularly anxious for news of the situation in Limassol, saying that he had it in mind to go there next day since it was there that the key lay to the ultimate success or failure of the coup – if a coup was to be successful, he said, it must be so within eight hours. That time having expired and with the outcome of events in Limassol at this stage uncertain, he was hopeful the coup would be defeated. He read the text of a broadcast he was about to make on Radio Free Paphos and gave me the text of a second message that he asked to be sent to HQ UN in New York requesting an urgent meeting of the Security Council to condemn the Greek 'Junta'. He also asked that Mr Weckman-Munoz, the Secretary General's Special Representative in Cyprus, and General Prem Chand, Commander UNFICYP, should visit him in Paphos next morning.

"I passed all these messages via the Troodos link to HQ UNFICYP. The day of 15 July ended with the BBC World Service still broadcasting that Makarios was dead, leaving myself as the only authoritative person claiming to have seen the President alive, seriously wondering whether I had been deceived by a lookalike and the implications of such a deceit.

"By dawn on 16 July the World Service was announcing that Makarios had been seen alive by a UN Officer. However, it wasn't until after the visit of Mr Weckman-Munoz and General Prem Chand to the Bishopric in mid-morning that any doubts about the reality were laid to rest.

"Overnight Limassol had fallen and the only resistance to the coup yet to be overcome was centred on Paphos where the now known presence of Makarios served as a rallying point. The National Guard now had to move fast against him to secure the Coup. It did so on two axes, one from Nicosia and one from Limassol. In addition, at about 1215 a Greek Cypriot gunboat and two MTBs opened fire on the Bishopric, but the ten rounds fell short. This, with the knowledge of the advancing National Guard, helped to make up Makarios' mind. An urgent message from him was delivered to me requesting UNFICYP to provide a helicopter to take him and his entourage to the British base at Akrotiri from whence he would leave Cyprus by air. No sooner had the message been relayed when Makarios and his entourage of three arrived in an old car at St Patrick's Camp. They were escorted to the Company Officers' Mess – some 100 metres from the Ops Room and the only radio link.

"The following three and a half hours were tense. The National Guard advance continued, focused on getting Makarios, who was being held in No 4 Company's camp. Intelligence was scarce, but the Company OPs were in position to give notice of any immediate presence around Paphos.

"Meanwhile negotiations continued between Makarios in the Officers' Mess, through myself, through the Troodos relay station and through HQ UNFICYP in Nicosia, and HQ UN in New York and James Callaghan, the British Foreign Secretary, in London. Eventually it was agreed all round

"I don't know who the airport needs protecting against most". 2nd Battalion, Cyprus, 1974.

that a helicopter would be provided to take Makarios from St Patrick's Camp to Akrotiri from whence he would proceed via Malta to London. A RAF helicopter duly arrived and, after being bade farewell by the lining party from No 4 Company, the President and his entourage departed at 1615."

Tension in the island remained high following the coup, which had increased the likelihood of a Turkish invasion. Everyone in the SBA was confined to the Area. The SBA Detachment was detailed to carry out extra duties, such as manning Entry Control Points, an OP on the British Military Hospital and a Guard on the British Forces Broadcasting station. Resupply convoys were run from Dhekelia to Episkopi, and also into Famagusta to collect bulk supplies from NAAFI. The UN Battalion was busy meeting the Greek Colonels in charge of Limassol and Paphos, and hearing their assurances that there was no intention of any military activities against the Turkish Cypriot communities.

At 0500 on 20 July news was received that the Turks were invading the north of the island. At 0600 two parachute battalions were dropped into the Turkish Enclave to reinforce it. At 0715 helicopters landed south of Kyrenia, followed by seaborne landings. Nicosia Airport was also bombed.

There was much fighting in Limassol, where the leaders of both sides had promised that neither would attack the other unless first attacked. The Battalion vehicles were stationed between them to remind them of their promise. It was the Greek National Guard who started the shooting and neither commander was able to restrain his men once firing had started. Furthermore, neither side was discouraged by the thought that UN troops were caught in the crossfire! At 1500 the TCF (Turkish Cypriot Fighters) surrendered to the National Guard. After much negotiation through Major Frisby, the Turks piled their arms in the streets and, under the supervision of No 1 Company, they were interned in the Town Stadium. In the process the Company was again fired on by the Greeks, an incident which was brought under control only when a Greek major set about his men with his fists!

Major Macfarlane received similar assurances in Paphos that neither side would attack and Lance Sergeant Smith, commanding the OP in the village of Mandria, was given the same promises. In Mandria, however, the Greeks soon adopted a different line and took Guardsmen Turton and Speight hostage to ensure the Turkish withdrawal; strong protests soon secured their release. The truce had broken down by early afternoon and by the next morning the Turks were ready to surrender.

Once again bad communications and the weak command on the Greek and Turkish sides made it hard to arrive at terms, but finally No 4 Company was allowed to collect the Turkish weapons. It was while doing this that Guardsman Lawson was killed by a weapon which went off among a pile of impounded arms. Despite the surrender terms an invasion by the Turkish Army seemed inevitable and it followed an air strike by the Turkish Air Force which narrowly missed 2nd Lieutenant Kerr and Lance Corporal Walker.

From Dhekelia Major Gibbs, with Major J.R.G.Crisp and No 3 Company, led an operation to evacuate British Service families from Famagusta in convoys supported by Ferrets and Saladins of the 16th/5th Lancers. Road repairs and damage on the approach route was extensive, so much of the evacuation was carried out on foot, but, in spite of this and the hazards of Turkish mortar fire and an air strike, the evacuation was completed successfully.

On 24 July No 2 (Support) Company, (by now wearing blue berets, having joined UNFICYP on the road to Nicosia), under command of Major R.J.Heywood, occupied Nicosia Airport which was in danger of attack from both the Turks and the Greeks, and which both sides coveted. The place was a shambles of burnt-out aeroplanes and looted shops, but the attack never came. Later that evening the rest of the SBA Detachment of the Battalion was ordered to join the UN Detachment of the Battalion and this took place in the early hours of the following day.

By the end of the month the situation began to stabilize and further Turkish advances were well outside the Coldstream area of responsibility. The Battalion set about consolidating with much sub-unit redeployment. Joint patrols with the 16th/5th Lancers were sent out in what was hoped to be the buffer zone between Nicosia and Kyrenia. A further redeployment took place on 13 August when the Battalion was ordered by the Commander of the UN Force, General Prem Chand, to establish section strength OPs in all the Turkish Cypriot and mixed villages throughout the zone. On the 15th the Turkish Army began its dual thrust eastwards and westwards. This set in train the problem of refugees, which became more acute day by day, with increasing numbers of Greeks Cypriots fleeing south and west. On the following day the Turkish Army consolidated near Famagusta, on their 'Attila Line'.

The Battalion was now faced with very formidable administrative problems, with twenty-seven different OP locations, all of which had to be supplied from Battalion resources. The Quartermaster, Captain P.J.Clifford, and his staff worked out an ingenious plan which resulted in many thousands of miles being travelled, but which enabled fresh rations to be eaten every day by every Guardsman in every location. Accommodation was another problem which was surmounted through the hard work of the Sappers.

The OPs were invariably welcome and were able to halt attacks by some of the irregular Greek Cypriot forces, EOKA(B), and thus avoid renewed flare-ups and possible further bloodshed. Companies changed locations at the end of August and it was announced that the Queen's Royal Irish Hussars would reinforce the British Contingent and would take over command of the Paphos District with Nos 1 and 3 Companies under command. The Battalion would have C Squadron under command in Limassol District. The Queen's Royal Irish Hussars arrived on 25 September, and the

2nd Battalion Officers on the occasion of the Colonel of the Regiment's visit, August 1974.

16/5th Lancers returned to England. The Battalion handed over command to 41 Commando Royal Marines on 30 October and the last flight departed for home on 8 November.

The success of the Battalion during the six-month tour lay in the unaccountable number of lives which were undoubtedly saved by the efforts of Coldstreamers, particularly junior officers and NCOs. Their conduct and achievements were also due in no small measure to the soundness of Battalion training which added a strong sense of discipline and self-respect to the natural good nature and humour of the Guardsmen. In recognition of their service during the tour Lance Sergeant R.Smith was awarded a Queen's Commendation and GOC's Commendations were awarded to Major J.R.Macfarlane, Major M.R.Frisby and Guardsman M.White.

An account of the hair-raising events of July 1974 would not be complete without reference to the very valuable and unusual source of information which came from No 3 Sonlion Street in Paphos, otherwise known as 'Mrs Squirrel's OP'. It was manned by Mrs Macfarlane and Mrs Robinson, the wife of CSM Robinson, who, with her family, had arrived in Cyprus only two days before the coup. With its panoramic view of the harbour and the only main road into and out of Paphos, the OP provided a constant stream of vital information to St Patrick's Camp during an unforgettable and thrilling ten days. Constantly under the threat of random fire from trigger-happy individuals, the ladies had the additional problems of food being scarce and hard to get, and the safety of four small boys. The OP was eventually withdrawn, but not before the occupants experienced a moment in history that held the major powers of the world in a state of high tension for some considerable time.

EPISKOPI GARRISON, 1988/90

by Charles Lomer

2nd Battalion

The 2nd Battalion (under Lieutenant Colonel Myles Frisby and later Charles Lomer) took over command from 1st Battalion The Royal Regiment of Fusiliers in early February 1988 in a very different scenario from its last visit in 1974. This time it had the opportunity to settle down in new surroundings to a routine, with the specific role of internal security duties. In practice these duties involved five platoons being permanently employed in essentially static guard duties in Episkopi Garrison, where the Battalion was based, at Government installations on Mount Troodos and at RAF Akrotiri. In addition, there was a myriad of island-wide operational contingency plans, ranging from reinforcement of 'essential facilities' to evacuating the British Embassy in Nicosia and close protection of the BBC World Service Relay Station.

While the occasional unruly crowd demonstration at Mount Troodos and a so-called 'terrorist bomb' at Berengeria quartering area generated some short-lived adrenalin, overall the role itself was dull, not least because the extant threat was less than in Central London. Routine responsibilities were met by means of a roulement system which saw two companies involved with security duties, a third free for company-level training and a fourth on leave. However, within this system, Guards of Honour for visiting VIPs had to be found, as did two full Guards for the Cyprus Queen's Birthday

Parade, acting as enemy for RMA Sandhurst exercises three times yearly and more regularly for visiting company training. There was also the annual and heavy administrative burden of the Troodos Walkabout, which in practice was an 'open to all' Services world-wide two-day cross-country marathon event, and a plethora of endless, lower-profile requirements which were nevertheless manpower-intensive.

Although scattered all over the island, company dry training and section field firing facilities were quite good, particularly on the Akamis Peninsula. But even there it became routine to lose half a day's firing because of Cypriot fishing boats maliciously remaining in the Danger Area; just occasionally the only solution was to encourage them to leave by means of a belt of GPMG tracer and the odd Carl Gustav round! One company enjoyed the benefit of an exercise in Jordan, marked by extraordinary desert temperatures and the fact that there were no safety arcs whatever. Happily, Support Company was also able to leave the island for annual support weapon concentrations in England. Battalion collective training was only achieved because of coincidental political imperatives; on the one hand a perceived political need to exercise British training rights outside Sovereign Base Areas, and on the other, because of the timely call on Mrs Thatcher by the Cypriot President seeking support for Cypriot European Community aspirations.

Living in Cyprus may have been something of a paradise for officers, but for young single Guardsmen it proved a strange environment and some never settled at all. Their barrack accommodation was poor and it is regrettable that in the end the only means of obtaining the funding required, in excess of £1 million, was to ensure that a visiting Parliamentary Select Committee got right inside a barrack block.

Messes thrived at every level and became a focal point for imaginative and pro-active social life. Married quarters areas also proved to be a centre of community activity. Most notable was Berengeria on the outskirts of Limassol where the majority of Battalion families lived. This extraordinary place was once a 'pre-fab' refugee camp during the 1974 War and from a distance was as depressing to the eye as one might have expected. Closer inspection was very different; the families there made living in Berengeria a source of pride, rather than complaint, and it was a vibrant, happy and highly successful community, in large part due to the tireless efforts of the Families Officer, Captain J.H.Todd, who lived there, and his staff.

Every conceivable sporting activity was either already present in Cyprus or provided by the Battalion through Beach Camps and good use of the PRI account when fair means and foul failed to obtain funding from Headquarters Cyprus. From polo to sailing and skiing, both snow and water, every member of the Battalion was encouraged, and where necessary forced, to try his hand at something new as a means of providing an interest to occupy the mind as well as the body during free time. A great number discovered new interests and further developed skills they already had, and, in virtually every area, individuals and the Battalion developed a near monopoly of silverware won.

As in every posting, even Cyprus had its downside. For some it was alien, too far from home, and they were unable to occupy themselves purposefully when not on duty. In hindsight this is perhaps no surprise, but the lesson learned is that while young officers will always reflect ever-changing trends in society, old-fashioned Coldstream leadership traditions, which place special responsibilities on platoon and company commanders for their Guardsmen, will always be valid. Young officers, platoon sergeants and section commanders learned quickly that the welfare of their Guardsmen came first, certainly before pursuing their own interests. Such essential principles were all the more important in the context of the Battalion's turnover being some 40 per cent per annum during the Cyprus tour.

It seems to be a sad fact of life that tragedy befalls those that least deserve it. This was certainly the case for those Battalion members who lost their lives, and perhaps worse, suffered dreadful injuries, in some cases irreparable, in the terrible carnage of a road accident which occurred as the dismounting Troodos Guard was descending the mountain and returning to Episkopi Garrison[3]. The resilience of the Battalion in overcoming a blow of this magnitude was remarkable, as indeed was the genuine hand of sympathy and friendship displayed by both the British community in Cyprus as a whole and the Cypriots island-wide. When disaster such as this strikes, the true strength, leadership and ability of the Quartermaster, the Families Officer and the Regimental Sergeant Major in particular are tested in depth, and here the Battalion simply could not have been better served through Major J.G.Savelle, Captain J.H.Todd and RSM T. Spensley respectively.

Moments to remember with a smile are many and varied, from the idiocy of Military Police Corporals who attempted to arrest a Colour Sergeant for not wearing his forage cap while making a telephone call from a public call box, to the hugely successful visit by the Regimental Band and its notable ability to draw crowds wherever it performed, to the Commanding Officer being stopped by Sovereign Base Police for speeding while driving the Colonel of the Regiment and the Regimental Lieutenant Colonel, to the Battalion winning the boxing in the Curium Amphitheatre as the sun set over the Mediterranean, and to the cricket team beating by one wicket an XI from RAF Akrotiri, which in practice had only four players from the base, the rest being imported on 'training exchanges' from the RAF Service team.

In many respects Cyprus was a force for good. It compelled the Battalion at every level to integrate with a large Tri-Service Headquarters and a wide variety of different civilian and Service organizations. The experience was beneficial to both the Battalion as an entity, large numbers of individuals within it, and its reputation. Equally, many outsiders became aware, both at the time and subsequently, of what a positive benefit the Battalion's presence was for them and their own organizations in terms of the example set. Overall and in spite of an uninspiring operational role and the desperate tragedy of the Troodos accident, the Battalion gained valuable experience and contributed as much during its tour. But Cyprus is no sunshine posting; there are command, leadership and welfare challenges of real substance which subsequent, well-publicized events involving following battalions were to demonstrate.

Note on Author

Colonel Charles Lomer was commissioned into the Coldstream Guards in 1969 and commanded the 2nd Battalion 1988–1990. He was Brigade Major, Household Division 1991–93 and retired in April 2000.

[3] The following members of the Battalion were killed or died of their injuries: Lance Sergeant M.Arnold; Lance Sergeant V.Horsfall; Guardsman M.Conroy; Guardsman D.French; Guardsman P.Kenny; Guardsman S.Lanston; Guardsman S.Shave and Guardsman M.Tackley.

RHODESIA, 1979–1980

by Richard Heywood

2nd Battalion

In November 1965 Ian Smith, the Prime Minister of Rhodesia, Britain's last colony in Africa, issued a long-expected Unilateral Declaration of Independence (UDI), as a result of the British Government's insistence that the African majority must be brought fully into the electoral process. The British Government's response, following pressure from Commonwealth leaders in black Africa, was to impose sanctions on Rhodesia, although ruling out the possibility of military action.

There followed a protracted civil war, which had reached something of a stalemate in January 1979 when the white Rhodesians agreed to approve a new constitution that would lead to an African-dominated Government. In April of that year Bishop Abel Muzorewa became Rhodesia's first black Prime Minister. In August the British Prime Minister, Margaret Thatcher, agreed that Robert Mugabe and Joshua Nkomo, the exiled leaders of the independence struggle, must be part of any future settlement, and Britain undertook to produce a constitution that would provide for genuine black majority rule, and also to prepare a plan for supervising elections in Rhodesia (Zimbabwe), which would be attended by Commonwealth observers.

This British political initiative to bring Rhodesia back from UDI and civil war was eventually hammered out at Lancaster House in December 1979; it ended with an agreement for a ceasefire and new elections, and was signed by all three black Rhodesian leaders, Bishop Abel Muzorewa, the caretaker Prime Minister, and the previously exiled leaders of the war, Robert Mugabe and Joshua Nkomo.

As a result of the agreement, the Ministry of Defence was invited to set up a monitoring force. It was necessary to convince the guerrillas in the bush to come out and take part in elections, and for a disciplined and organized force to observe the casting of votes. Only small, professional and sensitive teams would be effective and the MOD decided on an unusual plan. Several battalions and regiments in the United Kingdom provided their Commanding Officer and about a dozen hand-picked men to form teams.

The 2nd Battalion based at Caterham was commanded by Lieutenant Colonel W.E.Rous MBE. After many false alarms during November his team[4] eventually flew out to Salisbury just before Christmas 1979. Captain S.B.Fraser, though not then in the Battalion, was a member of the Force Headquarters.

The Coldstream party deployed up-country to various different tasks. The Commanding Officer and his staff were based at Umtali to monitor a Rhodesian Brigade in the area which had borne the brunt of the civil war. The young Platoon Commanders were given a torrid time working with ruthless, battle-hardened and extremely tough Rhodesian Army company and battalion

[4] It was one of the largest provided by a single unit, consisting of Major R.J.Heywood MBE, Major P.H.Mills, Lieutenant J.G.M.L.Dodson, Second Lieutenants T.J.Sheldon and H.G.Morgan-Grenville and twenty Warrant and Non-Commissioned Officers.

Coldstream members of the Ceasefire Monitoring Force, Rhodesia.

commanders, who were many years their senior and who the civil war had made particularly uncompromising. As well as acting as Second-in-Command Major Heywood, assisted by Company Sergeant Major Lord, oversaw the opening of the border with Mozambique, which was important for the direct link it provided to the coast at Beira. Most of his negotiations with officials from Mozambique were conducted in the middle of the border minefield. Major Mills, with a small team of non-commissioned officers, ran a terrorist assembly place, which was more successful than any other in persuading an enormous number of guerrillas to come out of the bush. The Rhodesian Army was convinced that our soldiers would not be able to survive the heat and isolation of the bush, let alone get the guerrillas to give themselves up to us. But the professionalism, bearing and determination of

Lance Corporal Deller in the marketplace at Umtali.

these small teams won the day and the whole Force was praised for the courage, nerve and self-discipline displayed by individuals.

The unique operation was an unqualified success. Some 20,000 guerrillas were collected into Assembly Places; a free and fair election took place and Mr Robert Mugabe, leader of the Zimbabwe African National Union (ZANU), came to power as Zimbabwe succeeded Rhodesia. The Commanding Officer was awarded the OBE following the safe return of all his men just three months after their deployment, and Second Lieutenant H.G.Morgan-Grenville was awarded a Commendation for Meritorious Service.

Note on Author

Brigadier Richard Heywood was commissioned into the Coldstream Guards in 1963 and retired in 1999. He was Brigade Major, Household Division, 1981–83 and commanded the 2nd Battalion from 1983–85 and held the appointment of Regimental Lieutenant Colonel Coldstream Guards from 1992–99.

FALKLAND ISLANDS TOUR, 1984

by Brian Barttelot

1st Battalion

In June 1984, after a year's Public Duties based at Caterham, the 1st Battalion, commanded by Lieutenant Colonel Sir Brian Barttelot Bt OBE, handed in its tunics and bearskins in exchange for winter warfare clothing and, after embarkation leave, set off on a five-month tour in the Falkland Islands. Most were flown to Ascension Island by the RAF and then completed the journey across the South Atlantic by sea aboard the SS *Uganda*, a ten-day cruise.

On taking over from The Royal Scots, No 1 Company, commanded by Major Charlie Macfarlane, found itself living afloat on a former oil rig service vessel (known as a coastel) in Stanley Harbour, its main task being the defence of the original airfield. No 2 Company under Major Nick Parsons was based at Fox Bay on West Falkland Island and thus separated from the rest of the Battalion. No 3 Company led by Major Willie Style was co-located with Battalion Headquarters at Goose Green, the objective of the fateful 3 PARA attack during the Falklands War of 1982 in which their Commanding Officer, Lieutenant Colonel H.Jones, was killed and subsequently awarded a posthumous VC. Apart from an *ad hoc* group made up from the Reconnaissance Platoon and volunteers, which was sent off down to South Georgia with Major Peter Hicks, Support Company was split up between the Rifle Companies. Headquarter Company was divided between Goose Green and Stanley, the capital, from where all the stores and rations were distributed (everything needed having to be flown or shipped in).

Following the expulsion of Argentinian Forces in 1982, there was no expectation of another invasion, but General de la Billière, who was Commander British Forces at the time, had good reason to believe that there remained a serious risk of sabotage attacks by Argentinian Special Forces. The

Battalion's main task therefore was to guard against such attacks and be ready to react and deal with any attempted incursion.

With no roads and the area of responsibility spread over many islands, speedy reaction could only be achieved with the aid of RAF Chinook helicopters, so as much time as possible was spent in practising helicopter deployments throughout the islands. At the same time the scope for field firing exercises was almost unlimited and there was no shortage of most types of ammunition. The Second-in-Command, Major Nick Emson, aided by Captain Richard Clowes, the Training Officer, made the most of this situation. Company live-firing exercises were invariably enlivened by support weapons and occasionally, because of very strong winds, the impact of mortar shells could be a little too close for comfort! The excitement was often further heightened by RAF fighter ground attack sorties and naval gunfire support. As a result a very high standard of field craft and field firing was achieved. On the Battalion's departure, General de la Billière wrote to the Commanding Officer, "You go back with a Battalion which is trained to the very highest operational standards".

Most were accommodated in portacabins, generally eight to a cabin, with showers and toilets in separate buildings. If you wanted to go to the loo in the middle of the night, with the 'roaring forties' blowing through the camp, you thought twice about it and, with outward opening doors to the portacabins, if you opened the door without holding onto the door handle it would probably be blown off its hinges!

In between exercises it was quite a struggle to keep everyone constructively occupied and happy.

The Major General talking to members of No 2 Company on training. The Company Commander is Major W.B. Style.

Falkland penguins. "Get your dressing!"

A Platoon Commander would set off on foot with his Guardsmen carrying all their equipment on week-long expeditions, 'yomping' over the very rough terrain to visit remote settlements all over the Islands. They would stop and make camp each night, everyone sleeping in individual 'bivvy bags'. The fishermen amongst them usually managed to catch sea trout which abounded in most of the rivers and streams. On arrival at a settlement the group would indulge in some community relations by helping to repair buildings or mending fences. The visit would end with a bit of a party when the 'fatted calf', or more likely, sheep, would invariably be killed and the expedition would set off back to base the following morning.

Inevitably there were quick reaction force and vulnerable point guard commitments, some of which involved living on the top of snow-covered mountains, protecting communication and radar stations; not a popular duty! Guarding RAF aircraft at Stanley airfield was a very manpower-intensive and sensitive commitment until the RAF and HQ British Forces eventually agreed to a less static form of defence.

1st Battalion: MT in the Falklands.

1st Battalion: No 1 Company marching to the ferry from the coastel.

Spare time was not easy to occupy. With a few exceptions in Stanley, all birds were of the feathered kind and few Guardsmen were really interested in wildlife, though most were keen to get a glimpse of the penguins. Football was just possible when the wind dropped, though the pitch at Goose Green was far from flat. Otherwise there were films and endless videos, occasional CSE Shows and plenty of time to write letters home.

Not to be forgotten and most isolated was the South Georgia Detachment. Three days sailing to the south-east and well inside the Antarctic Circle lies the island where all the trouble started. Two officers and twenty-four NCOs and Guardsmen survived there in quite reasonable British Antarctic Survey accommodation. They had no trouble and became quite proficient at langlauf skiing, igloo building and Arctic warfare skills generally. However, it was pretty lonely with only an occasional visit from a supply ship or RN warship. Weather permitting, they got a weekly mail drop from a RAF Hercules skimming over Cumberland Bay.

Despite the privations, loneliness and, for some, boredom of life in the Falklands, the Battalion,

1st Battalion: Remembrance Day, en route for home.

1st Battalion Remembrance Day en route for home. The Commanding Officer, Lieutenant Colonel Sir Brian Barttelot Bt, is in the centre.

as ever, rose to the occasion, made the most of what was there and sailed home in November with some relief but also satisfaction at an unusual and decidedly difficult job well done. Although many Guardsmen said at the time that they did not enjoy the tour, more than fifty per cent said that they did, and probably more in retrospect. They earned high praise from the General and his staff who seemed genuinely sorry to see them depart.

Note on Author

Colonel Sir Brian Barttelot, Bt. OBE. DL. served in the Regiment from 1961–1992, following his father and grandfather. He commanded the 1st Battalion 1982–84, which included operational tours in Northern Ireland and the Falkland Islands. He held the appointment of Regimental Lieutenant Colonel 1986–1992 and that of Colonel Foot Guards 1989–1992. He is President of the Sussex Branch of The Coldstream Guards Association.

HONG KONG, 1986–88

1st Battalion

In February 1986 the 1st Battalion, under Lieutenant Colonel Johnny Wardle, exchanged Caterham for Hong Kong replacing 1st Battalion The Cheshire Regiment for a two-year tour of duty in the Gurkha Field Force. The Battalion was the only British unit in the Field Force, which included three Gurkha Battalions stationed in Hong Kong. The military environment in the theatre was therefore extremely competitive, with the Gurkhas determined to outdo the UK Battalion at every opportunity. Another unusual challenge faced the families, who had to cope with a testing environment some 14,000 miles away from home, without the support of relatives and with a climate that could be severely depressing. As part of the preparations for the tour, the Stanley Fort Families Association was set up, and this proved an invaluable course of action, as over 300 wives moved with the Battalion.

1st Battalion: aerial view of New Territories, Hong Kong.

Training began in March, in preparation for the first tour on Frontier Duty in April. The Battalion's role was to maintain the integrity of the Land Border with the People's Republic of China, by preventing Illegal Immigrants (IIs) from getting into Hong Kong. The companies soon discovered that the Land Border included a lot of water on the flanks, as well as bogs, marshes, mud flats, fish ponds and flotsam!

The tally of IIs at once began to accumulate. Thirteen were captured in the first 24 hours of duty and the total at the end of the four-week tour was 632.

In between frontier tours the Battalion carried out internal security training, which included Company exercises in Brunei and Fiji.

In October 1986 the Battalion deployed on its second tour of Frontier Duty, which was to last for five weeks. Some 906 IIs were captured, but this total paled into insignificance with the haul of

Captain R.G. Clowes, Adjutant 1st Battalion, and Lieutenant the Hon R.F.D. Margesson at Victoria Island, Hong Kong.

1162 from the next tour, which was of seven weeks' duration, from March to May 1987. This latter total included seventeen who were actually captured in Stanley Fort. This was not believed at Battalion Headquarters, as the captures had taken place on 1st April!

The fourth and final tour on the Border lasted for five weeks from September to November 1987. During the night of 21/22 October the Battalion captured seventy IIs, which was the highest capture rate achieved for one night during any of the Battalion's Border tours. Although this had been the shortest tour, the final score of 1228 had surpassed all the others, making an overall grand total of 3928.

The Military must always be prepared for the unexpected and in December 1986 the versatility and flexibility of the Battalion were tested to the full. At midday on Friday 5 December it was announced that the Governor, Sir Edward Youde, had died in Beijing. The Battalion was detailed to provide the Bearer Party and, following rehearsals, it was duly despatched that afternoon. During dinner that evening the Commanding Officer was informed that the Acting Governor had agreed to Lady Youde's request for a State Funeral to be staged the following Tuesday.

There was no contingency plan and the Commanding Officer was therefore ordered to develop a plan overnight, and to brief the Commander British Forces at 0800 the next day, followed by a briefing to the Acting Governor and Executive Council at 0930. Members of the Recce Group were summoned from their various Messes and work started at 2100. Fortunately the Time Zones were favourable and so the Commanding Officer was able to ask Headquarters London District to fax a copy of the Churchill Funeral as an aide memoire. The London fax was down and so a favour was called in from the Hong Kong and Shanghai Bank, and as a result the financial wires were clogged for about an hour as some eighty pages of text were transmitted![5]

The document duly arrived at 0300, copies were made and recces began at dawn. Deadlines were just met and the plan accepted on the basis that any plan was better than no plan! The Sunday was 'learn to slow march day' for the Gurkhas, aided by every non-commissioned officer who could be deployed from the Battalion. The early morning rehearsal for the Marching Party of sixty took place at 0500 on Monday. One Gurkha Battalion had refused an offer of help and appeared with arms reversed in a totally unique and obviously incorrect position, which did not endear it to its formation Commander!

In the end all went well, although the gun carriage which was due to convey the coffin had collapsed at a private rehearsal on the Sunday, being riddled with rot and worm! The Battalion itself provided the Marching Party of sixty, the Corps of Drums, the Bearer Party and forty Marshals, and received glowing praise from The Major General, (Major General C.J.Airy) who was visiting Hong Kong at the time.

Away from Frontier Duty, the focus for the Battalion in 1987 was Limited War and the training during the year culminated in a five-day amphibious brigade exercise throughout the New Territories. Command of the Battalion had changed in August, with Colonel Wardle (who had been awarded the OBE in The Queen's Birthday Honours List) handing over to Lieutenant Colonel Edward Armitstead. Apart from training, the Battalion continued to participate in every available activity. Much sport was played, with considerable success, and a notable adventure training expedition took place, led by 2nd Lieutenant R.I.C.Tubbs, with the aim of climbing Mount Kinabalu in Sarawak, which was duly accomplished. Many individuals and families also took the opportunity to holiday in the exotic resorts of the Far East.

[5] Brigadier R.J.S. Wardle OBE, Recollections of 1st Battalion Coldstream Guards, 1985–87.

The Battalion handed over to 1st Battalion The Duke of Edinburgh's Royal Regiment in February 1988 and returned to London and Wellington Barracks. Everyone had worked hard, played hard and had taken full advantage of what Hong Kong had to offer. It had been a unique experience for all.

THE GULF WAR 1991

by Hugh Boscawen

When the Ministry of Defence thought up 'Options for Change' in 1990, many senior officials scoffed at the idea that the United Kingdom might deploy armoured forces out of the NATO area – or anywhere in divisional strength to fight a war.[6]

Shortly afterwards, on 2 August 1990, however, Republican Guard tanks of Saddam Hussein's Iraqi regime invaded Kuwait, an act that took most in the West by surprise. The United States and Britain rapidly sent aircraft and naval forces to the region to reinforce Saudi Arabia and the other Gulf States. Within a month it was clear that ground forces would be required and on 14 September the United Kingdom committed 7th Armoured Brigade to the Coalition forces in the Gulf.

At the time **1st Coldstream** was based in Wellington Barracks doing Public Duties and conversion courses to the Warrior vehicle before moving to Münster to take over from the Grenadiers in the Armoured Infantry role, but this plan was put on hold. The Battalion went on Christmas leave in December 1990, having heard the Commanding Officer, Lieutenant Colonel Iain McNeil, utter the famous words, "They won't need us in the Gulf. If they do, I'll eat my hat."

Preparations for Deployment

On the evening of 29 December a worried Picquet Officer telephoned the Second-in-Command, Major Hugh Boscawen, to summon him to a conference in Horse Guards at 1000 hours the following morning, a Sunday. He was there asked one basic question: "Could 1st Coldstream deploy with 520 men to look after prisoners on Operation GRANBY?" It did not take long to say that the Battalion could make the numbers and would be keen to go. Permission was granted to train and indent for equipment, but no order to deploy was given and no recall of personnel was allowed. Fortunately the *Daily Mirror* printed the story and the Battalion was soon back in Barracks! But at the outset, following the Second-in-Command's despatch of twelve FLASH signals on Day One, practical problems arose. A huge lorry-load of perforated steel 'sand tracking' arrived at Wellington Barracks; the only men to unload it were Sergeants' Mess members recovering from their New Year Ball!

Just under a month later the Battalion was on active service in the Gulf: a month after that, on 26 February, it was moving into Iraq as part of 1st (BR) Armoured Division.

Preparation began in earnest in early January 1991. Reorganization of the Battalion took place

[6] Over 35,500 British servicemen and women deployed in the Gulf in all. The author has drawn on: *1st Bn Coldstream Guards in the Gulf* 1991; letter by Brigadier I.H. McNeil, October 1999; Diary of Major H.G.R. Boscawen: *Operation DESERT SABRE,* Inspector General Doctrine & Training, 1993.

and more indents were submitted for equipment. Morale rose, as the Commanding Officer later wrote, "to the rafters"; men flooded back from courses and 'rejoins' offered themselves unconditionally. The task initially given was to guard the large numbers of prisoners of war that the United Kingdom contingent anticipated taking (an obligation placed on capturing nations by the Geneva Convention). At the same time it was clear that a makeshift brigade headquarters would have to be found from Battalion resources. The Commanding Officer was to command two other battalions in addition to the Coldstream in the hastily created Prisoner of War Guard Force (PWGF): 1st Battalion The Royal Highland Fusiliers and 1st Battalion The King's Own Scottish Borderers.

The Commanding Officer, acting full Colonel, departed to Riyadh on a reconnaissance and saw Major General Rupert Smith, commanding 1st (BR) Armoured Division, and the Commander British Forces Middle East, Lieutenant General Sir Peter de la Billière.

In the meantime the Battalion trained with a will in London. Although lectures on the background to Saddam Hussein's Iraq and desert navigation received close attention, the threat from the huge Iraqi chemical capability, well known from the Iran-Iraq War, concentrated the mind effectively. NBC lectures, fitness training wearing helmets and bergen rucksacks, and even time in the gas chamber were keenly attended.

Finally, on 18 January, the deployment of the Battalion to the Gulf was confirmed. The Commanding Officer and the Pre-Advance Party left that day while Major General Simon Cooper, commanding the Household Division, and the Colonel of the Regiment, Major General Sir George Burns, came to Wellington Barracks to say goodbye. Within a week the whole Battalion had left.

Saudi Arabia

Everyone deployed into the desert for acclimatization soon after arrival in the Force Maintenance Area at Al Jubayl in Saudi Arabia. The skills of battle-shooting, navigation, NBC, first aid and construction of defences all had to be adjusted to desert conditions. Weapon cleaning, carriage of equipment, driving over the different types of sand and even eating and drinking required thought and practice. Keeping the SA80 Rifle and Light Support Weapon clean and firing needed continuous effort and much ingenuity, and many theories were tried; both weapons were prone to frequent stoppages when exposed to sand. Tactics for desert as flat as a billiard table had to be devised. Wise ones (recalling Second World War pictures of 3rd Coldstream and 'Desert Rats' in sheepskin coats) brought combat jackets, but many found it very cold!

The camp soon began to look Guardsmanlike, in marked contrast to the dusty and disorganized Blackadder Lines and elsewhere, where the rear echelons of the British Army gave a poor impression, unlike their uniformly dressed, polite and saluting American Allies. Two Coldstream Quartermasters who had been in theatre for some time, Majors John Rigby and Brian Mather (the latter in 1st Armoured Division Signal Regiment), gave considerable help to the Battalion.

While in Al Jubayl the Battalion was visited by General de la Billière who impressed upon the Commanding Officer, Officers and Guardsmen that treatment of Iraqi prisoners was to be firm but fair; the parading of battered Allied pilots on television had shown what Iraqi treatment of prisoners was like.

In February a number of Royal Saudi Air Force interpreters joined the Battalion. They were followed by a group of Kuwaiti volunteers, from all walks of life, including members of the Kuwaiti Royal Family, many of whom told hair-raising tales of escapes and of Iraqi atrocities. A sharp reminder of the threat and a practical test of NBC drills occurred when a SCUD missile exploded

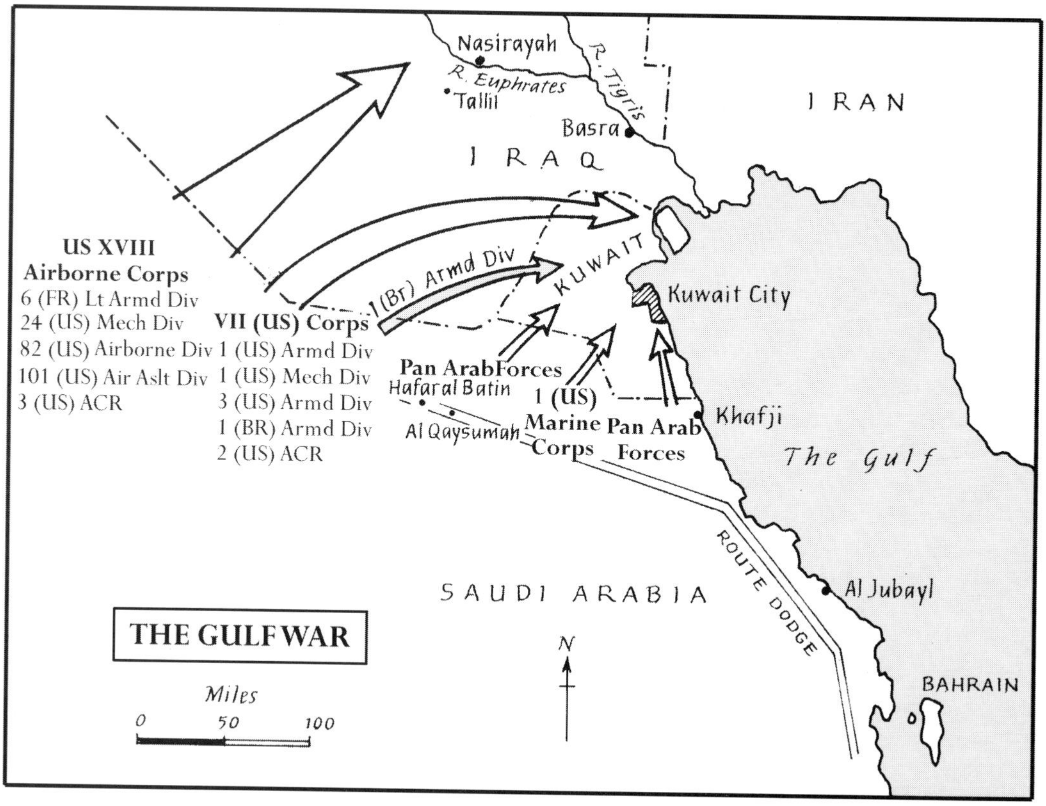

close to Al Jubayl docks, less than two miles from the Battalion, during the night of 15/16 February. Those who had not prepared their NBC equipment and respirators before bedtime were severely embarrassed and the Battalion Headquarters NBC staff and all ranks learned practical lessons!

On 18 February the Battalion vehicles drove 300 miles to Al Qaysumah where the British Prisoner of War Camp, named Maryhill Camp, was being built. The road (Main Supply Route (MSR) DODGE), two or three lanes wide for half the way, was densely packed with the transport of at least three army corps, and thousands of vehicles of every description fought for the limited road space.

The main body of the Battalion flew by C-130 Hercules to an airstrip near Maryhill Camp and some training continued at Al Qaysumah.

The bombing campaign and artillery raids to the north could clearly be heard at night and heralded an offensive, curiously reminiscent of reports of the First World War. Then, and later, the knowledge that the Allies had air superiority – supremacy – was immensely reassuring and made ground movement much easier.

The Ground War, 24 February–1 March 1991

On 22 February the Battalion joined 1st (BR) Armoured Division in its Forward Assembly Area, codenamed RAY, leaving a group from all three Battalions guarding Maryhill Camp. Companies moved into harbour areas in 'box' formation and final preparations took place.

The weather remained poor – overcast with rain and wind that picked up the fine gravel and acted like a sandblaster on exposed flesh. The sky, Colonel McNeil later wrote, was "an apocalyptic black, set against terrain that was flat without any relief of any kind from horizon to horizon, [and] set an atmosphere of impending doom. . . . It was testimony to discipline and good junior leadership that everyone remained very steady."

At 0400 hours on 24 February the ground war started: the long-awaited G Day had arrived. General Schwarzkopf's plan envisaged that VII(US) Corps would be the main effort, attacking left-flanking into Iraq on G + 1. 1st (US) Infantry Division was to breach the Iraqi defences so that three armoured divisions, 1st(US), 3rd(US) and 1st(BR), with 2nd(US) Armoured Cavalry Regiment, could exploit through the breach and attack the enemy's tactical, operational and strategic reserve divisions, including the Republican Guard, simultaneously. Other Allied forces attacked into Kuwait itself on G Day.

The Divisional Operation Order appeared on G Day and the Battalion Orders Group took place in a most unpleasant sandstorm. Colonel McNeil wrote:

> "After years of BAOR play-acting, this was the real thing. Too much to say – too little? Lives depended on one getting it right. . . . Orders were crisp, business-like and positive. But as I looked round these men, whom I genuinely liked, I wondered how many I would see again. . . . We all wore Arab head-dress, wrapped around the head, face and nose, so it was hardly a conventional sight."

For others at the Orders Group there was some excitement since the 'crusade' had begun, and the radio news had been reporting hourly the progress of the Parachute Regiment of the French Foreign Legion racing into Iraq on the left flank. The Divisional Commander's summary of the plan, repeated by the Commanding Officer, was inspiring: "Gentlemen. This rugby game is the hardest one we have ever played. When we leave the breach, the ball comes out of the ruck and the tryline is the Euphrates!"

The need to follow the armoured brigades closely in order to protect the Brigade Echelons and to collect prisoners had now been acknowledged and the Support Company Group, under Major Simon Vandeleur, was detached to join the Brigade Administrative Area of 4th Armoured Brigade. This Group comprised the Mortar and Anti-Tank Platoons, the Corps of Drums and a section of the Reconnaissance Platoon, and was detached until 1 March.

Although it had been planned that 1st Coldstream should move on G + 2 with the Divisional Administrative Area, the 6000 vehicles of this group, led by the Battalion, formed up in the 'buffer zone' on G + 1, 25 February 1991. NBC suits, overboots and helmets were donned. Not unexpectedly, news filtered through that the 1st(US) Infantry Division's attack had been so successful that all timings were advanced. Forty-eight hours 'Notice To Move' became two hours at a stroke! Part of the Reconnaissance Platoon drove ahead to collect the first prisoners, followed by a section from No 1 Company in Sea King helicopters.

The Battalion moved later. The going was poor and heavy rain led to delays and bogged vehicles, some in trenches containing dead Iraqis. When there was a halt close to the border a group of forty-eight Iraqis suddenly appeared, but fortunately surrendered. They were terrified, soaking and hungry, small in stature and elderly compared with the Guardsmen. When Major Jonathan Bourne-May's Land Rover drove over an anti-personnel mine, which blew the tyres off the trailer (the shrapnel just missing Company Sergeant Major Howick sitting in the back) and when armoured columns began crossing the route the decision was taken to halt until first light.

The Harbour Party and Battalion Main Body met up around 0900 hours on 26 February (G + 2) and a Divisional Prisoner of War Cage was set up. The move forward, some fifty miles, had taken over fourteen hours.

Elements of No 2 Company were flown forward to collect prisoners while Lieutenant Richard Bayliss and a section of No 3 Company drove to collect more from three different places. Movement was hindered by inaccurate grid references, the difficulties of navigating in totally featureless terrain, poor visibility – a very severe sand-storm blew that afternoon – compounded by many minefields and thousands of scattered, unexploded cluster bomblets. Later in the day two No 1 Company platoons under Captain Andrew Cumming and Lieutenant John Jeffcock were flown forward under command of the Company Second Captain, Lieutenant Mick Cocliff, to form a cage for 300 prisoners taken by 7th Armoured Brigade. Similar activities were to form the pattern for the next few days. Nevertheless, during that afternoon No 2 Company came across at least six groups of Iraqis who had not surrendered, some of whom opened fire. The Company moved on to round up 230 prisoners elsewhere; the ground-holding infantry divisions and 12th (Iraqi) Armoured Division on Objectives Bronze, Copper, Zinc and Brass had been destroyed.

During the night platoons and sections moved by helicopter, Land Rover or 4-tonne truck to collect groups of prisoners and the following day (27 February, G + 3) the Armoured Brigades approached Wadi Al Batin, a shallow valley in which the Iraq-Kuwaiti border lay. Most of the prisoners were dejected. Many had not eaten or had water for up to ten days. Earlier, during training, the Battalion had devised tactics for movement in a non-linear 'box' formation (for all-round defence, following Napoleon's *Bataillon Carré*). The improvised prisoner cages followed a less highbrow design, on the principle of the cartoonist Thelwell's 'Leg At Each Corner'; four 4-tonne trucks with machine guns were connected together with barbed wire to form a cage.

At 1000 hours on G + 3 the Battalion drove forty miles up Route FOX and found a new position (not without difficulty owing to minefields). Abandoned trenches and destroyed armoured vehicles

Major D.D.S.A. Vandeleur (left) and the Support Company Group meeting Major J.J.S. Bourne-May on their return to the Battalion, 1 Mar 91.

1st Battalion Company Commanders: Major S.D. Holborow and Major J.J.S. Bourne-May.

littered the route. Mines and bomblets lay in every position previously occupied by the Iraqis. The desert was so flat that it was possible to observe the curvature of the earth, but communications remained difficult: the Battalion could only get through to Division once every eight hours or so. On the 27th the Companies again sent out parties to collect prisoners: No 2 Company relieved Lieutenant David Key's No 7 Platoon of 1300 prisoners and during the night the Reconnaissance Platoon brought in another 170.

The news, early on 28 February (G + 4), that a ceasefire had been planned for 0800 hours (local time) came as a surprise, but the need to collect, process and transport prisoners from the various divisional objectives remained. Just before the ceasefire 1st (BR) Armoured Division cut the Basra-Kuwait road, and after just 100 hours the campaign was over. The Coldstream tasks continued and No 2 Company was able to relieve 32nd Heavy Regiment RA of another 1000 prisoners while No 3 Company shuttled prisoners from the Divisional Cage run by The King's Own Scottish Borderers to the VII(US) Corps Collection Point.

On 1 March the Battalion moved up to join Support Company, themselves with a sizeable cage, and prepared to drive into Kuwait.

Many junior Non-Commissioned Officers with a few Guardsmen had looked after much larger groups of prisoners. On one occasion Lance Corporal Lenthall and his section were left alone in the desert with a large number of prisoners. It was cold and wet. A Company Officer, arriving later, saw Corporal Lenthall teaching a huge phalanx of Iraqis foot drill to keep them warm, and heard him call ". . . and what's my name?" Hundreds of Iraqis shouted the answer in unison, "Lennie"!

Support Company Group

The Support Company Group joined 4th Armoured Brigade on 24 February and moved slowly through the breach on the night of 25/26 February. By 0900 hours on 26 February the Company found itself advancing across the Iraqi desert providing protection for the 500 vehicles of the 4th Brigade Administrative Area. By mid-morning reports were received of prisoners. Major Vandeleur and the Corps of Drums, under Lieutenant Robert Yorke, relieved an American artillery battalion

Jubilant Kuwaiti and Saudi interpreters attached to the Battalion hearing of the Cease Fire, 28 Feb 91.

of seventy prisoners. Lieutenant Yorke moved his platoon five miles to the MSR, traversing several poorly marked minefields and collecting another 130 Iraqis on the way. The rest of the Company advanced and gathered up 900 more prisoners, including two brigadiers. The forward Battlegroups brought in several hundred Iraqis during the night: US Military Policemen arrived next day to collect them. Feeding and providing water to such numbers was a major problem.

When the Company rejoined the Brigade Administrative Area that afternoon, elements of the 3rd Battalion The Royal Regiment of Fusiliers Battle group brought in 1500 prisoners, including one divisional and two brigade commanders. Company Sergeant Major Kevin Humphrey set up a cage in quick time and the miserable Iraqis were moved into it.

On 28 February, leaving the Mortar Platoon under Captain Mark Polglase to guard the cage, the Company Group moved forward, but soon had to leave the Drums with 300 prisoners taken by the 14th/20th King's Hussars Battle Group. Although food and particularly water for the Company Group and the prisoners were scarce, Battalion transport reached the two cages that night and next day, and at 1200 hours on 1 March Support Company rejoined the Battalion.

Kuwait

After another long drive, in drier weather, with the first appearance of the sun for some days, the Battalion stayed in the hills in North Central Kuwait from 1–4 March. It was close to an Iraqi brigade position and mines were a major hazard.

The move back to Al Qaysumah on 4 March via the main north-south Basra to Kuwait City 'motorway' over the Mutla Ridge, littered with the carnage of thousands of destroyed vehicles, military and civilian, caught attempting to escape out of Kuwait, was interesting.

Saudi Arabia and the Return Home

Since those who had been in theatre longest (over six months in some cases) were to be sent home first, the Battalion settled down to a period of training, first at Al Qaysumah where Maryhill Camp had to be guarded, and then in Al Jubayl, to which the Battalion returned on 13 March. Liaison with the US Allies took place and competitions were held. Support Company organized a patrol competition against the US Rangers, an élite force drawn from the whole of the US Army. The Anti-Tank Platoon triumphed in this arduous exercise held over a distance of fifty kilometres at night. Later, in a March and Shoot Competition against a US Marine Corps battalion, No 2 Company were convincing winners. The Allies were embarrassed to be beaten and one commanding officer ordered his men to 'show again'! Battalion cadre courses and field firing continued while companies guarded captured ex-Soviet equipment near Kuwait City.

The Battalion flew back to the United Kingdom over the period 3–8 April. Tragically, just before the Battalion returned home, Guardsman Napier of Number 2 Company was killed in a road accident in Al Jubayl, the only fatal casualty sustained by the Battalion in the Gulf.

The Home Front

The Battalion families, dispersed around the London area, kept in touch through Captain Clive Stevens' Families Office, and through the efforts made by many wives. With no censorship and husbands occasionally ringing home, the dangers of misleading rumours were considerable, but an authoritative daily recorded telephone message, and families activities kept people informed and reduced rumours to a minor nuisance. A visit to Wellington Barracks by Diana, Princess of Wales, in February 1991 provided a major boost to morale.

Gulf 1991

Most of the Battalion found the experience of the Gulf War fascinating. Although at first sight the role was undramatic, there was no shortage of danger or excitement. Along the way there were plenty of enemy, with chemical weapons, quite well-equipped armoured formations and millions of mines from which the Battalion was lucky to escape unscathed. Communications, movement and all manner of activities were as subject to the frictions of war as they had ever been. Fortunately there was little fight in most of the Iraqis the Battalion met; most had suffered badly from the bombing of their supply lines and had either been overrun or were keener to find food than to fight. The Republican Guard were more bullish, but not much more aggressive or effective. The Battalion nonetheless managed to find, guard, feed and transport some 7300 prisoners, perhaps 2000 of whom it took itself, sometimes under extraordinarily difficult conditions.

Lasting impressions included listening to the BBC World Service – and the American Forces Network – news every hour, the monotony of 4- and 10-man ration packs, the wonderful support in letters and the generous parcels from families, friends and unknown well-wishers from home. Bottled water and plastic plates, knives and forks were a war-winner for the individual; in marked contrast to previous campaigns (and the Battalion's 1989 Kenya exercise) very few suffered from sickness. The vehicles, many of which were twenty years old, performed reliably in the sand (only one breaking down irreparably) which was more than could be said for the Rifle and the Light Support Weapon. The morale of the Battalion and the sense of purpose were terrific. Many sights and smells were as unpleasant as in any war: the evidence of dejection and near-starvation of prisoners in defeat, the litter of an army destroyed, its charred hulks of tanks and guns, and discarded ammunition and rubbish was never far away.

The impression of being part of a huge, well-trained and supplied military formation on the Allied side, diverse in nationalities and equipment but immensely powerful, protected by air supremacy, and with high morale was very marked.

The members of the 1st Battalion who went to the Gulf were very proud of their contribution to the liberation of Kuwait and later to receive recognition in the form of the **Gulf 1991** blazon now on the Colours. In the post-'Options' Army, little respite was allowed and 1st Coldstream deployed to Northern Ireland in 1992 and Bosnia in 1993: for a time the sight of Guardsmen aged 21 with three (or more) campaign medal ribbons was commonplace.

Some months after the Gulf Colonel Iain McNeil addressed the Battalion and was disconcerted when the Officers and the Guardsmen did not fall out as expected. Major David Yorke, the Quartermaster and 'Old Soldier', then stepped forward and, recalling Colonel McNeil's words in December 1990, gave the Commanding Officer a hat to eat, which he did; fortunately it was made of meringue!

BOSNIA, 1993–1994

by Peter Williams

1st Battalion

During the 1990s the fall of the Berlin Wall gave new hope to many of the inhabitants of the Soviet bloc, but its consequences for the peoples of Yugoslavia were also momentous. First the Slovenes won their independence. Then in 1992 both Croatia and Bosnia-Herzegovina seceded from Yugoslavia. This in turn caused their local Serb populations to fight to break away from these new states, all too often ethnically cleansing the non-Serbs and bombarding their towns and cities, including the capital, Sarajevo. In fact no ethnic group showed itself to possess a monopoly either of virtue or of brutality.

British military involvement in the former Yugoslavia began when a medical unit was moved to Croatia as part of the UN Protection Force (UNPROFOR) Operation HAMDEN there. This was a humanitarian support operation and was followed later in 1992 by Operation GRAPPLE which saw the deployment to Bosnia from Germany of a Warrior-equipped armoured infantry battalion, 1st Battalion The Cheshire Regiment.

The apparently simple UNPROFOR mission was to support the humanitarian relief efforts of the UN High Commissioner for Refugees (UNHCR). However, the British troops soon found themselves in the midst of a complex and heavily armed conflict. Serbs, Croats and Bosniacs (Muslims) all fought for their own slice of their homeland, inflicting appalling violence and deprivation on their pre-war neighbours, not least in central Bosnia. Thousands died and about half the population found itself displaced either within the state's borders or beyond them. This then was the volatile and fluid civil war that the 1st Battalion found when we arrived in Bosnia for a six-month tour of duty in November 1993 taking over from 1st Battalion The Prince of Wales' Own Regiment of Yorkshire as the third Operation GRAPPLE battalion group. The main bases were in Vitez and Gornji Vakuf.

In Bosnia no two days were the same. Following the reopening on 25 November of Route

Guardsman Baxter on highway duty.

Diamond, the only main supply route, aid convoys rolled north for the first time in a month. Planning for this was detailed and designed to ensure that those living along the route received aid early on. The concept worked well and, despite difficult weather conditions, a considerable tonnage reached the UNHCR warehouse in Zenica. From here the Dutch Transport Battalion and the Coldstream MT Platoon were involved in secondary distribution to local municipalities. Included in the aid programme were three tons provided by two North-Eastern Branches of The Coldstream Guards Association which arrived in a meat van from Accrington.

Against a background of convoys there were always surprises. Included in this were two convoys put together by the Croat and Bosniac communities. Both were mounted in unsuitable vehicles of

1st Battalion Warrant Officers at Vitez.

which there were far too many. The Commanding Officer was involved in endless negotiations to secure their safe passage. Despite the discovery by the Bosniacs of ammunition in the Croat convoy, all went well until the extraction, when a Croat driver was killed by a sniper. The REME spent four days and nights in the mountains recovering the Bosniac convoy which had become bogged in. Fortunately they returned to camp in time for Christmas.

The festive season provided opportunities for the Battalion to entertain the local community. Parties were organized for both Croat and Bosniac children. The Corps of Drums performed at numerous events. These included a children's television show made by Vitez TV which also included the Adjutant, Captain J.E.J.N.Giles, in a starring role. As well as parties for children there were parties for the Press and local civil and military leaders.

Despite the festivities there was a major offensive by the Bosniacs just before Christmas. This involved some heavy shelling and, as a precautionary measure, Vitez bases went to State Red with all troops under hardened cover. This condition did not last long. No 1 Company at Gornji Vakuf had a much more difficult time over the preceding months. Croat artillery attacks against the Bosniacs caused them to adopt State Red on several occasions, notably one moment when the Company Second-in-Command noticed rounds creeping close to the base. Having duly ordered everyone to State Red, it was only a few minutes later when five rockets landed in the base damaging the Sergeants' Mess, washrooms, food stores and vehicle park, but leaving the Company unscathed. By coincidence the Company Liaison Officer was with the senior Croat commander at the time and they witnessed the attack. As a consequence he ordered an immediate halt to the firing. The attack was assessed as a mistake rather than deliberate targeting, despite the fact that Warrior armoured vehicles from No 1 Company had killed a Croat sniper earlier in the day.

Just before Christmas the four-man crew of a Mortar Platoon 432 armoured vehicle was abducted while it was dismounted monitoring the search of a convoy. In a planned operation they were taken away by a group of Bosniac soldiers protesting at the loss of their ambulanceman who had strayed into Croat lines and become a prisoner in the presence of another 432 crew. After a worrying three hours all four were safely returned.

The situation in Central Bosnia deteriorated seriously during the last fortnight of January as the Bosniac Army attempted to capture the Croat enclave around Vitez. Although both warring factions made great efforts to avoid rounds falling on the Battalion's two bases in the Lasva Valley, both outside Vitez, and on the Dutch-Belgium Transport Battalion's bases at Santici and Busovaca, it was a distinctly unsafe environment for convoy operations. Both in the Lasva area and in the Vrbas Valley, where Gornji Vakuf dominated the aid route, the free passage of humanitarian and UNPROFOR military vehicles was a ceaseless cause for concern.

Added to the risks of being caught up in someone else's war were the endless bureaucratic obstacles erected by the Serbs, Croats and Bosniacs (in descending order of magnitude) and the rise of civil unrest along Route Diamond in Bosniac areas. With the UNHCR managing to achieve no more than a fifth of its target tonnages for aid in the period from November to the end of January, it was no surprise that hungry locals gazed with envy on passing UNPROFOR military and UNHCR humanitarian convoys. In several Bosniac villages crowds attacked stalled or slow-moving aid vehicles and the route had to be closed as a result of civil unrest on a number of occasions, infuriating everyone involved in the humanitarian effort. Appeals to the Bosniac and Croat authorities to free up the route by stamping out civil disorder and excessive bureaucracy, despite endless solemn political agreements to do so, proved increasingly fruitless.

In late January 1994 the Foreign Secretary, Douglas Hurd, visited Vitez to assess the viability of the British contribution to the Bosnian aid programme. We were able to assure him that the Battalion had the means and determination to see the job through, but it was clear that our cautious optimism was more positive than the overall political mood.

Only a few days later the murder of Paul Goodall, a British convoy driver, in the regional capital, Zenica, delivered a further major blow to the humanitarian effort, while the Company base at Gornji Vakuf received some damage, but no casualties, during yet another Croat push to seize that shattered town.

Just as it seemed that things could only carry on getting worse, the tide began to turn. The arrival of Lieutenant General Sir Michael Rose as Commander Bosnia Herzegovina Command in late January, and a visit by the Defence Secretary, Malcolm Rifkind, soon afterwards brought a new sense of hope to the higher levels of the UN, justifying our long-held view that cautious optimism was in order. Although the war between the Bosniacs and Croats was to drag on until a peace accord came into effect on 25 February, with hindsight it is clear that the darkest days of the tour were fast receding.

General Rose was determined to shake up his command and saw the Coldstream Warriors as an asset to be employed to demonstrate his readiness to use force. Warrior companies were used to persuade the Serbs to back down and open checkpoints on the route into Sarajevo and to oblige the Croats to allow free access for desperately needed aid to reach the isolated mental hospitals in the Canadian Battalion's area. Finally, on 18 February, No 2 Company was detached from our command in order to play a part in the French-led Sector Sarajevo's operation to guard Serb weapon collection sites around the city following the UN-brokered deployment.

Meanwhile back in Central Bosnia our efforts shifted towards the implementation of the Bosniac-Croat peace accord. Both sides looked to UNPROFOR to lead them by the hand through what was to prove an enormously complex operation in which the key was to be fostering trust between the two parties. Freedom of movement for UN and civilian traffic on the main supply routes and implementing an effective ceasefire along mutually agreed frontlines were the first tasks, followed by the creation of buffer zones and the demilitarization of former flashpoints, notably Stari Vitez and Gornji Vakuf. So successful was this process, co-ordinated by UN-Bosniac-Croat joint commissions at all levels, that in March and April the flow of aid almost exceeded UNHCR targets and the physical protection of the route by UNPROFOR escort vehicles became a thing of the past.

In order to man all the new checkpoints and weapon collection sites and patrol the buffer zones a second British battalion, the 1st Battalion the Duke of Wellington's Regiment, and a second Light Dragoons Recce Squadron were sent into our area, as well as a Belgian Armoured Infantry Company. Areas of responsibility and tasks changed at a bewildering pace, but the Operations Officer proved to be equal to this extraordinary situation. Indeed, when the Prime Minister, John Major, visited on 18 March with the Defence Secretary, Malcolm Rifkind, he simply could not believe the changes brought about since early February.

While the peace process in Central Bosnia moved forward with a pace and degree of success that surprised everyone involved, the Battalion once again sent No 2 Company to Sarajevo. This time its mission was to escort convoys and to man observation posts on the Bosniac frontline, facing some of the same Serb positions that it had manned barely a fortnight earlier. The Company was to stay in Sarajevo until the end of April, earning high praise from the French Commander there. Elements of the Recce Platoon there were involved in a highly successful fighting withdrawal, when they were ambushed by the Serbs on the very morning that they were due to abandon their observation post.

If implementing the peace process in Central Bosnia was hectic, but largely unspectacular, there remained one last besieged enclave, the Maglaj Pocket, within our area. Subject to daily Serb artillery fire, its Bosniac and Croat defenders appealed to the UN for help, as no aid had got through, except by air drops, since late October 1993. Larry Hollingworth, the charismatic local UNHCR leader, worked ceaselessly with the Battalion's assistance to get aid convoys through to Maglaj, but without any success. It was only when the second British battalion arrived that it was possible to redeploy C Squadron the Light Dragoons to open up a base at Zepce, just south of Maglaj, from which an assessment of the Serb frontlines astride the severed aid routes to Maglaj could be made.

The presence of UNPROFOR troops in Zepce and later the insertion of British Special Forces into Maglaj, along with high-level political manoeuvrings, finally persuaded the Serbs to abandon their positions on the southern side of the Maglaj Pocket. On 19 March it suddenly became clear that the Serbs had pulled back overnight and the next day Larry Hollingworth took the first UNHCR convoy into Maglaj, protected by No 3 Company and the Light Dragoons. The convoy was met by an outpouring of emotion and sheer relief that must have rivalled those experienced in cities liberated by the Allies at the end of the Second World War. Maglaj became a No 3 Company town and its commander, Major the Hon R.F.D.Margesson, acquired the sort of respect and devotion normally given to royalty, although he denied letting it go to his head.

On the same day (the 20th) spectators gathered in the Sarajevo football stadium to watch an UNPROFOR team play a team representing Sarajevo city. They were to witness a unique event which achieved international acclaim. It was known that Serb artillery was trained on the stadium, but nevertheless on to the pitch marched the Regimental Band, resplendent in tunics and bearskins. The Band played for thirty minutes, at the end of which General Rose and the French Sector Commander Sarajevo came down personally to thank them. As General Rose said, "We see here today yet another small step on the path to normal life in this beautiful land. This is an irreversible process, because the people here have had enough of the senseless killing and destruction." The Band then departed for the airport to return to the United Kingdom. It was an unforgettable and poignant moment for all who were present.

With the peace process in Central Bosnia largely completed, although numerous problems still lay ahead for UN Civil Affairs, and with the relief of Maglaj achieved, the Battalion spent its last weeks reinforcing the trust between the Bosniac and Croat leaders and their communities. Bosnia was still a dangerous place and mines continued to cause tragic fatalities and injuries to UN and local personnel alike.

From a Household Division perspective our Operation GRAPPLE tour provided a tremendous wealth of experience for all who were lucky enough to be there. Over 800 Guardsmen, including fifty-three Foot Guards officers and a solitary Blues and Royals officer, had the chance to serve in the Battalion. The element of danger was ever present with the Battalion Group reporting more than 200 contacts, in over seventy of which self-defensive fire was returned; our impartiality was demonstrated by Guardsmen returning fire from Serb, Croat and Bosniac snipers when required, with some 4000 rounds, proving that the British Battalion was not going to stand any nonsense.

Everyone experienced great frustration at times, particularly when the warring parties refused to agree to each others' casualties being moved by our ambulances and when aid convoys were blocked. On the other hand we did help the UNHCR to move over 25,000 tonnes of aid up into Central Bosnia and protected a further 50,000 tonnes as it was redistributed within the region. Our liaison officers managed to move over 800 injured local people and to supervise the exchange of some 171 corpses.

Captain R.W. Yorke and a young recruit.

On 8 May we handed over to 2nd Battalion The Royal Anglian Regiment. At the end of six months we were very fortunate to be able to look back on a situation that had been very dangerous and almost hopeless at times, but which had improved out of all recognition by the time we handed over. This improvement was in no small measure due to the steadfast determination of all ranks to achieve the mission of creating the conditions for humanitarian aid to reach the people of our area. We all returned to Münster feeling that we had been privileged to be able to play our part at such a critical time in Bosnia's history and the thanks we received from everyone were a tribute to an achievement that was, quite rightly, Second to None.[7]

The Commanding Officer was awarded an OBE for his command of the Battalion. MBEs were awarded to Major M.G.Tucker, who was attached from the Royal Australian Regiment, and Sergeant Macrury, one of the Battalion

Guardsmen Brown and Ruddle with Petre Hoskin of Services Sound and Vision Corporation.

[7] During 1999 individuals from both the 1st Battalion and Number 7 Company were attached to 1st Battalion Irish Guards during their tours of duty in Kosovo and Bosnia respectively.

cooks from the Royal Logistic Corps. Lance Sergeant D.Waterhouse was awarded a Military Cross for his bravery in a shoot-out and Captain R.W. Yorke was awarded The Queen's Gallantry Medal.

Other awards for members of the Battalion were:

Mention in Despatches.
Captain S.J.H.Gill. Captain D.E.M.Guinness
Sergeant G.S.Crisford. Lance Sergeant S.J.May, Grenadier Guards.

Queen's Commendation for Brave Conduct.
Guardsman C.J.Andrews.

Queen's Commendation for Valuable Service.
Major A.J.B.Johnston. MBE. Major the Hon R.F.D.Margesson.
Lance Sergeant P.W.Murray. Grenadier Guards.

Joint Theatre Commander's Commendation.
Major A.J.B.Johnston, MBE. Captain C.R.Rumboll.
Captain (LE) L.Winter. Captain (LE) M.J.Manning. Lieutenant C.A.H.Philp.
Staff Sergeant I.Forbes. REME. Lance Corporal P.Fenwick.
Guardsman A.J.Deacon.

Force Commander's Commendation.
Lieutenant C.H.G.St George.

Note on Author
Colonel Peter Williams OBE joined the Coldstream Guards as a Regular Officer in September 1972. He commanded the 1st Battalion 1992–1994, which included the operational tour in Bosnia. He is currently Chief Strategic Policy at SHAPE.

CHAPTER TWELVE

HOME SERVICE, 1945–2000

by Edward Crofton

Organization

By the end of 1945 the Regiment consisted of four battalions. The **3rd Battalion** was the first Coldstream Battalion to come back to England, returning in March 1945 after an absence of nearly eight years. However, it was not to be left in peace for long and sailed for Palestine in October of that year. The following year saw the **4th Battalion** returning in July to Pirbright and its Farewell Parade; the **2nd Battalion** moved to Windsor in September and the **1st Battalion** to Caterham in December. In August 1945 Lieutenant General Sir Alfred Codrington, 72 years a Coldstreamer and Colonel of the Regiment since 1918, resigned the Colonelcy, aged 91, and was succeeded by Lieutenant General Sir Charles 'Budget' Loyd.

The ensuing fifty-four years since 1946 have seen massive changes in the everyday life of the nation and a general running down of the Armed Forces. Undoubtedly the two milestones during the period which have had the most serious repercussions for the Regiment have been the ending of National Service in 1959, which was the forerunner to the **3rd Battalion** being placed in 'suspended animation' in the same year, and 'Options for Change' which, thirty-two years later, in the Defence Review of 1991, brought the same fate for the **2nd Battalion** in 1993, together with the 2nd Battalions of both the Grenadier and Scots Guards. However, this time the three Regiments were permitted to retain an incremental Company, which would in the future carry the Colours and follow the customs and traditions of their parent Second Battalion. In the words of The Major General Commanding the Household Division, "The incremental Companies will have the capacity to operate independently for both Public Duties and Operations if necessary".[1]

So on 1 January 1994 Number 7 Company was born. Since then, not only has it undertaken an operational tour to Northern Ireland, but it has played a significant and distinguished part in all aspects of life in London District.

'Options for Change' was to have further far-reaching consequences in both ceremonial and training for both the Regiment and the Household Division. The Queen's Birthday Parade was reduced from eight to six Guards in 1993 and changes also took place in the composition and duties of The Queen's Guard.

The major training change concerned the Guards Depot, which moved from Caterham to Pirbright in 1960; since that time Pirbright has achieved a reputation every bit as revered as that of its predecessor! But in 1993 all Divisional depots were discontinued and Pirbright was redesignated

[1] *Guards Magazine*, Autumn, 1992.

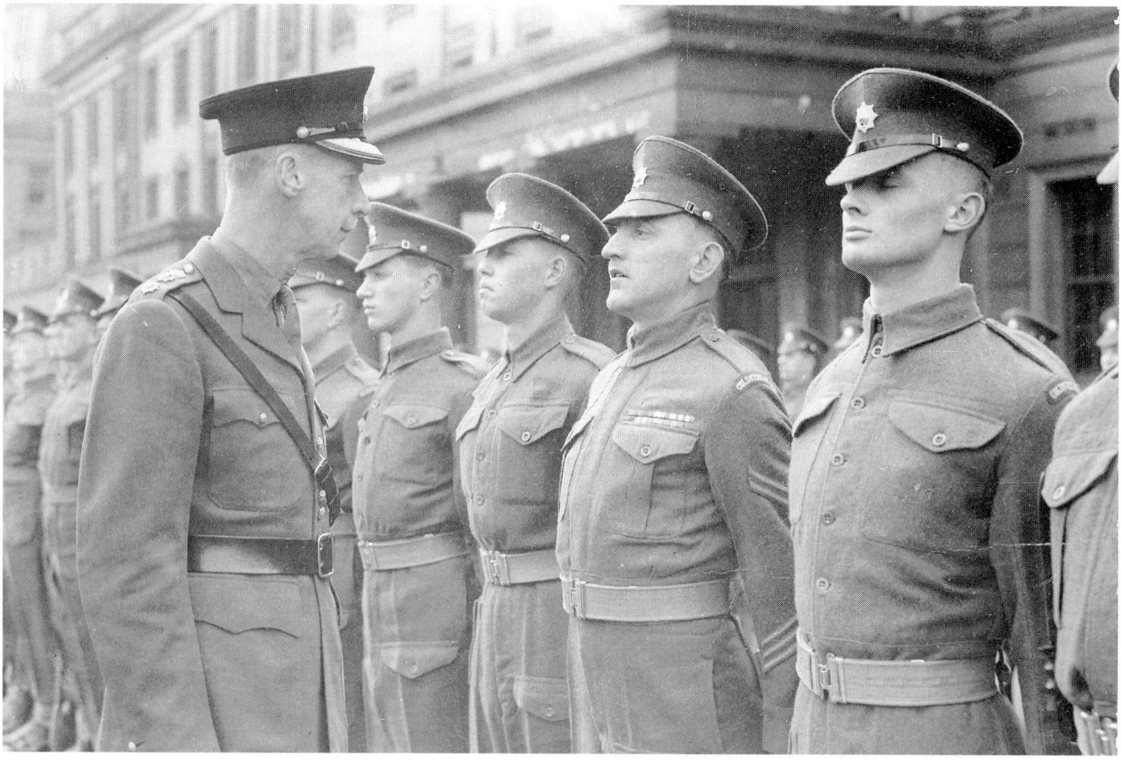

The Colonel of the Regiment, General Sir Charles Loyd, inspecting the 2nd Battalion at Wellington Barracks on St George's Day 1948.

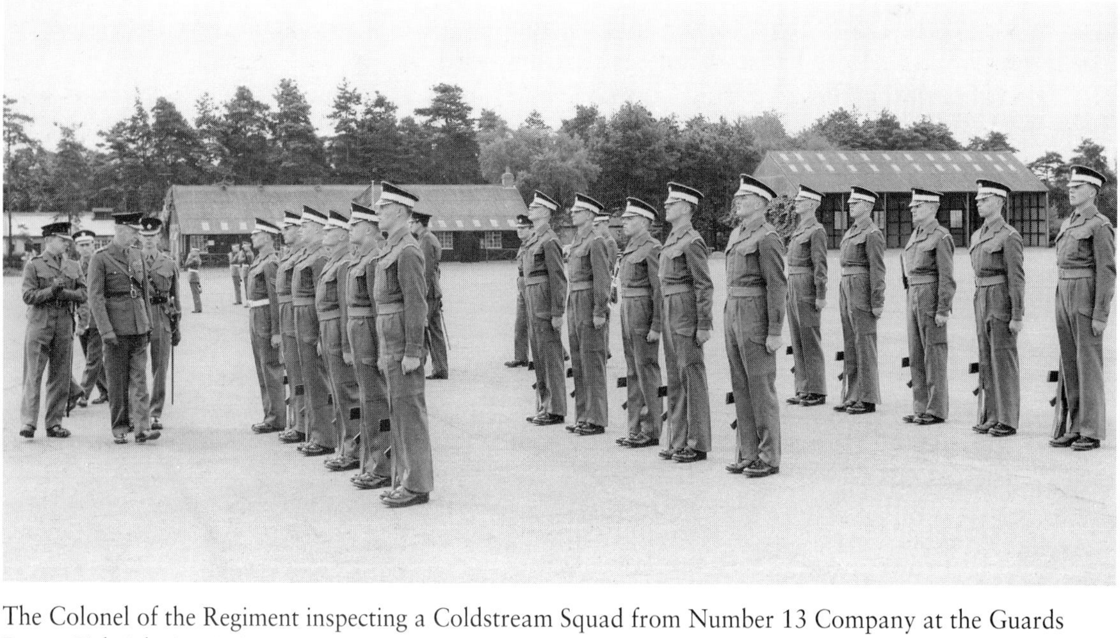

The Colonel of the Regiment inspecting a Coldstream Squad from Number 13 Company at the Guards Depot Pirbright in 1960.

1st Battalion, Caterham 1981/86; Commanding Officer's Parade.

No 4 Army Training Regiment. Sadly, this meant that Number 13 Company Coldstream Guards, together with the other Foot Guards Regimental Companies at the Guards Depot, would, as a formed entity, cease to exist. However, Number 13 Company continues to oversee the interest of all Coldstreamers at Pirbright and RMA Sandhurst, and the silk Company Colour is in the possession of the senior Coldstream Officer at either of the two establishments.

Coldstream recruits now undergo two phases of training, the first lasting twelve weeks at Pirbright, followed by a further twelve weeks at the Infantry Training Centre (ITC) Catterick, prior to joining either the 1st Battalion or Number 7 Company. Whereas Coldstream recruits at Pirbright

The last of many. Members of the 1st Battalion trained at Caterham when it was the Guards Depot. Left to right: Lieutenant D.R. Yorke (1959), Captain (QM) T.N. Storey (1953), Lieutenant Colonel J.J.B. Pope, (1956), Captain (QM) C.J. Louch (1958).

2nd Battalion; King's Birthday Parade 1947. The Captain of the Escort is Major J.A. Pelly, the Ensign, Lieutenant S.J. Mosley, and the Regimental Sergeant Major, A. Ramsden MC.

are under the auspices of No 13 Company, those at Catterick are likewise with No 14 Company.

Under the subsequent reorganization of Army Bands, the Foot Guards Regimental Bands have gained a Warrant Officer Class 1 Bandmaster. The Regimental Band, which is permanently stationed at Wellington Barracks, has been reduced from sixty-five in 1970 to forty-nine in 2000. Although all Army musicians belong officially to the Corps of Army Music, which came into being in 1994, the welfare of Coldstream musicians still remains firmly a Regimental responsibility. The venue for the training of musicians continues to be debated.

Far-reaching Ministry of Defence Reviews continue. The most recent has been the Strategic Defence Review in 1998, from which the Armed Forces have been structured to meet the new security challenges and the impact of scientific and technological developments.

Public Duties

The Regiment has of course played a leading part in the Nation's Ceremonial since 1945. The King's Birthday Parade resumed in 1947, with the participants wearing battledress; the 2nd Battalion found the Escort. Tunics were due to reappear in 1948, but that Parade was cancelled, as it also was in 1955. Coldstream Battalions have found the Escort in the following years: the 1st Battalion in 1954, 1964, 1972 (with all troops wearing black arm bands and the drums suitably draped following the death of The Duke of Windsor), 1982, 1989, and 1999; the 2nd Battalion in 1947, 1962, 1968, 1976, 1985, 1993 and Number 7 Company in 2000; and the 3rd Battalion in 1950, the Tercentenary Year of the formation of the Regiment, and 1959.

For the Tercentenary Year the 3rd Battalion was the only Battalion of the Regiment stationed in England and therefore carried out all the ceremonial to mark the occasion. The Annual Memorial Service was held in Westminster Abbey on the anniversary of the burial in the Abbey of the first

1967; 2nd Battalion Guard of Honour for General Ankrah, Chairman of the Revolutionary Council of Ghana. The Captain is Major H.M.C. Havergal and the Ensign Second Lieutenant M.R.A. Campbell.

Colonel of the Regiment. The next occasion was the King's Birthday Parade, followed at the beginning of July by His Majesty The King presenting New Colours to the Battalion on Horse Guards. The Parade was commanded by the Commanding Officer, Lieutenant Colonel W.A.G. Burns DSO MC, later to become the 26th Colonel of the Regiment. It was a near-run thing, as on the previous afternoon Colonel Burns had been hit in the throat by a cricket ball while wicket-keeping, and the next morning he could hardly speak. Fortunately, the doctor performed miracles and all was well!

Two further events marked a memorable year. In August a detachment of the Regiment paid a visit to both Berwick-upon-Tweed and Newcastle from where in 1650 five Companies from Colonel Fenwick's Regiment and five from Sir Arthur Hazelrigg's Regiment had joined the new Regiment of Colonel George Monck. Then in September the Old Colours of the 3rd Battalion were laid up in Exeter Cathedral.

Berwick-upon-Tweed also provided a highlight of the Regiment's 350th Anniversary Year in 2000 by according the Regiment the Freedom of the Borough. On 21 June the Regiment was also given the privilege as an individual Regiment of exercising its right to march through the City of London "with drums beating, Colours flying and bayonets fixed".[2]

Among many high-profile ceremonial occasions in which the Regiment has taken part, two involving the 2nd Battalion are worthy of particular mention. The first was the Vigil Duty at the Lying-in-State of His Majesty King George VI in 1952, and the second was the occasion in June 1984 when the Battalion provided no less than seven Guards of Honour over two days for the Heads of State attending the World Economic Summit in London.

There are rare occasions when a duty does not go entirely according to plan and one such occurred in the autumn of 1979 when Chairman Hua of China arrived on an official visit to the United Kingdom. The 2nd Battalion, which was stationed at Windsor, was detailed to provide the first ever Household Division Guard of Honour at Heathrow Airport. It took place on the evening of Sunday,

[2] The Regiment was originally granted this privilege on 18 March 1952 and is one of eight regiments to be so honoured. In 1968 the Regiment was granted the Freedom of the Burgh of Coldstream, and also, together with the other Foot Guards Regiments, the Freedom of the Borough of Windsor.

Colonel R.J.V. Crichton MC, Lieutenant of the Honourable Corps of Gentlemen at Arms, and Colonel A.B. Pemberton MBE, Lieutenant of The Queen's Body Guard of the Yeomen of the Guard.

28 October, and at the beginning of the weekend the Ensign, 2nd Lieutenant T.J.Sheldon, left written instructions for his orderly to take his kit to Heathrow where they would meet up. Unfortunately the message went astray.

An hour before H Hour the team assembled near the VIP Suite at Heathrow. The Guard Commander was Major R.J.Heywood and the Subaltern was Captain F.R.G.Johnston; 2nd Lieutenant Sheldon was also there, awaiting his orderly and his uniform. But as the minutes ticked by the kit did not materialize. The Guard Commander therefore set in train an emergency alternative, which involved the Subaltern acting as Ensign and carrying the Colour, while the Director of Music, Lieutenant Colonel R.A.Ridings, took over the less demanding duties of the Subaltern. Captain Johnston was well versed in the role of Ensign and a few minutes' Colour Drill soon had him up to a satisfactory standard. Lieutenant Colonel Ridings's sword drill was more of a problem, as Directors of Music never normally draw their swords, but he fortunately proved a quick learner.

Five minutes before the Guard of Honour was due to get on parade, the kit arrived from Caterham, but it was too late. Fortunately all subsequently went well. The Guard of Honour performed immaculately; the Prime Minister was very happy and The Major General was full of praise. Nevertheless, such a lapse obviously had the traditional consequences for 2nd Lieutenant Sheldon. However, when in due course Her Majesty The Queen heard about it, it was reported that, unlike Queen Victoria, she *was* amused and was impressed by the versatility displayed.[3]

When in London District, the Regiment has in the main been stationed at Wellington or Chelsea Barracks in London, and Victoria Barracks at Windsor; postings to Caterham and Pirbright have also featured. The 2nd Battalion was the first Battalion after a period of over twenty years to return to a refurbished Wellington Barracks in January 1985. The Barracks was officially re-opened by the 26th Colonel of the Regiment. The 2nd Battalion was succeeded in 1988 by the 1st Battalion, and so the Regiment was extremely fortunate to have had the benefit of being quartered for some six years in such a prestigious location at the heart of the capital. Both the 1st and 2nd Battalions were co-located in Chelsea Barracks in 1967 and 1972. Victoria Barracks, Windsor, has arguably been the most popular station of all. Pirbright has seen the 1st Battalion stationed there in 1947/48, and

[3] *You've Lost Your Name*, John Hook, page 8.

2nd Battalion departing Chelsea Barracks 1959.

the 2nd Battalion in 1956/57, and 1965/66. The 1st Battalion returned to Caterham in 1946 from Berlin, and also served there from 1981–1986, and the 2nd Battalion from 1978–1980.

Regimental Presentations of Colours have taken place at Windsor Castle in 1951, 1964, 1976, and 1999, and on Horse Guards Parade in 1985. The 1999 Ceremony will be remembered above all for the immense courage shown by the 27th Colonel of the Regiment, Lieutenant General the Hon Sir William Rous, only five days before his untimely death.

There are of course other activities for Battalions stationed in London District. Training exercises have become ever more frequent, both at home and overseas, thereby relieving the potential monotony of too much ceremonial and the subsequent effects on both recruiting and morale. In recent years Coldstream Battalions have participated on overseas exercises in places as far apart as Canada, North America, Cyprus, Sharjah, Kenya, Belize, Jamaica and The Gambia. The tour to the Falkland Islands in 1984 provided superb opportunities for live firing. In 2000 a Foot Guards

2nd Battalion training in Kenya 1992. Back row left to right: Drill Sergeant Bell, Colour Sergeant Nash, Staff Sergeant Forbes (REME), Major Tucker (RAR), Lance Sergeant Murr, Company Sergeant Major Emmerson. Front row: Sergeant Dingley, Guardsman Ducker, Sergeants Gough and Taylor.

Battalion or Incremental Company can generally reckon on one overseas training exercise a year. At home, outside of pre-planned training periods, support is very often given to other exercising units. Apart from Salisbury Plain, the principal training areas are Otterburn, Sennybridge and Thetford, augmented by Infantry Skill at Arms Camps at Wathgill in Yorkshire and Warcop in Cumbria. On local adventure training, budgetary restraints have taken their toll, resulting in the demise of Guards House Folda at Aviemore, but the Guards Adventure Training Camp at Fremington is still going strong.

Occasionally London-based Battalions have been required to assist the civil authorities. In 1947 both the 1st and 2nd Battalions assisted with the loading and delivery of meat supplies during the transport workers' strike. The following year the 2nd Battalion was called upon to assist the civil authorities by helping to unload ships during the dock strike. A further dock strike in 1949 saw the 3rd Battalion also involved with unloading.[4] Major I.D.Zvegintzov was awarded the MBE for his administrative skills during the two month fireman's strike in the winter of 1977/78. Major R.J.Heywood was similarly honoured, as the desk officer in the Ministry of Defence, who wrote and executed the entire plan for the whole of the United Kingdom. The winter of 1978/79 could have been particularly eventful for the 2nd Battalion, which had elements standing by to assist with the oil tanker dispute and the threatened flooding of the Thames. In May 1984 elements of the 2nd Battalion were rushed at a moment's notice to Wales to assist the Forestry Commission on fire-fighting duties. The security of Heathrow Airport has also been a regular commitment for the Household Division since the 1970s.

[4] On all these tasks the Guardsmen managed within a few days to exceed by a substantial margin the number of items handled by the civilian workforce.

Major T.A. Matheson and his Company training at Otterburn.

The links with the Senior Service begun by the 1st Colonel continue still, and in the twentieth century successful affiliations have been formed with a series of naval ships, starting with the frigate HMS *Falmouth*, continuing through the Type 22 frigate HMS *Brilliant*, (which served with distinction in the Falklands War of 1982) and on to HMS *Ocean*, an amphibious helicopter carrier of some 21,500 tons.

Current Army affiliations are with the 2nd Battalion The Royal Australian Regiment and with the Governor General's Foot Guards in Canada. It is hoped to re-establish the wartime links built up in Italy with the Pretoria Regiment in South Africa.

The strength of the Regiment has suffered many cuts since 1945, but in the year 2000 it is one of the best recruited in the British Army. However, it is at Regimental Headquarters that the most noticeable changes are to be seen. The appointment of Regimental Lieutenant Colonel is no longer an established post, but is held by a senior Coldstream officer serving elsewhere in the Army. The Superintending Clerk is also an appointment with history, and the Headquarters consists of only three established military posts (shortly to be reduced to two) up to and including the Regimental Quartermaster Sergeant, who has to run the stores as well as the Headquarters. The Regimental Adjutant and Assistant Regimental Adjutant are both Retired Officers and are part of a small civilian element. The Headquarters remains in Wellington Barracks and continues to oversee Regimental events and Coldstream Guards Association matters.

The Regiment continues, however, to meet the challenges and demands of a changing military and social environment brought about by a new world order, and the Coldstream Spirit is as strong as ever.

Extra-Regimental Employment (ERE)

One aspect of soldiering, whether at home or overseas, has been the opportunity to serve in ERE appointments. These can either take a traditional form such as a staff posting, or involve a less traditional scenario in some exotic part of the world. These latter appointments in particular have great recruiting value and the Regiment has been extremely fortunate in having been so well recruited over the years that many individuals of all ranks have been able to take advantage of what has been, and is, on offer.

Since 1945 Coldstreamers have been employed all over the world in a variety of appointments and units. Such diverse places of employment have included the West Africa Frontier Force, the Royal Brunei Malay Regiment and the United Nations at Panmunjon. Many stories, embellished or otherwise, have emanated from the experiences of those concerned and they, of course, whet the appetites of those coming after!

Coldstream Sport

Sport has played a major part in the character of the Regiment. Whether at home or abroad, individual Coldstreamers or Coldstream teams have participated to the best of their abilities, which in many cases have been considerable. Coldstreamers are not 'pot hunters', but there have been many notable, single and collective Coldstream sporting achievements through the decades which are worthy of mention. This article does not seek to cover them all – nor indeed field sports, which have themselves been character-forming for so many Coldstreamers – but tries to record as general and as varied a synopsis as possible.

Unlike some other Household Division Regiments, no Coldstreamer has ever played cricket for England. However, there can have been few better performers at Club level than Colonel A.C.Wilkinson, DSO, MC, GM, Lieutenant Colonel G.H.M. 'Buns' Cartwright and Colonel G.J.Edwards, who all played between the two world wars. G.N.Scott-Chad also was a renowned cricketer, who toured Jamaica with Lord Tennyson's team in 1932 and played county cricket for Norfolk in the 1920s and 1930s; he also represented Great Britain at squash in 1927. The Regiment can, however, claim two county cricket captains, G.E.S.Woodhouse and G.H.G.Doggart, who captained Somerset and Sussex respectively in the post-1945 years. M.D.Scott was awarded a Blue

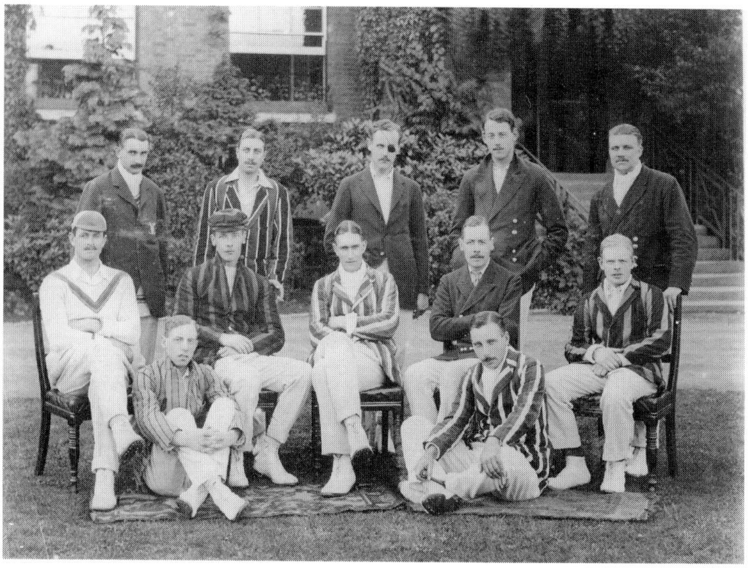

Coldstream Cricketers. Left in rear: Colonel A.C. Wilkinson; left front: Lieutenant Colonel G.H.M. Cartwright; left centre: Colonel G.J. Edwards. Also in picture is: Captain O.W.H. Leese, and the future 25th Colonel of the Regiment, Captain H.C. Loyd, seated between Colonels Cartwright and Edwards.

for cricket at Oxford in 1954, Second Lieutenant R.J.Heywood played for Norfolk and the Army in the 1960s, and more recently Captains S.A.F.Mitchell and C.H.G.St George have played for the Army and Combined Services; Captain St George captained both XIs for three consecutive years in the late 1990s.

Many Coldstreamers participated in the annual Guards Cricket Club Tour to Jersey, which was initiated by two eminent local Coldstreamers, Brigadier R.C.Lemprière-Robin and Major J.R.C.Riley. The Victoria College ground provided a perfect setting, being well suited to the visitors' style of play and there were many memorable moments over a period of some thirty years, including one unusual dismissal, that of Lieutenant Colonel H.M.C.Havergal being given out 'handled the ball'.

There have been several instances of equestrian success in the Regiment. Captain E.G.Christie-Miller rode 'Sprinkle Me' to victory in the Grand Military Gold Cup in 1909 and 1910. Polo has for long been a Regimental sport, both in this country and overseas, including in Egypt at the beginning of the twentieth century; particular success was achieved in the inter-Regimental Tournament in the 1960s.

Swimming and water polo have also been very popular. On the former, Lance Corporal R.Clayden, who joined in 1971, was a bronze medallist at the 1970 Commonwealth Games, and he was the British Army 100 metres free-style and backstroke champion in 1974. Both 1st and 2nd Battalion teams have been successful at water polo at varying times.

Athletics has seen some of the most notable Coldstream achievements. Olympians have included Lance Sergeant J.Ginty who competed in the 3000 metres steeplechase at the Berlin Games in 1936. Lieutenant Alistair McCorquodale was fourth in the 100 metres and 'the fastest white man in the world' at the White City in 1948. He was also a member of the 4 x 100 metres relay team which won the silver medal. Second Lieutenant P.G.S.Tower was the No 2 javelin thrower in the run-up to the Helsinki Olympics in 1952, but disagreed sartorially with the selectors who expected him to wear a tracksuit rather than grey flannels with an umbrella under his arm! Lieutenant J.M.Manningham-Buller was the Army Shot Put Champion in 1955. Only illness prevented I.J.R.Spofforth from fencing for Great Britain in the 1960 Rome Olympics; he won the individual and team gold medals at the Commonwealth Veterans Games in 1999. In 1982 Lieutenant C.C.Gore

1st Battalion athletics meeting Pirbright 1893. Left to right: Lieutenants S.H.J. Peel and J. Drummond-Hay.

represented the Army in the 200 metres event at the Inter-Service Championships, following his success at the 100 metres in the Army Championships. It was the first time for many years that an officer's name had appeared on that Cup.

The Regiment's main recruiting areas of the North-East and Yorkshire have ensured the prominence of Association Football in the Regiment's sporting world. Guardsman Fairbairn played professionally for Fulham in the 1930s, and Lance Sergeant T.Melling played for Newcastle in the 1950s and 1960s. On the executive side, P.D.Hill-Wood is chairman of Arsenal and Lance Sergeant L.McMenemy managed Southampton in the 1970s and 1980s; he was later appointed to the coaching staff of the full England Team, before finally taking charge of the Northern Ireland Squad in the 1990s.

Rugby Football, although not achieving the pre-eminence accorded to Association within the Regiment, has nevertheless flourished. An early rugby gladiator was Drum Major G.Carter of the 1st Battalion, who played for British Guiana during the Battalion's operational tour there in 1962, while more recently Lance Sergeant Berryman captained the British Army (Germany) XV.

Skiing is proving to be progressively popular, due in no small part to annual winter adventure training exercises in Germany and in Scotland. Enthusiasm has bred expertise and the Regiment is now experiencing increased success at Army Ski Meetings; winning the Infantry Championship in 2000, with its leading skier, Captain J.A.E. Rous, going on to represent the Army.

Of all the major sports, it is probably golf that has provided the Regiment with its most notable sporting success recently. For many years from 1945 the names of Lieutenant Colonel B.E.Luard MC and Major A.K.Barlow MC were synonymous with Coldstream golfing success, as winners of the Infantry Trophy several times in the 1950s and early 1960s. Coldstreamers of all ranks both past and present have represented the Regiment in the Colonel-in-Chief's Cup, which is competed for annually by the Household Division regiments. Following three consecutive years of success in the 1980s, the Regiment pulled off a double in 1999 by providing both teams of finalists, a feat which had not been achieved since 1936. The 'retired' just managed to overcome the 'servers', but it was a near-run thing! Success has continued with two Regimental teams reaching the 2000 semi-finals.

Mention must be made of cribbage, which is believed to have been introduced to the Regiment in Normandy in 1944 to prevent officers from losing money at poker. It then fell somewhat into abeyance before being re-introduced in the 2nd Battalion in Aden by three exponents from wartime days, the Commanding Officer, Lieutenant Colonel Sir Ian Jardine Bt, the Second-in-Command, Major E.I.Windsor Clive, and the Quartermaster, Major N.Duckworth. They strongly believed that young officers should master the etiquette and understand the tactical significance of the three phases, crust, cushion and hammer, and these together with other defining terms have been established as the guidelines of a Regimental tradition.

In the Sergeants's Mess euchre was a card game widely played. It has been defined in the Oxford Dictionary as a "cheating card game played by soldiers and low types" which left the rules very open for interpretation! New members of the Sergeants' Mess were invited to join three more senior and older members to make up a four and they then learned the game the hard way!

Enjoying all sports, from Olympics to euchre, is part of the Coldstream ethos, and long may it continue.

CHAPTER THIRTEEN

NORTHERN IRELAND, 1970–2000

by Edward Crofton

During the immediate post-war period Northern Ireland was a comparatively peaceful and pleasant station. However, in the late 1960s there were repeated clashes between the Catholic and Protestant communities, which the Royal Ulster Constabulary (RUC) found increasingly difficult to control. On 14 August 1969 Londonderry erupted, and Prime Minister Harold Wilson ordered troops into Ulster to restore order. Little was it realized then that service in Ulster would still be an open-ended commitment over thirty years later, in spite of the praiseworthy efforts of many to bring about peace in the intervening years. Between 1970 and 2000 the Regiment has been involved in seventeen operational and emergency tours lasting for periods of four to eighteen months in both rural and urban localities.

Belfast, 1970. 2nd Battalion

The 2nd Battalion arrived in West Belfast in July 1970 on its first four-month tour. As part of 39 Infantry Brigade, its main tasks were to keep the Protestants and Catholics apart and to stop terrorism, looting and vandalism. This required patrolling and vigilance 24 hours a day, both on

2nd Battalion, 1970. Mary Street. Left to right: Guardsmen Dare, Lewis and Heath.

2nd Battalion, 1970. 'Tea and sympathy'. Guardsman Seldon and local resident.

foot and in vehicles, snap road blocks and searches of vehicles, and house searches, generally in support of the RUC. Parallel with this successful policy was an effort to win over the confidence and friendship of the majority of citizens in the area. Children's outings and parties were organized by companies and their success was marked by the gratitude of the ordinary people, and by the hostility of the extremists who resented any attempt at normalizing relations between the Army and the people of Belfast. Foremost among these activities was the management of the Magnet Club, an inter-denominational youth club under the management of Lieutenant B.M. de L.Cazenove, CQMS L.Peake, SSI White APTC, and Lance Corporal K.Albrighton.

Tensions increased in August and the Commanding Officer, Lieutenant Colonel Colin Wallis-King, sent a signal to the padre asking him to pray for rain, in the hope that this would dampen the aggressive spirits of the locals. The result was startling and beyond all expectations. Most of the Battalion area was flooded and families had to be evacuated by the Guardsmen to welfare centres. The Regiment earned the genuine gratitude of the local residents for its part in the mopping up and subsequent redecoration of the houses of a number of elderly people. Lieutenant M.C.J.Willoughby and his men also earned the gratitude of the local community for their efforts in wading waist-high down the Clawney River to clear critical areas.

On 31 August the Battalion took part in its first large-scale search operation in support of the RUC, during which twenty-two houses were searched and finds made in six of them. Eleven individuals were arrested and the finds included six pistols, one shotgun, ten assorted grenades, about 2000 rounds of ammunition and various items of bomb-making equipment.

Incidents, both by day and by night, continued throughout the tour. They were largely minor, consisting of bottles, stones and petrol bombs being thrown at foot and mobile patrols, mostly by youths of both the religious denominations. In addition, both men and women were arrested for vandalism, abusive behaviour and drunkenness.

The Battalion left Belfast in November 1970. During the tour not one round of ammunition or CS gas had been fired, but over 1200 cars and nearly 400 houses had been searched; ninety-nine persons, one pony and a donkey had been arrested. However, not everything had been unfriendly,

2nd Battalion, 1970. Belfast floods. Lance Sergeant Carter giving assistance to locals.

and it was estimated that over 16,900 cups of tea had been given to members of the Battalion by the locals!

It had been a highly successful first tour in Ulster, for which the Commanding Officer was awarded the OBE. Lance Sergeant Cowling was also awarded the GOC's Commendation for his part, together with Guardsmen Griffiths, Taylor and Faulkner in rescuing a semi-conscious man from a house fire.

County Londonderry, 1970/72. 1st Battalion

Hardly had the 2nd Battalion departed than the 1st Battalion took its place the following month, but across the other side of the Province, based at McGilligan Camp, County Londonderry. Its role

2nd Battalion, 1970. HMS *Maidstone*.

on this the first of three tours within eighteen months was split between patrolling in the countryside of County Londonderry and duties in the city of Derry itself. This meant supporting the RUC in keeping the peace within the city and preventing illegal crossings of the border between Londonderry and Donegal.

In Ulster at this time soldiers were generally armed, one-third with rifles and two-thirds with batons. All wore helmets with plastic visors attached and leg padding, and most carried shields which were used in the manner of the Roman *Testudo*. Tactics were for heavy rubber bullets to be fired, followed up by snatch squads whose task was to seize rioters while they were still recovering from the effects of a rubber bullet. That was the theory – whether it always worked was another matter!

A significant factor of this, and any other peace-keeping scenario in the future, would be the responsibility which would devolve on to the junior ranks. It was the young Lance Corporal who would just as likely be put 'on the spot' as the young officer, and it is they probably more than anyone else who can take pride in the achievements of the British Army in Ulster over a generation.

The first full deployment of the Battalion was on 18 December 1970 to help contain any violence that might break out as a result of Lundy Day Celebrations.[1]

In mid-January 1971 the Battalion was deployed to Belfast to reinforce hard-pressed battalions there. Several platoons met the hostility and unpleasantness of an Irish mob, but they succeeded in arresting some of the rioters. The Battalion returned to Londonderry at the end of January, and, after further duties in the city and several battalion operations in the country, Easter remained a major test of the efficiency of the Security Forces.[2]

Both the Republicans and Protestants had been planning marches over Easter, the former to commemorate the Easter Rising and the latter by the Protestant Derry Apprentice Boys. These marches were designed for some days of rioting and the Battalion, together with 5 Light Regiment Royal Artillery and 1st Battalion The Royal Anglian Regiment, was deployed in the city for two Republican marches on Easter afternoon. The marches passed quietly until late on when several hundred youths attacked the platoon of soldiers, hijacked a bus and seemed all set for a long hard slog with the troops. The riot lasted for a couple of hours, during which time Lance Corporal Samson sustained a broken leg. Surprisingly, the trouble died down as quickly as it had begun and the rest of the evening and night passed quietly.

The Battalion was back in England by St George's Day. The Guardsmen had acquitted themselves well in very trying circumstances over the four months and the standards, discipline and self-respect required of Coldstreamers had proved their worth.

A significant factor of the tour had been the increasing amount of media attention on Security Force activities. This was not always helpful and was a forerunner of what would be the future norm. The appearance of TV cameras was invariably the cue for young yobbos to set up a disturbance. Some reporters and their team appreciated the problem, and were helpful and discreet. Others were not, and their presence merely prolonged the street violence. The 'PR Ambush' became all too common and led to a considerable shake-up in PR training. In future PR would be included

[1] The burning of an effigy of Colonel Lundy by the Protestant Apprentice boys, on the walls of the City overlooking the Catholic area of the Bogside, in commemoration of the successful Protestant defence of the city against the Catholics who supported King James II in 1689.

[2] Away from operations, the Battalion even managed to win the Northern Ireland major units football trophy, beating 3rd Battalion The Queen's Regiment 5–4 after extra time!

in work-up training, with the subsequent immense improvement over the years in the articulation shown by members of the Security Forces.

The programme of the 1st Battalion was rudely shattered when, on 8 December 1971, it was stood by at a week's notice to return to Ulster for a period of up to four months. The security situation had deteriorated alarmingly and violence had escalated to an unacceptable degree. Public Duties commitments were cancelled and the Battalion got down to some intensive shooting practice. At 0440 on Sunday 17 October the main body departed from Euston. By midnight the Battalion was complete in huts at Ballykinler, some 40 miles from Belfast, as Province Reserve.

On the 20th it was deployed to a disused factory on the outskirts of Londonderry. From there an operation was carried out in the Bogside and Creggan early the following day to arrest certain wanted men. These two areas had become extremely dangerous and were shortly to become so-called 'no-go areas' with significant consequences for the future. The Battalion suffered its first casualty, Guardsman Riley, who was shot but fortunately not seriously wounded. Five days later it moved to Ballykinler and deployed the following day to Newry to cover the funeral of three bank robbers. It returned, less a company, to Ballykinler, and one week later the two remaining companies were deployed for operations in Londonderry.

On 8 November the Battalion joined 8 Infantry Brigade in Londonderry, which was commanded by its former Commanding Officer, Brigadier Pat MacLellan, MBE. In Londonderry the three companies worked on a ten-day roulement between three locations; Fort George, which had previously been part of the naval dockyard, was the location of Battalion Headquarters and the company responsible for the Enclave Region west of the River Foyle, Brooke Park Library, together with a platoon location at Rosemount Police Station on the east edge of the Creggan Estate, and the factory compound of Blighs Lane which was wedged precariously on the side of a hill between the Creggan Estate above and the Bogside below. It was a constant target for sniper attacks from all sides.

In the early stages, two 'search and arrest' operations in battalion strength were conducted in the Creggan with the predictably violent reaction. Later the emphasis was on aggressive patrolling by night on the fringe of the Creggan and Bogside and also in the Enclave. A number of casualties were inflicted on terrorist snipers and nail bombers, and fifteen casualties (eight gunshot) on the Battalion. In one incident a patrol from Blighs Lane led by Second Lieutenant A.K.Jacques with Guardsmen Glendenning, Spring, Sullivan and Shepherd pursued a sniper who had been identified from a helicopter; they then flushed out and shot four further gunmen and made a fighting withdrawal intact back to base. For this action Second Lieutenant Jacques was awarded the Military Cross, Glendenning the Military Medal and the Guardsmen were all Mentioned in Despatches.

During the tour Captain the Hon T.H.Clifford was also Mentioned in Despatches. In another incident, a company 'pig' (armoured vehicle) was ambushed with a claymore-type landmine, followed by automatic fire. Company Sergeant Major K.Cockroft was shot through the left thigh, Guardsman Wilcox received a scalp wound and three others were injured in the blast. Later on that day a bullet passed clean through the steel helmet of Guardsman L.Smith, leaving chunks of metal embedded in his scalp. On both occasions fire was returned and at least one gunman hit.

In the midst of all this the Battalion rugby team took time off in the Army Cup to be beaten 86–0 by 9 Parachute Squadron, Royal Engineers!

Incidents of stone-throwing, nail bombs, sniping and ambushes continued to occur regularly throughout the tour and, although several members of the Battalion sustained injuries, these were fortunately not fatal. Guardsman Moulton's flak jacket saved him from the effects of a Thompson machine gun, Guardsman Firth was shot in the thigh, Guardsman Fawell in the shoulder (and was then listed as 'comfortable' when in hospital), while Lieutenant J.M.Turner-Bridger and Lance Sergeant Dalton both suffered hand injuries resulting from nail bombs. On another occasion Lieutenant Turner-Bridger's flak jacket miraculously saved him from further injury. No 3 Company had a scare when one of its platoon sergeants, Sergeant Pratt, and a Guardsman were left behind following a large-scale search operation in the Creggan. Sergeant Pratt had the presence of mind to commandeer a passing car at pistol point and so evade the fury of the fast-approaching mob.

In the historic events of Sunday 30 January 1972 the Battalion was deployed to help hold the 'containment line' by blocking off large portions of the city of Londonderry to forestall any trouble from the proposed Civil Rights March, should it arise. The repercussions continue thirty years later. In the words of the Commanding Officer, Lieutenant Colonel Michael Hicks OBE, "It was a trying and testing time". Colonel Hicks had commanded the Battalion on both tours.[3]

The tour ended in February 1972. Statistics recorded over the four months reveal that members of the Battalion were fired upon 1047 times and returned 410 rounds, fired 1661 baton rounds and used 350 tons of sand in constructing defences, drove 306,958 miles and checked 14,472 vehicles at road blocks. On 'Q' side, 15,500 pounds of sugar, 160,000 eggs, 18,000 loaves and 40 tons of potatoes had been consumed!

The early summer of 1972 witnessed appalling scenes of carnage on the streets of Ulster, coupled with the implementation of no-go areas in both Belfast and Londonderry. On 13 July Colonel Hicks handed over command of the Battalion to Lieutenant Colonel Peter Tower. On the 23rd Nos 2 and 3 Companies were on leave with No 1 to follow after dismounting Public Duties on the 25th. On the afternoon of the 24th the Battalion was ordered to be at 24 hours' notice to move to Northern Ireland from the 26th for an indefinite period.

The Commanding Officer's Recce Party, consisting of himself, the Company Commanders, Major R.N.F.Sweeting (No 1), Major J.R.Innes (No 2), Major J.J.B.Pope (No 3), the Operations Officer (formerly Adjutant) Captain A.C.Sainthill, the Quartermaster, Captain T.R.Forrest, together with drivers, departed early on the 27th. Arriving at RAF Aldergrove, they were directed to Londonderry where they were fortunate to be briefed by two Coldstreamers, the Commander of 8 Brigade, Brigadier Pat MacLellan, and his Deputy, Colonel Colin Wallis-King. The Battalion, less a small number who had been unaccountable on leave, was complete on the 29th and was moved into the Londonderry Model County Primary School. To say that it was bursting at the seams with its latest intake of 'pupils' is an understatement! Everybody set to work to improve its defences and therefore minimize the disadvantage of been overlooked by higher buildings on all sides.

On the 31st Operation MOTORMAN was launched in the Province. The Battalion's role was to promote the cordon to the west and south of the Creggan Estate as part of Operation CARCAN, the 8 Brigade operation to re-occupy the no-go areas of the Creggan and Bogside. The operation started in the early hours and occupation was virtually complete, with little resistance, by 0800. The Battalion subsequently consolidated the cordon position by providing road blocks and covering many miles on the perimeter of Londonderry. The IRA was reckoned to have been given adequate notice of Security Force intentions beforehand, so that its members had vanished over the Border. It was a question of when they would attempt to filter back through the cordon to claim their Social Security Benefit!

While Battalion Headquarters and No 1 Company were billeted in the Model School and two

[3] Brigadier W.M.E.Hicks, CB, OBE. Recollections of 1st Battalion Coldstream Guards, 1970–72.

Companies and the Corps of Drums were maintaining the cordon out in the enclave, sappers were busy constructing a new camp, overlooking the Creggan, for the Battalion to move into when the autumn term started. The security qualities of the new Creggan Camp were unconvincing – vulnerable to sniper fire from almost every side, with the portakabin huts offering no protection from fire. It was therefore decided that a 14-foot-high sandbag wall, comprising a third of a million sandbags, was the answer to the problem, and so furious sandbagging began under the drive of Regimental Sergeant Major A.Pickles.

However, the situation was cruelly exposed when, on 27 August, Sergeant A.Metcalfe was killed instantly by a bullet fired through a makeshift hessian screen by a sniper from a garden on the Creggan Estate. With the Regimental Sergeant Major much to the fore, efforts to make the camp safe were redoubled and the Battalion moved in on the 29th. The move to Creggan Camp coincided with a change of role, under which the Battalion took over responsibility for the southern sector of the Creggan estate, with neighbours 2nd Battalion Scots Guards being responsible for the Bogside. The Creggan was split into company areas, with roulement changes taking place regularly until the end of the tour.

Street patrolling in the Creggan was dangerous and unpleasant, and patrols had to contend with expert snipers who fired a single shot and were almost impossible to locate at one end of the scale, and abusive, foul-mouthed, stone-throwing children at the other. Inevitably there were casualties from both types of aggression. Guardsman Broom was shot through the leg by a low-velocity bullet. Guardsman Fulker had a remarkable escape when he was shot in the chest by an armalite bullet and, although it passed through his rib cage, the bullet did him no lasting damage and lodged in his flak jacket after passing through him. On 17 September a gunman seriously wounded Guardsman Bell of No 3 Company in the stomach, again with an armalite, but fire was returned almost instantaneously by the patrol, fatally wounding the gunman.

The Battalion returned to England at the end of September and went on leave prior to going to Berlin. Regimental Sergeant Major Pickles was subsequently awarded the MBE for Meritorious Service in Northern Ireland and the GOC awarded Commendations of Good Service to Lance Sergeant Mockford and Guardsman Newson of the Regimental Aid Post for the skill and care which they had both shown in tending so many of those injured during the Battalion's last two tours of duty in Northern Ireland.

West Belfast, 1972/73. 2nd Battalion

The 2nd Battalion returned to Northern Ireland and West Belfast in December 1972, under the command of Lieutenant Colonel Denis Lewey. Battalion Headquarters was in the familiar surroundings experienced on the 1970 tour of the Springfield Road RUC Station. The four companies were deployed in areas which had already become unpleasant by any standard. No 1, commanded by Major M.R.Frisby, was responsible for the Beechmount area, No 2 (Support), Major M.B.N.Howard, No 3, Major Sir Brian Barttelot Bt, the Clonard and Lower Shankhill, and No 4, Major M.W.F.Maxse, and later Major J.R.Macfarlane, a large area of West Belfast consisting mainly of Protestant housing estates.

All these areas were different in character and required differing tactics. Sadly the first three were all scenes of Battalion fatalities. Guardsman Doyle (No 1) was killed by a sniper on 21 February, as was Guardsman Brown (No 2) on 6 March. No 3 Company area was vulnerable to rocket and sniper fire from the Lower Falls, which, although outside the Battalion area, was a terrorist stronghold and one of the worst areas of Belfast. It was on this boundary that a ruthless ambush was laid by terrorists on 20 February. Two landrovers came under fire from several gunmen who were well concealed in buildings on the Falls Road. Guardsmen Pearson and Shaw were killed and Guardsman Falconer seriously injured. For his bravery during the ambush Guardsman Falconer was subsequently awarded the Military Medal.

It had been a very testing tour in an area of Northern Ireland where sniping, hijacking and bombing were the order of the day. However, the pre-tour training served the Battalion well and many casualties were undoubtedly averted due to the vigilance of all concerned. Apart from Guardsman Falconer, Major Howard was awarded a Mention in Despatches and Drummer Atkin a GOC's Commendation.

Staff Appointments

Although there were no Coldstream Battalions serving in Northern Ireland during 1974, members of the Regiment were serving in individual staff appointments. Major W.E.Rous was awarded the MBE following his tour of duty as the GSO 2 Operations at Headquarters Northern Ireland. In April the Regiment was greatly saddened to hear of the death of Captain Anthony Pollen while on duty in Londonderry.

West Belfast, 1975/6. 1st Battalion

The 1st Battalion returned to West Belfast in November 1975, with Battalion Headquarters once again in the Springfield Road RUC Station. Lieutenant Colonel Peter Gibbs had succeeded Lieutenant Colonel Peter Tower as Commanding Officer. The Battalion's area of responsibility included Springmartin, Ballymurphy, Whiterock and Broadway. The extensive work-up programme at Lydd and Hythe stood everyone in good stead over the ensuing four months and, in spite of some increased activity during the last fortnight of the tour, all returned safely to Chelsea Barracks via the LSL *Sir Geraint* at the beginning of March 1976.

Londonderry, 1976/78. 2nd Battalion

1976 was a busy year for the Regiment in Northern Ireland, as hardly had the 1st Battalion returned to the routine of London District than the 2nd Battalion began training for an 18-month tour in Londonderry, beginning in September. Lieutenant Colonel Malcolm Havergal took over command from Lieutenant Colonel the Hon Christopher Willoughby. Unlike a four-month roulement tour, this was to be an 'accompanied' tour, so that the overall Battalion strength was some 1100 with the requirement for over 200 married quarters.

The Battalion assumed responsibility for the RUC Division North Area from 1st Battalion The King's Regiment on 15 September. This consisted of around 176,000 acres and covered part of both County Londonderry and County Tyrone. It included the large urban centres of the predominantly Protestant-populated Waterside of Londonderry and the Roman Catholic stronghold of Strabane, a town which was the subject of two unfortunate statistics – more bomb explosions in proportion to its population than anywhere else in the Province and an unemployment rate of some 40 per cent, which was the highest in Europe. The area outside these two conurbations was rural.

To achieve the aim of assisting the RUC, the majority of the Battalion was based at Ebrington

2nd Battalion. Members of No 1 Company patrolling in Strabane, 1977.

Barracks in the Waterside. The four Companies rotated through a three-month cycle, with each Company spending slightly more than three weeks in each particular role.

The winter of 1976/77 was one of the coldest, whitest and wettest in the Province for a number of years. Despite these unpleasant conditions, the opposition remained active, subjecting the Battalion to a variety of incidents which increased as Christmas approached. Although the IRA declared a so-called 'Christmas truce', it planned a particularly vicious attack on New Year's Eve on the Nelm Drive Community Centre, to coincide with a New Year party that many Regimental families would be attending. Fortunately the 25lb device was spotted by an alert sentry, Guardsman A.Russell, and a major tragedy was thus averted. Guardsman Russell was subsequently awarded the GOC's Commendation.

2nd Battalion. Border Patrol, Londonderry, 1976/7.

In January a mobile patrol in Strabane was ambushed and Guardsman Hulme was slightly wounded. Of other casualties, Lance Corporal Lister was shot at and hit in the mouth by a pistol round whilst on rural duties in Enniskillen in April 1977, and in May Guardsman Daly had to jump from the top floor of a three-storey-high barrack block when it caught fire.

The Unionist strike in May gave the Battalion its busiest period. No 3 Company (Major P.H.Mills) as Brigade Reserve was deployed to Larne under 1st Battalion The Ulster Defence Regiment. In their place, the Battalion was reinforced by Z Company 1st Battalion The Royal Regiment of Fusiliers from the UK. However, the stoppage had a minimal effect in Londonderry and the immediate vicinity, and in general the RUC coped well with the situation. In July the Orange Day Marches passed off without serious incident.

Her Majesty The Queen visited the University of Coleraine in August as part of her Jubilee Tour and the Commanding Officer had command of eight companies and a Field Support Squadron Royal Engineers to search and clear the area beforehand. Thanks to the diligence of all concerned, no major incident took place.

September saw a string of finds and criminal arrests made in Strabane by No 2 (Support) Company (Major A.R.Mason) and the Sion Mills Force (the Recce and Assault Pioneer Platoons combined). As a result the town centre was reopened after many years of closure. Several casualties were undoubtedly averted in November, thanks to the alertness of Lance Corporal Clayden, who had recently joined the Battalion from the Guards Depot. He spotted a suspicious traffic cone on the Craigavon bridge. On inspection it proved to be a classic booby trap packed with high explosive. For his vigilance Lance Corporal Clayden was awarded the GOC's Commendation.

The Battalion handed over to 3rd Battalion The Royal Green Jackets at midnight on 16 March, thus completing the first Garrison tour by a Household Division Regiment in Northern Ireland during the current Emergency. Most people left the Province with mixed feelings, but everyone had made the most of what was offered in the difficult conditions which prevailed. Their achievements during the tour were highlighted by the award of the OBE to the Commanding Officer, a Mention in Despatches to Sergeant R.Cooper and the GOCs Commendation to Captain (QM) F.P.Horsfall, Sergeant A.Austin, and Lance Corporal R.McCormack, in addition to those already mentioned. Guardsmen Newton, Jeal and Baxter also received Royal Humane Society Awards for rescuing civilians from the River Foyle.

West Belfast, 1978/79. 1st Battalion

The 1st Battalion once again returned to West Belfast in October 1978, with Battalion Headquarters being based in Springfield RUC Station for the fourth time. Their area of responsibility contained the notorious hotspots of Turf Lodge, Whiterock and Ballymurphy. The events of the tour followed along traditional lines and, as the Commanding Officer, Lieutenant Colonel Martin Maxse MVO, tartly told a perhaps over-enthusiastic Public Relations Officer, "There are no public relations in the Springfield Road".

The Battalion found weapons, explosives and numerous different types of ammunition, apart from arresting many wanted men. The Commanding Officer had promised a new APC to whoever arrested the most wanted suspect. Sadly the prize remained unclaimed! Only two members of the Battalion suffered gunshot wounds and fortunately neither proved fatal. Guardsman Prendergast broke his thumb whilst stopping a bullet with his rifle and Guardsman Billingham was shot through the ankle when his landrover patrol was ambushed. An event which might also be remembered was the grenade that exploded outside the officers' lavatory at the Moyard base in Turf Lodge. Whether it was or was not occupied at the time cannot be confirmed!

West Belfast, 1982. 2nd Battalion

In March the 2nd Battalion, commanded by Lieutenant Colonel Richard Macfarlane, found itself once again in West Belfast. Two differences from previous tours were noted immediately. First, the size of the bases had increased as the Army had withdrawn and concentrated. The Battalion was therefore billeted in only two locations, Fort Whiterock and North Howard Street Mill, each location holding two companies. Battalion Headquarters of course remained traditionally located at the Springfield Road RUC Station. The other difference was the definite lead role of the RUC, with military support, which was very much a turn-around from previous tours.

Although the security situation had shown a marked improvement since the Battalion's last tour in the Province, the threat of sophisticated terrorist activity nevertheless remained, thereby occasioning no let-up in the need for a continued high level of alertness and vigilance. The importance of these attributes was soon reinforced by attacks on the company locations, which failed, and by other planned attacks which were prevented by pre-emptive action. The only casualty during the tour was Guardsman Gooderham who was seriously wounded by a bomb when he was opening the security barrier in the City Centre. His life was undoubtedly saved by his flak jacket, which absorbed much of the blast.

2nd Battalion, Belfast 1982. "I think that's where we left him" Regimental Sergeant Major J. Robinson and the Commanding Officer's Rover Group. Left to right: Sergeant Nightingale, Guardsman Ball, Lance Corporal McCoy, Guardsman Cook, RSM, Lance Sergeant Sapstead, Lance Corporals Goodenough and Birch.

2nd Battalion, Belfast 1982. Visit of the Colonel of the Regiment.

The tour featured regular finds of weapons and munitions, and several batches of explosives. The significant factor which was perhaps not appreciated at the time was the large number of arrests which subsequently led to charges connected with terrorist offences. The Battalion returned to Fallingbostel in August. For their part in the success of the tour, the Commanding Officer, Major E.B.L.Armitstead, Lance Sergeant D.Sleney and Lance Corporal J.Houchen were all Mentioned in Despatches.

South Armagh, 1982/83. 1st Battalion

Hardly had the 2nd Battalion departed than the 1st Battalion, under command of Lieutenant Colonel Sir Brian Barttelot, Bt. arrived in South Armagh on a five-month tour as part of 8 Brigade. It was the first time that a battalion from the Regiment had been deployed in that part of the Province. The Battalion's task was to support the RUC in maintaining law and order in what was universally known as 'bandit' country. Apart from the ever-present threat of murder attempts on police and soldiers, abductions, robberies, car hijacks, smuggling, cattle rustling, poaching and indiscriminate thuggery were commonplace.

2nd Battalion, Belfast 1982. Street patrol.

The diverse nature of the very scenic countryside and the rambling and often unrecognizable border, with forty-three crossing points in the Battalion area of responsibility, made it a perfect hunting ground for terrorists. Little significant intelligence could be gleaned from south of the border, from where Provisional IRA operations were almost invariably mounted. It was therefore very much a case of keeping the opposition guessing as to the Battalion's intentions. The local population, intimidated by the Provisional IRA, gave no recognition to the border, and for much of the time terrorists living on the other side could be kept informed of Security Force movements by sympathetic locals.

By day it was extremely dangerous to move about either in a vehicle or on foot, thereby running the risk of snipers. By night movement on foot was somewhat safer, but there was always the risk of running into some form of explosive device set off by remote control or by trip wire. Vehicles ran the risk of being blown up, particularly when crossing culverts, or being caught in impromptu illegal checkpoints. Helicopters were therefore crucially important and were the key element for the majority of deployment throughout the Battalion area.

The Battalion took over responsibility for South Armagh at the end of August, with Battalion Headquarters and No 1 Company located at Bessbrook Mill and the other Companies in Crossmaglen and Forkhill. September was an uneventful month, with the opposition doubtless carrying out their own recces. Hostilities began in earnest on 2 October, when an explosive device packed with 'dockyard confetti' was detonated by command wire in Crossmaglen as a patrol was passing by. Guardsman Lethaby suffered a broken leg in the blast, but the firing of the explosive was fortunately ill-timed and caused no other casualties.

A few days later, during a search, several barrels of smuggled Guinness were discovered which sadly had to be handed over as evidence! From then until Christmas a succession of shooting and bombing attacks took place. Guardsman Neville suffered a broken kneecap when 100lbs of explosive were detonated behind a wall. He was subsequently awarded the Queen's Gallantry Medal. Second Lieutenant W.O.C. Pearson-Gee had his binoculars and webbing struck by rounds when his patrol came under fire. Many lives were undoubtedly saved thanks to the eagle eyes of Lance Corporal Smallpage who spotted a catgut tripwire leading into a wall near the Dublin road

1st Battalion, South Armagh 1982/83. The result of Guardsman Neville's Bomb.

railway bridge. For his vigilance he was awarded the GOC's Commendation. The device in the wall was cleared and a further 100lbs of homemade explosive (HME) was recovered. On 20 December Guardsman Curless had the misfortune to lose an eye when a bomb exploded in Crossmaglen as his patrol was passing.

A steady flow of predictable incidents continued on into the New Year and on 5 January the Provisional IRA carried out its final murder attempt on a patrol in the area of Crossmaglen. Guardsman Lloyd was struck by a high velocity bullet which was stopped by his body armour. Although blown off his feet, he was unharmed. In the final week before the Battalion handed over to 40 Commando Royal Marines, the opposition made a last attempt to blow up the Dublin Belfast railway, which fortunately failed and 25 kilograms of HME was recovered. They also left a tractor with a load of straw bales parked by a road junction on the main route from Bessbrook to Crossmaglen. Three beer kegs were discovered partly concealed between the rear wheels and a further 45kg of HME was recovered.

The Battalion left South Armagh at the end of January 1983. Individuals had been bombed and shot at, and violent murders had continued to disrupt the lives of the local population. However, the Battalion's conduct of operations had proved to be extremely successful and the fact that no fatalities had been incurred during the tour in an area in which more members of the Security Forces had been killed than anywhere else in the Province spoke for itself. The successes achieved by the Battalion were reflected in the subsequent operational awards. Apart from those previously mentioned, the Commanding Officer was awarded the OBE, and Major O.R.StJ.Breakwell the MBE. Major M.H.Somervell and Sergeant R.McCormack were Mentioned in Despatches, and GOC's Commendations were awarded to Major G.C.Forestier-Walker, Major C.R.L.Lomer, Captain (QM) C.J.Louch, Second Lieutenant W.O.C.Pearson-Gee and Sergeant B.Nash.

South Armagh, 1986. 2nd Battalion

The tour began in July and the Battalion, commanded by Lieutenant Colonel Myles Frisby, OBE, was widely dispersed with companies located in both 39 and 8 Brigade areas. Battalion Headquarters and the Echelon were located in Drumadd Barracks, Armagh, No 1 Company was under operational control of 2nd Battalion Ulster Defence Regiment in South Armagh, No 2 (Support) Company had platoons in Newtownhamilton, Forkhill, Newry, Bessbrook and Armagh. No 3 Company, in 8 Brigade area, was located near Castlederg with a platoon at Strabane under operational control of 6 UDR, and No 4 Company was based at Ballykinler, with outstations under command of 3 UDR.

The first two weeks of the tour covered the Protestant marching season, for which Battalion Headquarters and two companies were deployed, but fortunately there was little trouble. The remainder of the tour followed the traditional pattern of life in that part of the Province, namely proximity bombs, hoaxes, explosive finds and incendiary attacks, car bombs and booby traps. The Commanding Officer and Regimental Sergeant Major C.Stevens were fortunate to escape injury when their patrol passed a device which failed to discharge its contents of commercial explosive and ball bearings. The Recce Platoon achieved the unenviable position of being the first troops deployed in Newry for six years.

The Battalion returned intact to Wellington Barracks at the end of August.

Belfast, 1988/9. 1st Battalion

September 1988 saw the 1st Battalion, under Lieutenant Colonel Edward Armitstead, once again in Belfast, but this time Battalion Headquarters broke with the tradition of being at RUC Springfield Road and was located in North Howard Street Mill. The Battalion area of responsibility was much larger than many with experience of previous Northern Ireland tours would have remembered. It stretched from the M1 outside Belfast to the north and down almost to Lisburn in the south. Company areas of responsibility covered all the well-known hot spots and the Battalion was augmented by an additional company from the Resident Battalion in Belfast, 1st Battalion The Duke of Wellington's Regiment.

The Battalion was almost immediately tested by the IRA, with two hoax bombs and an improvised explosive device (IED). Guardsman James of No 2 Company became the first casualty, when a command-detonated device exploded beside him, injuring his right eye and arm, but fortunately not seriously. The IRA continued its intense efforts to make the Battalion unwelcome. Fortunately the injuries were few and minor, with the exception of an individual in The Duke of Wellington's Regiment, who had to have a leg amputated.

Life for those in North Howard Street Mill was somewhat livened up in mid-November by the detonation of a 450lb car bomb. Extensive damage was caused to walls and ceilings inside the building, but the main structure survived remarkably well. The outer wall proved to be a useful barrier, so that much of the blast was deflected upwards. Amazingly there were only nine minor casualties. The damage was estimated to be in the region of £500,000 and would take several months to repair.

Apart from a brief lull over Christmas, IRA attacks continued at a fairly high level for the remainder of the tour. The majority of attacks were bombs of various sizes, detonated by command wire. One bomb which exploded on the outside wall of an observation post on top of the Divis tower block had been placed there from the flat below by two men with the help of magnets and a broomstick! Guardsman Halliwell received lacerations and a broken ankle when a device containing Semtex and hidden behind a bollard was detonated as his patrol passed by. Guardsman Gates was doubly lucky and was twice saved from serious injury, once when a device failed to explode properly, and again when he was knocked over by the blast of a bomb, but not injured.

The Battalion returned from Belfast at the end of January 1989, from a successful and uneventful tour, marred only in the final days by the tragic death of Guardsman Shaw as a result of an accident. Lance Sergeant A.Gray of the Corps of Drums was awarded a Mention in Despatches.

South Armagh, 1991. 2nd Battalion

The 2nd Battalion, commanded by Lieutenant Colonel Anthony Biggs, returned to South Armagh and came under command of Headquarters 3 Brigade in March. In addition to individuals from the other four Foot Guards Regiments and the Household Cavalry, the Battalion also took under command a battery from 4 Field Regiment Royal Artillery and a company from 1st Battalion The Black Watch. Battalion Headquarters and a company were based at Bessbrook Mill and the other companies were located at Forkhill, Newtownhamilton and Crossmaglen.

The Battalion had its first major incident within a fortnight of its arrival. A patrol from No 2 (Support) Company at Newtownhamilton was attacked near Conlon Hill. Four hundred rounds were fired at the patrol, and over 900 returned. On average, during its six months in South Armagh,

2nd Battalion, No 4 Company, South Armagh 1991. Left to right: Lieutenant J.F.B. Napier, Lance Sergeant Arscott, Lance Corporal Dart.

the Battalion was attacked or involved in a major incident of some sort about every ten days. Bases were mortared, grenades thrown, informants murdered and various finds made.

There were a number of IED attacks which came very close to killing members of the Battalion. One near Crossmaglen in June blew Lance Sergeant Cooper from the Corps of Drums into an adjacent field, but he miraculously escaped serious injury. Sadly, the one fatality was Lance Corporal S.Ware, who on 17 August was killed in a landmine explosion while on foot patrol east of Newtownhamilton. Long-distance foot patrols were carried out at an intensive and constant level, so that it was a very fit and lean Battalion by the end of the tour. Good patrolling and observation resulted in the substantial number of explosive devices that were discovered before they could be initiated; one such device contained over 1000lb of explosive.

2nd Battalion, South Armagh 1991, Bessbrook Mill.

2nd Battalion, South Armagh 1991, Rural patrol. Company Sergeant Major Emmerson with members of No 4 Company.

The Battalion also played a leading role in two major operations to rebuild the observation towers in the Border area. Other successful operations were run against smugglers and racketeers, and in one a cattle truck containing 134 sheep was apprehended. The driver was fined £2000 by the RUC and the sheep remained at the Forkhill base overnight, much to the amusement of those other members of the Household Division who were attached to No 1 Company!

Overall, it was another successful tour for the Regiment and this was reflected by the award of the OBE to the Commanding Officer with two Company Commanders, Major S.D.W.Mansbridge and Major J.J.C.Bucknall being Mentioned in Despatches, as was the Mechanical Transport Officer, Captain F.Shorrock. Company Sergeant Major K.Byrne and Sergeant K.Sample were both awarded the BEM; Lieutenant A.G.Barry, Sergeant R.P.Cooper, Lance Sergeant L.Hardeman, Lance Sergeant S.Lee, Lance Corporal K.Hoy and the Battalion Medical Officer, Captain A.S.Jacks RAMC, were all awarded the GOC's Commendation. In addition, WO1 R.Appleby was also awarded the MBE for his service as the Regimental Sergeant Major of 8 UDR.

East Tyrone, 1992. 1st Battalion

The Battalion had not expected to visit the Province in 1992 and, having moved from the UK to Germany in mid-October 1991, plans were underway early in 1992 for training at Soltau, prior to a visit to Canada. However, in February the Battalion, under the command of Lieutenant Colonel Peter Williams, was warned for an emergency tour. Pre-training started in May and it took over from 3rd Battalion The Parachute Regiment at the end of June. Initially, Battalion Headquarters and No 2 Company deployed to Cookstown, with No 3 Company in Dungannon. Support Company was also in Dungannon, under operational control of 1st Battalion The Royal Irish Regiment. No 1 Company was based in Portadown as 3 Brigade Reserve. The Battalion suffered a casualty earlier on in the tour when Guardsman Shore was hit when on foot patrol in Pomeroy. Although serious, the injury was fortunately not fatal.

An early aim of the tour was to ensure that the police and military boundaries coincided. On 6 August the Battalion assumed responsibility for the whole of RUC K Division. No 2 Company remained in Cookstown and assumed command of the Cookstown Sub Division, and No 1

Company assumed command of the Dungannon Sub-Station, with Tac Headquarters also located at Dungannon. No 3 Company moved to Portadown to become the 3 Brigade Operations Company. A platoon from No 1 Company was detached to the Light Infantry in South Armagh.

Throughout the tour the Battalion devoted a great deal of effort to restoring an air of normality to the relationship between the local population and the Army. By and large this bore fruit, although there was the occasional incident to remind individuals that local temperaments were fickle. Guardsman Hayes was hit in the face by a brick while on patrol in Cookstown and Second Lieutenant C.H.G.St George had his nose broken when he was assaulted. In November No 3 Company moved location for the third time when it was deployed to take over the running of the Border Crossing Point at Aughnacloy.

In December the IRA initiated a pre-Christmas bombing campaign, but its attempts were thwarted by a comprehensive series of vehicle checks. This resulted in an inordinate number of bomb hoaxes, with seven recorded on 23 December alone. At the Cookstown Vehicle Check Point Lance Corporal Selman was presented with a tin of 'Quality Street'. On opening it he discovered a device inside; this contained about 1kg of Semtex and had failed to go off. The Provisional IRA declared a ceasefire over Christmas and Boxing Day, and by the 30th the whole Battalion had departed from Northern Ireland.

The success of the tour can be gauged by the number of awards earned. The Commanding Officer, Major D.D.S.A.Vandeleur, Captain M.J.Manning (the Quartermaster), Captain G.C.C.Waters and Lance Sergeant M.Pollard, were all Mentioned in Despatches. GOC's Commendations were awarded to Staff Sergeant M.Fox, Sergeant N.Overton, Lance Sergeant A.Punting, Lance Corporal J.Davis and Guardsman B.Weaver.

South Armagh and Belfast, 1996.
1st Battalion and Number 7 Company

1996 saw the Regiment fully committed in Northern Ireland, with the 1st Battalion returning to South Armagh and Number 7 Company attached to 1st Battalion Scots Guards in West Belfast, both for six-month tours.

1st Battalion, March–September

The 1st Battalion, commanded by Lieutenant Colonel Hugh Boscawen, was first into the Province at the end of March, and once again assumed command of South Armagh with Battalion Headquarters at Bessbrook, and companies at Crossmaglen, Forkhill and Newtownhamilton. Many of the senior ranks had been junior ranks on previous Regimental tours in the area and their experiences were to prove invaluable. An IRA ceasefire had been operating for the past eighteen months and this had resulted in a greater degree of tolerance being shown to the Military by the locals.

The first months of the tour were ostensibly quiet, so that the extra-mural activities were able to include the Bessbrook Half Marathon, which consisted of some twenty-two laps of the Mill. The Battalion was involved in a very large search operation as part of the run-up to the multi-party Peace Forum Election on 30 May. Lance Corporal Bicknell had a narrow escape when he was struck on the head by a helicopter rotor blade. Fortunately he was wearing his combat helmet, thus averting a serious injury. Unlike on other tours, it was possible to get a few individuals of all ranks away on courses or adventure training.

1st Battalion, South Armagh 1996. Major W.J. Tower.

The Battalion returned to Germany at the end of September. The situation throughout the tour, despite two years of relative peace, had been highly volatile, with the very real risk of a return to full-scale violence between Catholics and Protestants. But, although the tour had not been without incident, the uneasy peace had been maintained. In the subsequent Northern Ireland Awards, the Commanding Officer and Lance Corporal P.Hobbs were awarded the Queen's Commendation for Valuable Service. Colour Sergeant D.Lyles and Lance Corporal R.Coates were awarded the GOC's Commendation.

No 7 Company, May–November

In February 1996 Number 7 Company Commander, Major Stephen Mansbridge, received a telephone call that the Company was to deploy with 1st Battalion Scots Guards on that Battalion's forthcoming tour in West Belfast. The news was greeted enthusiastically by the Company, as a large percentage had

Lance Sergeant Jobbins.

Lance Sergeant Bachaus.

never deployed on an operational tour before, many having only recently passed out from recruit training. The Company underwent a very comprehensive Northern Ireland training package before embarking for the Province at the beginning of May.

It assumed command of Fort Whiterock and the Woodbourne North Area, which included the notorious hot spots of Turf Lodge and Andersonstown. It was co-located with C Company 1st Battalion Scots Guards, with Battalion Headquarters being near Musgrove Park Hospital. The early weeks of the tour were uneventful, but elections in May and the subsequent marching season provided more activity, and the Company was deployed during the week of 12 July to contain public disorder throughout the city, after the Drumcree stand-off. During this period Fort Whiterock came under attack from some 200 missiles, including petrol bombs and paint bombs. The final month of the tour saw patrolling increased to pre-1994 Ceasefire levels, following the two bombs at Headquarters Northern Ireland in Lisburn. The Company returned to Chelsea Barracks in mid-November.

South Armagh, 1999/2000. 1st Battalion

The 1st Battalion under the command of Lieutenant Colonel Jonathan Bourne-May returned to South Armagh and 3 Brigade in mid-September 1999. Battalion Headquarters was once again located at Bessbrook Mill, together with Headquarter Company and No 2 Company (Major N.B.Henderson). No 1 Company (Major G.C.C.Waters) was at Forkhill, No 3 (Major R.W.Yorke QGM) at Crossmaglen, and the Corps of Drums on their own at Newtownhamilton.

The last time that Regular Battalions of the three senior Household Division Regiments had served together was in 2nd Guards Brigade in Malaya during 1948/49. However, between September and December 1999 3 Infantry Brigade was unofficially redesignated 3rd Guards Brigade, with 1st Battalion Grenadier Guards deployed in East Tyrone and 1st Battalion Scots Guards stationed at Ballykinler.

The Battalion arrived to an unfamiliar air of political optimism, brought about by the hope that the negotiations which were in full swing would achieve an acceptable and lasting situation to the Northern Ireland problem. Although the Provisional IRA had been on ceasefire for three years, the more hardline dissident republican groupings still retained the wherewithal and the intent to cause trouble. The Battalion's main tasks were to provide support to the RUC, who remained unable to conduct normal policing in the area without military support, and to man a series of surveillance towers along the South Armagh-Irish border.

For the Guardsman, a delicate balance had to be struck between military activity to provide security to the RUC and, at the same time, reducing the military profile in an attempt to foster an atmosphere of normality in keeping with the improving political situation. As ever, the Guardsmen proved, through a combination of patience, good humour and military skill, that they could effectively support the RUC on the ground without alienating the local population. The much-reduced number of complaints against the Army in South Armagh bore ample testimony to the success of this approach.

The fledgling Northern Ireland Assembly collapsed in January 2000 and the resulting political vacuum inevitably caused increased activity on the part of the dissident republican terrorists. The Battalion's emphasis for the last month of the tour reverted to the familiar anti-terrorist role. A significant increase in the threat, particularly from mortar attack on a company base or surveillance tower location, became evident as the opposition attempted to mount a successful attack in order to attract support for their cause. Extra troops were made available and patrolling and military activity generally increased considerably to prevent such an attack from taking place.

The tour ended in March 2000 and the Battalion returned to Victoria Barracks, Windsor. Although in many respects it was a very different tour from many of its predecessors, it had none-theless been an interesting and busy six months with a number of challenges. Fortunately there were no casualties, although a Lance Sergeant and five Guardsmen were severely shaken up towards the end of the tour when the helicopter in which they were travelling crash-landed. As ever, the Guardsmen played their part in full and lived up to the well-earned reputation of previous Regimental battalion tours of duty during what has been a long and protracted campaign.

Conclusion

"The only predictable thing about internal security duties in Northern Ireland is that unpredictable incidents will occur with predictable regularity."[4] This comment was made in the run-up to the 2nd Battalion's tour to Northern Ireland in July 1970, which was the first of seventeen visits by the Regiment to the Province. How prophetic these words have been. Throughout the dangers, hard-ships, highs and lows which have been endured over the past thirty years, the commitment and humour of the Guardsmen have never wavered. The reality of it all can be best be summed up in the words of Major John Savelle, who has spent some seven and half years of his Army service on operational duty in the Province, starting with the time of 'tea and sympathy' to the present 'Peace'. "For me it could all be best described as long periods of total boredom, peppered with bursts of intense activity, when one could hardly find time to draw breath."[5] Such has been the un-predictability of operational service in Northern Ireland.

[4] 2nd Battalion Notes, *Coldstream Gazette*, August 1970.

[5] Letter from Major John Savelle, MBE, December 1999.

CHAPTER FOURTEEN

350 YEARS A COLDSTREAMER

by John Hook and Peter Horsfall

"A soldier's life is terrible hard." A.A.Milne

This chapter might well be subtitled "Pay, Pensions, Provisions, Punishments, Paraphernalia, but not Politics" for it is our intention to try to portray the life and times of the ordinary Coldstreamer over the years. There will be no accounts here of wars, campaigns, strategies or a formal history of the Regiment, all of which is left to more erudite authors. Rather than giving a political background to battles, we aim to give some idea of what life was like for the soldier in the field.

It is well known that King George V awarded the title of 'Guardsman' to men of the Household Brigade in 1918 to acknowledge the part played by them during the 1914–18 war. Before that, they were known as 'Privates', but as Guardsman is a title we are proud of, may we be forgiven for using that term throughout this chapter?

Seventeenth Century

In his book *The History of the British Standing Army*, published in 1869, Colonel C.Walton begins his first chapter with the following:-

> "About ten o'clock on the morning of Saint Valentine's Day in the year 1661, there was to be seen on Tower Hill an ordinary London crowd collected round a small body of soldiers – only some hundred and seventy troopers, and nine hundred or a thousand infantry. The spectacle was neither very extensive nor very imposing, yet to us who can look back upon it and upon the stream of results which has flowed from it down the long page of the country's history, it is an event of the highest military and historical interest."

On that day when Monck's Regiment laid down their arms in the name of the Commonwealth and took them up again in the name of The King, it is recorded that there was great cheering, hats being thrown in the air, beating of drums and discharging of muskets, and shouts of "God save King Charles the Second!"

Though the cheering was for the restoration of The King, it could be that much of the jubilation was caused by a speech made by one of the Commissioners sent from Westminster for the event, an extract from which was:-

> "For which signal Services His Majesty and the whole Kingdom returned them not only their verbal but real thanks; The King having freely given them one weeks Pay by way

of Gratuity over and above their Wages, and the Parliament and Kingdom provided moneys for the Payment of the just Arrears Stated in the respective Accounts, which upon their disbanding should be forthwith paid for their use into their Officers hands."

The Wooden Horse. A form of military punishment in the seventeenth century under which the offender was sentenced to sit for hours in growing discomfort on the horse.

In 1650, when Monck's Regiment was formed, times were tough and troubled for everyone, and men in the New Model Army must have had to endure exceptional hardships. They had to face not only the resentments caused by the Civil War, but also the fierce hostility of the Scots with whom they were at war for the first ten years of their existence. It was a thankless campaign against a determined and elusive foe, and they did not even have the compensation of relaxing with the Scottish lassies. Fraternization was strictly forbidden and was punished by the guilty pair being bound together in irons and whipped.

Living conditions were harsh both on operations and in camp. Unless they were holding one of the fortresses or other smaller garrison, the soldiers lived in a billet with the local inhabitants and had to pay for their accommodation. This was hardly comfortable, as was described by Sir William Brereton:

> "The sluttiness and nastiness of this people is such that I cannot ommit the particularising thereof . . . their houses and halls and kitchens have such a noisome taste, a savour so strong, as it does offend you as soon as you come within their walls . . . To come into their kitchens and so see them dress their meat, and to behold the sink will be a sufficient supper, and will take off the edge of your stomach."[1]

Even when they arrived at Coldstream in December 1659, the men found that the regiment that had been there before had eaten all the victuals, and whilst the general was content to chew his tobacco, this did not satisfy the hunger of his troops, who reviled the poor town and vowed "it was justly called Cold-stream, being a place for good Christians to perish in".[2]

A common offence in the ranks was swearing. A Corporal was reported for using the word "by God" or "as God shall judge me" and sentenced to "ride the wooden horse".

During the years 1651–55 pay rates were 1s.6d a day for sergeants, one shilling for corporals, and 10d for Guardsman, but the latter would only receive 8d because he was issued with free 'fire and candle', as well as having to pay for his accommodation. Also from his pay was deducted

[1] *History of the British Standing Army.* Colonel Walton 1869
[2] *Life of General Monck, Duke of Albemarle,* Thomas Gumble.

the cost of the daily ration of bread or, more frequently, biscuit and cheese, usually one or two pounds of the former and a quarter or half a pound of the latter according to circumstances. The amount of the ration depended on the possibility of obtaining other victuals and, during campaigns, on the weight a soldier could carry. Occasionally gratuities were given for the successful accomplishment of difficult operations.

The seventeenth century Guardsman was just as resourceful as those of today, for cooking must have presented a problem. It was reported that "some of our soldiers brought a little raw meat with them and became excellent cooks, a back makes a dripping pan and a head-peece is a porrage pot". The 'back' was the armour used by troopers, or horsemen, and the 'head-peece' was the steel helmet worn by pikemen. Soldiers might be tempted to supplement their meagre rations by poaching, even stealing, but if caught could be punished by riding the wooden horse for an hour and to receive thirty stripes. Considering that in December 1657 there was no less than seven months' pay owing, soldiers were glad to live on biscuit and cheese, and, with nothing to purchase any extra, they must have been sorely tempted to risk punishment by poaching. Arrears of pay was serious because soldiers had to purchase their clothing.

Discipline was certainly harsh by today's standards, but it applied to civilians as much as to soldiers, and one could be hanged for picking pockets. Flogging was the standard punishment for minor military offences, and this would continue for another 230 years. Certain crimes such as insubordination or violence to superiors meant the death penalty by hanging or shooting, or (if one was lucky!) mutilation (by cutting off one's nose or ears), branding or deportation. The penalty for fighting in camp was to have a hand cut off.

When the number of offenders was inconveniently large, an example was made by selecting every tenth man by lot for punishment, or those involved would be made to dice for their lives; the men throwing the lowest numbers were forthwith shot or hanged and the rest released.

Flogging was the standard punishment until 1881 and was normally carried out by the Marshall's men or regimental provost. It was ordered that "stripes were to be smartly laid on, and in the case the Marshall's man does not lay them on smartly, he is to receive as many". That has all changed, but one punishment that has not is that the Coldstreamer of the seventeenth century was also liable to be awarded extra fatigues!

The Restoration in 1660 meant that the soldiers were for a while welcomed in the capital and treated as liberators, but it did not last long and they were soon being poorly treated over their accommodation, their pay and their pensions. Many old soldiers ended up as beggars and it was a welcome relief when Charles II built the Royal Hospital, Chelsea, for Army pensioners.

Legend has it that it was Nell Gwynne who persuaded Charles II to build the Royal Hospital for old soldiers after a maimed veteran came begging to the side of her coach. However, it was in fact Sir Stephen Fox, the Paymaster-General of the Forces, who should be credited with the original idea and who suggested that the King should donate a piece of land on which to erect the building. The King offered a site at Chelsea on which St James's College then stood, but then remembered, "Odso, I now recollect that I have already given that land to Mistress Nell here." "Yes, so you have, Charles," she responded, "but I willingly will give it back to you for so good a purpose." Shortly after, Charles built her a house in Pall Mall in exchange for that she had surrendered for the Hospital.

Begun in 1682 it was completed in 1690. In 1689 a general muster was taken throughout the Army of "men disabled by wounds in fight or other accident, or who, having served the Crown for twenty years had been judged unfit for service," and it was discovered that 579 soldiers had been admitted on to the pension list.

Originally there were 476 pensioners at the Hospital, 27 of whom were officers, 33 cavalrymen and 416 infantrymen. Of the Foot soldiers 32 Sergeants each received 2s.0d per week, 32 Corporals and 16 Drummers each 10d per week, and 336 Privates 8d per week, in addition to their food and clothing.[3]

Eighteenth Century

The eighteenth century saw few changes to the way of life of our Coldstream Guardsman, who spent much of his time overseas on various campaigns. But in 1783 his pay, which had remained virtually unchanged at 8d a day since Elizabethan times[4], was raised to the famous 'shilling a day', at which sum it would remain for another 100 years.

In the 1790s Napoleon began, like Hitler, to overrun Europe, and there was even a threat that he might try to invade England. This led the Government to look to the state of its army and it was decided in 1792 to start building barracks instead of having the soldiers scattered round the country in billets. They were not, however, at all popular with the troops and proved a mixed blessing.

The office of Barrack-Master[5] was established in 1792 and his responsibility was the construction of permanent barracks throughout Britain. By 1805 there were some 203 barracks. On the whole they were a great improvement on the hovels that had been the accommodation for the army in Ireland, but still were little more than stout walls and a roof. J.M.Brereton[6] writes:

> "No thought was given to basic facilities. Of 146 barracks in England and Scotland, 89 lacked any proper washing facilities for the men, while 77 had no means for washing dirty linen. In Ireland, conditions were even worse: 130 of the 139 barracks were devoid of men's ablution arrangements. Very often the soldier's only means of washing his person or his underclothes was by drawing water from a well in the barrack square. Especially in winter, there was little to encourage personal hygiene."[7]
>
> "The cramped barrack rooms were foetid with the stench of unwashed bodies, compounded with the odour of the dual-purpose tub which served as a urinal at night and a washtub by day.
>
> "In the smaller barracks one room was allotted to every eight men, in which they ate, slept, cleaned their arms and kit and stowed such worldly goods as they possessed. Regulations specified that each soldier should have a minimum space of 450 cubic feet: (a convict in prison was allowed 1,000.) Until the 1790s no beds were provided; instead, the men slept on straw-filled 'bolsters' or palliasses, which were refilled with fresh straw every two months. The only lighting was by candle. When bedsteads – wooden cots – were issued it was on the niggardly scale of one for every two men, so the term 'bedfellow' acquired a literal meaning."

[3] Serving soldiers had a halfpenny a week deducted from their pay to help pay for these pensions.

[4] It was 6d at the time of Crecy 1346.

[5] Unfortunately the first officer to hold this post misappropriated about £9m, and he also appointed a large number of assistant barrack-masters in places where no barracks were built nor planned.

[6] *The British Soldier*, J.M.Brereton.

[7] Even in the late 1940s only the first few men into the ablutions could obtain hot water for shaving. The rest took it in turns to collect a bucket of hot water from the cookhouse.

On 6 June 1780, during the Gordon Riots in London, the mobs burned down Newgate Prison and the Lord Mayor requested the Secretary of State for "some Horse and Foot in order to protect the Mansion House and the Bank of England". On 7 June the mob attacked the Bank, but the Guard was already in place and beat off the attack with some fatal casualties. From then on the Bank Picquet was furnished nightly by the Battalion finding public duties.

In the early days the march of the Picquet to the Bank caused annoyance to the public as they were jostled off the pavement, and as a result of complaints it was subsequently ordered that they should march in the roadway. In later years this caused annoyance to the drivers of vehicles, but the sight of the Picquet marching through the streets was a valuable reminder that the Gold Reserves of the Realm were considered so important that protection by the Brigade of Guards was justified.

During the last years when the Picquet marched to the Bank there were numerous stories about young subalterns who did not wish to be hindered when traffic lights were showing red, and rather than halt they would lead their men downstairs into the Underground entrance with the intention of coming up again on the opposite side – only to find that they had found their way down into the ladies' lavatory! For the last few years of the Picquet's existence, they travelled to and from the Bank by Army lorry; one author recalls that on more than one occasion the whole Bank Picquet travelled by Underground from St James's Park to the Bank!

Until 1963 the Picquet mounted in Guard Order and sentries were posted in ceremonial manner, but the decision was then taken to discontinue the tunic and bearskin and adopt a tactical order of dress more appropriate to its modern duties. On 31 July 1973 the Picquet was mounted for the last time.

Nineteenth Century

The nineteenth century saw many improvements to the way of life of a Guardsman, but not until the second half of the century. In the early 1800s the hard-working surgeons had to do their best for wounded soldiers within the confines of the state of medicine at that time. No anaesthetics were available if an amputation was necessary, and the only relief was a large drink and to bite on the bullet while the surgeon's assistant held the man down. A Sergeant in the Coldstream wrote a description of the operation he underwent when having his leg amputated at Bergen-up-Zoom in 1813:

> "They had got me fixed upon the end of a long barrack-room table, sitting upright, with the legs hanging down; a basin was brought for me to drink out of. I said, 'Sir, let me have a good draught'. He poured out nearly a pint of rum which I eagerly drank off. In an instant it raised up my spirits to an invincible courage . . . The serjeant was preparing to blindfold me 'Oh no,' I said, 'I shall sit still and see as well as the rest.' One of the surgeons sat on a stool, to hold the leg steady: the second ripped up my trousers and took down the stocking low enough, then he waited on the head surgeon . . . the tourniquet being placed painfully tight above the knee, he put his hand under the calf of the leg and setting the edge of the knife on the shin bone, at one heavy, quick stroke, drew it round till it met the shin bone again . . . the blood quickly following the knife, spread around and formed like a red fan, downwards . . . Next the surgeon with his hand, forced up the flesh towards the knee, to make way for the saw. When the saw was

applied, I found it extremely painful; it was worn out . . . it stuck as a bad saw would when sawing a green stick. I said, 'Oh, Sir, have you not a better saw?' He said he was sorry he had not, as they were all worn out. The bone got through, the next thing to be done was still more painful – that of tying up the ligatures: then followed the drawing down of the flesh to cover the end of the bone, and tightly strapped there with strips of sticking plaster; after this, strongly bandaged; thus ended the operation, which lasted about half an hour."

The sergeant was fitted with a free wooden leg and discharged with a pension of 1s per day.

On 14 July 1832 Regimental Headquarters issued an Order which gives some idea of the disciplining of Guardsmen:

"Battalions will have evening parades. In London the Battalions will always parade in Guard Order, when finding the public duties. No leave is to be given from church parade, inspection of necessaries, or surgeon's inspection, unless absolutely necessary. Men unfit for duty, or parade, caused by liquor, to be punished as drunk. When a drunkard appears in a suspicious state at evening parade, and that by leaving barracks he would probably get intoxicated, he must be kept in, and on no account be permitted to enter the canteen. . . . No soldier to have leave all night, and only six men a company to have leave from parade, or till twelve o'clock. To receive leave or other indulgence, the soldier must have been clear of all defaulters' lists for at least a month. To get a pass or furlough, he must have a good general character, and have been off the defaulter's list two months. Soldiers must have been two years in the Regiment, before they can apply for a pass."

In 1836 good conduct pay was introduced and this amounted to a penny (½p) per day for every five years' service, provided the soldier was of 'unblemished conduct'. The Duke of Wellington disapproved of this because he was not in favour of "bribing men to become good soldiers".

Pay rates remained virtually unchanged for over a hundred years and it was not until 1783 that some small increases were authorized. In fact the Pay Warrant for 1881 shows that Foot Guard Sergeants were paid 2s 6d per day, (2s 4d for Infantry Sergeants), Lance Corporals 1s 4d (1s 3d)

The men not only had to wear highly uncomfortable stocks, but also keep their hair in tight plaits, which required help to tie in place.

and Guardsmen 1s 1d, so it was accepted that a Guardsman received 1d a day more than Infantrymen of the Line!

The most important event in the 1850s was the Crimean campaign and some of the best information comes from a report by John Wyatt who was the Battalion Surgeon with the 1st Battalion throughout the campaign. He was not in the front line, but ran the hospital in what we would have known as A Echelon. Some of the rather old-fashioned wording is quoted directly from his report and should not be taken as indicative of the way the authors talk!

The Battalion arrived at Scutari on 29 April 1854 and was placed under tents. It spent six weeks here and the health of the Battalion continued unexceptionable, notwithstanding the heat frequently registering 104 degrees in the bell tents, each of which were occupied by fourteen men. Later that year a hurricane blew down the whole of the Battalion tents and the canvas of many were split into shreds by the violence of the wind. Eventually, after more tents had been issued, seventeen men occupied each of the bell-tents. (On the rare occasions that the authors ever lived in bell-tents, they were occupied by only eight men.)

During the summer the heat was excessive and a representation was also made respecting the injurious effects likely to be produced by the men continuing to wear the stiff regulation stocks[8], and the practice was discontinued. But they continued to fight in tunic and bearskin.

Wyatt describes how he carried out amputations on the battlefield using a wooden door balanced on two casks as his operating table – no great advance on conditions at Bergen-op-Zoom in 1813! The major problem, however, was sickness and some four soldiers died of cholera, dysentry or exhaustion to every one killed by enemy action. It is interesting that he reported:

> "The men suffered more in health from the imperfect state of their boots than from any other defect in clothing; having no change, their feet were perpetually sodden in moisture; and when the longboots were issued, they were too large and badly made. Great difficulty was experienced in inducing the men to take them off at night when asleep in their tents, on account of the cold, the thermometer sometimes ranging from 15 to 11 degrees Fahrenheit, and their wet feet often being swollen, were then constricted by the leather, and thus frost-bite induced, or sloughing of the toes, with sometimes an utter impossibility of subsequently removing the boots except by cutting the leather."[9]

At the end of his Report Surgeon Wyatt recorded several interesting 'Deductions':

> "Although not a recognised article of diet in the army, there is no doubt that a small quantity of tobacco issued daily to the soldier would have been very desirable. It has, in many instances, appeased the craving of hunger, both amongst the officers and men, at particular times, when the food was not most palatable; and the comfort of a smoke in the trenches was not to be despised, except by those unacquainted with the soothing influence of the weed."

He finally gave his personal opinion of the Coldstreamers with whom he had served for two and a half years:

[8] A high collar of very stiff material and most uncomfortable.

[9] Even today, 150 years later, argument still rages over the best footwear to use for such conditions.

"The author has expressed his convictions with freedom, because they have been founded on fact, but he trusts, not with too great presumption. Being unconscious of having evaded any part of the responsibilities of his anxious position, he claims the privilege of recording an unbiased opinion; and if in any way hereafter it may be conducive to the welfare of the men, he will derive all the satisfaction he can desire, ever remembering that it was his good fortune, under the Divine protection, to have been one of three of the Battalion, who served throughout a prolonged campaign, with those, who, by their patient endurance of untold hardship, their chivalrous devotion to discipline, and their undaunted bravery before the enemy, have so nobly perpetuated the application of the glorious motto of their Regiment 'Nulli Secundus'."

The weaknesses shown up by the Crimean War were many and among them was the inappropriate uniform they wore. So in 1884 the Army was trying out the new khaki uniform, copied from the Indian Army. It became permanent in 1902 and in 1910 webbing equipment replaced the old polished leather ammunition pouches. This did not mean any lightening of the Guardsmen's task of cleaning his kit, for he now had to blanco every bit of his 'Change of Quarter' order, polishing all the brass buckles and other fitments.

The Pay Warrant of 1881 had confirmed the rate of 1s.1d a day for our Guardsman, but he still saw little of it in his pocket because of 'stoppages', such as 6d (2½p) per day for his rations, 2d (1p) a day for laundry and unspecified amounts for barrack damages; these ranged from broken window panes to leaking urinal basins, and as late as 1950 a Guardsman had to show considerable courage if he wanted to find out at a Mess Meeting what the barrack damages were for.

In 1890 it was laid down that the soldier must officially receive a minimum of 2d (1p) a day in cash, but that was enough to buy him a pint of beer in those days.

He could, of course, try for promotion, but if that did not appeal, the most favoured appointment in the Army was probably that of officer's servant, which in the 1900s excused a man from ordinary duty and also earned an extra shilling a week; this increased to five shillings in 1947 and today is five pounds.

The great relief for a Guardsman was the abolition of flogging in 1881; it had been reduced in 1812 to a maximum of 300 lashes and in 1868 it was restricted to 'active service' only. Although flogging was now ended, the punishment of 'tattooing' was still retained for deserters, and Regimental Headquarters still possesses one of the machines. It is a series of needles in the shape of a 'D' about one and a half inches tall and spring-loaded with an extremely fierce spring. The needles, impregnated with permanent ink, or perhaps gunpowder, would penetrate about a quarter of an inch into a man's body, "two inches below and one in rear of the nipple of the left breast". The 'D' would be used on convicted deserters, whilst the letters 'BC' would be branded on the upper part of the right forearm of bad characters, who would then be discharged and the branding would prevent their fraudulent re-enlistment.

One of the biggest benefits for the Coldstreamer of the nineteenth century was the marked improvement in accommodation both for himself and his family. The improvements came initially as a result of an outbreak of cholera in 1832; the overcrowded barrack rooms were obviously a health threat and some families of Guardsmen were billeted out in cholera-infested areas. Separate married quarters were therefore provided within barracks as a temporary measure. The provision of married quarters in barracks then became official policy and the first official ones were built in 1860 as part of the new Chelsea Barracks then being constructed.

Twentieth Century

So we come to the twentieth century, much of it within living memory. The last 100 years must have brought greater changes for our Coldstreamer than all the previous 250 years, but there is no doubt that he is coping.

He is now paid not a shilling (5p) a day, but around £25 a day; but the cost of living has risen accordingly and also he earns every penny he gets because of the new skills and responsibilities that are expected of him. These skills are amazingly varied and demanding[10], and range from Rapid Response to radar and from nuclear warfare to internal security. He has to use his initiative as never before and his educational standards are higher than ever. It is arguable whether modern technology has made his job easier or more difficult.

The standard of food that he receives has certainly changed out of all recognition. 2668832 WO2 Arthur Haste, Master Cook of the 3rd Battalion, Guards Depot and 1st Battalion from 1951 to 1966, summed this up well, after a visit to the Battalion at Windsor in 1998.

> "I found a different world with so many things having changed. I was impressed with everything I saw, and was envious that things had been so different during my service . . . the ovens, steamers and fryers, all in shiny stainless steel, were a sight to behold. In 1945 we had big black, coke-fired ovens which had to be raked out to remove the clinkers every evening, and then banked up to keep them going through the night. The first job in the morning for the duty cooks was to take them out again and stoke them up ready for the day's cooking. They would be topped up with coke as necessary during the day. The fumes and dust from the hot coke at times was choking. On each occasion this was done, the red tiled floor had to be washed down.
>
> "I went with the 2nd Battalion to Malaya in 1948 and began to appreciate the easy life we had had in London! We had two 72" ranges and about eight Soyer boilers,[11] all wood-fired. Logs had to be split before they would go into the fire-boxes, and our cookhouse was a corrugated iron lean-to, about eight foot by twenty foot, with an earth floor.
>
> "Then in Egypt with the 3rd Battalion in 1951, we had similar ranges, but diesel-fired. The fire tended to go out on a fairly regular basis, and then re-ignite itself with a minor explosion that covered everything in soot. The result was always the same – sooty spuds, sooty stew and sooty cooks.
>
> "The rations today are far better and much more varied. We got ours from the RASC on Mondays, Wednesday and Fridays, and so at best had only three types of meat to offer the men.
>
> "In 1957, when I was Master Cook with the 1st Battalion in Germany, self-service was introduced; the first unit to initiate this was in Aldershot, and we laid claim to being second (in fact within hours of the first).
>
> "I was highly impressed with the Master Cook, his staff, and what they accomplish in the cookhouse these days. Probably jealous too of the highly technical and modern

[10] A Guardsman today is required to master up to sixty different skills.

[11] Soyer Stoves were invented and used in the Crimean War (1854–56) by Mr Soyer, head chef at the Reform Club, who went out to the Crimea with Florence Nightingale: so they were 'still going strong' a century later.

equipment I saw. I pride myself that we did our best with what we had in my day, and I personally never did hear any Guardsman boast that he had saved the lives of 600 men – because he had shot the cook!"

Home Service

When your authors joined the 2nd Battalion in Wellington Barracks after the Second World War the Battalion was well above establishment and duties did not come around over-frequently. This was just as well because the number of duties undertaken by the Battalion were as follows:

Magazine Guard – This was the arsenal near the Serpentine in Hyde Park and consisted of one Sergeant, two Corporals and three Guardsmen. It ceased to be used as an ammunition store and the guard was dispensed with in 1948.

Prisoner of War Guard – A large house on the Bayswater Road, near Notting Hill, was used as an interrogation centre for important Nazi prisoners of war.

Central London Recruiting Depot – A guard of two Non-Commissioned Officers and three Guardsmen who were stationed in the cells in the basement where any deserters picked up by the Military Police would be lodged overnight.

Queen's Guard – The Buckingham Palace detachment would post, if the Court was in Residence, two double-sentries in the front of the railings at the Palace, with a single sentry at either end of the railings, and a single sentry outside the guardroom. At night two single sentries were stationed in the gardens in the rear of the Palace. They were moved inside the railings in 1959, because of the trouble they had from tourists.

The St James's Detachment found two sentries under the Clock Tower, a single sentry outside Marlborough House while Queen Mary was still alive, double sentries outside Clarence House when Princess Elizabeth and Prince Philip lived there after their marriage, a single sentry outside York House and a single sentry outside the Guardroom.

Tower Guard – Two separate guards were found here, one the Spur Guard at the main entrance to the Tower, and the Main Guard which found sentries overnight but during the day were on stand-by in case anyone should attempt to steal the Crown Jewels.

The punishments of the Millennium bear no comparison with those of earlier times. Corporal punishment may have ended in 1881 – when in fact the last soldier to be flogged was a Coldstreamer – but until the 1950s the Coldstreamer who committed a serious crime was liable to a spell in the Military Prison at Shepton Mallet or the 'Glasshouse' at Aldershot, where he suffered considerable physical and mental hardship. Today it is a case of being sent to a Military Corrective Training Centre, where the emphasis is on 're-training' rather than simply being punished. One of the main punishments now is to fine offending soldiers – sometimes up to a month's pay; some disagree with this system as, in the case of married soldiers, the families suffer too. Another problem is to deal with an offender when on operations. In our time, particularly in Malaya, a Guardsman could be sentenced to up to 28 days' Field Punishment which worked effectively; if in camp, he was kept in the Guardroom, but would accompany his platoon if they were detailed for jungle patrols. There is no satisfactory solution to this problem, which is largely a matter of the Army adapting wisely to the changing attitudes of the time. Interestingly, the days of Guardsmen being locked up for minor offences on the barrack square seem to be over. Some of the old Sergeant Majors in the 'Great Parade Ground in the Sky' will be weeping at the thought!

Boy soldiers have served in the British Army since its formation, and for many years there was no limit as to the age at which they could enlist. According to Brereton there are records of infants of seven being attested as drummers, buglers or trumpeters, and ten-year-olds were quite common. In 1844 a limit of fourteen years was established and remained in force until the end of the 1940s.

In the 1960s, when civilian airlines, and on military operations the Royal Air Force, took over the responsibility for troop movements overseas, troopships were converted to educational cruise liners (their age and facilities debarring them from being used as cruise ships). So ended a long tradition of reasonably comfortable and enjoyable four-week trips to the Far East and other parts of the world. With up to 1,600 troops aboard and little call for fatigue parties, there was plenty of time for training, such as firing at balloons over the stern of the ship, and for entertainment such as deck concerts, boxing tournaments and so forth. Cabins were available for senior ranks, but soldiers were down in the lowest three or four decks in much more crowded accommodation.

When the 2nd Battalion sailed to Malaya in 1948 on the *Empire Trooper* the event created quite an interest, because the Guards very seldom served East of Suez (people forgot that we had been in Shanghai in 1927), and we were being sent out to deal with the Malayan Emergency. 'Manny' Shinwell was the Minister of War at that time and he decided to come down to Southampton to see us off. Imagine the scene on the troop deck, where in a space six foot by six foot, on one side there were three folding bunks six foot by two foot and the same on the other side, leaving a space two foot by six foot in the centre. We were told to lower the bunks and then each man lay on them. 'Manny' Shinwell thus had a clear run for himself and his entourage to sweep through the troop-decks unimpeded and unhindered. As he passed through our area I heard him say, "There seems to be plenty of space down here," but as soon as the six Guardsmen got out of their bunks there was no room to spare whatsoever!

But calls in foreign ports proved a great educational experience and the journey allowed men to acclimatize before reaching their destination. Flying meant that one could leave England in the middle of winter and arrive in the tropics a few hours later and the heat would strike as soon as the aircraft doors were opened.

Recruiting

It was felt that some comment should be made on the situation regarding recruiting in the Regiment in 2000, for the Coldstream is the best-recruited within the Guards Division, and probably in the Infantry as a whole. It was thought that to discover the reasons why the Regiment recruits in certain areas would be an easy one, but this has not proved to be the case. For example, at one time Bristol, Gloucester, Leeds, Leicester, Norfolk and Sheffield were among the best recruiting areas, but this is no longer so. Middlesbrough, Newcastle and Sunderland, always the most prolific areas for Coldstream recruits, still remain the best for providing fine young men for the Regiment.

Why has the pattern of recruiting changed so dramatically? It did not help when a few years ago the areas of responsibility for various Regiments were changed and the Coldstream were allotted the North-East and the South-West. Could this have been because we spent our early years in the North-East, formed there and were commanded by an officer who had been born in Devon? Sadly, the Grenadiers have been allocated Birmingham, Leicester and some other areas which were originally ours.

This raises the question as to why we have such strong branches of The Coldstream Guards Association in towns and cities in which we are no longer allowed to recruit. The assumption can be made that because battalions were billeted in or near the areas in question this encouraged men to select the Coldstream when enlisting. Another theory is that when battalions were stationed for any length of time in a particular town a number of men married local girls and returned to live in that area when discharged. A good example of this is Aldershot where the 3rd Battalion was stationed in the 1930s. Many members married local girls, settled there eventually and produced fine young sons who followed father into the Regiment. Needless to say, the local branch has benefited enormously and no doubt other branches can say the same.

Notwithstanding the rules relating to the allocation of areas for recruiting, family ties and friendship still account for the success in attracting a large proportion of Coldstreamers, and long may this continue.

It is intriguing to try to make comparisons between the qualities of past and present Guardsmen. Major Mick Manning, Quartermaster of the 1st Battalion, has been helpful in questioning numerous senior ranks and he found that some of the views expressed were surprising. Nevertheless, he agreed with them.

Most old soldiers, ourselves included, assume that the modern Guardsmen must be brighter and better educated than they were. This view was based on the amount of technical equipment in use nowadays, including sophisticated Armoured Personnel Carriers, weapons and method of communication. Surprisingly, this does not appear to be the case.

Major Manning, who was the Gunnery Officer of the 1st Battalion in Germany, carried out his survey with Warrant and Non-Commissioned Officers and the conclusion is that they, and he himself, are of the opinion that the intelligence level required of a soldier has changed very little. The reasoning for this is that the old equipment was in many ways more difficult to operate than that in use now. For example, tuning in on a radio now is simpler, as the station required is 'keyed-in' rather than the old 'hit and miss' methods of the past; sights on modern weaponry are far more sophisticated and thus more accurate than arms which had fore and back sights to contend with.

First Line Maintenance on modern Personnel Carriers is little different to that used in the past, and the same can be said of most guns and small arms. A most important change appears to be in the levels of trust placed in junior Non-Commissioned Officers, and the best example of this has been in Northern Ireland. In 1969, when the troubles began, small patrols had to be commanded by an officer, warrant officer or full sergeant, whereas nowadays it is not uncommon for a lance corporal to command such a sub-unit. One reason for this is that methods of communication back to a headquarters are now much better and more reliable.

All those questioned in the survey agreed that the qualities required in a Guardsman remain the same as always – dynamism, self-reliance, physical fitness, energy, loyalty, integrity, courage of course, and plenty of initiative. We have no doubt that the Coldstreamer of today possesses the same qualities and the same overriding pride in his Regiment as did the Coldstreamer of 1650.

Those joining the Regiment nowadays are in most cases coming from a 'soft' civilian environment. For example the days of walking or riding a bicycle to school have virtually disappeared, children now being delivered by car or public transport. Soft 'trainer'-type footwear does nothing to prepare infantrymen for the types of boots issued on commencing training; initial training has had to be extended to allow recruits to get used to boots.

Moving the Guards Depot from Caterham to Pirbright, an 'open' camp, has not helped the instructional staff in any way whatsoever. The following humorous quote about Caterham Barracks says more in a serious way than as a joke: "It's the only place in the world which looks like a prison, where you're treated like a criminal, and yet you spend the rest of your life telling everyone how much you enjoyed it!" A proven fact is that when you left Caterham you felt 'ten feet tall' because you had survived such a tough environment.

If you mention the Guards Depot to any pre-war Guardsman he would recall the barrack room with twenty iron beds; three coir 'biscuits' for a mattress; his Trained Soldier, his introduction to the box crease in his trousers; the long puttee; evening 'shining parade' with a grilling on Regimental history; and sleeping on his uniform to obtain the perfect creases. Prior to Lights Out came the nightly cry "Stand by your beds" for hands and foot inspection. Then the constant changing khaki and buff equipment for drill, vest and shorts for P.T., khaki undress for education, canvas overalls and web equipment for musketry, and back to khaki for second drill period.[12]

In entering the new Millennium it is worth mentioning some of the aspects of modern-day soldiering. Extraordinary as it sounds, some Guardsmen joining the battalion from basic training are married with children. As they qualify for married quarters at eighteen this means more work for the administration staff. One asks the question – is a young couple ready to take on the responsibility of running a house, with or without children?

Those commissioned after serving in the ranks are now known as Late Entry (LE) officers, and there are far more opportunities for the good soldier to gain promotion. Interestingly, at the time of writing this book two LE officers are with the Irish Guards in Germany, one with the Scots Guards in Ireland and five more are serving away from the Regiment. There are four serving in the 1st Battalion.

Similarly, the openings for Warrant Officers Class One are out of all proportion to the strength of the Regiment. For many years there have been at least twenty Coldstream Warrant Officers serving away from the Regiment at the same time, and until recently we provided both the Academy Sergeant Major at Sandhurst and the Garrison Sergeant Major London District. These are recognized as the two senior RSM posts in the British Army.

Old soldiers visiting Wellington and Victoria Barracks have been pleasantly surprised at the excellent accommodation provided for even the most junior Guardsman. It is now commonplace for one, two, three or four-man rooms – with toilet and bathroom facilities for about every four men. This is a vast improvement on barrack rooms of thirty-two men with a urinal for about sixty-four and a W.C. between many more. Baths were even scarcer. Although food and accommodation are charged for and bills raised against soldiers when they are in the base camp or barracks, nobody complains about this whilst the standards are high. It goes without saying that when on operations the accommodation is either non-existent or very poor.

One decision about room inspections and kit layouts no longer being part of the daily routine has

[12] Letter from Sergeant J.V.Kelley, formerly Orderly Room Sergeant of the 3rd Battalion, December 1999.

not helped to maintain standards. Although unpopular with many junior ranks, the making up of 'bedding blocks' and regular inspections created excellent habits, both whilst serving and after becoming a civilian! As for blanket-shaking five minutes after reveille, the two authors still do this until this day (in their dreams anyhow)!

Earlier in the chapter mention was made that a Guardsman's pay is over £25 a day. This sounds good, but one has to realize that in theory anyhow a soldier is on call 365 days a year. Now that civilians have a minimum hourly rate of £3.60p this puts the soldiers' pay into realistic terms. The normal leave allowance is thirty days with an extra mandatory twenty-eight days' embarkation or posting leave and an additional twenty-eight days after an operational tour. With the 'overstretch' in the Army as a whole the latter tours are occurring fast and furious. Proof of the latter is apparent when one sees the large amount of campaign medals worn in the Regiment.

Almost forty per cent of the 1st Battalion are married, of which thirty-five per cent live in married quarters. Some of the other five per cent are purchasing their own houses and/or live in private accommodation by choice. Sadly, some of the junior ranks, with children, qualify for financial support from the social services. Happily, a Guardsman can afford a pint, or two, not like in 1890 when it had to be laid down that he was to receive an income of 2d a day!

Not many years ago boys' service, including Junior Leaders and Junior Soldiers Regiments, was done away with. This was sad as many senior ranks in the Regiment started life in these units. When General Sir Michael Rose was the Adjutant General in the late 1990s he reintroduced these and there is every reason to think that this regiment, and many others, will benefit enormously. The pity is that the minimum age is sixteen and a half. As mentioned earlier, it was fourteen and this was only raised in line with the school-leaving age.

Nowadays the opportunities for sport of any type and adventurous training are enormous. Individuals and teams from the Regiment continue to do well in numerous events. We are always well represented in the London Marathon and make a lot of money for charities. The pace stick team from the 1st Battalion won the 1999 World Championship and was rewarded with a trip to South Africa to train teams there. Platoons and Companies from the Regiment have visited too many places to list here.

Two problems for the future. Firstly, how will the serving soldiers react to homosexuals being allowed to serve in the Armed Forces? Secondly, will women be allowed to serve in infantry regiments? Certainly, in the 'politically correct' climate that now exists, life for the officers and non-commissioned officers will not become easier. No doubt they will meet these challenges as well as their predecessors.

350 Years On

Much has changed during the last 100 years and the Coldstreamer of today lives a very different life to his forbear of 1900, let alone 1650. But one thing has not changed over the 350 years and that is his spirit and also the spirit of the Regiment. Every member of it has always been determined in peace and war to be 'Second to None' in maintaining the qualities that really matter in life – *courage*, self-discipline, honesty, *loyalty* and pride in being a Coldstreamer.

Notes on Authors

John Hook joined the Regiment in September 1945. He served with all three Regular battalions before ending up at Regimental Headquarters as Superintending Clerk, and was discharged in 1972. He then became a Judge's clerk for twenty-four years and in 1976 became a member of the Queen's Body Guard of the Yeomen of the Guard and served for 22 years, finishing as a Messenger Sergeant Major. He was awarded the Royal Victorian Medal. He is Secretary of the Bath Branch of The Coldstream Guards Association.

Major Peter Horsfall enlisted in the Regiment as a Drummer Boy at the age of 16 in 1946. His military career saw service with the 2nd Battalion and also at the Guards Depot, RMA Sandhurst and two tours of duty at Mons Officer Cadet School, the latter of these as the Regimental Sergeant Major. In 1972 he was given a Regular Quartermaster Commission in the Regiment and also awarded the MBE. He was Quartermaster of the 2nd Battalion from 1975–1978, and of the Guards Depot from 1978 until his retirement from the Army in 1980. In the same year he was appointed Staff Superintendent at the House of Lords and held that appointment until his retirement in 1995.

CHAPTER FIFTEEN

THE REGIMENT – TODAY AND TOMORROW

by Tom Mollo and James Rous

The year 2000 marks the 350th anniversary of the Coldstream Guards and the start of a new millennium. These two ideas of continuity and change can be said to sum up the Regiment of today: the 1st Battalion has recently returned from active service in South Armagh, where it was equipped with some of the most advanced equipment used by the Army, while Number 7 Company, based in Chelsea Barracks, has been carrying out the more traditional task of Public Duties. The Regiment in recent years has indeed proved itself to be equally adept in these two distinct areas of 'green' and 'red' soldiering, illustrating the versatility and professionalism of our soldiers of which we are so proud.

Before we look to what the future holds for our Regiment, we must examine first the state of play at the end of the 1990s. The current structure was shaped by the 1991 'Options for Change' Government White Paper. Most notably this placed the 2nd Battalion into suspended animation in 1993. However, Number 7 Company was created at this time as an incremental company and maintains the Colours and customs of the 2nd Battalion, so that when the time comes the 2nd Battalion will be re-established with ease! The Regimental Band survived 'Options for Change', albeit at a reduced size. Within the 1st Battalion are reflected changes which occurred Army-wide, for example, the disappearance of Coldstream cooks and clerks since the births of the Royal Logistic Corps and the Adjutant General's Corps respectively. All in all, the Coldstream Guards has been lucky enough to have preserved its identity, through what has been a period of amalgamation and disbandment for many others, and we remain the oldest British Regiment in continuous existence.

The 1st Battalion consists of three rifle companies, Number 4 (Support) Company, Headquarter Company and the Corps of Drums. Each rifle company consists of three platoons, and Number 4 (Support) Company consists of the Mortar Platoon, the Anti-Tank Platoon, the Reconnaissance Platoon and the Signal Platoon. Headquarter Company consists of the Battalion Headquarters (including the Regimental Administration Office), the Quartermaster's Department, the Mechanical Transport Platoon, the Light Aid Detachment, the Training Wing, the Regimental Police Staff, the Gymnasium Staff, the Medical Centre, the Mess Staff and the Corps of Drums, which is currently the Machine Gun Platoon. Number 7 Company has the structure of a rifle company with increased administrative support. Regimental Headquarters has been reduced in size over the last few years, but continues to provide support to Coldstreamers past and present. The Band now consists of forty-nine musicians, after a reduction in the scale of all regimental bands which occurred in 1987. The

Regimental Association continues to thrive and currently consists of thirty-six branches, including many extremely loyal Coldstreamers worldwide in Canada, South Africa, Hong Kong, Australia and New Zealand.

An examination of the recent commitments of the Regiment reveals the diverse and complicated demands facing the Coldstreamer of today. The size of the Regiment was reduced as a result of 'Options for Change' and the desire for a peace dividend following the end of the Cold War. But the world has not proved itself to be a safer place; indeed, in 1991 the 1st Battalion was deployed to the Gulf to take part in a conventional warfare operation. The Regiment has completed seventeen tours in Northern Ireland, many of which have involved reinforcing other battalions. In the Balkans the 1st Battalion deployed to Bosnia in 1993–4; more recently the best part of a company deployed to Kosovo with 1st Battalion Irish Guards, and seventeen Coldstreamers reinforced the Household Cavalry Regiment in Bosnia. In 1995 the 1st Battalion provided The Queen's Royal Lancers with a platoon for service with the United Nations contingent in Cyprus. In April 2000 Number 8 Company, consisting of Company Headquarters and two Coldstream platoons and one platoon from the Irish Guards, formed as part of 1st Battalion Scots Guards in Wellington Barracks. So, in terms of active service the Regiment continues to be busy: however, the nature of UN, NATO and other peace-keeping commitments requires Coldstreamers to operate in unfamiliar environments, within and alongside varied organizations, and with complex rules of engagement. Add to these the intellectual challenges posed by technological advances, and it becomes clear that the nature of a Coldstreamer's operational duty today is vastly different from what has been seen in the past.

Throughout this period, on the other hand, the obligations of Public Duties in London and Windsor have remained largely unchanged. London ceremonial continues to foster the traditional qualities of discipline and turnout for which the Foot Guards enjoy world-wide renown. 1999 saw the 1st Battalion Trooping its Colour and 2000 was the turn of Number 7 Company in the Foot Guards' traditional tribute to their Colonel-in-Chief on her Official Birthday. Guards of Honour are still provided for State Visits and for other State occasions such as the State Opening of Parliament. Young officers can still be seen during periods of Spring Drills being put through their paces by Drill Sergeants!

The changes in the shape of soldiering are also marked in non-operational fields. The end of the Cold War has altered the disposition of the British Army around the world. As the strength of the British Army base in Germany has decreased, so the variety of locations open for training has increased. Coldstreamers now serve in many corners of the globe and recent years have seen large-scale training taking place in areas including Canada, Belize, Jamaica and the Falkland Islands. Furthermore, the end of the Cold War has allowed British troops to exercise in Poland and Hungary. Battle Group-level exercises in Poland produced the spectacle of trainloads of Coldstreamers and their armoured vehicles moving east through Germany and across the Polish border – to a rapturous welcome!

The Regiment continues to support adventurous training and sport, firstly because it is accepted that these activities enhance the operational effectiveness of the soldiers by fostering team spirit, willpower, self-confidence and leadership. In addition, the high regard in which such activities are held in the Regiment stems in part from an acceptance of the doctrine that "soldiering must be fun"! Whenever possible, teams and individuals are encouraged to take part in the sports in which they excel, from inter-company up to Army level, in sports including football, squash, rugby, golf and tennis. Although the workload remains high for all elements of the Regiment, it has still been possible to run some very successful adventurous training: in one year expeditions were mounted to Corsica, Italy, South Africa, Cyprus and Bavaria. Each year, if operational commitments allow, a team is sent to Val d'Isère in order to take part in the Infantry Alpine Skiing Training Camp and Championships. Recent years have seen great successes for the team; however, their significance is small in comparison to the spectacle of a Guardsman, probably a novice skier, completing a World Cup standard downhill course after only six weeks of skiing, travelling at speeds of up to sixty miles an hour.

In no area is the contrast between progress and tradition more marked than in that of equipment. This has set great challenges for the Quartermaster's Department! Some of the equipment used by soldiers today is almost unrecognizable to generations of Coldstreamers past. In the last few years every individual has witnessed the introduction of a new rifle and new combat clothing. The introduction of the Warrior infantry fighting vehicle has created the armoured infantry role. Over the next few years the process of digitization will transform the battlefield as new communications equipment is introduced: every individual will have a radio and all commanders will be required to be computer literate in order to operate their portable ruggedized 'laptops'. On the other hand Coldstreamers continue to wear real bearskin caps, and the tunic which has had the same basic pattern since 1856! Guardsmen continue to wear the buff belt while the rest of the Army have adopted plastic ones. Our Corps of Drums still uses the rope tension drums rather than the modern rod tension drums used everywhere else in the Armed Forces, the result of a triumph of common sense by the 27th Colonel!

The pattern of life also exemplifies a healthy blend of past and present. The Battalion is woken up by the duty drummer sounding Reveille before breakfast in a modern and well-equipped cookhouse. Training during the day is as likely to involve a Queen's Guard check parade as it is to consist of Armoured Fighting Vehicle (AVF) recognition on the Anti-Tank Platoon's computer simulators. Those who are unlucky enough to be on Commanding Officer's Orders go through the same form-up and procedure as their predecessors, but find that the process of military law has altered over the years in keeping with modern legislation. The Battalion Forecast of Events will include both modern additions, such as mandatory briefs for all ranks on 'Health and Safety at Work', 'Equal Opportunities' and 'Drug Awareness', and more traditional red-letter days such as Black Sunday, Hanging the Brick and St George's Day. A Non-Commissioned Officer may find himself on one day running a range on the Small Arms Trainer (an indoor computer-generated range) and on the next as Sergeant-in-Waiting for his company, maintaining the In-Waiting book in the same way as generations of his predecessors.

Coldstreamers have had to rise to the challenges of becoming proficient in the use of increasingly advanced technologies on the battlefield, keeping pace with modern legislation and matching the ever-changing nature of the Regiment's commitments. However, as recruits in training, while serving with the Colours, and in meeting these challenges, they continue to identify strongly with the ethos that has inspired their predecessors to perform some of the extreme acts of unselfishness, commitment and heroism that have shaped the narrative of this book.

The Coldstream is in a healthy state for the future, continuing to recruit more and better soldiers than any other infantry regiment. In meeting modern technical and operational challenges with the traditional Coldstream approach of high standards and professionalism, the Coldstreamer of today is no less of a giant than his predecessors of old. The Regiment is set to add many more fine years to its glorious first three hundred and fifty.

Note on Authors

Captain Tom Mollo was commissioned into the Coldstream Guards in 1995. He served with the 1st Battalion in Germany, Northern Ireland and Windsor. In 1998 he was appointed Temporary Equerry to The Queen and the Regimental Recruiting Officer. He retired from the Army in August 2000.

Captain James Rous was commissioned into the Coldstream Guards in 1996. He was posted to the 1st Battalion, at that time in Northern Ireland, and then Germany, where he served as a platoon commander. On returning to Windsor he was appointed Regimental Signals Officer. He succeeded Captain Mollo as Temporary Equerry to The Queen and Regimental Recruiting Officer.

APPENDIX A

BATTLE HONOURS

by Lewis Pearce

Although Battle Honours date back to the seventeenth century, they were not carried on Colours until 1813, and they have been awarded at varying intervals after the battle concerned. Not all the Battle Honours awarded are carried on the Colours. In the case of both the First and Second World Wars Regiments had the unenviable task of having to select only ten from each of the many awarded to appear on the Colours. Since around 1890 it has been the custom to deck the Colours with a laurel wreath on the anniversaries of certain campaigns, battles and actions in which the Regiment has distinguished itself. There are forty such occasions in the Coldstream.

Coldstream Battle Honours

The Regiment has a total of 113 Battle Honours, 44 of which (shown in capital letters) are borne upon the Queen's and Regimental Colours.

TANGIER 1680, NAMUR 1695, GIBRALTAR 1704-5 OUDENARDE, MALPLAQUET, DETTINGEN, THE SPHINX (superscribed 'EGYPT'), LINCELLES, TALAVERA, BARROSA, FUENTES d'ONOR, SALAMANCA, NIVE, PENINSULA, WATERLOO, ALMA, INKERMAN, SEVASTOPOL, TEL-EL-KEBIR, EGYPT 1882, SUAKIN 1885, MODDER RIVER, SOUTH AFRICA 1899–1902

First World War

Mons, RETREAT FROM MONS, MARNE 1914, AISNE 1914, YPRES 1914, 17; Langemarck 1914, Gheluvelt, Nonne Bosschen, Givenchy 1914, Neuve Chapelle, Aubers, Festubert 1915, LOOS, Mount Sorel, SOMME 1916, 18; Flers-Courcelette, Morval, Pilckem, Menin Road, Poelcapelle, Passchendaele, CAMBRAI 1917, 18; St Quentin, Bapaume 1918, ARRAS 1918, Lys, HAZEBROUCK, Albert 1918, Scarpe 1918, Drocourt-Queant, HINDENBURG LINE, Havrincourt, Canal du Nord, Selle, Sambre, France and Flanders 1914–18.

Second World War

Dyle, Defence of Escaut, DUNKIRK 1940, Cagny, MONT PINCON, Quarry Hill, Estry, Heppen, Nederrijn, Venraij, Meijel, Roer, RHINELAND, Reichswald, Cleve, Goch, Moyland, Hochwald, Rhine, Lingen, Uelzen, NORTH-WEST EUROPE 1940, 44–45; Egyptian Frontier 1940, SIDI

BARRANI, Halfaya 1941, TOBRUK 1941, 1942; Msus, Knightsbridge, Defence of Alamein Line, Medenine, Mareth, Longstop Hill 1942, Sbiba, Steamroller Farm, TUNIS, Hamman Lif, North Africa 1940–43, SALERNO, Battipaglia, Cappezano, Volturno Crossing, Monte Camino, Calabritto, Garigliano Crossing, MONTE ORNITO, Monte Piccolo, Capture of Perugia, Arezzo, Advance to Florence, Monte Domini, Catarelto Ridge, Argenta Gap, ITALY 1943–45.

Post War

GULF 1991

Note on Author

Lewis Pearce enlisted in the Coldstream in 1972 as a Junior Guardsman, and completed 22 years of adult service in 1996, attaining the rank of Sergeant. The latter part of his service was spent as the Orderly Room Clerk in Regimental Headquarters, following earlier service in the 2nd Battalion. He is Secretary of the London Branch of The Coldstream Guards Association.

APPENDIX B

VICTORIA CROSS & GEORGE CROSS HOLDERS

by Lewis Pearce

Crimean War

3968 Private William STANLAKE VC DCM (sometimes known as Stanlack or Stanlock)
Brevet Major (later Lieutenant Colonel) John Augustus CONOLLY VC
Brevet Major (later Lieutenant General) Gerald Littlehales GOODLAKE VC
4787 Private George STRONG VC

First World War

5854 Lance Corporal (later Lance Sergeant) George Harry WYATT VC
6840 Lance Corporal Frederick William DOBSON VC
6738 Lance Sergeant (later Sergeant) Oliver BROOKS VC
Major and Brevet Lieutenant Colonel (later Brigadier General) John Vaughan CAMPBELL VC CMG DSO
15067 Lance Corporal Thomas WHITHAM VC
Lieutenant (later Honorary Captain) Cyril Hubert FRISBY VC
20810 Private (Acting Lance Corporal) Thomas Norman JACKSON VC

Second World War

Lieutenant (Temporary Captain) Ian Oswald LIDDELL VC
2657545 Warrant Officer Class 2 (CSM) Peter Harold WRIGHT VC
War Substantive Major/Temporary Lieutenant Colonel (Acting Brigadier) Arthur Frederick Crane NICHOLLS GC

APPENDIX C

COLONELS OF THE REGIMENT

by Lewis Pearce

It is impossible to pick out particular individuals from among the twenty-eight Colonels of the Regiment during the 350 years of its existence, but mention should be made of three great Coldstreamers in this century who between them served no less than 76 years as Colonel.

Lieutenant General Sir Alfred Codrington GCVO KCB (Colonel 1918–1945) was commissioned in 1873 and saw active service in Egypt (1882), South Africa (1899–1900), where he was severely wounded, and the First World War, where he commanded Third Army in UK. During his twenty-

The 24th Colonel of the Regiment, Lieutenant General Sir Alfred Codrington GCVO KCB.

The 25th Colonel of the Regiment, General Sir Charles Loyd GCVO KCB DSO MC.

The 26th Colonel of the Regiment, Major General Sir George Burns GCVO CB DSO OBE MC.

The 27th Colonel of the Regiment, Lieutenant General the Hon Sir William Rous KCB OBE.

seven years as Colonel, he showed tremendous pride in being a Coldstreamer and saw the Association well established. His father and his son both served in the Regiment.

General Sir Charles Loyd GCVO KCB DSO MC (Colonel 1945–1966) joined the Regiment in 1910 and during the First World War established an outstanding record as a fighting soldier, winning a DSO and MC and being three times Mentioned in Despatches. In World War Two he commanded 2nd Division in France and then became GOC-in-C Southern Command and GOC London District where he was responsible for uniting the Household Cavalry and the Brigade of Guards to form the Household Division. His son Julian also served in the Regiment.

Major General Sir George Burns GCVO CB DSO OBE MC (Colonel 1966–1994) was another very fine fighting soldier, winning a MC in France in 1940 and a DSO in Italy in 1943. He devoted his life to the Regiment and the Regiment was devoted to him, particularly the members of the Association, where his enthusiasm and bonhomie became legendary.

"'George Burns, The Coldstreamer' was in every sense 'Second to None.'" These words were written by his successor as Colonel, **Lieutenant General the Honourable Sir William Rous KCB OBE**, who sadly died of cancer, aged 60, after only five years as Colonel. But he too showed in that short time an immense pride in the Coldstream and in being the 27th Colonel. His son, James, is now serving in the Regiment.

COLONELS OF THE REGIMENT 1650–2000

1. George Monck, Duke of Albemarle, KG, Captain General, 1650–1669.
2. William, Earl of Craven, Lieutenant General, 1669–1689.
3. Thomas Talmash (or Tolemache), Lieutenant General, 1689–1694.
4. John, Lord Cutts, Lieutenant General, 1694–1706.
5. Charles Churchill, General, 1707–1714.
6. The Right Honourable William, Earl Cadogan, KT, Lieutenant General, 1714–1722.
7. Richard Lumley, Earl of Scarborough, KG, 1722–1740.
8. HRH, William, Duke of Cumberland, KG, Field Marshal, 1740–1741.
9. Charles, 3rd Duke of Marlborough, KG, 1742–1744.
10. The Right Honourable William Keppel, Earl of Albemarle, 1744–1755.
11. James O'Hara, 2nd Lord Tyrawley, Field Marshal, 1755–1773.
12. The Right Honourable John Waldegrave, 3rd Earl Waldegrave, KG, General, 1773–1784.
13. HRH, Frederick, Duke of York, KG, Field Marshal, 1784–1805.
14. HRH, Frederick Adolphus, Duke of Cambridge, KG, Field Marshal, 1805–1850.
15. John Byng, Earl of Strafford, GCB, Field Marshal, 1850–1860.
16. Colin, Lord Clyde, GCB, General, 1860–1863.
17. Sir William Maynard Gomm, GCB, Field Marshal, 1863–1875.
18. Sir William Codrington, GCB, General, 1875–1884.
19. The Right Honourable Sir Thomas Steel, GCB, General, 1884–1890.
20. The Honourable Sir Arthur Hardinge, KCB, CIE, General, 1890–1892.
21. Sir Frederick C. Stephenson, GCB, General, 1892–1911.
22. Lord William Frederick Ernest Seymour, KCVO, General, 1911–1915.
23. Evelyn Edward Thomas, 7th Viscount Falmouth, 1915–1918.
24. Sir Alfred Codrington, GCVO, KCB, Lieutenant General, 1918–1945.
25. Sir Charles Loyd, KCB, KCVO, DSO, MC, General, 1945–1966.
26. Sir George Burns, GCVO, CB, DSO, OBE, MC, Major General, 1966–1994.
27. The Honourable Sir William Rous, KCB, OBE, Lieutenant General, 1994–1999.
28. Sir Michael Rose, KCB, CBE, DSO, QGM, General, 1999–

APPENDIX D

THE COLOURS

by Bill Corbould

The State Colours

The State Colours of the Coldstream Guards are thought to have been presented to the Regiment by King William IV. They are carried by Guards of Honour, (not formed from The Queen's Guard) mounted on Her Majesty The Queen on State occasions. The State Colours are kept at Regimental Headquarters.

a. First State Colour

Gules (Crimson); in the centre the Star of the Order of the Garter proper, within the Union Wreath or, ensigned with the Crown, in each of the four corners a Sphinx argent, between two branches of laurel fructed and tied with a riband or. In the centre below the Star of the Order of the Garter, on a scroll azure, the word 'Egypt' or, with the following distinctions:

Lincelles, Talavera, Barrosa, Peninsula, Waterloo

b. Second State Colour

Gules (Crimson); in the centre the Star of the Order of the Garter proper, within the Union Wreath or, ensigned with the Crown, in each of the four corners, a Sphinx argent between two branches of laurel fructed and tied with a riband or, superscribed 'Egypt' also or, with the following honorary distinctions in addition to those borne on the First State Colour:

Alma, Inkerman, Sevastopol

Battalion Colours

Each Battalion has two Colours which are held within the Battalion and are carried on ceremonial occasions. The Queen's (or King's) Colour is crimson and the Regimental Colour is the Union Flag. Both are embroidered with 44 of the Regiment's 113 Battle Honours, as at Appendix A.

Number 7 Company, which was formed on 1st January 1994 when the 2nd Battalion was placed in 'suspended animation', was then given the privilege of continuing to carry the Colours of the 2nd Battalion, as well as maintaining its customs and traditions.

New Colours were presented to both the 1st Battalion and Number 7 Company by The Queen at Windsor Castle on 20 May 1999.

Company Colours

In addition to the Battalion Colours, each Company has its own Company Colour, made of either silk or bunting. The bunting Colours are used to mark Company Headquarters in peace and war, while those of silk are used as points on ceremonial parades. Each is a small version of the Union Flag and is embroidered with the number and badge of the Company, but does not carry any Battle Honours.

The Commanding Officer also has his own Colour in silk, which is used to mark Battalion Headquarters. In addition there are two silk Colours, one for the Colonel of the Regiment and the other for the Regimental Lieutenant Colonel. Both Colours are carried only when these two officers are on parade.

Note on Author

Lieutenant Colonel Bill Corbould was commissioned into the Regiment in 1941. He served in the 2nd Battalion in Italy 1944–45 and was twice wounded. He transferred to The Parachute Regiment in 1958. He is President of the Aldershot Branch of The Coldstream Guards Association.

APPENDIX E

COLDSTREAM UNIFORMS, 1650–2000

by Julian Paget

The Coldstreamer of 1650 was not a particularly military-looking figure, for, apart from his weapons, he was dressed very much as a civilian, his clothing depending on the whim (and the purse) of the Colonel of his Regiment.

If he was a Musketeer, he wore a broad-brimmed, felt hat with one or more red feathers at the back, a loose red jacket, dark blue breeches and shoes or high boots. He carried a heavy musket, weighing some thirteen pounds and so cumbersome that he had to use an aiming rest to fire it; slung round him was a belt of twelve charges of gunpowder (known as 'the Twelve Apostles').

About a third of each regiment were Pikemen, and they wore light armour[1] consisting of a helmet, a 'breast' and a 'back'. They carried a 16-foot pike intended to keep cavalry at bay, abandoned in 1770.

The Coldstreamer was recognizable by two features. First the feathers in his hat were red, whereas those of the Royal Regiment, later the Grenadier Guards, were white. Second, Coldstream officers at that time, being part of the New Model Army, wore white ribbons on their shoulders, and the Grenadiers, being Royalist, wore red.

When grenadier companies were formed in 1678 they wore first a mitre cap and then a bearskin with a white plume. The light companies (formed in the 1770s) wore green plumes.

In 1768 several changes occurred and distinctions between regiments became more evident. Breeches became white and the headgear was a tricorne hat. Coldstream officers and men began from 1772 to wear their buttons in pairs and the loops on the jackets were also in pairs, with the First Guards being single and the Third Guards in threes. The Guardsmen also had pewter buttons inscribed 'Coldstream Guards'.

The next major change came in 1832 when it was decided that all companies of the Coldstream and Third Guards, and not just the grenadier companies, should wear the bearskin cap. The First Guards already had a white plume on the left, since this had always been the custom in the grenadier companies. The Coldstream chose a red plume on the right, while the Third Guards had no plume. This meant that when the three regiments were in line in their traditional positions (First Guards on the right, Coldstream on the left, with the Third Guards in the centre) all the plumes faced inwards and the commander could identify each regiment, be it on parade or in battle.

Regiments also wore distinctive badges on each side of the collar of their coatee and the Coldstream chose a white rose.[2] They also wore their buttons in pairs, and this has continued ever since, so that, at least in Home Service clothing, each regiment is clearly identifiable.

[1] Abandoned in 1660

[2] Worn today on the shoulder.

A further distinction came in 1834 with the introduction of the Forage Cap; this gave the opportunity for the Coldstream to use the Garter star, which had been granted to them in 1696 by King William III and also to wear a distinctive cap band. The First Guards chose red, as being the Royal colour, and the Coldstream opted for white.

Such was the order of dress in which Coldstreamers fought in the Crimean War in 1854, but it was clearly totally unsuitable for the campaigns in Egypt, Sudan and South Africa at the end of the century. Tropical clothing was therefore introduced in 1882, with pith helmets and then slouch hats, on both of which the Coldstream wore a red plume.

Home Service clothing remained, of course, for ceremonial duties, but from 1902 khaki Service Dress was issued with plus fours and puttees. Regimental designations were adopted on the shoulders together with Roman numerals to denote the battalion. Leather equipment was replaced by webbing.

The Second World War brought Battle Dress, with webbing gaiters replacing puttees, and denims being used for fatigues. A variety of headgear appeared, in particular berets in various hues. Designations and numerals to indicate battalions were used as in 1914–1918, and divisional signs were also worn on the shoulders.

The 1960s brought Combat Dress with the Disruptive Pattern Material (DPM) smock and trousers following later, and this is still in use. It aims at maximum anonymity with regard to both rank and regiment, and only the cap or beret offers an identification that the wearer is a Coldstreamer.

APPENDIX F

THE REGIMENTAL BAND AND CORPS OF DRUMS

by David Marshall

The Regimental Band was formed in 1785 when twelve German musicians were enlisted by The Duke of York, Colonel of the Regiment, and were sent to England to replace the eight civilian performers, who had up to that time provided the music for the King's Guard. They were led by Music Master Christopher Eley, remembered today for his slow march 'Duke of York'.

Mr Eley was succeeded by John Weyrauch in 1800 who in turn was followed by James Denman in 1815. Thomas Lindsay was appointed Bandmaster in 1818. Under his guidance, the Coldstream Band became renowned for its woodwind section, producing most famously Henry Lazarus, who later became principal clarinettist with the Opera Orchestra in 1840.

The German connection remained strong until 1825 when the first English conductor was appointed. Charles Godfrey served for thirty-eight years and was founder of the dynasty that was to have such a marked influence on military music. When he completed his military service in 1834

The Coldstream 'German Band' at St James's Palace, 1790.

the officers of the Regiment retained him as a civilian bandmaster until his death at the age of 73. He was succeeded in 1863 by his second son, Frederick Adolphus.

After more than half a century of Godfreys, Cadwallader Thomas, who had joined the Coldstream Band in 1853, took up the post of Bandmaster. He was another outstanding musician and clarinettist who had the misfortune to serve between, and thus be overshadowed by, the two Godfreys and the next incumbent, John Mackenzie Rogan.

Mackenzie Rogan was the first Bandmaster in the Brigade of Guards to be granted a substantive commission, being promoted to the rank of 2nd Lieutenant in 1904. After rising through the ranks, he retired as a Lieutenant Colonel. Never before had a serving bandmaster or director of music attained this rank. For twenty years Colonel Mackenzie Rogan was the Senior Director of Music of the Brigade of Guards. During this period he was responsible for the Massed Bands of the Brigade at the funeral of Queen Victoria, the coronation and funeral of King Edward VII and the coronation of King George V. He retired in 1920 and was succeeded by Lieutenant Robert Evans. By that time the strength of the Band had risen over the years to sixty-five.

Robert Evans had served in the Coldstream Guards as a musician and, after holding appointments as Bandmaster with The Highland Light Infantry and the Royal Garrison Artillery at Plymouth, he returned to the Regiment as Director of Music from 1920 to 1930. His successor was Lieutenant James Causley Windram. In January 1942 Major Windram was appointed Senior Director of Music of the Brigade of Guards, but it was to be a tragically short-lived appointment. On 18 June 1944, during a service in the Guards Chapel, at which Major Windram was conducting a section of the Band, a German V 1 rocket crashed through the roof and exploded. Among the 120 fatalities were Major Windram and five of the musicians, a further twelve members of the Band being injured.

Douglas Pope, Bandmaster of the Royal Army Service Corps, was immediately flown home from Italy where he was on tour playing to Allied troops and became Director of Music. In 1960 he was appointed Senior Director of Music of the Brigade of Guards. On his retirement in 1963 he was succeeded by Captain Trevor Sharpe, who, apart from his many appearances at State functions, Tattoos and massed bands events, achieved a degree of fame for conducting the Band in the playing of the signature tune for the television series 'Dad's Army'.

In 1974 Major Sharpe was promoted to Lieutenant Colonel on his appointment as Director of Music at Kneller Hall and was succeeded by Captain Richard Ridings, who in turn was promoted to Lieutenant Colonel in 1976 on his appointment as Senior Director of Music, Household Division. Under his direction the Regimental Band undertook many international commitments which included tours to North America, Australia and New Zealand. Captain Roger Swift succeeded Colonel Ridings in 1985 and during his time as Director of Music the Regimental Band became the first band to tour Japan as guests of the Japan Orchestral Society. Major Swift was succeeded by Captain David Marshall in 1990. Since then, in addition to the many Public and State Duties, the Band has also undertaken a further four visits to Japan and one to Australia and North America. Captain Ian McElligott succeeded Major Marshall as Director of Music in 1999.

As with all British Military Bands, the musicians are also trained as Regimental Medical Assistants. During the Gulf War in 1991 the Band deployed in a casualty evacuation role. In 1994 it flew to war-torn Bosnia to play at a football match in the Olympic Stadium in Sarajevo to participate in the festivities to celebrate the lifting of the blockade, within range of Serb guns directed on the stadium! The gesture won international acclaim, television pictures of the symbolic event being shown around the world.

The strength of the Regimental Band in 1970 was still sixty-five, but by 1987 this had become forty-nine – a significant reduction. Within that number there are today a variety of groups specializing in strings, fanfare trumpets and dance music. Many of the musicians are graduates with degrees in music, or have been members of top-class brass bands before enlisting.

The Band has been immensely fortunate to have had the services of so many outstanding musicians during its long and distinguished history and it remains a supremely important element of the Regiment.

Regimental Music

The Regimental Slow March 'Figaro' was taken from Mozart's Opera *The Marriage of Figaro* and was adopted by the Regiment in 1805.

The Regimental Quick March 'Milanollo' was composed in February 1846 by Johann Valentin Hamm and was dedicated by him to Miss Teresa Milanollo, one of two sisters, who were both musically gifted. Teresa was born in Sarigliano near Turin in 1827, and she and her younger sister Maria achieved considerable international fame playing violin duets, which included a visit to England in 1845. Their individual playing talents earned them the respective nicknames of Madamoiselle Adagio and Madamoiselle Staccato![1]

Miss Teresa Milanollo.

'Milanollo-Marsch', originally composed for the piano, was published later in 1846 by sons of B.Schott, who had agents in such centres of musical excellence as Vienna, and also had a shop in London at 159 Regent Street.[1] The official arrangement as a Regimental March was authorized in 1882.

THE CORPS OF DRUMS

Unlike the Regimental Band, the Corps of Drums is part of the Battalion and, as such, has always been available whenever needed on the line of march. Drummers initially signalled the Commanding Officer's tactical orders; later drum and fife regulated the soldiers' day in camp or quarters, something which continues to this day with Long Reveille. The turn into the nineteenth century saw bugles slowly replaced by signalling drums. Drummers at this stage were established to companies. When first they functioned as a Corps is not apparent, but it is generally thought to have been at

[1] Letter from Major Richard Powell, 26 April 1999

about the time of the Cardwell Reforms of 1872. Napoleon, though, is known to have massed his drummers on the battlefield to good effect.[2]

'The Drums' date from 1650 when the Regiment contained one Drum Major and twenty Drummers. Their current establishment is twenty-eight. They were trained as machine gunners in their secondary role, but have invariably formed a rifle platoon on active service. Although their training in a secondary role as machine gunners ceased at the end of 1999 their operational role for the future is still under debate. One drummer is established to No 7 Company.

Coldstreamers have been pre-eminent in the world of drums music for the greater part of the twentieth century. Battle, Poole and Shrimpton, all outstanding composers, were followed between the two World Wars by such as W.Godden, who became the Senior Drum Major in the British Army. After the Second World War Drum Majors H.Appleby and T.Birkett maintained the Coldstream pre-eminence, with the latter famed for the composition of 'Hazelmere' and 'The Adjutant', only relaxing his composing in the 1990s with his final marches 'Buttons in Twos' and 'The 27th Colonel'.

Coldstream Drum Majors post-1945 have continued to influence not only their own Regiment but also many other Regiments throughout the Army. Perhaps the best known in a distinguished list are A.Austin, G.Carter, S.Ward, P.Kirk and J.McIllree MBE. Many others not named have been a part of this unique Coldstream History.

Note on Author

Major David Marshall has had a distinguished career in military music which spans four decades. He has, in turn, been Director of Music to the Bands of the Royal Armoured Corps and Royal Corps of Transport. He was appointed Director of Music to the Band of the Coldstream Guards in 1990 and retired from the Army in 1999.

[2] Letter from Major Richard Powell, 9 December 1999.

APPENDIX G

THE COLDSTREAM GUARDS ASSOCIATION

by Christopher Louch

Colonel C.S.O.Monck commanded the Coldstream Guards in 1913 and at a dinner given to the National Reserve of the Regiment after a review by His Majesty King George V on the 28 April 1913 he announced his intention of forming an Association of Coldstreamers. The announcement was enthusiastically received.

The Objectives of the Association were drawn up by the Committee in April 1913 and were:

To foster a spirit of comradeship among all ranks of the Regiment, past and present.
To organize meetings of members of each Branch.
To make the Regiment known and so to assist in recruiting.
To assist members who are leaving, or who have left the Regiment, to obtain employment.
To bring to the notice of Headquarters any case deserving of assistance from Regimental Funds which are at the disposal of the Lieutenant Colonel Commanding.

Brigadier General C.S.O. Monck, the Founder of the Old Coldstreamers Association.

These Objectives have stood the test of time for, although the wording has slightly changed, the meaning is still the same.

The Rules for the Association were also drawn up by the first Committee, were published in June 1913, and were as follows:

1. All Coldstreamers, past and present, of at least three years' service are eligible to become members. Serving members will be Honorary Members. All elections to be subject to the final approval of the Headquarters Committee.
2. Subscriptions for Members and Honorary members will be 2/- (10p) per year, payable before the 1st April in each year. Officers, past and present, may become Life Members on a payment of £2.2s 0p (Two Guineas) or upwards.
3. Members in arrears with the annual subscription to be struck off the roll.
4. The Headquarters Committee is formed as follows:
   President: The Regimental Lieutenant Colonel.
   Vice President and Chairman of Committee: to be elected at the Annual General Meeting and to hold office for one year.
   Members: One Officer per Battalion. One WO or NCO per Battalion. One Representative of each Branch Committee. Regimental Adjutant. Regimental Sergeant Major (Superintending Clerk).
   Treasurer: Regimental Adjutant.
   Honorary Secretary: Regimental Sergeant Major.
   This Committee is the governing body of The Association.
5. Branch Committees to consist of a President, an Honorary Secretary, and three or more members.
6. A Branch may be formed in any district or town under the authority of the Headquarters Committee.
7. The Presidents of local Branches are responsible for the funds of their Branches.
8. A General Meeting of the Association will be held annually in London during the month of May.
9. Annual Meetings of Branches are to be held in April, and their annual reports will be forwarded so as to reach the Honorary Secretary of the Headquarters Committee by 1st May.

On the 12 June 1913 another Committee Meeting was held and it was decided to proceed with the formation of the following Branches:

Birmingham	–	President – Sir Francis Newdegate GCMG.
Newcastle	–	President – Brigadier General H.C.Surtees CB CMG DSO MVO DL.
Sheffield	–	President – Lieutenant Colonel W.J.F.Ramsden.
Exeter	–	President – Major L.C.Garratt

Major C.E.Pereira was elected to be President of the London Branch.

The First Annual General Committee Meeting was held at Regimental Headquarters on 15 December 1913 when representatives attended from the newly formed Branches. The badge to be worn by members was selected at this meeting. It was also arranged that an inaugural dinner would be given to each Branch, at the expense of the Central Fund. It had already been announced that such a Dinner would be given to the London Branch on the 20 March 1914.

So by the end of 1913 we had the concept, formation and established Branches of the Old Coldstreamers' Association.

Company Sergeant Major Field leading a party of members of the Birmingham Branch for the Presentation of the 1914 Star by Lieutenant General Sir Alfred Codrington, May 1919.

On 24 June 1914, under the Presidency of Sir Robert Walker Bt, the Hull Branch was formed. Sergeant Luck, the Coldstream Recruiter there at the time, assisted him and eight members were enrolled. (It is interesting to note that then as now the Recruiting Sergeants were very active in the Branches of The Association with some serving as the Secretary.)

The first Report on The Old Coldstreamers' Association (the forerunner of the *Coldstream Gazette*) was published in 1920 and covered the time from 1913 through the First World War and the Armistice Parades. Throughout this time the Branches continued, with assistance from Regimental Headquarters, even though the staff were severely tried by the extra duties during the War.

In 1919 the Colonel of the Regiment, Lieutenant General Sir Alfred Codrington, and the Regimental Lieutenant Colonel, Colonel J.Steele, visited Birmingham, Sheffield and Hull, accompanied by the Regimental Band. Parades were held for the presentation of 1914 Mons Stars. The number of members had now swelled, as 500 Coldstreamers were on parade at Birmingham. At Sheffield a Dinner was given in the evening at the Grand Hotel at which 200 attended, and the Hull Branch membership had risen from the original 8 to 133.

The Branches were now looking for permanent places for their meetings and functions, the most fortunate being the Hull Branch whose President, Major Sir Robert Walker Bt, donated the new club premises at 26 Park Street which General Codrington as Colonel of the Regiment accepted as a gift to the Association. It is also noted that at this Presentation a Loyal Message was sent to the Regiment's Colonel in Chief, as follows:

> "To the Equerry in Waiting, Royal Train, Liverpool. The Members of the Hull Branch, Old Coldstreamers' Association, assembled at the opening of clubhouse, a gift of Sir Robert Walker Bt, send respectful greeting and devoted loyalty to His Majesty, their Colonel in Chief."

The following reply was received:

> "General Sir Alfred Codrington, Old Coldstreamers Club Hull. The King sincerely thanks you and those who join you, for your loyal message. His Majesty hopes that every success will attend the new club. Equerry, Royal Train."

On 18 September 1919 a General Meeting of the Association was held at Regimental Headquarters when the Headquarters Committee and all Branches were well represented. Various propositions were discussed and then embodied in the new pamphlet of Rules which was issued in May 1920. Among the most important alterations were:

1. Length of service with the Regiment, as a qualification for membership, was abolished. It was decided that character during service was not to be emphasized in the case of a man who proved himself a good citizen.
2. Payment of arrears of subscriptions was a question for Branches.
3. Branches to be permitted to increase the annual subscriptions, but this must be brought to the notice of the Headquarters Committee.

It was obvious that the social climate after the War had changed and that Branches had to adapt to local conditions.

Membership of the Association flourished. Most of the serving members joined the London Branch, so that between the Branch formation and first Report in 1920, its membership stood at 1014. Many who were now no longer serving and who resided too far from any Branch made use of the London Branch as a link with the Regiment. Some lived in Canada and Australia, but the link proved "once a Coldstreamer always a Coldstreamer".

Many cases of Coldstreamers in distress were now being brought to the attention of the Headquarters and grants were made from all funds which were at the disposal of the Regimental Lieutenant Colonel. Many Members were also assisted in finding employment so that the Objectives that had been laid down by Colonel Monck and his Committee in 1913 were now being met.

The next Report of the Old Coldstreamers' Association was published covering from 1920 to 1922 and it was obvious that the numbers were increasing. By May 1924 the Annual Report of the Old Coldstreamers' Association had grown with very full Reports on the Regiment and the three Battalions on sports, shooting, promotions and other activities. The Reports from the Branches covered all activities throughout the year, including the speeches made by senior Officers at Branch Annual Dinners. Nominal Rolls and Financial Statements were also published. The Regimental Band was constantly requested and played at dinners and other functions in aid of the Association, but sometimes, as today, the cost of travel was not always taken into consideration.

In 1919, when the memory of the First World War was still fresh in the mind, it was felt that there should be a Memorial in London to those Guardsmen who had lost their lives between 1914 and 1918. A Brigade of Guards Committee was set up under the Chairmanship of Field Marshal HRH The Duke of Connaught, Colonel of the Grenadier Guards and Senior Colonel of the Household Brigade. The Members were Colonels of the other Guards Regiments, that of the Coldstream being Lieutenant General Sir Alfred Codrington KCB KCVO. The General Officers who had commanded the Brigade of Guards and Lieutenant Colonels commanding the Regiments were also on the Committee. In February 1920 an appeal for funds was launched and various sculptors were asked to submit designs. The one submitted by Mr Ledward was accepted.

The Guards Division Memorial was unveiled on 16 October 1926 by HRH The Duke of Connaught, who had been nominated by the Colonel-in-Chief. At what was an impressive ceremony 6000 Past and Present Members of the Household Brigade were on parade. Massed pipers played the lament 'Flowers of the Forest' and 'Last Post' and 'Reveille' were sounded. Guardsmen slow-marched forward with wreaths to honour the dead and these were placed on the Memorial by the Colonels of the respective Regiments.

On 16 September 1928 a Divine Service was held at the Guards Chapel. Members of the London Branch of the Old Coldstreamers' Association and their families attended, numbering over 500. The music was provided by the Regimental Band and the choir by the Corps of Drums of the 2nd Battalion.

After the Service the Coldstreamers formed up by Battalions and marched, headed by the Band and Corps of Drums, via Birdcage Walk and Storeys Gate to the Guards Division Memorial. On arrival the Colonel of the Regiment, Lieutenant General Sir Alfred Codrington, laid a floral tribute in the form of a Coldstream Star on the Memorial in memory of the Coldstreamers who fell in the Great War. 'Last Post' and 'Reveille' were sounded by the Corps of Drums and the Parade then marched past the Memorial and back to Wellington Barracks where it was dismissed.

After the Parade the Sergeants' Mess of the 2nd Battalion entertained those members who had travelled a long distance to be at the Service and March. Thus the London Branch Memorial Parade was established, but it was not until after the Second World War that other Branches travelled to Wellington Barracks to participate in the Service and Parade.

It is of interest to note that on the Parade on 14 September 1930 three holders of the Victoria Cross were present; Colonel J.V.Campbell VC CMG DSO ADC and the Wreath Bearers Mr O.Brooks VC and Mr G.H.Wyatt VC.

The Service and Parade have continued to this day with the exception of the years 1940 to 1946, with the only change being that the date is now fixed for the second Sunday in May.

After the First World War Branch Dinners became annual events. Senior officers attended, the Loyal Toast and a Toast to the Regiment were drunk, and Loyal Greetings were sent to the Colonel-in-Chief.

Many Branches to this day still hold their Annual Dinner and the procedure remains the same. Some now include the Ladies, and some, through reasons of locality and distance have lunches or buffets, but as always the Coldstream Spirit remains.

The Annual Report of the Old Coldstreamers Association continued to be published each year until 1935. These had become very comprehensive, not only concerning the Branches, but also on the Regiment and Battalions. The 1920s and 1930s had seen more Branches established throughout the country, and membership of the Association had increased. Employment and Welfare were the predominant areas covered by the Association through what were hard and difficult years. A Brigade of Guards Employment Society was established with the National Association for Employment of Ex-Regular Soldiers Sailors and Airmen. This was the forerunner of what is now the Household Division Employment Agency and the Forces Employment Agency.

In 1930 Major M.F.Trew was appointed Regimental Adjutant. His previous posting had been Company Commander of Number 1 Company in the 2nd Battalion. On the Battalion's return from Shanghai in 1928, and to keep in contact with those members with whom he had served for five years, he published a *Number 1 Company Gazette* with Regimental News, with the main object of keeping the past members in touch with the Company. This proved to be a popular experiment.

The circulation of the Old Coldstreamers' Association Reports was limited and Major Trew, after his success with his *Number 1 Company Gazette*, and with the approval of the Regimental Lieutenant Colonel, Colonel J.E.Gibbs MC, launched the *Coldstream Gazette*. This was published twice yearly with Edition No 1 in January 1931, and No 2 the following September. It was sent out free of charge to all past officers of the Regiment, all annual subscribers to the Old Coldstreamers'

The Colonel of the Regiment inspecting Old Coldstreamers on the occasion of his inspection of the Regiment at Chelsea Barracks on 13 July 1936.

Association and to all Reservists. A certain number of copies were supplied to all Branches of the Association, Battalions and Depot Companies. It was also pointed out that Reservists, on being discharged, might still wish to receive a copy and it would be supplied to them on application at a charge of sixpence per year. The sixpence was to be sent in stamps and the two Gazettes would then be forwarded to them post free. The Gazette did of course in some way duplicate the information in the Annual Reports of The Old Coldstreamers' Association, but more importantly it covered not only the previous six months but published what would be happening by date and venue in the future. It also featured Officers, Warrant Officers and Non-Commissioned Officers promotions, appointments and postings. Welfare and Employment featured strongly, with emphasis on those who had not already joined Branches of the Association.

In 1936 the Annual Report of the Old Coldstreamers' Association was discontinued and the *Coldstream Gazette* became the Association Journal. The Gazette grew in size but continued to be published twice yearly with a special edition in November 1938 to celebrate the Silver Jubilee of the Association.

In 1939 an order went out to all Branches from Regimental Headquarters that the Old Coldstreamers' Association would close down for the duration of hostilities, and all books and accounts would be sent to Regimental Headquarters. But Branches did great work looking after wounded Coldstreamers throughout the War, and the London Branch published a 16-page booklet entitled *A Short Record of the London Branch Activities during World War II (1939–1945)*. In 1945 the prisoners of war returning to the United Kingdom were all written to and visited by Branch members who gave help and assistance as necessary. By early 1946 Branch Committees were supplemented by Coldstreamers who had returned, Annual General Meetings were held, reunions and activities planned. The London Branch held a dinner at the Seymour Hall on 28 September 1945 at which 600 past and present Coldstreamers attended, of which three were Lieutenant Generals, Sir Charles Loyd, Sir Arthur Smith and Sir Oliver Leese. The London Branch was not able to have an Annual Dinner in 1946 due to the fact that it could not find a venue to cater for the numbers attending and the problems caused by food rationing. In place of a reunion with a 'get together' a running buffet was held at the Duke of York's Headquarters, King's Road.

In May 1947 the 17th Edition, the first for seven years, of the *Coldstream Gazette* was published.

The Annual Memorial Service, 1950. The March from Westminster Abbey to Horse Guards. The Wreath Bearers are CSM P. Wright VC and RSM C. Knowles MC.

After the Second World War, when the Regiment still consisted of men from the five War Battalions as well as those from the Training Battalion, it was inevitable that the numbers in the Branches greatly increased, continuing the camaraderie set up during six long years of hostilities.

The Tercentenary of the Regiment in 1950 was not only celebrated by the Regiment, but also saw many activities and parades organized by the Old Coldstreamers' Association. One such Parade in which the Association took part on 5 July was the Presentation of New Colours to the 3rd Battalion on Horse Guards Parade by His Majesty King George VI. The Battalion was commanded by Lieutenant Colonel W.A.G.Burns DSO MC, later to become the 26th Colonel of the Regiment. This was the first Presentation to be shown on television and the Battalion was accompanied on parade

His Majesty The King inspecting Old Coldstreamers on 5 July 1950. In attendance on His Majesty are Colonel E.R. Hill, Regimental Lieutenant Colonel, Brigadier L.M. Gibbs, President of the London Branch, and behind him General Sir Charles Loyd, Colonel of the Regiment, and Lieutenant Colonel Sir Michael Adeane, Private Secretary to His Majesty.

by Number 13 Company, Number 16 Company and a Coldstream Detachment from 1 (Guards) Independent Parachute Company. On the left of the Parade, forming the largest contingent, were members of the Old Coldstreamers' Association with rows of medals glinting in the grey light of the morning. The command came to 'March off the Colours' and then began the most moving part of the Parade. To the strains of 'Auld Lang Syne' the Colours passed under Horse Guards Arch, which brought back memories of the past years and a lump in the throat for those who had served in the Battalion since the Colours had last been presented in 1936.

After His Majesty The King had inspected all Coldstreamers on parade and the New Colours had been presented, the Battalion was formed into threes and the Parade marched past their Colonel-in-Chief, to the Regimental March. The Old Coldstreamers' Association was congratulated on its bearing and marching which was described as a most stirring and heart-warming sight.

In the Tercentenary Year the Regiment and the Association broke with tradition and held the Annual Memorial Sunday Service at Westminster Abbey, and afterwards marched to the Guards Memorial to lay the wreath. The Wreath Bearers on the Parade were CSM P.Wright VC and RSM C.Knowles MC. Throughout the year Old Coldstreamers were on parade from Newcastle to Exeter and dinners and functions abounded. For those who were members of the Regiment both past and present it was a memorable year.

With the continuation of National Service the numbers in the Association continued to grow with new Branches being formed. Some Branches found the need to have sub-Branches such as Manchester with Bolton and Bury, Reading with Oxford, and Essex with London.

At the Annual General Meeting of the Association in 1954 it was decided that the Association should be called 'The Coldstreamers' Association'. The decision to leave out the 'Old' was made because it was felt that it was incorrect, since Coldstreamers can join whether serving with the Colours or not. The name remained in that form until 1977 when it was changed to its present title of 'The Coldstream Guards Association'.

With the end of National Service in 1961, the 3rd Battalion being placed in suspended animation in 1959 and the strengths of the 1st and 2nd Battalions being reduced, the future of the Association could have faltered, but this did not happen.

The Annual Memorial Service 2000. The March from Wellington Barracks to Horse Guards Parade. The Colonel of the Regiment, General Sir Michael Rose, precedes the Wreath Bearers, Mr P. Cassells (right) and Mr W. Makin (left) from the Liverpool Branch of The Coldstream Guards Association.

2000. The March Past the Colonel of the Regiment on return to Wellington Barracks.

Over the last 87 years The Coldstream Guards Association has stood the test of time and the Objectives of the Association as laid down by Colonel Monck have not changed. The welfare of Coldstreamers, their dependents and widows has always been, and will always be, one of the main aims. The Association has prospered throughout its history and will continue to be an integral part of the Regiment. Its success has been achieved through the values of all those who have served in the Regiment and who have carried them on within the Association whether as Presidents, Vice Presidents, Chairmen, Secretaries, Committees and Members.

The Secretaries meet once a year in London at the Annual Secretaries Conference which is chaired by the Regimental Lieutenant Colonel as President of the Association. This has been moved to the last Saturday in October and a full day is devoted to the planning of the Association year, as well as full discussion of propositions and points put forward by Branches.

Coldstream Guards Association Days are held each year generally at Pirbright, with the annual Horse Race Meeting in October at York, at which the Association has a sponsored race. The Coldstream Guards Association Sweepstake first started by Mr A.Ruddock of the York Branch is held on this occasion and raises money for all the Branch Welfare Funds.

Times have changed, but with serving soldiers joining and supporting Branches, and Coldstream Recruiting Sergeants continuing to be active Members of respective Branch Committees, The Coldstream Guards Association will always be there for all Coldstreamers both Past and Present.

Note on Author

Major Christopher Louch enlisted in the Regiment in 1958. He served with the 1st and 2nd Battalions, and the Guards Depot, and was promoted to WO1 Garrison Sergeant Major in Hong Kong. In 1980 he was given a Regular Quartermaster Commission in the Regiment. He was Quartermaster of the 2nd Battalion from 1975–1978 and retired in 1988. In the same year he was appointed Assistant Regimental Adjutant and became the Honorary Secretary of The Coldstream Guards' Association. He was an outstanding Editor of the *Coldstream Gazette* for many years. He died suddenly in May 2000 just before Memorial Sunday.

COLDSTREAM GUARDS ASSOCIATION BRANCHES

	Formed
Aldershot	1957
Ashington	1973
Bath	1930
Birmingham	1913
Bradford	1948
Bristol	1954
Canada	1974
Doncaster	1937
Dorset and West Hants	1950
Essex	1959
Exeter	1938
Gloucester	1953
Huddersfield	1948
Hull	1914
Isle of Wight	1993
King's Lynn	1981
Leeds	1946
Leicester	1922
Liverpool	1927
London	1913
Manchester	1938
Middlesbrough	1931
Newcastle	1913
North East Lancs	1928
Norwich	1928
Plymouth and Cornwall	1913
Reading and Oxford	1926
Sheffield	1913
Shropshire	1930
Suffolk	1934
Sunderland	1922
Sussex	1927
Watford	1985
Windsor	1935
Yeovil and Taunton	1996
York	1955

SELECT BIBLIOGRAPHY

A great many books 'have been used to compile this history and it is not proposed to list them all. Some readers may wish, however, to read further about some subject mentioned and the bibliography below lists some of the books that provide more information and are not too heavy reading. They are shown more or less in chronological order for easier reference:

1.	Early History of the Coldstream Guards	G. Davies	1923
2.	The Story of the Guards	Julian Paget	1976
3.	Record of the Coldstream Guards	E.R.Hill	1950
4.	History of the British Army. 1899–1927	Sir John Fortescue	
5.	Wellington's Peninsular War	Julian Paget	1990
6.	Hougoumont	Julian Paget	1992
7.	Origins and Services of the Coldstream Guards	D.McKinnon	1833
8.	The Coldstream Guards. 1885–1914	Sir John Hall	1929
9.	Colours and Customs of the Coldstream Guards	E.R.Hill	1950
10.	The British Soldier	J.M.Brereton	1985
11.	The Coldstream Guards. 1914–1918	Sir John Ross	1928
12.	The History of the Guards Division in the Great War 1914–1918	C.Headlam	1924
13.	Morale. A Study of Men and Courage	John Baynes	1927
14.	Far from a Donkey. The Life of Sir Ivor Maxse	John Baynes	1995
15.	The Guards Division	Mike Chappell	1955
16.	Field Marshal Earl Haig	Philip Warner	1991
17.	The Coldstream Guards. 1920–1946	Michael Howard and John Sparrow	1951
18.	El Alamein to the River Sangro	Field Marshal Montgomery	1947
19.	No Dishonourable Name	David Quilter	1947
20.	The Campaign in Italy	Eric Linklater	1951
21.	A Distant Drum	Jocelyn Pereira	1948
22.	The Story of the Guards Armoured Division	The Earl of Rosse and E.R.Hill	1956

23.	Sixth Guards Tank Brigade	Patrick Forbes	1950
24.	Normandy to the Baltic	Field Marshal Montgomery	1948
25.	The Second World War. Vols I–VI	Winston S.Churchill	1949
26.	The Coats Mission	Sir Jeffrey Darell	1990
27.	History of the Glider Pilot Regiment	Claude Smith	1992
28.	This is the SAS	Tony Geraghty	1982
29.	G Patrol	Michael Crichton-Stuart	1958
30.	The Desert My Dwelling Place	David Lloyd Owen	
31.	War Behind Enemy Lines	Julian Thompson	1998
32.	He Who Dares	David Sutherland	1998
33.	Ill Met By Moonlight	I.W.S.Moss	1950
34.	A War of Shadows	I.W.S.Moss	1952
35.	Fight Another Day	J.M.Langley	1974
36.	M.I.9	M.R.D.Foot and J.M.Langley	1979
37.	Guardsmen of the Sky	J.N.P.Watson	1997
38.	SOE. 1940–1946	M.R.D.Foot	1984
39.	SOE. Recollections and Reflections. 1940–1945	J.G.Beevor	1981
40.	Coldstream Guards. 1946–1970	Richard Crichton	1978
41.	Fighting for Peace	Michael Rose	1998
42.	Standards, Guidons and Colours of the Household Division	N.P.Dawnay	1975
43.	You've Lost Your Name!	John G.Hook	1992
44.	Hard to Believe – Too Old at Sixteen	Peter Horsfall	1999
45.	They Died With Their Boots Clean	Gerald Kersh	1941
46.	History of the British Standing Army	Colonel C.Walton	1869

INDEX

References in italics refer to illustrations. Ranks shown are those at the time of the history rather than those attained later.

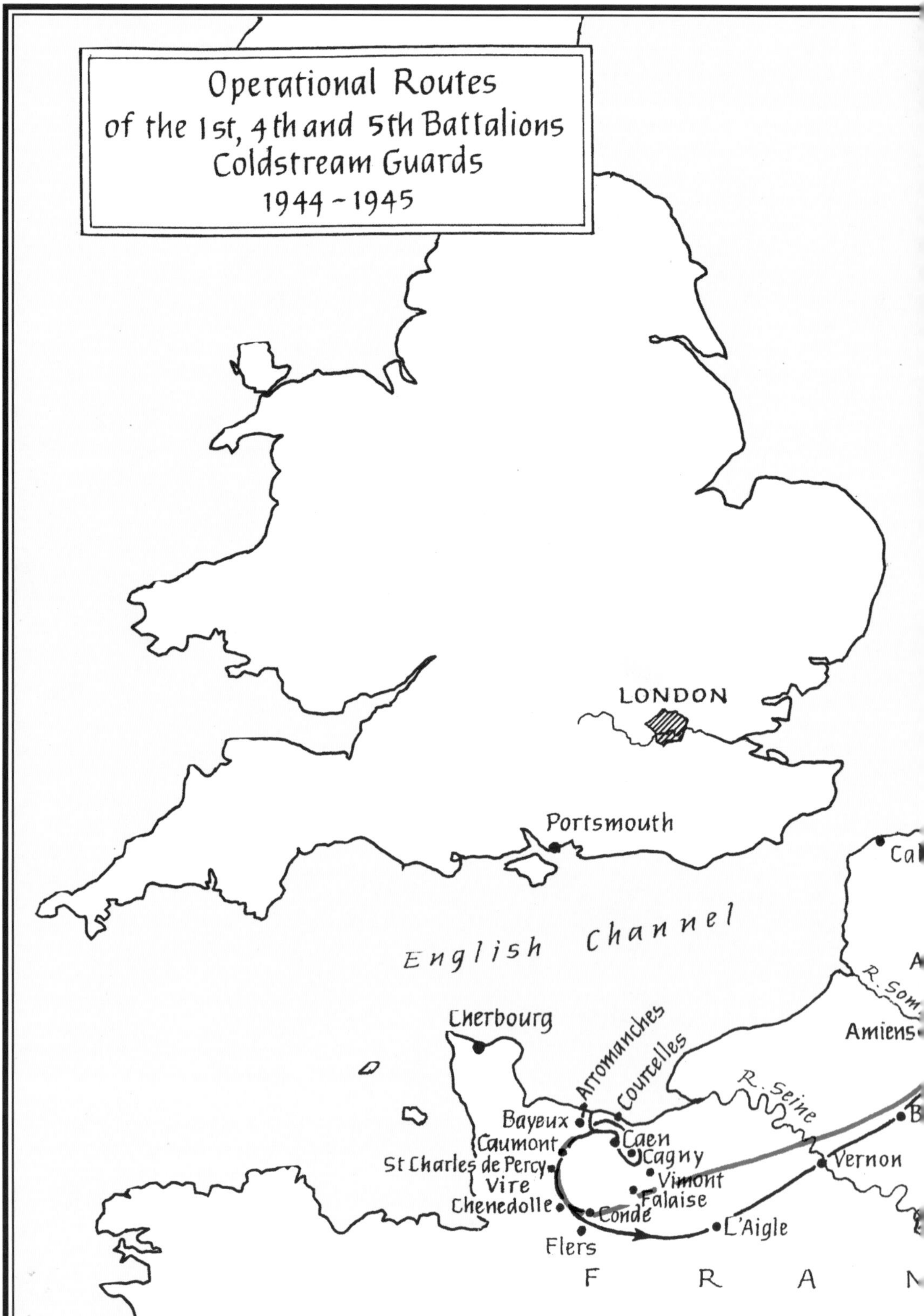
Operational Routes
of the 1st, 4th and 5th Battalions
Coldstream Guards
1944 – 1945
LONDON
Portsmouth
English Channel
Cherbourg
Arromanches
Courcelles
Bayeux
Caumont
St Charles de Percy
Vire
Chenedolle
Caen
Cagny
Vimont
Falaise
Conde
Flers
L'Aigle
Vernon
R. Seine
Amiens
R. Som
F R A N